PLAYFAIR
CRICKET ANNUAL
1983
36th edition

EDITED BY GORDON ROSS

Statistics by
Barry McCaully, Brian Heald and Brian Croudy

Front cover: David Gower. Phot

D0257116

PICK THE BEST
NATWEST BANK TROPHY TEAM
OF ENGLAND PLAYERS
AFTER THE FIRST TWO YEARS
OF THE COMPETITION

*(the term 'England' means players who are qualified
to play for England)*

£1000 TO BE WON

Prizes: 1st: £300   2nd: £200   3rd: £150   4th: £100
Plus twenty-five prizes of £10 each

How to enter: Pick the best NatWest Bank Trophy team from the
40 cricketers shown below who played in the competition in the
first two seasons. Then write in 20 words what you think is the
greatest virtue of 60-overs cricket.

Write the names on the entry form on the opposite page with
your name and address and post to the address shown.

Your Choice
Bill Athey, David Bairstow, Ian Botham, Geoff Boycott, Mike
Brearley, Alan Butcher, Geoff Cook, Nick Cook, Norman Cowans,
Brian Davison, Peter Denning, Phil Edmonds, Keith Fletcher,
Graeme Fowler, Mike Gatting, Graham Gooch, Ian Gould, David
Gower, Ian Greig, Eddie Hemmings, David Hughes, Robin
Jackman, Trevor Jesty, Allan Lamb, Wayne Larkins, David Lloyd,
Vic Marks, Geoff Miller, Chris Old, Derek Pringle, Derek Randall,
Brian Rose, Jack Simmons, Chris Tavaré, Bob Taylor, Les Taylor,
Derek Underwood, Peter Willey, Bob Willis, Barry Wood.

Rules
Judging: Each entry will be considered by a panel of cricket
experts and the entry which, in the opinion of the judges,
constitutes the best NatWest Trophy team will be adjudged the
winner. The decision of the judges is final and binding; no
correspondence will be entered into. Employees of Macdonald &
Co (Publishers) Ltd and their families are not eligible to
compete.
Proof of entry: All entries must be on the entry form provided.
Proof of posting is not proof of entry.

ENTRY FORM

Your team in batting order, with a captain:

1

2

3

4

5

6

7

8

9

10

11

Write in no more than 20 words what you think is the greatest virtue of 60-overs cricket.

Closing date: 12.00 noon Wednesday, 14 September 1983

Your name and address:

....

....

....

Post to: The Editor
Playfair Cricket Annual Competition
Queen Anne Press
Macdonald & Co (Publishers) Ltd
Maxwell House
74 Worship Street
London EC2A 2EN

One hundred small businesses will receive Business Development Loans from NatWest today.

And tomorrow. And the next day. And the day after.

THE ASHES LOST

by Gordon Ross

Australia's success in the fight for the Ashes this winter was not altogether unexpected. In fact, the most carping critics had expressed the opinion that England were unlikely to win a single Test. Happily, they were wrong – just – and Bob Willis put his finger on the pulse of the problem when he said that we seem unable at the moment to produce opening batsmen and fast bowlers in England. What is the reason for this? The development of modern Huttons and Washbrooks, Stathams and Truemans is certainly not restricted by financial difficulties. There is more money in the Test arena now than was ever dreamed of by the great players of the past. Admittedly, it must be mentioned that there is far more vicious short-pitched fast bowling than there used to be. Brian Statham's distinguished Test career was not measured by the number of bouncers he bowled, but by the number of wickets he took. The world authorities seem totally unwilling to legislate against the excessive use of the bouncer, and certainly Packer's television build-up to the recent series was tantamount to a declaration of war. In the event, then, opening batsmen were bent on preserving their skins as well as not getting out, and scoring runs. There would, however, appear to be no rational reason for the dearth of fast bowlers, except that one-day cricket has nurtured a breed of bowlers who have found it just as effective to keep runs down as to take wickets – 200 for no wicket is just as good for the fielding side in a one-day game as 200 for 9, except in the rare case of a tie.

In addition, there were probably more 'passengers' on this England tour than ever before, prompting the critics to raise their voices once again on the subject of those chosen – and more important still – some of those left behind. The search must begin straight away for new talent. A process for the development of really fast bowlers must be devised. There was no greater supporter of a genuine speed attack than Len Hutton; after all, he took the triumvirate of Statham, Trueman and Tyson to Australia with devastating results. There is continual talk of the lack of interest in the three-day County Championship, but its preservation (whether it is a three-day

5

or a four-day match) is absolutely vital to school batsmen in how to build an innings and bowlers in how to take wickets.

One heartening aspect of the tour was the superb catching by both sides. The remarkable catch by David Hookes in the last Test when he ran away from the ball to get into position for its downward path, finally taking the ball with one hand, must rank as one of the great catches of all time. Millions of television viewers were exhilarated by that piece of cricket.

To return, then, to the Home Front in the summer of 1982. The double Test series first with India and then with Pakistan were interesting enough with England winning both series, one to nothing against India and two-one against Pakistan. It was very much a batsman's series against India. Botham led the charge with 208, 128 and 67 at an average of 134.33. But already the writing was on the wall for the England attack. Even in the third Test when India were without Gavaskar, they scored 410, and the England bowling figures for the series were food for thought up and down the corridors of Lord's and elsewhere. Willis took 15 wickets at 22, an admirable performance, but as for the rest . . . well . . . they are best forgotten. Against Pakistan, they were certainly better, again because of the ever-dependable Willis, and because Botham came off with the ball this time – 28 wickets between them. Seven other bowlers took 18 between them. The team for Australia was shortly due to be announced, so in all fairness to the selectors, they were desperately short of class bowling which subsequent events proved overwhelmingly. Significantly, on the batting front, Gower failed to score a hundred in any of the six Tests – an enigma in a sense in view of his ability, lacking only in the application to build.

The internal domestic competitions produced a cross-section of winners. Middlesex, the County Championship, Surrey, the NatWest Trophy, Somerset, the Benson and Hedges, and Sussex, the John Player League. An interesting point is that neither Derbyshire, nor Surrey, the first two winners of the NatWest Trophy, had ever won its predecessor, the Gillette Cup. Nine counties won the Gillette Cup – Sussex, Yorkshire, Warwickshire, Kent, Lancashire, Gloucestershire, Northamptonshire, Middlesex and Somerset, so with Derbyshire and Surrey's success, this leaves six counties who have won neither – Essex, Glamorgan, Hampshire, Leicestershire, Nottinghamshire, and Worcestershire. Both Leicestershire and Essex have won the Benson and Hedges and Worcestershire and Hampshire, the John Player League. So only Glamorgan and Nottinghamshire have yet to win one of the one-day competitions.

The two Lord's Finals were almost identical in scoring and in one-sidedness. Both were won by 9 wickets, and at no time was the side batting first – Warwickshire in the NatWest and Nottinghamshire in the Benson and Hedges – likely to make much of a match of it. So NatWest, in two years, have experienced both sides of the coin – high drama and a desperate finish in their first year; an academic result in their second.

On May 29, at Worcester, Glenn Turner, Worcestershire's marvellous New Zealander, scored 311 against Warwickshire – his one hundredth century in first-class cricket. He became the 19th player to perform this feat (Zaheer made it 20 during the winter), the second non-Englishman (Bradman was the first) and the first New Zealander. At 35, Turner became the third youngest, after Hammond and Compton. Not surprisingly, his 311 was the highest ever hundredth century, and the first time he had passed 300, although in the West Indies in the winter of 1971-72 he scored four double centuries, being out in the last two at the same score – 259. 69 of his 100s were scored for Worcestershire, and 33 of them actually on the Worcester ground. He was in the unique position, by virtue of having played for New Zealand, to score a hundred against every English county and this he did, though he never made a hundred on a Kent ground.

On the sponsorship front, this summer will be the last for two established sponsors. Prudential are making this summer's Prudential World Cup their last sponsorship in cricket, and Schweppes terminate their association with the County Championship at the end of this season. NatWest, on the other hand, have increased the sum of their sponsorship to bring in more Minor Counties. Now, instead of the first round consisting of seven matches with a number of First-Class Counties getting a bye, there will be sixteen matches, with all the First-Class Counties competing, Scotland coming in for the first time to join Ireland, and eight more Minor Counties to join five who usually participate. The draw has been arranged to provide only one match between First-Class Counties – Worcestershire v Nottinghamshire at Worcester. So there are fifteen opportunities for a David to beat a Goliath.

Sri Lanka v England 1981–82

TEST MATCH

PLAYED AT COLOMBO, 17, 18, 20, 21 FEBRUARY
ENGLAND WON BY 7 WICKETS

SRI LANKA

Batsman	1st innings		2nd innings	
*B. Warnapura	c Gower b Willis	2	c Gooch b Emburey	38
S. Wettimuny	c Taylor b Botham	6	b Willis	9
R.L. Dias	c Cook b Willis	0	c Taylor b Underwood	77
L.R.D. Mendis	lbw b Botham	17	c Willis b Emburey	27
R.S. Madugalle	c Gower b Underwood	65	c Cook b Emburey	3
A. Ranatunga	b Underwood	54	c Fletcher b Emburey	2
D.S. de Silva	c Gower b Underwood	3	c Fletcher b Underwood	1
A.L.F. de Mel	c Fletcher b Underwood	19	c Gower b Emburey	2
L.W. Kaluperuma	c Cook b Underwood	1	c Taylor b Emburey	0
†H.M. Goonatillake	not out	22	not out	2
G.R.A. de Silva	c Emburey b Botham	12	c Willis b Underwood	0
Extras	(B2, LB4, NB9, W2)	17	(LB6, NB8)	14
Total		**218**		**175**

ENGLAND

Batsman	1st innings		2nd innings	
G.A. Gooch	lbw b de Mel	22	b G. de Silva	31
G. Cook	c Kaluperuma b de Mel	11	lbw b de Mel	0
C.J. Tavaré	b de Mel	0	st Goonatillake b G. de Silva	85
D.I. Gower	c Goonatillake b D. de Silva	89	not out	42
*K.W.R. Fletcher	c Warnapura b G. de Silva	45	not out	0
I.T. Botham	b de Mel	13		
†R.W. Taylor	not out	31		
J.E. Emburey	lbw b G. de Silva	0		
P.J.W. Allott	c Kaluperuma b D. de Silva	3		
D.L. Underwood	c Mendis b D. de Silva	0		
R.G.D. Willis	run out	0		
Extras	(B3, NB6)	9	(B4, LB8, NB1)	13
Total		**223**	**(3 wkts)**	**171**

BOWLING

ENGLAND	O	M	R	W		O	M	R	W
Willis	19	8	46	2	—	9	3	24	1
Botham	12.5	1	28	3	—	12	1	37	0
Allott	13	3	44	0	—	—	—	—	—
Emburey	19	3	55	0	—	25	11	33	6
Underwood	18	6	28	5	—	37.5	15	67	3
SRI LANKA									
de Mel	17	2	70	4	—	13.1	4	33	1
Warnapura	3	1	9	0	—	1	0	1	0
D. de Silva	27.5	11	54	3	—	15	5	38	0
Kaluperuma	9	1	29	0	—	12	3	40	0
G. de Silva	30	12	52	2	—	17	6	46	2

FALL OF WICKETS

	SL 1st	ENG 1st	SL 2nd	ENG 2nd
1st	9	34	30	3
2nd	11	34	113	84
3rd	29	60	140	167
4th	34	120	167	—
5th	133	151	169	—
6th	149	200	170	—
7th	181	207	172	—
8th	183	216	173	—
9th	190	216	174	—
10th	218	223	175	—

New Zealand v Australia 1981–82

FIRST TEST MATCH

PLAYED AT WELLINGTON 26, 27, 28 FEBRUARY, 1, 2, MARCH

MATCH DRAWN

NEW ZEALAND

B.A. Edgar lbw b Alderman	55
J.G. Wright c Chappell b Yardley	38
J.F.M. Morrison b Thomson	15
*G.P. Howarth not out	58
J.V. Coney lbw b Yardley	1
M.D. Crowe run out	9
R.J. Hadlee b Thomson	21
†I.D.S. Smith c Chappell b Yardley	11
B.L. Cairns not out	19
M.C. Snedden did not bat	
E.J. Chatfield did not bat	
Extras (B5, LB19, NB11, W4)	39
Total (7 wkts dec)	**266**

AUSTRALIA

G.M. Wood b Cairns	41
B.M. Laird not out	27
J. Dyson not out	12
*G.S. Chappell did not bat	
K.J. Hughes did not bat	
A.R. Border did not bat	
†R.W. Marsh did not bat	
D.K. Lillee did not bat	
B. Yardley did not bat	
T.M. Alderman did not bat	
J.R. Thomson did not bat	
Extras (LB2, NB3)	5
Total (1 wkt)	**85**

BOWLING

AUSTRALIA	O	M	R	W		FALL OF WICKETS		
							NZ	AUS
							1st	1st
Thomson	26	13	35	2	—			
Alderman	44	20	93	1	—			
Lillee	15	5	32	0	—	1st	86	65
Chappell	8	2	18	0	—	2nd	120	—
Yardley	23	10	49	3	—	3rd	149	—
NEW ZEALAND						4th	162	—
Hadlee	7	2	15	0	—	5th	186	—
Snedden	8	1	24	1	—	6th	212	—
Cairns	11	4	20	1	—	7th	246	—
Chatfield	8	5	7	0	—	8th	—	—
Crowe	4	1	14	0	—	9th	—	—
						10th	—	—

SECOND TEST MATCH
PLAYED AT AUCKLAND, 12, 13, 14, 15, 16 MARCH
NEW ZEALAND WON BY 5 WICKETS

AUSTRALIA

B.M. Laird c Smith b Troup	38	lbw b Hadlee	39
G.M. Wood b Cairns	9	c Snedden b Cairns	100
J. Dyson b Snedden	33	b Cairns	33
K.J. Hughes c Smith b Troup	0	b Cairns	17
*G.S. Chappell run out	32	c Edgar b Hadlee	24
A.R. Border run out	0	c Howarth b Morrison	38
†R.W. Marsh b Troup	33	c Crowe b Hadlee	3
B. Yardley b Hadlee	25	c Coney b Hadlee	0
J.R. Thomson lbw b Hadlee	13	lbw b Hadlee	4
D.K. Lillee c Crowe b Troup	9	c Smith b Morrison	5
T.M. Alderman not out	0	not out	0
Extras (LB2, NB16)	18	(B4, LB5, NB8)	17
Total	**210**		**280**

NEW ZEALAND

B.A. Edgar c & b Yardley	161	c Lillee b Yardley	29
J.G. Wright c Yardley b Lillee	4	c Laird b Alderman	4
J.F.M. Morrison b Lillee	11	c Marsh b Lillee	8
*G.P. Howarth run out	56	c Chappell b Yardley	19
J.V. Coney b Yardley	73	not out	5
M.D. Crowe c Wood b Lillee	2		
R.J. Hadlee c Chappell b Yardley	25	not out	6
†I.D.S. Smith lbw b Yardley	5		
B.L. Cairns c Lillee b Alderman	14	b Border	34
M.C. Snedden not out	18		
G.B. Troup c Border b Alderman	4		
Extras (B4, LB7, NB2, W1)	14	(LB4)	4
Total	**387**	**(5 wkts)**	**109**

BOWLING

N. ZEALAND	O	M	R	W		O	M	R	W	FALL OF WICKETS			
											AUS	NZ	AUS	NZ
Hadlee	20	7	38	2	—	28	9	63	5		1st	1st	2nd	2nd
Troup	18.3	3	82	4	—	15	4	31	0	1st	19	15	106	4
Cairns	17	7	38	1	—	44	10	85	3	2nd	75	35	167	17
Snedden	12	5	26	1	—	8	2	22	0	3rd	76	122	196	44
Howarth	1	0	8	0	—	4	2	4	0	4th	120	276	202	97
Coney	—	—	—	—	—	4	1	6	0	5th	120	291	241	103
Morrison	—	—	—	—	—	35	16	52	2	6th	131	326	254	—
AUSTRALIA										7th	173	345	254	—
Thomson	23	8	52	0	—	—	—	—	—	8th	187	352	260	—
Alderman	24.3	4	59	2	—	7	0	30	1	9th	203	366	277	—
Lillee	39	7	106	3	—	13	5	32	1	10th	210	387	280	—
Yardley	56	22	142	4	—	7.4	2	40	2					
Border	3	0	11	0	—	2	1	3	1					
Chappell	5	2	3	0										

THIRD TEST MATCH
PLAYED AT CHRISTCHURCH, 19, 20, 21, 22 MARCH
AUSTRALIA WON BY 8 WICKETS

AUSTRALIA

B.M. Laird	c Smith b Troup	12	c Edgar b Snedden	31
G.M. Wood	c Crowe b Hadlee	64	c Coney b Hadlee	15
J. Dyson	c Hadlee b Snedden	1	not out	14
*G.S. Chappell	c Smith b Coney	176	not out	3
K.J. Hughes	b Hadlee	12		
A.R. Border	b Snedden	6		
†R.W. Marsh	c Cairns b Hadlee	23		
B. Yardley	c Cairns b Hadlee	8		
J.R. Thomson	b Hadlee	25		
D.K. Lillee	c & b Hadlee	7		
T.M. Alderman	not out	1		
Extras	(B2, LB8, NB8)	18	(B2, LB2, NB2)	6
Total		**353**	(2 wkts)	**69**

NEW ZEALAND

B.A. Edgar	c Dyson b Alderman	22	c Marsh b Alderman	11
J.G. Wright	c Marsh b Lillee	13	b Alderman	141
J.F.M. Morrison	lbw b Thomson	8	lbw b Chappell	4
*G.P. Howarth	c Alderman b Thomson	9	c Wood b Border	41
J.V. Coney	b Lillee	0	b Border	0
M.D. Crowe	c Marsh b Lillee	0	b Yardley	9
R.J. Hadlee	c Marsh b Thomson	40	c Alderman b Yardley	0
†I.D.S. Smith	b Thomson	0	c Wood b Yardley	0
B.L. Cairns	run out	3	lbw b Yardley	16
M.C. Snedden	b Alderman	32	b Border	20
G.B. Troup	not out	0	not out	8
Extras	(B8, LB2, NB11, W1)	22	(B4, LB7, NB9, W2)	22
Total		**149**		**272**

BOWLING

N. ZEALAND	O	M	R	W		O	M	R	W
Hadlee	28.5	5	100	6	—	8	2	10	1
Troup	11	1	53	1					
Snedden	18	2	89	2	—	4	0	15	1
Cairns	21	3	74	0	—	9	1	28	0
Coney	8	2	15	1	—	1	0	2	0
Morrison	3	0	4	0	—	2	1	6	0
Wright	—	—	—	—	—	1	0	2	0
Crowe	—	—	—	—	—	0.3	0	0	0
AUSTRALIA									
Thomson	21	5	51	4	—	19	5	54	0
Alderman	19.2	8	63	2	—	23	5	66	2
Lillee	12	6	13	3	—	—	—	—	—
Chappell	—	—	—	—	—	18	5	30	1
Yardley	—	—	—	—	—	27	7	80	4
Border	—	—	—	—	—	10.3	4	20	3

FALL OF WICKETS

	AUS 1st	NZ 1st	NZ 2nd	AUS 2nd
1st	50	33	21	24
2nd	57	57	36	60
3rd	82	57	129	—
4th	128	57	133	—
5th	145	67	162	—
6th	237	82	166	—
7th	256	82	166	—
8th	340	87	215	—
9th	352	149	249	—
10th	353	149	272	—

Pakistan v Sri Lanka 1981–82

FIRST TEST MATCH

PLAYED AT KARACHI, 5, 6, 7, 9, 10 MARCH
PAKISTAN WON BY 204 RUNS

PAKISTAN

Mansoor Akhtar c Goonatillake b de Mel	6	c Mendis b D.S. de Silva	23
Rizwan-uz-Zaman c Goonatillake b Ratnayeke	42	c Goonatillake b de Mel	10
Saleem Malik b D.S. de Silva	12	not out	100
*Javed Miandad c Goonatillake b de Mel	4	st Goonatillake b D.S. de Silva	92
Wasim Raja c Dias b de Mel	31	not out	12
Haroon Rashid run out	153		
†Saleem Yousuf c Goonatillake b D.S. de Silva	4		
Tahir Naqqash c Mendis b D.S. de Silva	57		
Iqbal Qasim lbw b D.S. de Silva	1	c sub (Wijesuriya) b D.S. de Silva	56
Rashid Khan c Madugalle b G.R.A. de Silva	59		
Tauseef Ahmed not out	5		
Extras (LB9, W4, NB9)	22	(B5, LB1, W1, NB1)	8
Total	**396**	**(4 wkts dec)**	**301**

SRI LANKA

*B. Warnapura lbw b Tahir	13	b Tahir	0
S. Wettimuny c Mansoor b Rashid	71	c Saleem b Rashid	14
R.L. Dias lbw b Iqbal	53	lbw b Tahir	19
R.S. Madugalle c Saleem b Rashid	29	c Tauseef b Iqbal	18
J.R. Ratnayeke c Rizwan b Iqbal	24	c Saleem b Wasim	0
L.R.D. Mendis c Rashid b Tahir	54	c Saleem b Iqbal	15
A. Ranatunga st Saleem b Tauseef	13	c Saleem b Tauseef	33
D.S. de Silva b Tauseef	26	st Saleem b Iqbal	12
†H.M. Goonatillake c Saleem b Tahir	14	b Wasim	13
A.L.F. de Mel run out	9	c Javed b Iqbal	2
G.R.A. de Silva not out	10	not out	0
Extras (B1, LB12, W3, NB12)	28	(B9, LB11, W1, NB2)	23
Total	**344**		**149**

BOWLING

SRI LANKA	O	M	R	W		O	M	R	W
de Mel	28	2	124	3	—	23.2	3	100	1
Ratnayeke	16	6	49	1	—	5.4	2	20	0
D.S. de Silva	38	8	102	4	—	26	3	99	3
G.R.A. de Silva	17.2	2	69	1	—	35	5	74	0
Warnapura	2	0	9	0					
Wettimuny	2	0	21	0					
PAKISTAN									
Tahir	32	11	83	3	—	9	1	34	2
Rashid	26	7	53	2	—	8	3	25	1
Iqbal	28	7	88	2	—	15.1	8	27	4
Tauseef	21.4	6	64	2	—	12	1	39	1
Wasim	5	1	28	0	—	3	2	1	2

FALL OF WICKETS

	PAK	SL	PAK	SL
	1st	1st	2nd	2nd
1st	6	24	16	1
2nd	46	120	53	27
3rd	53	152	107	41
4th	72	199	268	68
5th	113	221	—	91
6th	126	242	—	121
7th	230	285	—	125
8th	232	308	—	139
9th	359	322	—	149
10th	396	344	—	149

SECOND TEST MATCH
PLAYED AT FAISALABAD, 14, 15, 16, 18, 19 MARCH
MATCH DRAWN

SRI LANKA

S. Wettimuny b Wasim	157	c Ashraf b Tahir	13
†H.M. Goonatillake c Salim b Iqbal	27	b Iqbal	56
R.L. Dias c Salim b Iqbal	98	c Mohsin b Tahir	7
*L.R.D. Mendis b Iqbal	16	run out	0
R.S. Madugalle not out	91	lbw b Iqbal	12
A. Ranatunga b Iqbal	0	c Ashraf b Tauseef	2
A.N. Ranasinghe c Javed b Iqbal	6	c Javed b Tauseef	5
A.L.F. de Mel c Salim b Iqbal	4	not out	25
D.S. de Silva lbw b Rizwan	25	st Ashraf b Tauseef	8
L.W. Kaluperuma b Rizwan	0	not out	11
G.R.A. de Silva lbw b Rizwan	5		
Extras (LB11, W2, NB12)	25	(LB9, W1, NB5)	15
Total	**454**	**(8 wkts dec)**	**154**

PAKISTAN

Rizwan-uz-Zaman b G.R.A. de Silva	36	b de Mel	16
Mohsin Khan c Wettimuny b de Mel	12	c de Mel b D.S. de Silva	74
Salim Malik b de Mel	23	lbw b de Mel	4
*Javed Miandad c Ranatunga b D.S. de Silva	18	c Madugalle b D.S. de Silva	36
Wasim Raja c Madugalle b D.S. de Silva	22	c Wettimuny b D.S. de Silva	0
Haroon Rashid c de Mel b D.S. de Silva	25	b D.S. de Silva	0
†Ashraf Ali b Ranasinghe	58	not out	29
Tahir Naqqash c de Mel b G.R.A. de Silva	1	c sub (B.N. Perera) b D.S. de Silva	13
Iqbal Qasim run out	5		
Rashid Khan not out	43	not out	3
Tauseef Ahmed c Madugalle b D.S. de Silva	18		
Extras (LB1, NB8)	9	(B3, LB7, NB1)	11
Total	**270**	**(7 wkts)**	**186**

BOWLING

PAKISTAN	O	M	R	W	O	M	R	W
Tahir	26	4	108	0	13	3	53	2
Rashid	13	3	52	0	1	0	4	0
Iqbal	65	18	141	6	30	9	51	2
Tauseef	12	3	35	0	14	4	18	3
Wasim	26	6	66	1	—	—	—	—
Javed	1	0	1	0	—	—	—	—
Rizwan	12	3	26	3	5	2	13	0
SRI LANKA								
de Mel	23	4	73	2	17	2	71	2
Ranasinghe	7	1	23	1	5	0	17	0
D.S. de Silva	32	3	103	4	18	2	59	5
G.R.A. de Silva	24	10	38	2	4	1	20	0
Kaluperuma	6	0	24	0				

FALL OF WICKETS

	SL 1st	PAK 1st	SL 2nd	PAK 2nd
1st	77	19	19	24
2nd	294	54	44	40
3rd	304	83	82	132
4th	341	116	82	132
5th	341	124	86	132
6th	355	154	104	137
7th	385	156	114	174
8th	446	185	114	—
9th	448	222	—	—
10th	454	270	—	—

THIRD TEST MATCH

PLAYED AT LAHORE 22, 23, 25, 26, 27 MARCH

PAKISTAN WON BY AN INNINGS AND 102 RUNS

SRI LANKA

B. Warnapura c Mohsin b Imran	7	c Javed b Tauseef	26
S. Wettimuny c Iqbal b Imran	20	c Majid b Imran	41
R.S.A. Jayasekera b Imran	0	b Imran	2
R.L. Dias c Tauseef b Imran	109	c Wasim b Tauseef	9
R.S. Madugalle c Ashraf b Imran	0	b Tauseef	5
L.R.D. Mendis c & b Tauseef	26	c Mudassar b Tauseef	5
D.S. de Silva b Imran	7	not out	36
A.L.F. de Mel st Ashraf b Iqbal	34	lbw b Imran	0
†H.M. Goonatillake b Imran	15	c & b Imran	21
J.R. Ratnayake not out	1	b Imran	0
R.G.C.E. Wijesuriya lbw b Imran	0	b Imran	3
Extras (LB11, W6, NB4)	21	(B4, LB2, W1, NB3)	10
Total	**240**		**158**

PAKISTAN

Mudassar Nazar c Madugalle b de Silva	37
Mohsin Khan b Ratnayeke	129
Majid Khan c sub (Ranasinghe) b Ratnayeke	63
*Javed Miandad c Goonatillake b de Mel	26
Zaheer Abbas b Ratnayeke	134
Wasim Raja c Goonatillake b de Mel	1
Imran Khan c Mendis b de Mel	39
†Ashraf Ali not out	45
Tahir Naqqash not out	1
Iqbal Qasim did not bat	
Tauseef Ahmed did not bat	
Extras (B5, LB5, W10, NB5)	25
Total (7 wkts dec)	**500**

BOWLING

PAKISTAN	O	M	R	W		O	M	R	W	FALL OF WICKETS			
											SL	PAK	SL
											1st	1st	2nd
Imran	29.3	8	58	8	—	22.5	3	58	6				
Tahir	10	0	54	0	—	6	0	22	0	1st	17	79	56
Iqbal	12	4	21	1	—	1	0	1	0	2nd	17	230	78
Mudassar	8	1	23	0	—	—	—	—	—	3rd	79	247	84
Tauseef	12	1	50	1	—	25	7	58	4	4th	83	297	90
Wasim	5	1	13	0	—	6	4	9	0	5th	141	306	93
Majid	—	—	—	—	—	1	0	3	0	6th	171	406	95
SRI LANKA										7th	209	494	96
de Mel	28	3	120	3	—	—	—	—	—	8th	231	—	142
Ratnayeke	28	3	121	3	—	—	—	—	—	9th	239	—	142
de Silva	39	4	129	1	—	—	—	—	—	10th	240	—	158
Wijesuriya	24	3	105	0	—	—	—	—	—				

England v India 1982

FIRST CORNHILL TEST MATCH
(GOLDEN JUBILEE MATCH)

PLAYED AT LORD'S, 10, 11, 12, 14, 15 JUNE
ENGLAND WON BY 7 WICKETS

ENGLAND

G. Cook lbw b Kapil Dev	4	lbw b Kapil Dev	10
C.J. Tavaré c Viswanath b Kapil Dev	4	b Kapil Dev	3
A.J. Lamb lbw b Kapil Dev	9	not out	37
D.I. Gower c Viswanath b Kapil Dev	37	not out	14
I.T. Botham c Malhotra b Madan Lal	67		
D.W. Randall c Parkar b Kapil Dev	126		
D.R. Pringle c Gavaskar b Doshi	7		
P.H. Edmonds c Kirmani b Madan Lal	64		
†R.W. Taylor c Viswanath b Doshi	31	c Malhotra b Kapil Dev	1
P.J.W. Allott not out	41		
*R.G.D. Willis b Madan Lal	28		
Extras (B1, LB5, NB9)	15	(LB2)	2
Total	**433**	**(3 wkts)**	**67**

INDIA

*S.M. Gavaskar b Botham	48	c Cook b Willis	24
G.A. Parkar lbw b Botham	6	b Willis	1
D.B. Vengsarkar lbw b Willis	2	c Allott b Willis	157
G.R. Viswanath b Botham	1	c Taylor b Pringle	3
Yashpal Sharma lbw b Pringle	4	b Willis	37
A. Malhotra lbw b Pringle	5	c Taylor b Willis	0
Kapil Dev c Cook b Willis	41	c Cook b Botham	89
R.J. Shastri c Cook b Willis	4	b Allott	23
†S.M.H. Kirmani not out	6	c Gower b Willis	3
S. Madan Lal c Tavaré b Botham	0	lbw b Pringle	15
D.R. Doshi c Taylor b Botham	0	not out	4
Extras (LB1, NB4)	5	(LB2, NB11)	13
Total	**128**		**369**

BOWLING

INDIA	O	M	R	W		O	M	R	W
Kapil Dev	43	8	125	5	—	10	1	43	3
Madan Lal	28.1	6	99	3	—	2	1	2	0
Shastri	34	10	73	0	—	2	0	9	0
Doshi	40	7	120	2	—	5	3	11	0
Yashpal Sharma	3	2	1	0					
ENGLAND									
Botham	19.4	3	46	5	—	31.5	7	103	1
Willis	16	2	41	3	—	28	3	101	6
Pringle	9	4	16	2	—	19	4	58	2
Edmonds	2	1	5	0	—	15	6	39	0
Allott	4	1	15	0	—	17	3	51	1
Cook					—	1	0	4	0

FALL OF WICKETS

	ENG	IND	IND	ENG
	1st	1st	2nd	2nd
1st	5	17	6	11
2nd	18	21	47	13
3rd	37	22	107	18
4th	96	31	110	—
5th	149	45	252	—
6th	166	112	252	—
7th	291	116	254	—
8th	363	116	275	—
9th	363	128	341	—
10th	433	128	369	—

SECOND CORNHILL TEST MATCH

PLAYED AT OLD TRAFFORD, 24, 25, 26, 27, 28 JUNE
MATCH DRAWN

ENGLAND

G. Cook b Doshi	66
C.J. Tavaré b Doshi	57
A.J. Lamb c Viswanath b Madan Lal	9
D.I. Gower c Shastri b Madan Lal	9
I.T. Botham b Shastri	128
D.W. Randall c Kirmani b Doshi	0
G. Miller c Vengsarkar b Doshi	98
D.R. Pringle st Kirmani b Doshi	23
P.H. Edmonds c Kirmani b Madan Lal	12
†R.W. Taylor not out	1
*R.G.D. Willis c Gavaskar b Doshi	6
Extras (B2, LB5, NB9)	16
Total	**425**

INDIA

*S.M. Gavaskar c Tavaré b Willis	2
R.J. Shastri c Cook b Willis	0
D.B. Vengsarkar c Randall b Pringle	12
G.R. Viswanath c Taylor b Botham	54
†S.M.H. Kirmani b Edmonds	58
Yashpal Sharma b Edmonds	10
S.M. Patil not out	129
Kapil Dev c Taylor b Miller	65
S. Madan Lal b Edmonds	26
S.V. Nayak not out	2
D.R. Doshi did not bat	
Extras (B6, LB2, W3, NB10)	21
Total (8 wkts)	**379**

BOWLING

INDIA	O	M	R	W	
Kapil Dev	36	5	109	0	—
Madan Lal	35	9	104	3	—
Nayak	12	1	50	0	—
Doshi	47.1	17	102	6	—
Shastri	23	8	44	1	—
ENGLAND					
Willis	17	4	94	2	—
Pringle	15	4	33	1	—
Edmonds	37	12	94	3	—
Botham	12	4	86	1	—
Miller	16	4	51	1	—

FALL OF WICKETS

	ENG	IND
	1st	1st
1st	106	5
2nd	117	8
3rd	141	25
4th	161	112
5th	161	136
6th	330	173
7th	382	269
8th	413	366
9th	419	—
10th	425	—

THIRD CORNHILL TEST MATCH
PLAYED AT THE OVAL, 8, 9, 10, 12, 13 JULY
MATCH DRAWN

ENGLAND

G. Cook c Shastri b Patil	50	c Yashpal Sharma b Kapil Dev	8
C.J. Tavaré b Kapil Dev	39	not out	75
A.J. Lamb run out	107	b Doshi	45
D.I. Gower c Kirmani b Shastri	47	c & b Nayak	45
I.T. Botham c Viswanath b Doshi	208		
D.W. Randall st Kirmani b Shastri	95		
D.R. Pringle st Kirmani b Doshi	9		
P.H. Edmonds c sub (G.A. Parkar) b Doshi	14		
†R.W. Taylor lbw b Shastri	3		
P.J.W. Allott c Yashpal Sharma b Doshi	3		
*R.G.D. Willis not out	1		
Extras (B3, LB5, NB10)	18	(B6, LB8, NB4)	18
Total	**594**	**(3 wkts dec)**	**191**

INDIA

R.J. Shastri c Botham b Willis	66	c Taylor b Willis	0
D.B. Vengsarkar c Edmonds b Botham	6	c Taylor b Pringle	16
G.R. Viswanath lbw b Willis	56	not out	75
Yashpal Sharma c Gower b Willis	38	not out	9
S.M. Patil c sub (N.R. Taylor) b Botham	62		
†S.M.H. Kirmani b Allott	43		
Kapil Dev c Allott b Edmonds	97		
S. Madan Lal c Taylor b Edmonds	5		
S.V. Nayak b Edmonds	11	c Taylor b Pringle	6
D.R. Doshi not out	5		
*S.M. Gavaskar absent hurt			
Extras (B3, LB5, NB13)	21	(LB3, NB2)	5
Total	**410**	**(3 wkts)**	**111**

BOWLING

INDIA	O	M	R	W		O	M	R	W
Kapil Dev	25	4	109	1	—	19	3	53	1
Madan Lal	26	8	69	0	—	11	6	17	0
Nayak	21	5	66	0	—	5.3	0	16	1
Patil	14	1	48	1	—				
Doshi	46	6	175	4	—	19	5	47	1
Shastri	41.3	8	109	3	—	16	3	40	0
ENGLAND									
Willis	23	4	78	3	—	4	0	16	1
Botham	19	2	73	2	—	4	0	12	0
Allott	24	4	69	1	—	4	1	12	0
Pringle	28	5	80	0	—	11	5	32	2
Edmonds	35.2	11	89	3	—	13	5	34	0

FALL OF WICKETS

	ENG 1st	IND 1st	ENG 2nd	IND 2nd
1st	96	21	12	0
2nd	96	134	94	18
3rd	185	135	191	43
4th	361	232	—	—
5th	512	248	—	—
6th	534	378	—	—
7th	562	394	—	—
8th	569	396	—	—
9th	582	410	—	—
10th	594	—	—	—

TEST MATCH AVERAGES

ENGLAND v INDIA 1982

ENGLAND

	M	I	NO	Runs	HS	Avge	100	50	Ct	St
I.T. Botham	3	3	0	403	208	134.33	2	1	1	—
G. Miller	1	1	0	98	98	98.00	—	1	—	—
D.W. Randall	3	3	0	221	126	73.66	1	1	1	—
A.J. Lamb	3	5	1	207	107	51.75	1	—	—	—
C.J. Tavaré	3	5	1	178	75*	44.50	—	2	2	—
P.J.W. Allott	2	2	1	44	41*	44.00	—	—	2	—
D.I. Gower	3	5	1	152	47	38.00	—	—	2	—
P.H. Edmonds	3	3	0	90	64	30.00	—	1	1	—
G. Cook	3	5	0	138	66	27.60	—	2	5	—
R.G.D. Willis	3	3	1	35	28	17.50	—	—	—	—
D.R. Pringle	3	3	0	39	23	13.00	—	—	—	—
R.W. Taylor	3	4	1	36	31	12.00	—	—	9	—

	Overs	Mdns	Runs	Wkts	Avge	Best	5 wI	10 wM
R.G.D. Willis	88	13	330	15	22.00	6-101	1	—
D.R. Pringle	82	22	219	7	31.28	2-16	—	—
I.T. Botham	93.3	16	320	9	35.55	5-46	1	—
P.H. Edmonds	102.2	35	261	6	43.50	3-89	—	—
G. Miller	16	4	51	1	51.00	1-51	—	—
P.J.W. Allott	49	9	147	2	73.50	1-51	—	—
G. Cook	1	0	4	0	—	—	—	—

INDIA

	M	I	NO	Runs	HS	Avge	100	50	Ct	St
S.M. Patil	2	2	1	191	129*	191.00	1	1	—	—
Kapil Dev	3	4	0	292	97	73.00	—	3	—	—
G.R. Viswanath	3	5	1	189	75*	47.25	—	3	5	—
D.B. Vengsarkar	3	5	0	193	157	38.60	1	—	4	—
S.M.H. Kirmani	3	4	1	110	58	36.66	—	1	4	3
S.M. Gavaskar	3	3	0	74	48	24.66	—	—	2	—
Yashpal Sharma	3	5	1	98	38	24.50	—	—	2	—
R.J. Shastri	3	5	0	93	66	18.60	—	1	2	—
S. Madan Lal	3	4	0	52	26	13.00	—	—	—	—
S.V. Nayak	2	3	1	19	11	9.50	—	—	1	—
D.R. Doshi	3	3	2	9	5*	9.00	—	—	—	—
G.A. Parkar	1	2	0	7	6	3.50	—	—	1	—
A. Malhotra	1	2	0	5	5	2.50	—	—	2	—

	Overs	Mdns	Runs	Wkts	Avge	Best	5 wI	10 wM
D.R. Doshi	157.1	38	455	13	35.00	6-102	1	—
Kapil Dev	133	21	439	10	43.90	5-125	1	—
S.M. Patil	14	1	48	1	48.00	1-48	—	—
S. Madan Lal	102.1	30	291	6	48.50	3-99	—	—
R.J. Shastri	116.3	29	275	4	68.75	3-109	—	—
S.V. Nayak	38.3	6	132	1	132.00	1-16	—	—
Yashpal Sharma	3	2	1	0	—	—	—	—

18

INDIAN TOUR AVERAGES 1982

All first-class matches: Played 12, Won 1, Drawn 10, Lost 1

BATTING AND FIELDING

	M	I	NO	Runs	HS	Avge	100	50	Ct	St
G.R. Viswanath	9	12	3	561	106*	62.33	2	4	8	—
S. Madan Lal	9	15	10	309	58*	61.80	—	2	1	—
D.B. Vengsarkar	9	13	2	610	157	55.45	1	4	9	—
S.M. Gavaskar	8	10	—	438	172	43.80	1	1	3	—
Yashpal Sharma	9	15	5	418	77	41.80	—	3	6	—
Kapil Dev	8	11	—	438	97	39.81	—	3	5	—
S.V. Nayak	10	13	6	253	67*	36.14	—	1	3	—
G.A. Parkar	7	14	2	433	146	36.08	1	2	7	1
A. Malhotra	8	15	1	462	154*	33.00	1	2	5	—
S.M.H. Kirmani	9	12	3	265	65	29.44	—	2	11	4
R.J. Shastri	9	15	2	359	74	27.61	—	3	6	—
S.M. Patil	9	16	1	390	129*	26.00	1	1	1	—
P. Roy	7	12	—	174	51	14.50	—	1	1	—
D.R. Doshi	9	4	2	11	5*	5.50	—	—	—	—
N.S. Yadav	7	2	1	1	1*	1.00	—	—	—	—
Randhir Singh	5	3	—	0	0	—	—	—	—	—

BOWLING

	Type	O	M	R	W	Avge	Best	5 wI	10 wM
S. Madan Lal	RFM	246.1	49	763	22	34.68	4-28	—	—
D.R. Doshi	SLA	345.3	78	1003	25	40.12	6-102	1	—
Kapil Dev	RFM	255.4	45	810	20	40.50	5-39	2	—
R.J. Shastri	SLA	269.5	69	634	15	42.26	3-109	—	—
S.V. Nayak	RM/LB	205.3	39	645	14	46.07	5-54	1	—
Randhir Singh	RM	131	24	418	7	59.71	2-50	—	—
N.S. Yadav	OB	195	33	604	7	86.28	3-77	—	—

Also bowled: S.M. Gavaskar 5-0-23-0; A. Malhotra 9-1-37-1; S.M. Patil 60-9-155-4; P. Roy 1-0-14-0; D.B. Vengsarkar 0.2-0-2-0; Yashpal Sharma 10-2-32-0.

England v Pakistan 1982

FIRST CORNHILL TEST MATCH

PLAYED AT EDGBASTON, 29, 30, 31 JULY, 1 AUGUST
ENGLAND WON BY 113 RUNS

ENGLAND

D.W. Randall	b Imran	17	b Imran	105
C.J. Tavaré	c Javed b Qadir	54	c Mohsin b Imran	17
A.J. Lamb	c Bari b Sikander	6	lbw b Tahir	5
D.I. Gower	c Bari b Imran	74	c Mudassar b Tahir	13
I.T. Botham	b Imran	2	lbw b Tahir	0
M.W. Gatting	b Imran	17	c Bari b Tahir	5
G. Miller	b Imran	47	b Tahir	5
I.A. Greig	c sub (Haroon) b Imran	14	b Qadir	7
E.E. Hemmings	lbw b Imran	2	c Mansoor b Qadir	19
†R.W. Taylor	lbw b Imran	1	c Qadir b Raja	54
*R.G.D. Willis	not out	0	not out	28
Extras	(B4, LB10, W6, NB18)	38	(B10, LB11, W7, NB5)	33
Total		**272**		**291**

PAKISTAN

Mudassar Nazar	lbw b Botham	0	lbw b Botham	0
Mohsin Khan	c Willis b Botham	26	lbw b Botham	35
Tahir Naqqash	c Taylor b Greig	12	c & b Hemmings	39
Mansoor Akhtar	c Willis b Hemmings	58	c Taylor b Botham	10
Javed Miandad	c Willis b Hemmings	30	run out	0
Zaheer Abbas	lbw b Greig	40	c Taylor b Willis	4
Wasim Raja	c Tavaré b Willis	26	c Gower b Willis	16
*Imran Khan	c Taylor b Willis	22	b Miller	65
†Wasim Bari	not out	16	c Taylor b Botham	12
Abdul Qadir	lbw b Greig	7	c Randall b Miller	9
Sikander Bakht	c Hemmings b Greig	1	not out	1
Extras	(B5, LB2, W1, NB5)	13	(LB3, NB5)	8
Total		**251**		**199**

BOWLING

PAKISTAN	O	M	R	W		O	M	R	W
Imran Khan	25.3	11	52	7	—	32	5	84	2
Tahir	15	4	46	1	—	18	7	40	5
Sikander	18	5	58	1	—	13	5	34	0
Mudassar	5	2	8	0	—	—	—	—	—
Qadir	29	7	70	1	—	40	10	100	2
Raja	—	—	—	—	—	2.3	2	0	1
ENGLAND									
Botham	24	1	86	2	—	21	7	70	4
Greig	14.2	3	53	4	—	4	1	19	0
Willis	15	3	42	2	—	14	2	49	2
Hemmings	24	5	56	2	—	10	4	27	1
Miller	2	1	1	0	—	7.4	1	26	2

FALL OF WICKETS

	ENG	PAK	ENG	PAK
	1st	*1st*	*2nd*	*2nd*
1st	29	0	62	0
2nd	37	29	98	0
3rd	164	53	127	38
4th	172	110	137	54
5th	179	164	137	66
6th	228	198	146	69
7th	263	217	170	98
8th	265	227	188	151
9th	271	248	212	178
10th	272	251	291	199

SECOND CORNHILL TEST MATCH

PLAYED AT LORD'S, 12, 13, 14, 15, 16 AUGUST
PAKISTAN WON BY 10 WICKETS

PAKISTAN

Mohsin Khan c Tavaré b Jackman	200	not out		39
Mudassar Nazar c Taylor b Jackman	20			
Mansoor Akhtar c Lamb b Botham	57			
Javed Miandad run out	6	not out		26
Zaheer Abbas b Jackman	75			
Haroon Rashid lbw b Botham	1			
*Imran Khan c Taylor b Botham	12			
Tahir Naqqash c Gatting b Jackman	2			
†Wasim Bari not out	24			
Abdul Qadir not out	18			
Sarfraz Nawaz did not bat				
Extras	13	(B3, LB8, NB2)	(B1, LB10, W1)	12
Total (8 wkts dec)	428	(0 wkts)		77

ENGLAND

D.W. Randall b Sarfraz	29	b Mudassar		9
C.J. Tavaré b Sarfraz	8	c Javed b Imran		82
A.J. Lamb c Haroon b Tahir	33	lbw b Mudassar		0
*D.I. Gower c Mansoor b Imran	29	c Wasim b Mudassar		0
I.T. Botham c Mohsin b Abdul	31	c Sarfraz b Mudassar		69
M.W. Gatting not out	32	c Wasim b Mudassar		7
D.R. Pringle c Haroon b Abdul	5	c Javed b Abdul		14
I.A. Greig lbw b Abdul	3	lbw b Mudassar		2
E.E. Hemmings b Sarfraz	6	c Wasim b Imran		14
†R.W. Taylor lbw b Abdul	5	not out		24
R.D. Jackman lbw b Imran	0	c Haroon b Abdul		17
Extras	46	(B11, LB12, W13, NB10)	(B10, LB19, W5, NB4)	38
Total	227			276

BOWLING

ENGLAND	O	M	R	W		O	M	R	W
Botham	44	8	148	3	—	7	0	30	0
Jackman	36	5	110	4	—	4	0	22	0
Pringle	26	9	62	0	—	—	—	—	—
Greig	13	2	42	0	—	—	—	—	—
Hemmings	20	3	53	0	—	2.1	0	3	0
PAKISTAN									
Imran	23	4	55	2	—	42	13	84	2
Sarfraz	23	4	56	3	—	14	5	22	0
Tahir	12	4	25	1	—	7	4	6	0
Abdul	24	9	39	4	—	37.5	15	94	2
Mudassar	4	1	6	0	—	19	7	32	6

FALL OF WICKETS			
	P	E	E
	1st	1st	2nd
1st	53	16	9
2nd	197	69	9
3rd	208	89	9
4th	361	157	121
5th	364	173	132
6th	380	187	171
7th	382	197	180
8th	401	217	224
9th	—	226	235
10th	—	227	276

THIRD CORNHILL TEST MATCH
PLAYED AT HEADINGLEY, 26, 27, 28, 30, 31 AUGUST
ENGLAND WON BY 3 WICKETS

PAKISTAN

Mohsin Khan c Taylor b Botham	10	c Taylor b Willis	0
Mudassar Nazar b Botham	65	c Botham b Willis	0
Mansoor Akhtar c Gatting b Willis	0	c Randall b Botham	39
Javed Miandad c Fowler b Willis	54	c Taylor b Botham	52
Zaheer Abbas c Taylor b Jackman	8	lbw b Botham	4
Majid Khan lbw b Jackman	21	c Gower b Botham	10
*Imran Khan not out	67	c Randall b Botham	46
†Wasim Bari b Jackman	23	c Taylor b Willis	7
Abdul Qadir c Willis b Botham	5	b Jackman	17
Sikander Bakht c Tavaré b Willis	7	c Gatting b Marks	7
Ehteshamuddin b Botham	0	not out	0
Extras (B1, LB7, W4, NB3)	15	(LB6, W4, NB7)	17
Total	**275**		**199**

ENGLAND

C.J. Tavaré c sub (Haroon) b Imran	22	c Majid b Imran	33
G. Fowler b Ehteshamuddin	9	c Wasim b Mudassar	86
M.W. Gatting lbw b Imran	25	lbw b Imran	25
A.J. Lamb c Mohsin b Imran	0	lbw b Mudassar	4
D.I. Gower c sub (Haroon) b Sikander	74	c Wasim b Mudassar	7
I.T. Botham c sub (Haroon) b Sikander	57	c Majid b Mudassar	4
D.W. Randall run out	8	lbw b Imran	0
V.J. Marks b Abdul	7	not out	12
†R.W. Taylor c Javed b Imran	18	not out	6
R.D. Jackman c Mohsin b Imran	11		
*R.G.D. Willis not out	1		
Extras (B4, LB10, W2, NB8)	24	(B19, LB16, W1, NB6)	42
Total	**256**	**(7 wkts)**	**219**

BOWLING

ENGLAND	O	M	R	W		O	M	R	W	FALL OF WICKETS			
											PAK	ENG	PAK	ENG
Willis	26	6	76	3	—	19	3	55	3		1st	1st	2nd	2nd
Botham	24.5	9	70	4	—	30	8	74	5	1st	16	15	0	103
Jackman	37	14	74	3	—	28	11	41	1	2nd	19	67	3	168
Marks	5	0	23	0	—	2	1	8	1	3rd	119	69	81	172
Gatting	8	2	17	0	—	2	1	4	0	4th	128	77	85	189
PAKISTAN										5th	160	146	108	189
Imran	25.2	7	49	5	—	30.2	8	66	3	6th	168	159	115	189
Ehteshamuddin	14	4	46	1	—					7th	207	170	128	199
Sikander	24	5	47	2	—	20	4	40	0	8th	224	209	170	—
Abdul	22	5	87	1	—	8	2	16	0	9th	274	255	199	—
Mudassar	4	1	3	0	—	22	7	55	4	10th	275	256	199	—

TEST MATCH AVERAGES

ENGLAND

	M	I	NO	Runs	HS	Avge	100	50	Ct	St
G. Fowler	1	2	0	95	86	47.50	—	1	1	—
C.J. Tavaré	3	6	0	216	82	36.00	—	2	3	—
D.I. Gower	3	6	0	197	74	32.83	—	2	2	—
D.W. Randall	3	6	0	168	105	28.00	1	—	3	—
I.T. Botham	3	6	0	163	69	27.16	—	2	1	—
R.W. Taylor	3	6	2	108	54	27.00	—	1	12	—
G. Miller	1	2	0	52	47	26.00	—	—	1	—
M.W. Gatting	3	6	1	111	32*	22.20	—	—	3	—
V.J. Marks	1	2	1	19	12*	19.00	—	—	—	—
E.E. Hemmings	2	4	0	41	19	10.25	—	—	2	—
D.R. Pringle	1	2	0	19	14	9.50	—	—	—	—
R.D. Jackman	2	3	0	28	17	9.33	—	—	—	—
A.J. Lamb	3	6	0	48	33	8.00	—	—	1	—
I.A. Greig	2	4	0	26	14	6.50	—	—	—	—
R.G.D. Willis	2	3	3	29	28*	—	—	—	3	—

	Overs	Mdns	Runs	Wkts	Avge	Best	5 wI	10 wM
G. Miller	9.4	2	27	2	13.50	2-26	—	—
R.G.D. Willis	74	14	222	10	22.20	3-55	—	—
I.T. Botham	150.5	33	478	18	26.55	5-74	1	—
I.A. Greig	31.2	6	114	4	28.50	4-53	—	—
R.D. Jackman	105	30	247	8	30.87	4-110	—	—
V.J. Marks	7	1	31	1	31.00	1-8	—	—
E.E. Hemmings	56.1	12	149	3	49.66	2-56	—	—
M.W. Gatting	10	3	21	0	—	—	—	—
D.R. Pringle	26	9	62	0	—	—	—	—

PAKISTAN

	M	I	NO	Runs	HS	Avge	100	50	Ct	St
Mohsin Khan	3	6	1	310	200	62.00	1	—	4	—
Imran Khan	3	5	1	212	67*	53.00	—	2	—	—
Javed Miandad	3	6	1	178	54	35.60	—	2	4	—
Mansoor Akhtar	3	5	0	154	58	30.80	—	2	2	—
Wasim Bari	3	5	2	82	24*	27.33	—	—	8	—
Zaheer Abbas	3	5	0	131	75	26.20	—	1	—	—
Wasim Raja	1	2	0	42	26	21.00	—	—	—	—
Tahir Naqqash	2	3	0	53	39	17.66	—	—	—	—
Mudassar Nazar	3	5	0	85	65	17.00	—	1	1	—
Majid Khan	1	2	0	31	21	15.50	—	—	2	—
Abdul Qadir	3	5	1	56	18*	14.00	—	—	1	—
Sikander Bakht	2	4	1	16	7	5.33	—	—	—	—
Haroon Rashid	1	1	0	1	1	1.00	—	—	3	—
Eteshamuddin	1	2	1	0	0*	0.00	—	—	—	—
Sarfraz Nawaz	1	—	—	—	—	—	—	—	1	—

	Overs	Mdns	Runs	Wkts	Avge	Best	5 wI	10 wM
Wasim Raja	2.3	2	0	1	0.00	1-0	—	—
Mudassar Nazar	54	18	104	10	10.40	6-32	1	—
Tahir Naqqash	52	19	117	7	16.71	5-40	1	—
Imran Khan	178.1	48	390	21	18.57	7-52	2	—
Sarfraz Nawaz	37	9	78	3	26.00	3-56	—	—
Abdul Qadir	160.5	48	406	10	40.60	4-39	—	—
Ehteshamuddin	14	4	46	1	46.00	1-46	—	—
Sikander Bakht	75	19	179	3	59.66	2-47	—	—

PAKISTAN TOUR AVERAGES 1982

All first-class matches: Played 15, Won 5, Drawn 6, Lost 4

BATTING AND FIELDING

	M	I	NO	Runs	HS	Avge	100	50	Ct	St
Mudassar Nazar	11	16	6	825	211*	82.50	4	2	4	—
Zaheer Abbas	9	12	3	664	148*	73.77	2	4	2	—
Mohsin Khan	13	20	3	1248	203*	73.41	4	4	5	—
Imran Khan	9	8	4	291	67*	72.75	—	2	—	—
Javed Miandad	10	13	6	450	105*	64.28	1	3	14	—
Mansoor Ahktar	11	17	2	595	153	39.66	1	5	5	—
Haroon Rashid	10	13	3	331	90	33.10	—	2	8	—
Wasim Bari	11	7	2	162	45	32.40	—	—	22	7
Majid Khan	11	17	3	403	88	28.78	—	1	8	—
Wasim Raja	12	12	2	247	50*	24.70	—	1	5	—
Tahir Naqqash	6	4	—	65	39	16.25	—	—	3	—
Abdul Qadir	12	9	3	93	21*	15.50	—	—	3	—
Saleem Yousuf	4	4	1	38	15*	12.66	—	—	5	2
Salim Malik	5	7	1	68	25*	11.33	—	—	4	—
Sikander Bakht	12	7	2	29	9	5.80	—	—	3	—
Iqbal Qasim	7	4	1	9	5	3.00	—	—	2	—
Jalaluddin	3	2	—	10	10	5.00	—	—	—	—
Sarfraz Narwaz	6	1	—	7	7	3.50	—	—	1	—

Also batted: Two matches: Ehtesham-Ud-Din 0, 0*; Intikhab Alam 4, 0.

BOWLING

	Type	O	M	R	W	Avge	Best	5 wI	10 wM
Mudassar Nazar	RM	139	35	368	21	17.52	6-32	1	—
Imran Khan	RF	290.3	76	621	35	17.74	7-52	2	—
Abdul Qadir	LBG	542.4	123	1187	57	20.82	7-44	4	1
Sarfraz Narwaz	RFM	127	24	351	16	21.93	6-92	1	—
Sikander Bakht	RFM	326	86	959	27	35.51	4-68	—	—
Tahir Naqqash	RFM	160	44	537	15	35.80	5-40	1	—
Iqbal Qasim	SLA	161.1	36	434	12	36.16	5-52	1	—
Wasim Raja	LBG	117.4	30	346	9	38.44	3-34	—	—

Also bowled: Ehtesham-Ud-Din 28-9-81-1; Intikhab Alam 6-0-17-1; Jalaluddin 56-19-123-4; Javed Miandad 3-0-16-0; Majid Khan 22-9-57-2; Mansoor Akhtar 16.3-6-43-1; Mohsin Khan 5-0-32-1; Salim Malik 1-0-5-0; Zaheer Abbas 0.1-0-0-0.

Prudential Trophy One-Day Internationals 1982

ENGLAND v INDIA AT LEEDS 2/6/82

India 193 (Kapil Dev 60, Botham 4-56)
England 194-1 (Wood 78*, Tavaré 66)
Result: England won by 9 wickets

ENGLAND v INDIA AT THE OVAL 4/6/82

England 276 (Lamb 99, Gower 76, Kapil Dev 4-39)
India 162-8 in 55 overs (Madan Lal 53*)
Result: England won by 114 runs

ENGLAND v PAKISTAN AT TRENT BRIDGE 17/7/82

Pakistan 250-6 in 55 overs (Zaheer 53, Mudassar 51)
England 252-3 (Lamb 118)
Result: England won by 7 wickets

ENGLAND v PAKISTAN AT OLD TRAFFORD 19/7/82

England 295-8 in 55 overs (Gatting 76)
Pakistan 222 (Wasim Raja 60)
Result: England won by 73 runs

PROPOSED FUTURE CRICKET TOURS

TO ENGLAND	ENGLAND TOURS OVERSEAS
1984 West Indies	1983-84 Pakistan and New Zealand
1985 Australia	
1986 New Zealand and India	

OTHER TOURS

1983-84 West Indies to India	1984-85 West Indies to Pakistan
Australia to West Indies	India to West Indies

India v Sri Lanka 1982–83

TEST MATCH

PLAYED AT MADRAS, 17, 18, 19, 21, 22 SEPTEMBER
MATCH DRAWN

SRI LANKA

*B. Warnapura	c Yashpal Sharma b Madan Lal	4	c Yashpal Sharma b Kapil Dev	6
†H.M. Goonatillake	c Patil b Kapil Dev	7	c sub (K. Srikkanth) b Kapil Dev	0
R.L. Dias	c Arun Lal b Doshi	60	c Gavaskar b Shukla	97
L.R.D. Mendis	lbw b Doshi	105	b Shukla	105
A. Ranatunga	c Vengsarkar b Doshi	25	c Kirmani b Doshi	15
R.S. Madugalle	c Madan Lal b Doshi	46	c Patil b Doshi	4
A.N. Ranasinghe	c Arun Lal b Doshi	0	b Kapil Dev	77
D.S. de Silva	c Gavaskar b Madan Lal	49	not out	46
J.R. Ratnayeke	lbw b Kapil Dev	23	c Yashpal Sharma b Kapil Dev	6
A.L.F. de Mel	not out	18	b Doshi	12
G.R.A. de Silva	c Viswanath b Kapil Dev	0	b Kapil Dev	14
Extras	(LB4, NB5)	9	(B4, LB5, W1, NB2)	12
Total		**346**		**394**

INDIA

*S.M. Gavaskar	c de Mel b D.S. de Silva	155	not out	4
Arun Lal	b de Mel	63	c Dias b de Mel	1
D.B. Vengsarkar	run out	90	c & b de Mel	5
G.R. Viswanath	c Warnapura b D.S. de Silva	9	lbw b de Mel	2
S.M. Patil	not out	114	run out	46
Yashpal Sharma	c Goonatillake b de Mel	17	not out	31
Kapil Dev	c Goonatillake b Ratnayeke	31	c Goonatillake b de Mel	30
S. Madan Lal	not out	37	c & b D.S. de Silva	9
†S.M.H. Kirmani			b de Mel	5
R. Shukla	did not bat			
D.R. Doshi	did not bat			
Extras	(B11, LB8, W2, NB29)	50	(NB2)	2
Total	(6 wkts dec)	**566**	(7 wkts)	**135**

BOWLING

INDIA	O	M	R	W		O	M	R	W
Kapil Dev	22.5	2	97	3	—	24.3	3	110	5
Madan Lal	16	1	72	2	—	7	1	43	0
Doshi	30	8	85	5	—	38	4	147	3
Patil	2	0	13	0	—	—	—	—	—
Shukla	22	4	70	0	—	27	5	82	2
SRI LANKA									
de Mel	28	2	133	2	—	14	0	68	5
Ratnayeke	19	1	75	1	—	5	0	36	0
G.R.A. de Silva	17	2	78	0					
Warnapura	9	3	27	0					
D.S. de Silva	48	4	162	2	—	9	1	29	1
Ranasinghe	7	0	29	0					
Ranatunga	1	0	12	0	—				

FALL OF WICKETS

	SL	IND	SL	IND
	1st	1st	2nd	2nd
1st	11	156	6	3
2nd	11	329	47	16
3rd	164	347	157	78
4th	203	363	198	90
5th	204	403	202	94
6th	204	488	291	125
7th	281	—	340	130
8th	304	—	361	—
9th	346	—	362	—
10th	346	—	394	—

Yashpal Sharma kept wicket after tea on the first day, and also on the fourth day, when he took two catches.

Pakistan v Australia 1982–83

FIRST TEST MATCH

PLAYED AT KARACHI 22, 23, 24, 26, 27 SEPTEMBER 1982
PAKISTAN WON BY 9 WICKETS

AUSTRALIA

G.M. Wood c Wasim b Imran	0	c sub (Salim) b Abdul	17
B.M. Laird run out	32	c Mansoor b Imran	3
J. Dyson b Iqbal	87	b Abdul	6
*K.J. Hughes c Wasim b Iqbal	54	c Wasim b Abdul	14
A.R. Border not out	55	c sub (Salim) b Abdul	8
G.M. Ritchie c Haroon b Abdul	4	b Iqbal	17
†R.W. Marsh b Tahir	19	lbw b Imran	32
B. Yardley b Javed b Tahir	0	lbw b Abdul	0
R.J. Bright c Haroon b Tahir	2	run out	32
G.F. Lawson c Wasim b Tahir	0	run out	11
J.R. Thomson st Wasim b Abdul	14	c Wasim b Iqbal	18
Extras (B4, LB10, W1, NB2)	17	(B2, LB19)	21
Total	**284**		**179**

PAKISTAN

Mohsin Khan handled ball	58	not out	14
Mansoor Akhtar c Bright b Thomson	32	not out	26
Haroon Rashid c Laird b Yardley	82		
Javed Miandad b Lawson	32		
Zaheer Abbas c Marsh b Lawson	91		
Mudassar Nazar not out	52	c Border b Thomson	5
*Imran Khan c Yardley b Bright	1		
Tahir Naqqash st Marsh b Bright	15		
†Wasim Bari c Marsh b Bright	0		
Abdul Qadir run out	29		
Iqbal Qasim not out	2	(NB2)	2
Extras (B4, LB8, W1, NB12)	25		
Total (9 wkts dec)	**419**	**(1 wkt)**	**47**

BOWLING

PAKISTAN	O	M	R	W		O	M	R	W	FALL OF WICKETS			
											A	P	A	P
Imran	23	3	38	1	—	12	5	17	2		1st	1st	2nd	2nd
Tahir	16	3	61	4	—	7	3	17	0	1st	0	43	10	5
Mudassar	13	0	33	0	—	—	—	—	—	2nd	71	168	20	—
Abdul	21.4	1	80	2	—	26	7	76	5	3rd	169	188	32	—
Iqbal	26	10	55	2	—	21.5	6	48	2	4th	202	277	45	—
AUSTRALIA										5th	211	328	72	—
Thomson	29	5	103	1	—	3	1	16	1	6th	249	329	72	—
Lawson	39	10	93	2	—	—	—	—	—	7th	249	351	73	—
Bright	36	8	96	3	—	5	0	14	0	8th	255	353	137	—
Yardley	23	2	98	1	—	3	1	9	0	9th	255	404	160	—
Border	1	0	4	0	—	—	—	—	—	10th	284	—	179	—
Hughes	—	—	—	—	—	0.1	0	6	0					

SECOND TEST MATCH

PLAYED AT FAISALABAD 30 SEPTEMBER, 1, 2, 4, 5, OCTOBER 1982
PAKISTAN WON BY AN INNINGS AND 3 RUNS

PAKISTAN

Mohsin Khan c Marsh b Lawson	76
Mudassar Nazar c Hughes b Border	79
Mansoor Akhtar c Marsh b Lawson	111
Javed Miandad c Laird b Lawson	6
Zaheer Abbas b Sleep	126
Haroon Rashid c Laird b Lawson	51
*Imran Khan not out	24
Tahir Naqqash not out	15
†Wasim Bari did not bat	
Abdul Qadir did not bat	
Iqbal Qasim did not bat	
Extras (B4, LB1, NB8)	13
	—
Total (6 wkts dec)	501

AUSTRALIA

B.M. Laird lbw b Abdul	8	c Mudassar b Abdul	60
G.M. Wood c Wasim b Mudassar	49	c Wasim b Iqbal	22
J. Dyson c Mudassar b Iqbal	23	b Iqbal b Abdul	43
A.R. Border c Javed b Imran	9	c Haroon b Abdul	31
*K.J. Hughes c Imran b Abdul	11	lbw b Abdul	7
G.M. Ritchie run out	34	not out	106
P.R. Sleep lbw b Imran	0	c Mohsin b Abdul	29
†R.W. Marsh b Abdul	0	run out	8
R.J. Bright c Haroon b Abdul	0	c sub (Salim) b Iqbal	0
G.F. Lawson c Zaheer b Iqbal	14	lbw b Abdul	0
J.R. Thomson not out	1	st Wasim b Abdul	11
Extras (B8, LB6, W2, NB3)	19	(LB7, W1, NB5)	13
	—		—
Total	168		330

BOWLING

AUSTRALIA	O	M	R	W		O	M	R	W	FALL OF WICKETS			
Thomson	23	5	79	0	—	—	—	—	—				
Lawson	33	6	96	4	—	—	—	—	—				
Sleep	36	3	159	1	—	—	—	—	—		*P*	*A*	*A*
Bright	41	15	107	0	—	—	—	—	—		1st	1st	2nd
Border	11	3	47	1	—	—	—	—	—	1st	123	20	73
PAKISTAN										2nd	181	82	125
Imran	14	6	16	2	—	10	5	20	0	3rd	201	96	133
Tahir	15	4	21	0	—	9	1	25	0	4th	356	113	162
Abdul	42	14	76	4	—	50.4	12	142	7	5th	428	123	218
Iqbal	25	11	28	2	—	46	18	97	2	6th	482	123	290
Mudassar	7	2	8	1	—	9	3	26	0	7th	—	124	309
Zaheer	—	—	—	—	—	3	0	5	0	8th	—	124	309
Javed	—	—	—	—	—	1	0	2	0	9th	—	167	310
										10th	—	168	330

28

THIRD TEST MATCH

PLAYED AT LAHORE, 14, 15, 16, 18, 19 OCTOBER 1982
PAKISTAN WON BY 9 WICKETS

AUSTRALIA

G.M. Wood c Javed b Abdul	85	c Mudassar b Jalaluddin	30
B.M. Laird lbw b Abdul	28	lbw b Tahir	6
J. Dyson b Jalaluddin	10	lbw b Tahir	51
A.R. Border lbw b Imran	9	st Wasim b Abdul	6
*K.J. Hughes b Tahir	29	st Wasim b Abdul	39
G.M. Ritchie lbw b Imran	26	lbw b Imran	19
†R.W. Marsh c sub (Iqbal Sikhander) b Imran	1	c Mudassar b Jalaluddin	12
B. Yardley c Haroon b Jalaluddin	40	b Imran	21
G.F. Lawson not out	57	c sub (Iqbal Sikhander) b Imran	8
J.R. Thomson lbw b Jalaluddin	0	not out	5
T.M. Alderman b Imran	7	c Zaheer b Imran	0
Extras (B5, LB13, W1, NB5)	24	(B4, LB5, NB8)	17
Total	316		214

PAKISTAN

Mohsin Khan b Border	135	lbw b Lawson	14
Mudassar Nazar lbw b Lawson	23	not out	39
Abdul Qadir c Laird b Yardley	1		
Mansoor Akhtar lbw b Lawson	12	not out	2
Javed Miandad c Hughes b Alderman	138		
Zaheer Abbas c Yardley b Alderman	52		
Haroon Rashid c Ritchie b Thomson	15		
*Imran Khan not out	39		
Tahir Naqqash not out	7		
†Wasim Bari did not bat			
Jalaluddin did not bat			
Extras (B3, LB13, W2, NB27)	45	(B4, LB5)	9
Total (7 wkts dec)	467	(1 wkt)	64

BOWLING

PAKISTAN	O	M	R	W		O	M	R	W	FALL OF WICKETS				
											A	*P*	*A*	*P*
											1st	*1st*	*2nd*	*2nd*
Imran	24.2	10	45	4	—	20	6	35	4	1st	85	92	21	55
Tahir	18	4	65	1	—	16	3	39	2	2nd	120	93	55	—
Mudassar	6	1	17	0	—	2	0	5	0	3rd	140	119	64	—
Jalaluddin	19	4	77	3	—	16	8	15	2	4th	140	269	138	—
Abdul	37	7	86	2	—	35	7	102	2	5th	197	392	157	—
Zaheer	2	0	2	0	—	1	0	1	0	6th	202	402	170	—
AUSTRALIA										7th	203	442	189	—
Thomson	19	1	73	1	—	5	0	24	0	8th	264	—	203	—
Lawson	35	4	91	2	—	7	1	21	1	9th	264	—	203	—
Alderman	34	4	144	2	—	3	0	10	0	10th	316	—	214	—
Yardley	27	6	102	1	—									
Border	4	1	12	1	—									

Australia v England 1982–83

FIRST TEST MATCH

PLAYED AT PERTH, 12, 13, 14, 16, 17 NOVEMBER

MATCH DRAWN

ENGLAND

G. Cook c Dyson b Lillee	1	c Border b Lawson	7
C.J. Tavaré c Hughes b Yardley	89	c Chappell b Yardley	9
D.I. Gower c Dyson b Alderman	72	lbw b Lillee	28
A.J. Lamb c Marsh b Yardley	46	c Marsh b Lawson	56
I.T. Botham c Marsh b Lawson	12	b Lawson	0
D.W. Randall c Wood b Yardley	78	b Lawson	115
D.R. Pringle b Lillee	0	not out	47
G. Miller c Marsh b Lillee	30	c Marsh b Yardley	0
†R.W. Taylor not out	29	b Yardley	31
*R.G.D. Willis c Lillee b Yardley	26	b Lawson	0
N.G. Cowans b Yardley	4	lbw b Chappell	36
Extras (B7, LB9, W2, NB6)	24	(B5, LB11, W2, NB11)	29
Total	**411**		**358**

AUSTRALIA

G.M. Wood c & b Willis	29	c Taylor b Willis	0
J. Dyson lbw b Miller	52	c Cowans b Willis	12
A.R. Border c Taylor b Botham	8	not out	32
*G.S. Chappell c Lamb b Willis	117	not out	22
K.J. Hughes c Willis b Miller	62		
D.W. Hookes lbw b Miller	56		
†R.W. Marsh c Cook b Botham	0		
G.F. Lawson b Miller	50		
B Yardley c Lamb b Willis	17		
D.K. Lillee not out	2		
T.M. Alderman did not bat			
Extras (B4, LB1, W1, NB25)	31	(LB1, NB6)	7
Total (9 wkts dec)	**424**	**(2 wkts)**	**73**

BOWLING

AUSTRALIA	O	M	R	W		O	M	R	W
Lillee	38	13	96	3	—	33	12	89	1
Alderman	43	15	84	1	—				
Lawson	29	6	89	1	—	32	5	108	5
Chappell	3	0	11	0	—	2.3	1	8	1
Yardley	42.4	15	107	5	—	41	10	101	3
Border	—	—	—	—	—	7	2	21	0
Hookes	—	—	—	—	—	1	0	2	0
ENGLAND									
Willis	31.5	4	95	3	—	6	1	23	2
Botham	40	10	121	2	—	6	1	17	0
Cowans	13	2	54	0	—	3	1	15	0
Pringle	10	1	37	0	—	2	0	3	0
Miller	33	11	70	4	—	4	3	8	0
Cook	4	2	16	0	—				
Lamb	—	—	—	—	—	1	1	0	0

FALL OF WICKETS

	E	A	E	A
	1st	*1st*	*2nd*	*2nd*
1st	14	63	10	2
2nd	109	76	51	22
3rd	189	123	77	
4th	204	264	80	
5th	304	311	151	
6th	323	311	229	
7th	342	374	242	
8th	357	414	292	
9th	406	424	292	
10th	411	—	358	

SECOND TEST MATCH
PLAYED AT BRISBANE, 26, 27, 28, 30 NOVEMBER, 1 DECEMBER
AUSTRALIA WON BY 7 WICKETS

ENGLAND

C.J. Tavaré c Hughes b Lawson		1	c Marsh b Lawson	13
G. Fowler c Yardley b Lawson		7	c Marsh b Thomson	83
D.I. Gower c Wessels b Lawson		18	c Marsh b Thomson	34
A.J. Lamb c Marsh b Lawson		72	c Wessels b Thomson	12
I.T. Botham c Rackemann b Yardley		40	c Marsh b Thomson	15
D.W. Randall c Lawson b Rackemann		37	c Yardley b Thomson	4
G. Miller c Marsh b Lawson		0	c Marsh b Lawson	60
†R.W. Taylor c Lawson b Rackemann		1	c Hookes b Lawson	3
E.E. Hemmings not out		15	b Lawson	18
*R.G.D. Willis c Thomson b Yardley		1	not out	10
N.G. Cowans c Marsh b Lawson		10	c Marsh b Lawson	5
Extras (LB2, W1, NB14)		17	(B8, LB8, W1, NB25)	52
Total		**219**		**309**

AUSTRALIA

K.C. Wessels b Willis		162	b Hemmings	46
J. Dyson b Botham		1	retired hurt	4
A.R. Border c Randall b Willis		0	c Botham b Hemmings	15
*G.S. Chappell run out		53	c Lamb b Cowans	8
K.J. Hughes c Taylor b Botham		0	not out	39
D.W. Hookes c Taylor b Miller		28	not out	66
†R.W. Marsh c Taylor b Botham		11		
B. Yardley c Tavaré b Willis		53		
G.F. Lawson c Hemmings b Willis		6		
C.G. Rackemann b Willis		4		
J.R. Thomson not out		5		
Extras (B2, LB8, NB8)		18	(B2, LB5, NB5)	12
Total		**341**	(for 3 wkts)	**190**

BOWLING

AUSTRALIA	O	M	R	W		O	M	R	W	FALL OF WICKETS			
											E	A	E	A
Lawson	18.3	4	47	6	—	35.3	11	87	5					
Rackemann	21	8	61	2	—	12.2	3	35	0		*1st*	*1st*	*2nd*	*2nd*
Thomson	8	0	43	0	—	31	6	73	5	1st	8	4	54	60
Yardley	17	5	51	2	—	40.4	21	50	0	2nd	13	11	144	77
Chappell	—	—	—	—	—	6	2	8	0	3rd	63	94	165	83
Hookes	—	—	—	—	—	2	0	4	0	4th	141	99	169	—
ENGLAND										5th	152	130	194	—
Willis	29.4	3	66	5	—	1	0	24	0	6th	152	151	201	—
Botham	22	1	105	3	—	15.5	1	70	0	7th	178	271	226	—
Cowans	6	0	36	0	—	9	1	31	1	8th	191	310	285	—
Hemmings	33.3	6	81	0	—	29	9	43	2	9th	195	332	295	—
Miller	19.3	4	35	1	—	3	0	10	0	10th	219	341	309	—

THIRD TEST MATCH
PLAYED AT ADELAIDE, 10, 11, 12, 14, 15 DECEMBER
AUSTRALIA WON BY 8 WICKETS

AUSTRALIA

K.C. Wessels c Taylor b Botham		44	c Taylor b Botham	1
J. Dyson c Taylor b Botham		44	not out	37
*G.S. Chappell c Gower b Willis		115	not out	26
K.J. Hughes run out		88		
G.F. Lawson c Botham b Willis		2	c Randall b Willis	14
A.R. Border c Taylor b Pringle		26		
D.W. Hookes c Botham b Hemmings		37		
R.W. Marsh c Hemmings b Pringle		3		
B. Yardley c Gower b Botham		38		
R.M. Hogg not out		14		
J.R. Thomson c & b Botham		3		
Extras (LB6, WB18)		24	(NB5)	5
Total		**438**	**(2 wkts)**	**83**

ENGLAND

C.J. Tavaré c Marsh b Hogg		1	c Wessels b Thomson	0
G. Fowler c Marsh b Lawson		11	c Marsh b Lawson	37
D.I. Gower c Marsh b Lawson		60	b Hogg	114
A.J. Lamb c Marsh b Lawson		82	c Chappell b Yardley	8
I.T. Botham c Wessels b Thomson		35	c Dyson b Yardley	58
D.W. Randall b Lawson		0	c Marsh b Lawson	17
G. Miller c Yardley b Hogg		7	lbw b Lawson	17
†R.W. Taylor c Chappell b Yardley		2	not out	3
D.R. Pringle not out		1	c Marsh b Thomson	9
E.E. Hemmings b Thomson		0	c Wessels b Lawson	0
*R.G.D. Willis b Thomson		1	c Marsh b Lawson	10
Extras (LB5, NB11)		16	(B7, LB6, W3, NB15)	31
Total		**216**		**304**

BOWLING

ENGLAND	O	M	R	W		O	M	R	W
Willis	25	8	76	2	—	8	1	17	1
Botham	36.5	5	112	4	—	10	2	45	1
Pringle	33	5	97	2	—	1.5	0	11	0
Miller	14	2	33	0	—	—	—	—	—
Hemmings	48	17	96	1	—	4	1	5	0
AUSTRALIA									
Lawson	18	4	56	4	—	24	6	66	5
Hogg	14	2	41	2	—	19	5	53	1
Thomson	14.5	3	51	3	—	13	3	41	2
Yardley	21	7	52	1	—	37	12	90	2
Border	—	—	—	—	—	8	2	14	0
Hookes	—	—	—	—	—	3	1	9	0

FALL OF WICKETS				
	A	E	E	A
	1st	1st	2nd	2nd
1st	76	1	11	3
2nd	138	21	90	37
3rd	264	140	118	—
4th	270	181	236	—
5th	315	181	247	—
6th	355	194	272	—
7th	359	199	277	—
8th	391	213	289	—
9th	430	213	290	—
10th	438	216	304	—

FOURTH TEST MATCH

PLAYED AT MELBOURNE, 26, 27, 28, 29, 30 DECEMBER

ENGLAND WON BY 3 RUNS

ENGLAND

G. Cook c Chappell b Thomson	10	c Yardley b Thomson	26
G. Fowler c Chappell b Hogg	4	b Hogg	65
C.J. Tavaré b Yardley b Thomson	89	b Hogg	0
D.I. Gower c Marsh b Hogg	18	c Marsh b Lawson	3
A.J. Lamb c Dyson b Yardley	83	c Marsh b Hogg	26
I.T. Botham c Wessels b Yardley	27	c Chappell b Thomson	46
G. Miller c Border b Yardley	10	lbw b Lawson	14
D.R. Pringle c Wessels b Hogg	9	c Marsh b Lawson	42
†R.W. Taylor c Marsh b Yardley	1	lbw b Thomson	37
*R.G.D. Willis not out	6	not out	8
N.G. Cowans c Lawson b Hogg	3	b Lawson	10
Extras (B3, LB6, W3, NB12)	24	(B2, LB9, NB6)	17
Total	**284**		**294**

AUSTRALIA

K.C. Wessels b Willis	47	b Cowans	14
J. Dyson lbw b Cowans	21	c Tavaré b Botham	31
*G.S. Chappell c Lamb b Cowans	0	c sub (Gould) b Cowans	2
K.J. Hughes b Willis	66	c Taylor b Miller	48
A.R. Border b Botham	2	not out	62
D.W. Hookes c Taylor b Pringle	53	c Willis b Cowans	68
†R.W. Marsh b Willis	53	lbw b Cowans	13
B. Yardley b Miller	9	b Cowans	0
G.F. Lawson c Fowler b Miller	0	c Cowans b Pringle	7
R.M. Hogg not out	8	lbw b Cowans	4
J.R. Thomson b Miller	1	c Miller b Botham	21
Extras (LB8, NB19)	27	(B5, LB9, W1, NB3)	18
Total	**287**		**288**

BOWLING

AUSTRALIA	O	M	R	W		O	M	R	W
Lawson	17	6	48	0	—	21.4	6	66	4
Hogg	23.3	6	69	4	—	22	5	64	3
Yardley	27	9	89	4	—	15	2	67	0
Thomson	13	2	49	2	—	21	3	74	3
Chappell	1	0	5	0	—	1	0	4	0
ENGLAND									
Willis	15	2	38	3	—	17	0	57	0
Botham	18	3	69	1	—	25.1	4	80	2
Cowans	16	0	69	2	—	26	6	77	6
Pringle	15	2	40	1	—	12	4	26	1
Miller	15	5	44	3	—	16	9	30	1

FALL OF WICKETS

	E	A	E	A
	1st	1st	2nd	2nd
1st	11	55	40	37
2nd	25	55	41	39
3rd	56	83	45	71
4th	217	89	128	171
5th	227	180	129	173
6th	259	261	160	190
7th	262	276	201	190
8th	268	276	262	202
9th	278	278	282	218
10th	284	287	294	288

FIFTH TEST MATCH

PLAYED AT SYDNEY, 2, 3, 4, 6, 7 JANUARY

MATCH DRAWN

AUSTRALIA

K.C. Wessels c Willis b Botham	19	lbw b Botham	53
J. Dyson c Taylor b Hemmings	79	c Gower b Willis	2
*G.S. Chappell lbw b Willis	35	c Randall b Hemmings	11
K.J. Hughes c Cowans b Botham	29	c Botham b Hemmings	137
D.W. Hookes c Botham b Hemmings	17	lbw b Miller	19
A.R. Border c Miller b Hemmings	89	c Botham b Cowans	83
†R.W. Marsh c & b Miller	3	c Taylor b Miller	41
B. Yardley b Cowans	24	c Botham b Hemmings	0
G.F. Lawson c & b Botham	6	not out	13
J.R. Thomson c Lamb b Botham	0	c Gower b Miller	12
R.M. Hogg not out	0	run out	0
Extras (B3, LB8, W2)	13	(LB7, NB4)	11
Total	**314**		**382**

ENGLAND

G. Cook c Chappell b Hogg	8	lbw b Lawson	2
C.J. Tavaré b Lawson	0	lbw b Yardley	16
D.I. Gower c Chappell b Lawson	70	c Hookes b Yardley	24
A.J. Lamb b Lawson	0	c & b Yardley	29
D.W. Randall b Thomson	70	b Thomson	44
I.T. Botham c Wessels b Thomson	5	lbw b Thomson	32
G. Miller lbw b Thomson	34	not out	21
†R.W. Taylor lbw b Thomson	0	not out	28
*R.G.D. Willis c Border b Thomson	1	c Marsh b Yardley	95
E.E. Hemmings c Border b Yardley	29		
N.G. Cowans not out	0		
Extras (B4, LB4, NB12)	20	(B1, LB10, W1, NB11)	23
Total	**237**	(7 wkts)	**314**

BOWLING

ENGLAND	O	M	R	W		O	M	R	W	FALL OF WICKETS			
											A	E	A	E
											1st	1st	2nd	2nd
Willis	20	6	57	1	—	10	2	33	1					
Cowans	21	3	67	1	—	13	1	47	1	1st	39	8	23	3
Botham	30	8	75	4	—	10	0	35	1	2nd	96	23	38	55
Hemmings	27	10	68	3	—	47	16	116	3	3rd	150	24	82	104
Miller	17	3	34	1	—	49.3	12	133	3	4th	173	146	113	155
Cook	—	—	—	—	—	2	1	7	0	5th	210	163	262	196
AUSTRALIA										6th	219	169	350	260
Lawson	20	2	70	3	—	15	1	50	1	7th	262	170	357	261
Hogg	16	2	50	1	—	13	6	25	0	8th	283	220	358	—
Thomson	14.5	2	50	5	—	13	3	30	2	9th	251	232	382	—
Yardley	14	4	47	1	—	37	6	139	4	10th	314	237	382	—
Border	—	—	—	—	—	16	3	36	0					
Chappell	—	—	—	—	—	1	0	6	0					
Hookes	—	—	—	—	—	2	1	5	0					

TEST MATCH AVERAGES

AUSTRALIA

	M	I	NO	Runs	HS	Avge	100	50	Ct	St
K.J. Hughes	5	8	1	469	137	67.00	1	3	2	—
D.W. Hookes	5	8	1	344	68	49.14	—	4	2	—
G.S. Chappell	5	10	2	389	117	48.62	2	1	8	—
K.C. Wessels	4	8	0	386	162	48.25	1	1	8	—
A.R. Border	5	9	2	317	89	45.28	—	3	4	—
J. Dyson	5	10	2	283	79	35.37	—	2	4	—
B. Yardley	5	7	0	141	53	20.14	—	1	6	—
R.W. Marsh	5	7	0	124	53	17.71	—	1	28	—
G.M. Wood	1	2	0	29	29	14.50	—	—	1	—
G.F. Lawson	5	8	1	98	50	14.00	—	1	3	—
R.M. Hogg	3	5	3	26	14*	13.00	—	—	1	—
J.R. Thomson	4	6	1	42	21	8.40	—	—	1	—
C.G. Rackemann	1	1	0	4	4	4.00	—	—	1	—
D.K. Lillee	1	1	1	2	2*	—	—	—	1	—
T.M. Alderman	1	did not bat								

	Overs	Mdns	Runs	Wkts	Avge	Best	5 wI	10 wM
J.R. Thomson	127.4	22	411	22	18.68	5-50	2	—
G.F. Lawson	230.4	51	687	34	20.20	6-47	4	1
R.M. Hogg	107.3	26	302	11	27.45	4-69	—	—
B. Yardley	292.2	91	793	22	36.04	5-107	1	—
G.S. Chappell	14.3	3	44	1	44.00	1-8	—	—
D.K. Lillee	71	25	185	4	46.25	3-96	—	—
C.G. Rackemann	33.2	11	96	2	48.00	2-61	—	—
T.M. Alderman	43	15	84	1	84.00	1-84	—	—
D.W. Hookes	8	2	20	0	—	—	—	—
A.R. Border	31	7	71	0	—	—	—	—

ENGLAND

	M	I	NO	Runs	HS	Avge	100	50	Ct	St
D.W. Randall	4	8	0	365	115	45.62	1	2	3	—
D.I. Gower	5	10	0	441	114	44.10	1	3	4	—
A.J. Lamb	5	10	0	414	83	41.40	—	4	5	—
G. Fowler	3	6	0	207	83	34.50	—	2	1	—
E.E. Hemmings	3	6	1	157	95	31.40	—	1	2	—
I.T. Botham	5	10	0	270	58	27.00	—	1	9	—
D.R. Pringle	3	6	2	108	47*	27.00	—	—	1	—
C.J. Tavaré	5	10	0	218	89	21.80	—	2	2	—
G. Miller	5	10	1	193	60	21.44	—	1	3	—
R.W. Taylor	5	10	3	135	37	19.28	—	—	13	—
N.G. Cowans	4	7	1	68	36	11.33	—	—	3	—
R.G.D. Willis	5	9	3	63	26	10.50	—	—	4	—
G. Cook	3	6	0	54	26	9.00	—	—	1	—

	Overs	Mdns	Runs	Wkts	Avge	Best	5 wI	10 wM
R.G.D. Willis	166.3	28	486	18	27.00	5-66	1	—
G. Miller	171	50	397	13	30.53	4-70	—	—
N.G. Cowans	107	14	396	11	36.00	6-77	1	—
I.T. Botham	213.5	35	729	18	40.50	4-75	1	—
E.E. Hemmings	188.3	59	409	9	45.44	3-68	—	—
D.R. Pringle	73.5	12	214	4	53.50	2-97	—	—
A.J. Lamb	1	1	0	0	—	—	—	—
G. Cook	6	3	23	0	—	—	—	—

Benson & Hedges
World Series Cup

AUSTRALIA v NEW ZEALAND AT MELBOURNE 9/1/83

New Zealand 181 in 44.5 overs (J.G. Wright 54, C.G. Rackemann 4-39)
Australia 182-2 in 46.4 overs (K.C. Wessels 79, J. Dyson 78*)
Result: Australia won by 8 wickets

AUSTRALIA v ENGLAND AT SYDNEY 11/1/83

Australia 180 in 46.4 overs
England 149 in 41.1 overs
Result: Australia won by 31 runs

ENGLAND v NEW ZEALAND AT MELBOURNE 13/1/83

New Zealand 239-8 in 50 overs (J.G. Wright 55)
England 237-8 in 50 overs (D.I. Gower 122)
Result: New Zealand won by 2 runs

ENGLAND v NEW ZEALAND AT BRISBANE 15/1/83

England 267-6 in 50 overs (D.I. Gower 158)
New Zealand 213 in 48.2 overs
Result: England won by 54 runs

AUSTRALIA v ENGLAND AT BRISBANE 16/1/83

England 182 in 46.4 overs (D.W. Randall 57)
Australia 184-3 in 41 overs (D.W. Hookes 54*)
Result: Australia won by 7 wickets

AUSTRALIA v NEW ZEALAND AT SYDNEY 18/1/83

New Zealand 226-8 in 50 overs (J.J. Crowe 56, G.M. Turner 55)
Australia 179 in 45.3 overs (D.W. Hookes 68, K.C. Wessels 58, B.L. Cairns 4-16)
Result: New Zealand won by 47 runs

ENGLAND v NEW ZEALAND AT SYDNEY 20/1/83

New Zealand 199 in 47.2 overs (B.A. Edgar 74, R.G.D. Willis 4-23)
England 200-2 in 42.4 overs (A.J. Lamb 108*, C.J. Tavaré 83*)
Result: England won by 8 wickets

AUSTRALIA v NEW ZEALAND AT MELBOURNE 22/1/83

New Zealand 246-6 in 50 overs (J.G. Wright 84)
Australia 188 in 44.1 overs (K.C. Wessels 62, G.B. Troup 4-54)
Result: New Zealand won by 58 runs

AUSTRALIA v ENGLAND AT MELBOURNE 23/1/83

England 213-5 in 37 overs (A.J. Lamb 94, D.W. Randall 51*)
Australia 217-5 in 34.4 overs (J. Dyson 54, A.R. Border 54, D.W. Hookes 50)
Result: Australia won by 5 wickets

AUSTRALIA v ENGLAND AT SYDNEY 26/1/83

England 207 in 41 overs
Australia 109 in 28.3 overs
Result: England won by 98 runs

ENGLAND v NEW ZEALAND AT ADELAIDE 29/1/83

England 296-5 in 50 overs (D.I. Gower 109, I.T. Botham 65, T.E. Jesty 52*)
New Zealand 297-6 in 48.5 overs (R.J. Hadlee 79, G.P. Howarth 50)
Result: New Zealand won by 4 wickets

AUSTRALIA v ENGLAND AT ADELAIDE 30/1/83

England 228-6 in 47 overs (D.I. Gower 77)
Australia 214-7 in 47 overs (D.W. Hookes 76)
Result: England won by 14 runs

AUSTRALIA v NEW ZEALAND AT ADELAIDE 31/1/83

New Zealand 199-9 in 50 overs (G.M. Turner 84)
Australia 153 in 44 overs
Result: New Zealand won by 46 runs

ENGLAND v NEW ZEALAND AT PERTH 5/2/83

England 88-7 in 23 overs
New Zealand 89-3 in 20.3 overs
Result: New Zealand won by 7 wickets

AUSTRALIA v NEW ZEALAND AT PERTH 6/2/83

Australia 191-9 in 50 overs
New Zealand 164 in 44.5 overs
Result: Australia won by 27 runs

Final Qualifying Table

	P	W	L	Pts
New Zealand	10	6	4	12
Australia	10	5	5	10
England	10	4	6	8

THE FINALS

AUSTRALIA v NEW ZEALAND AT SYDNEY 9/2/83

New Zealand 193-7 in 49 overs (J.V. Coney 58*)
Australia 155-4 in 33.1 overs (K.J. Hughes 63)
Result: Australia won by 4 wickets (match reduced to 38 overs because of rain)

AUSTRALIA v NEW ZEALAND AT MELBOURNE 13/2/83

Australia 302-8 in 50 overs (S.B. Smith 117, G.M. Wood 91)
New Zealand 153 in 39.5 overs (B.L. Cairns 52)
Result: Australia won by 149 runs

Australia won the final series 2-0

Congratulations, Surrey, on winning the 1982 NatWest Bank Trophy.

ENGLAND v NEW ZEALAND
1929–30 TO 1978

SERIES BY SERIES

Season		Visiting Captain	P	E W	A W	D
1929-30	In New Zealand	A.H.H. Gilligan (E)	4	1	0	3
1931	In England	T.C. Lowry (NZ)	3	1	0	2
1932-33	In New Zealand	D.R. Jardine (E)	2	0	0	2
1937	In England	M.L. Page (NZ)	3	1	0	2
1946-47	In New Zealand	W.R. Hammond (E)	1	0	0	1
1949	In England	W.A. Hadlee (NZ)	4	0	0	4
1950-51	In New Zealand	F.R. Brown (E)	2	1	0	1
1954-55	In New Zealand	L. Hutton (E)	2	2	0	0
1958	In England	J.R. Reid (NZ)	5	4	0	1
1958-59	In New Zealand	P.B.H. May (E)	2	1	0	1
1962-63	In New Zealand	E.R. Dexter (E)	3	3	0	0
1965	In England	J.R. Reid (NZ)	3	3	0	0
1965-66	In New Zealand	M.J.K. Smith (E)	3	0	0	3
1969	In England	G.T. Dowling (NZ)	3	2	0	1
1970-71	In New Zealand	R. Illingworth (E)	2	1	0	1
1973	In England	B.E. Congdon (NZ)	3	2	0	1
1974-75	In New Zealand	M.H. Denness (E)	2	1	0	1
1977-78	In New Zealand	G. Boycott (E)	3	1	1	1
1978	In England	M.G. Burgess (NZ)	3	3	0	0
	At Lord's		8	4	0	4
	At The Oval		6	3	0	3
	At Manchester		4	2	0	2
	At Leeds		4	3	0	1
	At Birmingham		2	2	0	0
	At Nottingham		3	2	0	1
	At Christchurch		10	5	0	5
	At Auckland		10	3	0	7
	At Wellington		4	2	1	1
	At Dunedin		2	1	0	1
	In England		27	16	0	11
	In New Zealand		26	11	1	14
	Total		53	27	1	25

HIGHEST INNINGS TOTALS

England			New Zealand		
593-6d	Auckland	1974-75	551-9d	Lord's	1973
562-7d	Auckland	1962-63	484	Lord's	1949
560-8d	Christchurch	1932-33	469-9d	Lord's	1931
550	Christchurch	1950-51	440	Wellington	1929-30
548-7d	Auckland	1932-33	440	Nottingham	1973
546-4d	Leeds	1965	417-8d	Christchurch	1950-51
540	Auckland	1929-30	413	Birmingham	1965
482	The Oval	1949			
463-9	Lord's	1973			
454	Lord's	1931			

LOWEST INNINGS TOTALS

England			New Zealand		
64	Wellington	1977-78	26	Auckland	1954-55
181	Christchurch	1929-30	47	Lord's	1958
187	Manchester	1937	65	Christchurch	1970-71
190	Lord's	1969	67	Leeds	1958
221	Birmingham	1958	67	Lord's	1978

HIGHEST INDIVIDUAL INNINGS FOR ENGLAND

336*	W.R. Hammond	at Auckland	1932-33
310*	J.H. Edrich	at Leeds	1965
227	W.R. Hammond	at Christchurch	1932-33
216	K.W.R. Fletcher	at Auckland	1974-75
206	L. Hutton	at The Oval	1949
196	G.B. Legge	at Auckland	1929-30
181	M.H. Denness	at Auckland	1974-75
178	K.W.R. Fletcher	at Lord's	1973
164*	D.L. Amiss	at Christchurch	1974-75
163	K.F. Barrington	at Leeds	1965

A total of 55 centuries have been scored for England.

HIGHEST INDIVIDUAL INNINGS FOR NEW ZEALAND

206	M.P. Donnelly	at Lord's	1979
176	B.E. Congdon	at Nottingham	1973
175	B.E. Congdon	at Lord's	1973
136	C.S. Dempster	at Wellington	1929-30
123	G.P. Howarth	at Lord's	1978
122	G.P. Howarth	at Auckland	1977-78
121	J.M. Parker	at Auckland	1974-75
120	C.S. Dempster	at Lord's	1931
117	J.W.E. Mills	at Wellington	1929-30

A total of 21 centuries have been scored for New Zealand.

A CENTURY IN EACH INNINGS OF A MATCH
FOR ENGLAND
Nil

122	G.P. Howarth	at Auckland	1977-78
102			

A CENTURY ON DEBUT IN SERIES
FOR ENGLAND

122	G.O. Allen	at Lord's	1931
137	L.E.G. Ames	at Lord's	1931
117	H. Sutcliffe	at The Oval	1931
114	J. Hardstaff, jr	at Lord's	1937
121	J.D. Robertson	at Lord's	1949
103	R.T. Simpson	at Manchester	1949
100	P.E. Richardson	at Birmingham	1958
104*	C.A. Milton	at Leeds	1958
126	K.F. Barrington	at Auckland	1962-63
131*	P.H. Parfitt	at Auckland	1962-63
125	B.R. Knight	at Auckland	1962-63
310*	J.H. Edrich	at Leeds	1965
138	D.L. Amiss	at Nottingham	1973
139	A.W. Greig	at Nottingham	1973
111	D.I. Gower	at The Oval	1978

FOR NEW ZEALAND

117	J.W.E. Mills	at Wellington	1929-30

RECORD WICKET PARTNERSHIPS FOR ENGLAND

1st	147	L. Hutton & R.T. Simpson at The Oval	1946
2nd	369	J.H. Edrich & K.F. Barrington at Leeds	1965
3rd	245	W.R. Hammond & J. Hardstaff at Lord's	1937
4th	266	M.H. Denness & K.W.R. Fletcher at Auckland	1974-75
5th	242	W.R. Hammond & L.E.G. Ames at Christchurch	1932-33
6th	240	P.H. Parfitt & B.R. Knight at Auckland	1962-63
7th	149	A.P.E. Knott & P. Lever at Auckland	1970-71
8th	246	L.E.G. Ames & G.O. Allen at Lord's	1931
9th	163*	M.C. Cowdrey & A.C. Smith at Wellington	1962-63
10th	59	A.P.E. Knott & N. Gifford at Nottingham	1973

RECORD WICKET PARTNERSHIPS FOR NEW ZEALAND

1st	276	C.S. Dempster & J.W.E. Mills at Wellington	1929-30
2nd	131	B. Sutcliffe & J.R. Reid at Christchurch	1950-51
3rd	190	B.E. Congdon & B.F. Hastings at Lord's	1973
4th	142	M.L. Page & R.C. Blunt at Lord's	1931
5th	177	B.E. Congdon & V. Pollard at Nottingham	1973
6th	117	M.G. Burgess & V. Pollard at Lord's	1973
7th	104	B. Sutcliffe & V. Pollard at Birmingham	1965
8th	104	A.W. Roberts & D.A.R. Moloney at Lord's	1937
9th	64	J. Cowie & T.B. Burtt at Christchurch	1946-47
10th	57	F.L.H. Mooney & J. Cowie at Leeds	1949

HIGHEST RUN AGGREGATE IN A TEST RUBBER

England in England	469 (Av. 78.16)	L. Hutton	1949
England in New Zealand	563 (Av. 563.00)	W.R. Hammond	1932-33
New Zealand in England	462 (Av. 77.00)	M.P. Donnelly	1949
New Zealand in New Zealand	341 (Av. 85.25)	C.S. Dempster	1929-30

BEST INNINGS BOWLING FIGURES

England in England	7-32	D.L. Underwood (Lord's)	1969
England in New Zealand	7-75	F.S. Trueman (Christchurch)	1962-63
New Zealand in England	6-67	J. Cowie (Manchester)	1937
New Zealand in New Zealand	6-26	R.J. Hadlee (Wellington)	1977-78

TEN WICKETS OR MORE IN A MATCH FOR ENGLAND

12-97	D.L. Underwood at Christchurch	1970-71
12-101	D.L. Underwood at The Oval	1969
11-65	G.A.R. Lock at Leeds	1954-55
11-70	D.L. Underwood at Lord's	1969
11-84	G.A.R. Lock at Christchurch	1958-59
11-140	I.T. Botham at Lord's	1978
10-149	A.W. Greig at Auckland	1974-75

TEN WICKETS OR MORE IN A MATCH FOR NEW ZEALAND

10-100	R.J. Hadlee at Wellington	1977-78
10-140	J. Cowie at Manchester	1937

HIGHEST MATCH AGGREGATE	1293-34 wkts at Lord's	1931
LOWEST MATCH AGGREGATE	390-30 wkts at Lord's	1958

GLENN TURNER'S 100 CENTURIES

On May 29 at Worcester, Glenn Turner, Worcestershire's New Zealand opening batsman, scored 311 against Warwickshire. This was Turner's 100th century in first-class cricket. He became the nineteenth player to perform this feat, the second non-Englishman (Bradman was the first) and the first New Zealander. Turner's innings was the highest ever 100th century and at 35 he became the third youngest, after Hammond and Compton.

The following is a progressive list of his centuries:

1	106*	Worcestershire v Middlesex	(Worcester)	1968
2	167	Otago v Wellington	(Dunedin)	1968-69
3	123	South Island v West Indians	(Dunedin)	1968-69
4	124	New Zealanders v Middlesex	(Lord's)	1969
5	100	New Zealand v Pakistan	(Dacca)	1969-70
6	122	Worcestershire v Essex	(Worcester)	1970
7	137	Worcestershire v Hampshire	(Southampton)	1970
8	154*	Worcestershire v Gloucestershire	(Bristol)	1970
9	112	Worcestershire v Leicestershire	(Worcester)	1970
10	106	Worcestershire v Warwickshire	(Birmingham)	1970
11	118	Worcestershire v Somerset	(Worcester)	1970
12	110*	Worcestershire v Northamptonshire	(Wellingborough)	1970
13	142*	Worcestershire v Derbyshire	(Chesterfield)	1970
14	140	Worcestershire v Yorkshire	(Worcester)	1970
15	133*	Worcestershire v Warwickshire	(Worcester)	1970
16	179	Worcestershire v Pakistanis	(Worcester)	1971
17	101	Worcestershire v Essex	(Worcester)	1971
18	101*	Otago v Wellington	(Wellington)	1971-72
19	202	New Zealanders v WIBC President's XI	(Montego Bay)	1971-72
20	223*	New Zealand v West Indies	(Kingston)	1971-72
21	259	New Zealand v Guyana	(Georgetown)	1971-72
22	259	New Zealand v West Indies	(Georgetown)	1971-72
23	111	Worcestershire v Cambridge University	(Cambridge)	1972
24	156	Worcestershire v Warwickshire	(Worcester)	1972
25	122	} Worcestershire v Warwickshire	(Birmingham)	1972
26	128*			
27	170	Worcestershire v Gloucestershire	(Bristol)	1972
28	154	Worcestershire v Essex	(Leyton)	1972
29	107	Worcestershire v Nottinghamshire	(Nottingham)	1972
30	132	Otago v Auckland	(Auckland)	1972-73
31	131	Otago v Wellington	(Dunedin)	1972-73
32	151*	New Zealanders v D.H. Robins' XI	(Eastbourne)	1973
33	143	New Zealanders v Worcestershire	(Worcester)	1973
34	153*	New Zealanders v MCC	(Lord's)	1973
35	111	New Zealanders v Northamptonshire	(Northampton)	1973
36	121*	New Zealanders v Surrey	(The Oval)	1973
37	109*	Worcestershire v Glamorgan	(Cardiff)	1973
38	110	Worcestershire v Leicestershire	(Leicester)	1973
39	106*	Worcestershire v Essex	(Chelmsford)	1973
40	140	Worcestershire v Nottinghamshire	(Worcester)	1973
41	106*	New Zealanders v Tasmania	(Launceston)	1973-74

42 101 } 43 110* }	New Zealand v Australia	(Christchurch)	1973-74
44 138 ret hurt }	Worcestershire v Kent	(Worcester)	1974
45 202*	Worcestershire v Cambridge University	(Cambridge)	1974
46 181	Worcestershire v Gloucestershire	(Cheltenham)	1974
47 135 } 48 108 }	Otago v Northern Districts	(Gisborne)	1974-75
49 105 } 50 186* }	Otago v Central Districts	(Dunedin)	1974-75
51 100*	Worcestershire v Nottinghamshire	(Worcester)	1975
52 214*	Worcestershire v Oxford University	(Worcester)	1975
53 154*	Worcestershire v Glamorgan	(Swansea)	1975
54 177*	Otago v Wellington	(Wellington)	1975-76
55 104	Otago v Auckland	(Dunedin)	1975-76
56 115	Otago v Northern Districts	(Dunedin)	1975-76
57 121*	Otago v Indians	(Dunedin)	1975-76
58 117	New Zealand v India	(Christchurch)	1975-76
59 169	Worcestershire v Nottinghamshire	(Nottingham)	1976
60 135*	Worcestershire v Somerset	(Bath)	1976
61 150	Worcestershire v Sussex	(Hove)	1976
62 120	Worcestershire v Northamptonshire	(Northampton)	1976
63 113	New Zealand v India	(Kanpur)	1976-77
64 177*	Northern Districts v Central Districts	(Napier)	1976-77
65 153	Worcestershire v Hampshire	(Worcester)	1977
66 141*	Worcestershire v Glamorgan	(Swansea)	1977
67 131	Worcestershire v Somerset	(Worcester)	1977
68 127	Worcestershire v Northamptonshire	(Northampton)	1978
69 155*	Worcestershire v Hampshire	(Portsmouth)	1978
70 150	Worcestershire v Surrey	(Worcester)	1978
71 101	Worcestershire v Essex	(Chelmsford)	1978
72 202*	Worcestershire v Warwickshire	(Birmingham)	1978
73 115	Worcestershire v Gloucestershire	(Worcester)	1978
74 148*	Worcestershire v Yorkshire	(Worcester)	1979
75 109	Worcestershire v Lancashire	(Southport)	1979
76 118	Worcestershire v Sussex	(Worcester)	1979
77 131	Worcestershire v Surrey	(Guildford)	1979
78 120	Worcestershire v Leicestershire	(Leicester)	1979
79 150*	Worcestershire v Nottinghamshire	(Worcester)	1979
80 108	Worcestershire v Warwickshire	(Worcester)	1979
81 135	Worcestershire v Glamorgan	(Worcester)	1979
82 136	Otago v Auckland	(Alexandra)	1979/80
83 228*	Worcestershire v Gloucestershire	(Worcester)	1980
84 100	Worcestershire v Middlesex	(Worcester)	1980
85 115	Worcestershire v Yorkshire	(Bradford)	1980
86 101	Worcestershire v Warwickshire	(Birmingham)	1980
87 182*	Worcestershire v Derbyshire	(Worcester)	1980
88 168	Worcestershire v Essex	(Colchester)	1980
89 103*	Worcestershire v Kent	(Worcester)	1980
90 104*	Worcestershire v Sussex	(Worcester)	1981
91 101	Worcestershire v Essex	(Worcester)	1981
92 168	Worcestershire v Yorkshire	(Worcester)	1981
93 161 } 94 101 }	Worcestershire v Northamptonshire	(Stourbridge)	1981
95 111	Worcestershire v Gloucestershire	(Worcester)	1981

96	130*	Worcestershire v Glamorgan	(Swansea)	1981
97	147*	Worcestershire v Warwickshire	(Worcester)	1981
98	139			
99	239*	Worcestershire v Oxford University	(Oxford)	1982
100	311*	Worcestershire v Warwickshire	(Worcester)	1982

Of his 100 centuries, 69 have been scored for Worcestershire of which 33 have been made at Worcester. He scored 64 of the centuries in the County Championship and although he has scored a century against every county, including his own, Turner has never made a century on a Kent ground. He scored 13 centuries for Otago, one for Northern Districts and one for South Island. Seven centuries were scored in Tests and nine for New Zealand teams on tours.

MINOR COUNTIES
FINAL TABLE

	P	W	L	D	NR	Pts	Avge
Oxfordshire	10	4	2	4	0	56	5.60
Wiltshire	10	4	4	2	1	51	5.10
Dorset	10	4	1	4	1	48	4.80
Berkshire	10	3	4	3	0	47	4.70
Hertfordshire	10	3	0	6	1	47	4.70
Suffolk	10	3	2	5	0	46	4.60
Cambridgeshire	10	3	2	5	0	44	4.40
Somerset II	8	2	0	5	1	31	3.87
Durham	10	1	1	8	0	37	3.70
Lincolnshire	8	2	2	4	0	26	3.25
Shropshire	10	1	0	7	2	31	3.10
Lancashire II	8	1	0	4	3	24	3.00
Devon	10	2	3	3	2	29	2.90
Norfolk	10	1	2	6	1	29	2.90
Cheshire	12	2	1	8	1	34	2.83
Staffordshire	10	1	0	7	2	25	2.50
Bedfordshire	10	1	3	6	0	23	2.30
Northumberland	12	0	2	7	3	23	1.91
Buckinghamshire	12	1	5	6	0	19	1.58
Cornwall	10	0	3	5	2	13	1.30
Cumberland	8	0	2	5	1	10	1.25

This isn't a bouncer!

Congratulations to Surrey on winning the NatWest Bank Trophy.

SURREY WIN THE
SECOND NATWEST TROPHY

Inevitably, the second NatWest Bank Trophy Final had none of the high drama of the first – it couldn't possibly have matched an occasion when, after a full day's cricket, the scores were levelled on the last ball. This time Surrey were far too good for their opponents, Warwickshire, and the result was determined long before the last ball was bowled.

But even if the Final lacked tense excitement some of the earlier matches did not. In fact, the Yorkshire v Worcestershire game at Headingley in the Second Round was described as producing one of the most astonishing turn-arounds even limited over cricket has ever seen. When play began again on the second day after a rain-interrupted first day, Yorkshire were 40 for 4, needing a further 247 runs from 44 overs for a victory that not even their most fervent supporter could ever have contemplated. To score 247 runs when batting second with only 44 overs remaining is difficult enough, even with all ten wickets standing, but with the four leading batsmen out, the task seemed monumental. Nevertheless, Yorkshire dashed home in cavalier fashion to reach the target – 290 for 7, with three balls to spare. The hero (The Man of the Match – it just had to be!) was David Bairstow who fell, with all guns firing, only 8 runs short of a century. Even so, the victory wasn't attributable only to Bairstow. Neil Hartley scored 58, Chris Old 55 not out, and Graham Stevenson 28 not out. Yorkshire folk will place this day in the County's history along with great matches and great players of their halcyon days – the days of Holmes, Sutcliffe, Leyland, Mitchell, Wood and Verity.

As is usual in Cup cricket there were some surprises. Sussex being brushed aside at Hove to be beaten by 9 wickets by Nottinghamshire was one of them. Clive Rice, unfit, and not expected to bowl, did bowl, and took 6 for 18 – the best bowling figures in the competition after the first two seasons. Hampshire's 6 wicket victory over Derbyshire, the holders, in the first defence of their title, was another, and then Gloucester did at Trent Bridge what Nottinghamshire had done at Hove; they won by 9 wickets. So Nottinghamshire had figured in two 9 wicket victories – one for; one against.

Yet probably the most talked about innings of the competition – in fact of the whole season – was that played by Alvin Kallicharran at Taunton where Somerset were the odds-on favourites in the Quarter-Finals. Warwickshire, set to score 260, lost both openers with the score at 30. Enter Kallicharran and Amiss to add 153. Kallicharran reigned supreme, to reach 141 not out when Warwickshire achieved this totally unexpected but meritorious victory. Many people who were there said it was the greatest innings they had ever seen. Warwickshire, not having a very good season and plagued by injuries, thus had the bonus of a Semi-Final at Edgbaston, even though Yorkshire were favourites. Once again the favourites went down after a disastrous start – 29 for 3; 52 for 4; 99 for 6. Thank Heaven once again for Bairstow – 49 not out this time, and 33 by Carrick, enabling Yorkshire to score a respectable 216 for 9 in the prescribed 60 overs. But Warwickshire's opening partnership of 139 soon put paid to that. David Smith, who had not enjoyed the best of fortune during the season, came good with 113; Andy Lloyd made 66 and Warwickshire were home with plenty to spare, by 7 wickets.

But all this time Surrey had been disposing of one opponent after another in a clinical fashion. No-one sat up and took much notice when they beat Durham (although Durham are a very good Minor County side) by 111 runs, but it was a major performance when they beat Northants by 6 wickets, also at The Oval. This time another David Smith scored a century and there was justified confidence when Surrey were then drawn at Southampton, but it was tempered with the thought that Hampshire were a pretty good side especially if their two West Indians, Gordon Greenidge and Malcolm Marshall, delivered the goods, as well they can. But when Hampshire were 38 for 4 a wobble had started which even David Turner's 51 could only marginally steady. Jackman roared in to take 6 for 22 and Surrey cruised home by 8 wickets. Then came the devastating blow. At The Oval in the Semi-Final, Middlesex were shot out for 80 by Sylvester Clarke to lose by 125 runs. Surrey were stronger favourites to beat Warwickshire at Lord's than most of Lester Piggott's Derby rides, and they did precisely that, having played in four consecutive Cup Finals at Lord's and lost the previous three. It was high time for the pendulum to swing and it did, decisively. At one time it looked as though this great occasion could end just after lunch – Warwickshire were 74-8 as Surrey brought in a third bowler to make his presence felt. David Thomas took 3 wickets for 7 runs in 3 overs and was Denis Compton's Man of the Match. Asif Din and Gladstone Small saved a lunch-time retreat by taking the score to 136 and then it became 158. Surrey revelled in the afternoon sunlight to ease gently home by 9 wickets. Alan Butcher must have thought he had done enough towards a trip to Australia by scoring 86. The Selectors, apparently, did not. So three NatWest matches in the season ended with 9 wicket victories – quite an unusual triumvirate.

1982 RESULTS

FIRST ROUND

Bedfordshire v Somerset at Bedford

Bedfordshire 153-9 in 60 overs
Somerset 154-6
Result: Somerset won by 4 wickets
Man of the Match: R. Dethridge
Adjudicator: J.M. Parks

Leicestershire v Norfolk at Leicester

Norfolk 164-7 in 60 overs (Parvez Mir 55, Taylor 4-34)
Leicestershire 166-2 (Gower 65*)
Result: Leicestershire won by 8 wickets
Man of the Match: D.I. Gower
Adjudicator: R.T. Simpson

Middlesex v Cheshire at Enfield

Cheshire 104 (Edmonds 5-12)
Middlesex 106-2 (Slack 54*)
Result: Middlesex won by 8 wickets
Man of the Match: P.H. Edmonds
Adjudicator: A.V. Bedser

Northamptonshire v Ireland at Northampton

Ireland 155
Northamptonshire 156-3 (Willey 72*)
Result: Northamptonshire won by 7 wickets
Man of the Match: P. Willey
Adjudicator: D.B. Close

Surrey v Durham at The Oval

Surrey 279-7 in 60 overs (Lynch 129, Roope 77, Davis 5-51)
Durham 168-6 in 60 overs (Greensword 73)
Result: Surrey won by 111 runs
Man of the Match: M.A. Lynch
Adjudicator: R.E. Marshall

Sussex v Nottinghamshire at Hove

Sussex 113 (Rice 6-18)
Nottinghamshire 114-1
Result: Nottinghamshire won by 9 wickets
Man of the Match: C.E.B. Rice
Adjudicator: C.A. Milton

Warwickshire v Cambridgeshire at Birmingham

Warwickshire 300-6 in 60 overs (Amiss 135, Lloyd 64, Humpage 52)
Cambridgeshire 180 (McEvoy 52)
Result: Warwickshire won by 120 runs
Man of the Match: D.L. Amiss
Adjudicator: B.L. D'Oliveira

SECOND ROUND
Essex v Kent at Chelmsford

Essex 269-7 in 60 overs (Fletcher 97)
Kent 139 (Turner 4-23, Phillip 4-26)
Result: Essex won by 130 runs
Man of the Match: K.W.R. Fletcher
Adjudicator: J.M. Parks

Glamorgan v Warwickshire at Cardiff

Glamorgan 169 (Ontong 54)
Warwickshire 170-4 (Lloyd 52)
Result: Warwickshire won by 6 wickets
Man of the Match: T.A. Lloyd
Adjudicator: C.A. Milton

Hampshire v Derbyshire at Southampton

Derbyshire 239-5 in 60 overs (Kirsten 110*, Wright 56)
Hampshire 242-4 (Greenidge 83, Rice 59)
Result: Hampshire won by 6 wickets
Man of the Match: P.N. Kirsten
Adjudicator: F.J. Titmus

Middlesex v Lancashire at Lord's

Middlesex 204-9 in 60 overs (Brearley 66)
Lancashire 202-9 in 60 overs (Cowans 4-26)
Result: Middlesex won by 2 runs
Man of the Match: N.G. Cowans
Adjudicator: B.L. D'Oliveira for the first two days, then Gordon Ross

Nottinghamshire v Gloucestershire at Nottingham

Nottinghamshire 142
Gloucestershire 145-1 (Stovold 76*, Broad 59)
Result: Gloucestershire won by 9 wickets
Man of the Match: A.W. Stovold
Adjudicator: C. Washbrook

Somerset v Leicestershire at Taunton

Somerset 271-5 in 60 overs (Denning 73, Marks 51*)
Leicestershire 208-9 in 60 overs (Gower 60, Garner 4-23)
Result: Somerset won by 63 runs
Man of the Match: V.J. Marks
Adjudicator: P.J. Sharpe

Surrey v Northamptonshire at The Oval

Northamptonshire 239-5 in 60 overs (Willey 55, Cook 50)
Surrey 242-4 (Smith 103*)
Result: Surrey won by 6 wickets
Man of the Match: D.M. Smith
Adjudicator: D.B. Close for two days, then the umpires – D.G.L. Evans & B.J. Meyer

Yorkshire v Worcestershire at Leeds

Worcestershire 286-5 in 60 overs (Turner 105)
Yorkshire 290-7 (Bairstow 92, Hartley 58, Old 55*, Inchmore 4-47)
Result: Yorkshire won by 3 wickets
Man of the Match: D.L. Bairstow
Adjudicator: J.A. Jameson

QUARTER-FINALS

Gloucestershire v Middlesex at Bristol

Middlesex 215-9 in 60 overs
Gloucestershire 212-8 (Broad 98)
Result: Middlesex won by 3 runs
Man of the Match: B.C. Broad
Adjudicator: J.A. Jameson

Hampshire v Surrey at Southampton

Hampshire 119 (Turner 51, Jackman 6-22)
Surrey 120-2 (Smith 62*)
Result: Surrey won by 8 wickets
Man of the Match: R.D. Jackman
Adjudicator: J.M. Parks

Somerset v Warwickshire at Taunton

Somerset 259-9 in 60 overs (Botham 85, Marks 55, Ferreira 4-53)
Warwickshire 261-5 (Kallicharran 141*, Amiss 59)
Result: Warwickshire won by 5 wickets
Man of the Match: A.I. Kallicharran
Adjudicator: C.A. Milton

Yorkshire v Essex at Leeds

Essex 132 (Turner 50*)
Yorkshire 133-1 (Moxon 78*)
Result: Yorkshire won by 9 wickets
Man of the Match: M.D. Moxon
Adjudicator: C. Washbrook

SEMI-FINALS

Surrey v Middlesex at The Oval

Surrey 205-9 in 60 overs (Butcher 53, Daniel 4-24)
Middlesex 80 (Clarke 4-10)
Result: Surrey won by 125 runs
Man of the Match: S.T. Clarke
Adjudicator: J.M. Parks

Warwickshire v Yorkshire at Birmingham

Yorkshire 216-9 in 60 overs (Boycott 51)
Warwickshire 219-3 (Smith 113, Lloyd 66)
Result: Warwickshire won by 7 wickets
Man of the Match: K.D. Smith
Adjudicator: B.L. D'Oliveira

NATWEST BANK TROPHY FINAL
PLAYED AT LORD'S, 4 SEPTEMBER
SURREY WON BY 9 WICKETS

WARWICKSHIRE

K.D. Smith	hit wkt b Thomas	12
T.A. Lloyd	lbw b Jackman	2
A.I. Kallicharran	c Howarth b Knight	19
D.L. Amiss	b Thomas	0
†G.W. Humpage	c Richards b Thomas	0
P.R. Oliver	run out	2
Asif Din	lbw b Jackman	45
A.M. Ferreira	lbw b Clarke	8
C. Lethbridge	c Howarth b Knight	4
G.C. Small	c Richards b Clarke	33
*R.G.D. Willis	not out	8
Extras (B8, LB11, NB6)		25
		—
Total (57.2 overs)		158

SURREY

A.R. Butcher	not out	86
G.P. Howarth	c Oliver b Lethbridge	31
D.M. Smith	not out	28
*R.D.V. Knight	did not bat	
M.A. Lynch	did not bat	
†C.J. Richards	did not bat	
D.J. Thomas	did not bat	
G. Monkhouse	did not bat	
S.T. Clarke	did not bat	
R.D. Jackman	did not bat	
K.S. Mackintosh	did not bat	
Extras (LB4, NB10)		14
		—
Total (34.4 overs) (1 wkt)		159

Man of the Match: D.J. Thomas
Adjudicator: D.C.S. Compton

BOWLING

SURREY	O	M	R	W		FALL OF WICKETS		
							WA	SY
Clarke	11.2	5	17	2				
Jackman	12	2	27	2		1st	3	80
Thomas	11	1	26	3		2nd	32	—
Monkhouse	8	0	36	0		3rd	42	—
Knight	12	3	14	2		4th	48	—
Mackintosh	3	0	13	0		5th	51	—
WARWICKSHIRE						6th	52	—
Willis	7	0	23	0		7th	67	—
Small	8	0	60	0		8th	74	—
Ferreira	6	0	16	0		9th	136	—
Lethbridge	6	1	23	1		10th	158	—
Kallicharran	6.4	1	23	0				

NATWEST BANK TROPHY
PRINCIPAL RECORDS

Highest innings total: 306-8 off 60 overs, Essex v Hertfordshire (Hitchin) 1981.

Highest innings total by a Minor County: 187 off 55.4 overs, Durham v Lancashire (Manchester) 1981.

Highest innings total by a side batting second: 290-7 off 59.3 overs, Yorkshire v Worcestershire (Leeds) 1982.

Highest innings total by a side batting first and losing: 286-5 Worcestershire v Yorkshire (Leeds) 1982.

Lowest innings total: 75 off 45.5 overs, Ireland v Gloucestershire (Clontarf, Dublin) 1981.

Lowest innings total by a First-class County: 80 Middlesex v Surrey (Oval) 1982.

Biggest victory: 191 runs: Essex beat Hertfordshire (Hitchin) 1981. 9 wickets: Nottinghamshire beat Sussex (Hove) 1982; Yorkshire beat Essex (Leeds) 1982; Surrey beat Warwickshire (Lord's) 1982.

Highest individual innings: 141* A.I. Kallicharran, Warwickshire v Somerset (Taunton) 1982.

Highest individual innings by a Minor County player: 80 S.R. Atkinson, Durham v Lancashire (Manchester).

Centuries: 11 centuries have been scored in the competition.

Record Wicket Partnerships

1st	184	G.A. Gooch & B.R. Hardie, Essex v Hertfordshire (Hitchin)	1981
2nd	123	J.G. Wright & P.N. Kirsten, Derbyshire v Northamptonshire (Lord's)	1981
3rd	153	A.I. Kallicharran & D.L. Amiss, Warwickshire v Somerset (Taunton)	1982
4th	139	D.S. Steele & G. Miller, Derbyshire v Suffolk (Bury St Edm'ds)	1981
5th	166	M.A. Lynch & G.R.J. Roope, Surrey v Durham (Oval)	1982
6th	73	A.W. Stovold & P. Bainbridge, Gloucestershire v Ireland (Dublin)	1981
7th	102	D.L. Bairstow & C.M. Old, Yorkshire v Worcestershire (Leeds)	1982
8th	46*	C.M. Old & G.B. Stevenson, Yorkshire v Worcestershire (Leeds)	1982
9th	62	Asif Din & G.C. Small, Warwickshire v Surrey (Lord's)	1982
10th	81	S. Turner & R.E. East, Essex v Yorkshire (Leeds)	1982

Best bowling: 6-18 C.E.B. Rice, Nottinghamshire v Sussex (Hove) 1982.
6-22 R.D. Jackman, Surrey v Hampshire (Southampton) 1982.

Hat-tricks: Nil.

Most wicket-keeping dismissals: 6 (5 ct 1 st) R.W. Taylor, Derbyshire v Essex (Derby).

GILLETTE CUP WINNERS

1963 Sussex	1969 Yorkshire	1975 Lancashire
1964 Sussex	1970 Lancashire	1976 Northamptonshire
1965 Yorkshire	1971 Lancashire	1977 Middlesex
1966 Warwickshire	1972 Lancashire	1978 Sussex
1967 Kent	1973 Gloucestershire	1979 Somerset
1968 Warwickshire	1974 Kent	1980 Middlesex

NATWEST BANK TROPHY WINNERS

1981 Derbyshire	1982 Surrey

NATWEST BANK TROPHY
PRINCIPAL RECORDS 1963-1982

(including those in the former Gillette Cup)

Highest innings total: 371-4 off 60 overs, Hampshire v Glamorgan (Southampton) 1975.

Highest innings total by a Minor County: 229-5 off 60 overs, Devon v Cornwall (Exeter) 1980.

Highest innings total by a side batting second: 297-4 off 57.1 overs, Somerset v Warwickshire (Taunton) 1978.

Highest innings total by a side batting first and losing: 292-5 off 60 overs, Warwickshire v Somerset (Taunton) 1978.

Lowest innings total: 41 off 20 overs, Cambridgeshire v Buckinghamshire (Cambridge) 1972; 41 off 19.4 overs, Middlesex v Essex (Westcliff) 1972; 41 off 36.1 overs, Shropshire v Essex (Wellington) 1974.

Lowest innings total by a side batting first and winning: 98 off 56.2 overs, Worcestershire v Durham (Chester-le-Street) 1968.

Highest individual innings: 177 C.G. Greenidge, Hampshire v Glamorgan (Southampton) 1975.

Highest individual innings by a Minor County player: 132 G. Robinson, Lincolnshire v Northumberland (Jesmond) 1971.

Centuries: 93 were scored in the Gillette Cup. 11 have been scored in the NatWest Bank Trophy.

Record Wicket Partnerships

1st	227	R.E. Marshall & B.L. Reed, Hampshire v Bedfordshire (Goldington)	1968
2nd	223	M.J. Smith & C.T. Radley, Middlesex v Hampshire (Lord's)	1977
3rd	160	B. Wood & F.C. Hayes, Lancashire v Warwickshire (Birmingham)	1976
4th	234	D. Lloyd & C.H. Lloyd, Lancashire v Gloucestershire (Manchester)	1978
5th	166	M.A. Lynch & G.R.J. Roope, Surrey v Durham (Oval)	1982
6th	105	G.S. Sobers & R.A. White, Nottinghamshire v Worcestershire (Worcester)	1974
7th	107	D.R. Shepherd & D.A. Graveney, Gloucestershire v Surrey (Bristol)	1973
8th	69	S.J. Rouse & D.J. Brown, Warwickshire v Middlesex (Lord's)	1977
9th	87	M.A. Nash & A.E. Cordle, Glamorgan v Lincolnshire (Swansea)	1974
10th	81	S. Turner & R.E. East, Essex v Yorkshire (Leeds)	1982

Hat-tricks: J.D.F. Larter, Northamptonshire v Sussex (Northampton) 1963
D.A.D. Sydenham, Surrey v Cheshire (Hoylake) 1964
R.N.S. Hobbs, Essex v Middlesex (Lord's) 1968
N.M. McVicker, Warwickshire v Lincolnshire (Birmingham) 1971

Seven wickets in innings: 7-15 A.L. Dixon, Kent v Surrey (The Oval) 1968. P.J. Sainsbury, Hampshire v Norfolk (Southampton) 7-30 in 1965 and R.D. Jackman, Surrey v Yorkshire (Harrogate) 7-33 in 1970 have also achieved this feat.

Most 'Man of the Match' awards: 7 C.H. Lloyd (Lancashire); 6 B.L. D'Oliveira (Worcestershire) and B. Wood (Lancashire); 5 M.C. Cowdrey (Kent), A.W. Greig (Sussex) and R.D.V. Knight (Gloucestershire and Surrey).

WINNERS OF THE 1982 PICK-A-TEAM COMPETITION

First Prize: £300   Scott Miller, 92 Collesdene Avenue, Joppa, Edinburgh.

Second Prize: £200   Andrew Milner, 5 Benson Close, Lichfield, Staffordshire.

Third Prize: £150   Robert Chorley, 69 Bedford Gardens, London W8.

Fourth Prize: £100   Sandra Young, 3 Thomson Place, Rosyth, Fife.

25 Runners-up: £10 each

Richard Yarr, 11 Catherine Street, Brighouse, West Yorkshire; M.R. Haselup, Elbury, Brue Avenue, Bruton, Somerset BA10 0HZ; Paul Jones, 9 Douglas Road, Hollywood, Birmingham B47 5JY; Andrew McNeill, 29 Harry Arke House, Oldbury, Warley, West Midlands; Stewart Longhurst, 28 Gwyther Street, Pembroke Dock, Dyfed; E.E.G. Boucher, Rest Harrow, Church Road, Colaton, Raleigh, Sidmouth, Devon; J.G. Worricker, 131 Burdon Lane, Cheam, Surrey SM2 7DB; Andrew Farmer, 116 Colchester Road, Leyton, London E10 6HD; Mrs. Margaret Baker, 5 St. Edmunds Gate, Attleborough, Norfolk; A.P. Harvey, 32 Fordwich Hill, Hertford, Herts SG14 2BQ; R.T. Tarleton, 61 Tyne Road, Oakham, Rutland, Leicestershire; Martin Fox, 61 Stainburn Crescent, Leeds LS17 6NT; Paul Wheeldon, 124 Queen's Road, Ashton-Under-Lyne, Tameside OL6 8EL; Martin Buckman, 90 Auckland Drive, Lower Bevendean, Brighton, Sussex BN2 4JG; B.D. Eley, 25 Limebrest Avenue, Thornton, Lancashire FY5 5AT; D.H. Woodhead, 2 Healey Wood Gardens, Brighouse, West Yorkshire HD6 3SR; R.P. Oates, 6 Loxley Street, Batley, West Yorkshire; James LeBlanc, 147 Ongar Road, Brentwood, Essex; I.C. Bolton, 'Bracton', Hill Waye, Gerrards Cross, Bucks SL9 8BJ; John Shelford, 37 Houghton Street, Blackburn, Lancashire BB2 3OQ; Charles Bolden, 5 Drayton Road, Sunderland SR6 8HE; Stephen Percival, 27 Leslie Close, Hagbourne Park, Freshbrook, Swindon, Wiltshire; J.R. Laslett, Clampers, High Road, Cookham, Maidenhead, Berkshire; M.J. Chant, 49 Plaistow Avenue, Hodge Hill, Birmingham B36 8HQ; N. Murphy, 9 Thirlmere Avenue, Workington, Cumbria CA14 3HY.

THE WINNING TEAM

(1) Graham Gooch, (2) Glenn Turner, (3) Viv Richards, (4) Allan Lamb, (5) Clive Lloyd (Captain), (6) Clive Rice, (7) Ian Botham, (8) David Bairstow, (9) Richard Hadlee, (10) Joel Garner, (11) Derek Underwood.

There were 1,377 entries.

SOMERSET'S BENSON & HEDGES AGAIN!

Somerset became the first County to win the Benson & Hedges Cup in two successive years when they thoroughly outplayed Nottinghamshire (in their first Final) to win by 9 wickets. It could hardly be more comprehensive than that. Perhaps the occasion was a bit too much for the players of Nottinghamshire especially as their two star players, Richard Hadlee and Clive Rice, were a long way from being fully fit. Their score of 130 – a poor batting performance – was never likely to be anywhere near enough against the immense strength of Somerset's batting, and after Denning had largely got himself out with the score at 27, Roebuck and Richards batted with a fluency and freedom that had an air of inevitability about it. Thus, once again, Benson & Hedges have missed a cliff-hanger Final, although some of their earlier round games have had tension enough.

Somerset had put Sussex out with similar certainty in the Semi-Final at Taunton, winning this one by 8 wickets, Joel Garner having run amok against the Sussex batting. Yet Somerset had not headed their own zonal table. This went to Middlesex with four wins out of four, and they must have been joint, or even clear favourites after this. But those old Cup fighters, Lancashire, put them out in the Quarter-Finals at Lord's. It is interesting that only one of the four Group Leaders progressed as far as the Semi-Finals – Derbyshire, Kent and Middlesex had all fallen before. But how close Nottinghamshire came to disaster is reflected in the score against Leicestershire in the Quarter-Finals – Nottinghamshire 156; Leicestershire 154-9 in 55 overs – victory for Notts by the slender margin of 2 runs.

When Lancashire were 88 for 1 at Trent Bridge in the Semi-Final with Clive Lloyd next man in, Notts could have been in trouble, but the Lancashire batting faded away with French picking up four catches behind the stumps. After that it wasn't too difficult. So Somerset are poised for three in a row now, a feat Lancashire achieved in the Gillette Cup – the only instance to date of a hat-trick in either the Gillette, NatWest, Benson & Hedges or John Player.

Yet the County with the most Gold Awards is Kent with 37, followed by Lancashire and Somerset with 33 each. Lowest in the list is Northants with only 19. It is rather surprising that no County has won fewer Benson & Hedges games than Northamptonshire.

1982 RESULTS

8 MAY

Gloucestershire v Glamorgan at Bristol
Gloucestershire 187 in 54.2 overs
Glamorgan 183 in 54.2 overs
Result: Gloucestershire won by 4 runs
Gold Award: J.H. Childs

Kent v Hampshire at Canterbury
Kent 217-9 in 55 overs
Hampshire 198 in 53.3 overs
Result: Kent won by 19 runs
Gold Award: N.R. Taylor

Lancashire v Scotland at Manchester
Lancashire 156-0 in 49.2 overs
Scotland 154 in 54 overs
Result: Lancashire won by 10 wickets
Gold Award: C.E.H. Croft

Leicestershire v Derbyshire at Leicester
Leicestershire 233-5 in 54 overs
Derbyshire 232-6 in 55 overs
Result: Leicestershire won by 5 wickets
Gold Award: M.A. Garnham

Northamptonshire v Nottinghamshire at Northampton
Nottinghamshire 234-7 in 55 overs
Northamptonshire 195 in 53.3 overs
Result: Nottinghamshire won by 39 runs
Gold Award: A.J. Lamb

Somerset v Combined Universities at Taunton
Somerset 150-2 in 34.5 overs
Combined Universities 147 in 50.2 overs
Result: Somerset won by 8 wickets
Gold Award: D.J.S. Taylor

Surrey v Essex at The Oval
Surrey 276-6 in 55 overs
Essex 191-8 in 55 overs
Result: Surrey won by 85 runs
Gold Award: M.A. Lynch

Yorkshire v Worcestershire at Leeds
Worcestershire 210-8 in 54 overs
Yorkshire 209-9 in 54 overs
Result: Worcestershire won by 2 wickets
Gold Award: G.B. Stevenson

15 MAY

Derbyshire v Minor Counties at Derby
Derbyshire 202-2 in 38.5 overs
Minor Counties 201 in 54.3 overs
Result: Derbyshire won by 8 wickets
Gold Award: G. Miller

Essex v Kent at Chelmsford
Kent 180-5 in 52.5 overs
Essex 178 in 51.3 overs
Result: Kent won by 5 wickets
Gold Award: D.L. Underwood

Hampshire v Sussex at Bournemouth
Sussex 248-9 in 55 overs
Hampshire 129 in 43.4 overs
Result: Sussex won by 119 runs
Gold Award: P.W.G. Parker

Middlesex v Somerset at Lord's
Middlesex 99-4 in 37.4 overs
Somerset 98 in 39.3 overs
Result: Middlesex won by 6 wickets
Gold Award: N.F. Williams

Nottinghamshire v Warwickshire at Nottingham
Nottinghamshire 244-7 in 55 overs
Warwickshire 205 in 50.3 overs
Result: Nottinghamshire won by 39 runs
Gold Award: S.B. Hassan

Worcestershire v Leicestershire at Worcester
Leicestershire 278-3 in 55 overs
Worcestershire 272-8 in 55 overs
Result: Leicestershire won by 6 wickets
Gold Award: J.C. Balderstone

Combined Universities v Gloucestershire at Oxford
Gloucestershire 300-4 in 55 overs
Combined Universities 216-8 in 55 overs
Result: Gloucestershire won by 84 runs
Gold Award: A.W. Stovold

Scotland v Northamptonshire at Titwood
Northamptonshire 259-5 in 55 overs
Scotland 82 in 39.2 overs
Result: Northamptonshire won by 177 runs
Gold Award: W. Larkins

22 MAY

Essex v Hampshire at Chelmsford
Essex 131-9 in 53.3 overs
Hampshire 130 in 52.2 overs
Result: Essex won by 1 wicket
Gold Award: S. Turner

Glamorgan v Combined Universities at Cardiff
Glamorgan 232-5 in 55 overs
Combined Universities 86 in 28.4 overs
Result: Glamorgan won by 146 runs
Gold Award: J.A. Hopkins

Leicestershire v Yorkshire at Leicester
Leicestershire 210-4 in 53 overs
Yorkshire 207-9 in 55 overs
Result: Leicestershire won by 6 wickets
Gold Award: G. Boycott

Northamptonshire v Lancashire at Northampton
Lancashire 105-2 in 36.1 overs
Northamptonshire 102 in 37.5 overs
Result: Lancashire won by 8 wickets
Gold Award: B.W. Reidy

Warwickshire v Scotland at Birmingham
Warwickshire 167-1 in 38 overs
Scotland 166 in 53.1 overs
Result: Warwickshire won by 9 wickets
Gold Award: D.L. Amiss

Minor Counties v Worcestershire at Wellington
Worcestershire 226 in 55 overs
Minor Counties 129 in 48.3 overs
Result: Worcestershire won by 97 runs
Gold Award: D. Nicholls

22 & 24 MAY

Gloucestershire v Middlesex at Bristol
Middlesex 229-6 in 54.2 overs
Gloucestershire 226-3 in 55 overs
Result: Middlesex won by 4 wickets
Gold Award: J.M. Brearley

Surrey v Sussex at The Oval
Sussex 235-7 in 53.2 overs
Surrey 231 in 55 overs
Result: Sussex won by 3 wickets
Gold Award: I.J. Gould

25 MAY

Glamorgan v Somerset at Swansea
Somerset 174-8 in 55 overs
Glamorgan 162 in 54.3 overs
Result: Somerset won by 12 runs
Gold Award: I.T. Botham

Kent v Surrey at Canterbury
Kent 220-9 in 54.4 overs
Surrey 217 in 54.4 overs
Result: Kent won by 1 wicket
Gold Award: C.S. Cowdrey

Lancashire v Warwickshire at Manchester
Lancashire 239-8 in 55 overs
Warwickshire 201 in 50.5 overs
Result: Lancashire won by 38 runs
Gold Award: A. Kennedy

Sussex v Essex at Hove
Essex 327-2 in 55 overs
Sussex 213 in 42.2 overs
Result: Essex won by 114 runs
Gold Award: G.A. Gooch

Worcestershire v Derbyshire at Worcester
Derbyshire 284-6 in 55 overs
Worcestershire 278-9 in 55 overs
Result: Derbyshire won by 6 wickets
Gold Award: B. Wood

Scotland v Nottinghamshire at Titwood
Nottinghamshire 242-6 in 55 overs
Scotland 149-8 in 55 overs
Result: Nottinghamshire won by 93 runs
Gold Award: C.E.B. Rice

Combined Universities v Middlesex at Cambridge
Middlesex 107-1 in 33 overs
Combined Universities 105 in 44.4 overs
Result: Middlesex won by 9 wickets
Gold Award: P.H. Edmonds

25 & 26 MAY

Yorkshire v Minor Counties at Bradford
Yorkshire 193-4 in 52.3 overs
Minor Counties 192-8 in 55 overs
Result: Yorkshire won by 6 wickets
Gold Award: C.W.J. Athey

27 MAY

Derbyshire v Yorkshire at Chesterfield
Derbyshire 181-3 in 42 overs
Yorkshire 178 in 55 overs
Result: Derbyshire won by 7 wickets
Gold Award: J.H. Hampshire

Hampshire v Surrey at Southampton
Surrey 207-8 in 55 overs
Hampshire 194-7 in 55 overs
Result: Surrey won by 13 runs
Gold Award: G.R.J. Roope

Nottinghamshire v Lancashire at Nottingham
Nottinghamshire 216-8 in 55 overs
Lancashire 194-9 in 55 overs
Result: Nottinghamshire won by 22 runs
Gold Award: R.J. Hadlee

Somerset v Gloucestershire at Taunton
Somerset 307-6 in 55 overs
Gloucestershire 294-7 in 55 overs
Result: Somerset won by 14 runs
Gold Award: P.W. Denning

Minor Counties v Leicestershire at Wellington
Minor Counties 187-7 in 55 overs
Leicestershire 56 in 26.2 overs
Result: Minor Counties won by 131 runs
Gold Award: S. Davis

27 & 28 MAY

Sussex v Kent at Hove
Sussex 305-6 in 55 overs
Kent 252 in 48.5 overs
Result: Sussex won by 53 runs
Gold Award: N.R. Taylor

Warwickshire v Northamptonshire at Birmingham
Warwickshire 259-4 in 52.4 overs
Northamptonshire 258-8 in 55 overs
Result: Warwickshire won by 6 wickets
Gold Award: W. Larkins

28 MAY

Middlesex v Glamorgan at Lord's
Middlesex 199-3 in 51 overs
Glamorgan 195-8 in 55 overs
Result: Middlesex won by 7 wickets
Gold Award: M.W. Gatting

The zonal points table is on page 166

QUARTER-FINALS – 16 JUNE

Derbyshire v Sussex at Derby
Derbyshire 194-6 in 53.4 overs
Sussex 190 in 55 overs
Result: Derbyshire won by 4 wickets
Gold Award: P.W.G. Parker

Kent v Somerset at Canterbury
Somerset 208-7 in 54.4 overs
Kent 207 in 54.2 overs
Result: Somerset won by 3 wickets
Gold Award: N.R. Taylor

Middlesex v Lancashire at Lord's
Lancashire 191-9 in 55 overs
Middlesex 139 in 48 overs
Result: Lancashire won by 51 runs
Gold Award: C.H. Lloyd

16 & 17 JUNE

Nottinghamshire v Leicestershire at Nottingham
Nottinghamshire 156 in 53.4 overs
Leicestershire 154-9 in 55 overs
Result: Nottinghamshire won by 2 runs
Gold Award: G.J. Parsons

SEMI-FINALS – 30 JUNE

Somerset v Sussex at Taunton
Somerset 112-2 in 36.1 overs
Sussex 110 in 41.1 overs
Result: Somerset won by 8 wickets
Gold Award: J. Garner

Nottinghamshire v Lancashire at Nottingham
Nottinghamshire 184-6 in 53.1 overs
Lancashire 182 in 54.4 overs
Result: Nottinghamshire won by 4 wickets
Gold Award: R.J. Hadlee

THE BENSON & HEDGES CUP FINAL
PLAYED AT LORD'S, 24 JULY
SOMERSET WON BY 9 WICKETS

NOTTINGHAMSHIRE

P.A. Todd	b Garner	2
R.T. Robinson	c Richards b Dredge	13
D.W. Randall	b Marks	19
B. Hassan	c Taylor b Dredge	26
*C.E.B. Rice	b Marks	27
J.D. Birch	b Moseley	7
R.J. Hadlee	b Garner	11
†B.N. French	c Taylor b Botham	8
E.E. Hemmings	b Botham	1
K.E. Cooper	b Garner	3
M. Hendrick	not out	0
Extras (LB5, W7, NB1)		13
Total (50.1 overs)		130

SOMERSET

P.W. Denning	c French b Hendrick	22
P.M. Roebuck	not out	53
I.V.A. Richards	not out	51
*B.C. Rose	did not bat	
I.T. Botham	did not bat	
V.J. Marks	did not bat	
N.F.H. Popplewell	did not bat	
†D.J.S. Taylor	did not bat	
J. Garner	did not bat	
C.H. Dredge	did not bat	
H.R. Moseley	did not bat	
Extras (LB5, W1)		6
Total (33.1 overs) (1 wkt)		132

Gold Award: V.J. Marks

BOWLING

SOMERSET	O	M	R	W		FALL OF WICKETS	
						NT	SM
Garner	8.1	1	13	3			27
Botham	9	3	19	2	1st	3	27
Dredge	11	2	35	2	2nd	40	—
Moseley	11	2	26	1	3rd	40	—
Marks	11	4	24	2	4th	86	—
NOTTINGHAMSHIRE					5th	102	—
Hadlee	9	0	37	0	6th	106	—
Hendrick	8	1	26	1	7th	122	—
Cooper	5.1	0	41	0	8th	123	—
Rice	6	2	11	0	9th	130	—
Hemmings	5	0	11	0	10th	130	—

BENSON & HEDGES CUP
PRINCIPAL RECORDS

Highest innings total: 350-3 off 55 overs, Essex v Combined Universities (Chelmsford) 1979.

Highest innings total by a side batting second: 291-5 off 53.5 overs, Warwickshire v Lancashire (Manchester) 1981.

Highest innings total by a side batting first and losing: 288-9 off 55 overs, Lancashire v Warwickshire (Manchester) 1981.

Lowest completed innings total: 56 off 26.2 overs, Leicestershire v Minor Counties (Wellington) 1982.

Highest individual innings: 198* G.A. Gooch, Essex v Sussex (Hove) 1982.

Record Wicket Partnerships

1st	241	S.M. Gavaskar & B.C. Rose, Somerset v Kent (Canterbury)	1980
2nd	285*	C.G. Greenidge & D.R. Turner, Hampshire v Minor Counties (South) (Amersham)	1973
3rd	268*	G.A. Gooch & K.W.R. Fletcher, Essex v Sussex (Hove)	1982
4th	184*	D. Lloyd & B.W. Reidy, Lancashire v Derbyshire (Chesterfield)	1980
5th	134	M. Maslin & D.N.F. Slade, Minor Counties (East) v Nottinghamshire (Nottingham)	1976
6th	114	M.J. Khan & G.P. Ellis, Glamorgan v Gloucestershire (Bristol)	1975
7th	149*	J.D. Love & C.M. Old, Yorkshire v Scotland (Bradford)	1981
8th	109	R.E. East & N. Smith, Essex v Northamptonshire (Chelmsford)	1977
9th	81	J.N. Shepherd & D.L. Underwood, Kent v Middlesex (Lord's)	1975
10th	80*	D.L. Bairstow & M. Johnson, Yorkshire v Derbyshire (Derby)	1981

Hat-tricks: G.D. McKenzie, Leicestershire v Worcestershire (Worcester) 1972. K. Higgs, Leicestershire v Surrey (Lord's) 1974. A.A. Jones, Middlesex v Essex (Lord's) 1977. M.J. Procter, Gloucestershire v Hampshire (Southampton) 1977. W. Larkins, Northamptonshire v Combined Universities (Northampton) 1980. E.A. Moseley, Glamorgan v Kent (Cardiff) 1981.

Seven wickets in an innings: 7-12 W.W. Daniel, Middlesex v Minor Counties (East) (Ipswich) 1978, 7-22 J.R. Thomson, Middlesex v Hampshire (Lord's) 1981, 7-32 R.G.D. Willis, Warwickshire v Yorkshire (Birmingham) 1981.

Most 'Gold' awards: 11 B. Wood (10 for Lancashire, 1 for Derbyshire), 9 J.H. Edrich (Surrey).

BENSON & HEDGES CUP WINNERS

1972 Leicestershire	1978 Kent
1973 Kent	1979 Essex
1974 Surrey	1980 Northamptonshire
1975 Leicestershire	1981 Somerset
1976 Kent	1982 Somerset
1977 Gloucestershire	

SUSSEX WIN THE
JOHN PLAYER

It is often said – and justifiably so – that the three-day County Championship and the 40-over (restricted bowler's run-up) on a Sunday afternoon are poles apart. It is interesting, however, that Middlesex and Leicestershire, first and second respectively in the County Championship, should be second and third in the John Player, on the basis, presumably, that a good side can adapt. Sussex became the ninth County to win the John Player, creeping up from fifth in the previous season. They became the sixth County to win this competition in six years, after Leicestershire and Kent had helped themselves to four out of five in the first five seasons. The performance by Sussex well deserved success. They won 14 out of 16 matches, with one no-result and only one defeat. This occurred at Horsham in mid-June when Worcester won a fine match by 3 wickets – Sussex 206-8 in 40 overs; Worcestershire 208-7 in 39 overs. Worcestershire, however, did not sustain this standard and finished 15th in the table. The most surprising drop was by Warwickshire – 3rd in 1981; 17th in 1982. Middlesex and Leicestershire achieved the reverse; they moved up to 2nd and 3rd from 15th and 14th.

JOHN PLAYER LEAGUE FINAL TABLE

	P	W	L	NR	TIE	Pts
Sussex (5)	16	14	1	1	0	58
Middlesex (15)	16	11	4	1	0	46
Leicestershire (14)	16	9	6	1	0	38
Essex (1)	16	9	7	0	0	36
Kent (7)	16	9	7	0	0	36
Hampshire (6)	16	8	6	0	2	36
Nottinghamshire (10)	16	8	6	1	1	36
Northamptonshire (17)	16	8	7	1	0	34
Somerset (2)	16	8	8	0	0	32
Glamorgan (10)	16	6	7	3	0	30
Lancashire (12)	16	6	7	2	1	30
Derbyshire (4)	16	6	9	1	0	26
Surrey (7)	16	6	9	0	1	26
Gloucestershire (16)	16	5	9	2	0	24
Worcestershire (10)	16	5	10	1	0	22
Yorkshire (7)	16	3	10	2	1	18
Warwickshire (3)	16	3	11	2	0	16

1981 positions in brackets.

JOHN PLAYER LEAGUE
PRINCIPAL RECORDS

Highest innings total: 307-4 off 38 overs. Worcs v Derbyshire (Worcester) 1975.
Highest innings total by a side batting second: 301-6 off 39.3 overs, Warwickshire v Essex (Colchester) 1982.
Highest innings total by a side batting first and losing: 299-4 off 40 overs, Essex v Warwickshire (Colchester) 1982.
Lowest completed innings total: 23 off 19.4 overs, Middlesex v Yorkshire (Leeds) 1974.
Highest individual innings: 163* C.G. Greenidge, Hampshire v Warwickshire (Birmingham) 1979.

Record Wicket Partnerships

1st	224	J.A. Ormrod and D.N. Patel, Worcestershire v Hampshire (Southampton)	1982
2nd	179	B.W. Luckhurst & M.H. Denness, Kent v Somerset (Canterbury)	1973
3rd	215	W. Larkins & R.G. Williams, Northamptonshire v Worcestershire (Luton)	1982
4th	175	M.J.K. Smith & D.L. Amiss, Warwickshire v Yorkshire (Birmingham)	1970
5th	163	A.G.E. Ealham & B.D. Julien, Kent v Leicestershire (Leicester)	1977
6th	121	C.P. Wilkins & A.J. Borrington, Derbyshire v Warwickshire (Chesterfield)	1972
7th	101	S.J. Windaybank & D.A. Graveney, Gloucestershire v Nottinghamshire (Nottingham)	1981
8th	95*	D. Breakwell & K.F. Jennings, Somerset v Nottinghamshire (Nottingham)	1976
9th	86	D.P. Hughes & P. Lever, Lancashire v Essex (Leyton)	1973
10th	57	D.A. Graveney & J.B. Mortimore, Gloucestershire v Lancashire (Tewkesbury)	1973

Four wickets in four balls: A. Ward, Derbyshire v Sussex (Derby) 1970.
Hat-tricks (excluding above): R. Palmer, Somerset v Gloucestershire (Bristol) 1970. K.D. Boyce, Essex v Somerset (Westcliff) 1971. G.D. McKenzie, Leicestershire v Essex (Leicester) 1972. R.G.D. Willis, Warwickshire v Yorkshire (Birmingham) 1973. W. Blenkiron, Warwickshire v Derbyshire (Buxton) 1974. A. Buss, Sussex v Worcestershire (Hastings) 1974. J.M. Rice, Hampshire v Northamptonshire (Southampton) 1975. M.A. Nash, Glamorgan v Worcestershire (Worcester) 1975. A. Hodgson, Northamptonshire v Sussex (Northampton) 1976. A.E. Cordle, Glamorgan v Hampshire (Portsmouth) 1979. C.J. Tunnicliffe, Derbyshire v Worcestershire (Derby) 1979. M.D. Marshall, Hampshire v Surrey (Southampton) 1981.
Eight wickets in an innings: 8-26 K.D. Boyce, Essex v Lancashire (Manchester) 1971.

JOHN PLAYER LEAGUE CHAMPIONS

1969	Lancashire	1976	Kent
1970	Lancashire	1977	Leicestershire
1971	Worcestershire	1978	Hampshire
1972	Kent	1979	Somerset
1973	Kent	1980	Warwickshire
1974	Leicestershire	1981	Essex
1975	Hampshire	1982	Sussex

MIDDLESEX ARE THE
COUNTY CHAMPIONS

At Worcester, where many an Overseas cricketer has had his first experience of playing cricket in England in the shadow of the world-famous cathedral, Mike Brearley came out of the mist and into retirement, having just hit the winning run and having led Middlesex to the Schweppes County Championship – a fitting testimony to his marvellous career in cricket for Cambridge University, Middlesex and England. There was a time when their followers fully expected Middlesex to win more than one honour in this summer of 1982, but although Brearley was involved in a great number of memorable one-day games, this was probably the one he most wanted to win – the competition which is the supreme test of all-round skill, maintained from April until September. Few devotees, at the beginning of the season, would have expected Leicestershire to be the County chasing them home, but that is what happened.

Mike Brearley has been described as a ruthless captain – but then so many of the great captains have had this approach, and Brearley achieved the success all captains strive for. There is little doubt that Middlesex will sorely miss his leadership and his ability to score runs when they are most needed, not to mention his uncanny understanding of the foibles of individual players, those playing both with and against him, which made him such a master of strategy.

But all praise, too, to Leicestershire, who came with a late run to challenge Middlesex. Rain plays such an important part in the outcome of Championships and on a day towards the end of the season when only one match enjoyed a full day's cricket, it was at Taunton, that Leicestershire easily beat Somerset, as Middlesex watched the rain at Lord's. It was Cook's spinners which bowled Somerset out and many thought him a possible for Australia having taken 80 wickets at 22.90. But the Selectors did not. A great deal more will surely be heard of him. It was a wonderful season for Davison (now a qualified English player for Test cricket) who scored 1789 runs at an average of 57.70. He hit seven County Championship centuries. Balderstone hit four. Gower, surprisingly, only one. This is the reservation which so many old players have about

66

Gower – the number of times he is in the forties, fifties and even sixties and seventies, when he should be getting a hundred. But how worth watching he is when he is in full flight.

The unlucky Gatting (as far as Test cricket is concerned) had a good season for Middlesex with an average of 67. Daniel and Edmonds each took 71 wickets and Emburey 74, but the young man to highlight their season, of course, was Cowans – from the Second Eleven to the England team in a few short (or long) strides! Although they never really threatened to catch the two leaders, Hampshire nonetheless showed a marked improvement all round to finish third. A wonderful season for Trevor Jesty – a batting average of 48.22, 34 wickets at 21.47, and six centuries which, when added up, surely should have produced a trip to Australia. Trevor Jesty may well ask 'What on earth do I have to do to be selected, except as an afterthought?'

At the other end of the scale, Warwickshire finished seventeenth, as they had done in 1981; Glamorgan dropped from fourteenth to sixteenth (a few problems here), and Gloucestershire from thirteenth to fifteenth.

SCHWEPPES COUNTY CHAMPIONSHIP FINAL TABLE

	P	W	L	D	Bonus points Bt	Bw	Pts
1—Middlesex (4)	22	12	2	8	59	74	325
2—Leicestershire (8)	22	10	4	8	57	69	286
3—Hampshire (7)	22	8	6	8	48	74	250
4—Nottinghamshire (1)	22	7	7	8	44	65	221
5—Surrey (6)	22	6	6	10	56	62	214
6—Somerset (3)	22	6	6	10	51	66	213
7—Essex (5)	22	5	5	12	57	75	212
8—Sussex (2)	22	6	7	9	43	68	207
9—Northamptonshire (15)	22	5	3	14	61	54	195
10—Yorkshire (10)	22	5	1	16	48	51	179
11—Derbyshire (12)	22	4	3	15	45	64	173
12—Lancashire (16)	22	4	3	15	48	55	167
13—Kent (9)	22	3	4	15	55	63	166
14—Worcestershire (11)	22	3	5	14	43	54	141
15—Gloucestershire (13)	22	2	9	11	46	55	133
16—Glamorgan (14)	22	1	8	13	43	60	119
17—Warwickshire (17)	22	0	8	14	58	53	111

1981 positions in brackets.
Worcestershire total includes 12pts from match reduced to one innings.

COUNTY CHAMPIONS

The earliest winners of the title were decided usually by the least matches lost. In 1888 an unofficial points table was introduced and in 1890 the Championship was constituted officially. Since 1977 it has been sponsored by Schweppes.

Year	County	Year	County	Year	County
1864	Surrey	1898	Yorkshire	1948	Glamorgan
1865	Nottinghamshire	1899	Surrey	1949	Middlesex / Yorkshire
1866	Middlesex	1900	Yorkshire		
1867	Yorkshire	1901	Yorkshire	1950	Lancashire / Surrey
1868	Nottinghamshire	1902	Yorkshire		
1869	Nottinghamshire / Yorkshire	1903	Middlesex	1951	Warwickshire
		1904	Lancashire	1952	Surrey
1870	Yorkshire	1905	Yorkshire	1953	Surrey
1871	Nottinghamshire	1906	Kent	1954	Surrey
1872	Nottinghamshire	1907	Nottinghamshire	1955	Surrey
1873	Gloucestershire / Nottinghamshire	1908	Yorkshire	1956	Surrey
		1909	Kent	1957	Surrey
1874	Gloucestershire	1910	Kent	1958	Surrey
1875	Nottinghamshire	1911	Warwickshire	1959	Yorkshire
1876	Gloucestershire	1912	Yorkshire	1960	Yorkshire
1877	Gloucestershire	1913	Kent	1961	Hampshire
1878	Undecided	1914	Surrey	1962	Yorkshire
1879	Nottinghamshire / Lancashire	1919	Yorkshire	1963	Yorkshire
		1920	Middlesex	1964	Worcestershire
1880	Nottinghamshire	1921	Middlesex	1965	Worcestershire
1881	Lancashire	1922	Yorkshire	1966	Yorkshire
1882	Nottinghamshire / Lancashire	1923	Yorkshire	1967	Yorkshire
		1924	Yorkshire	1968	Yorkshire
1883	Nottinghamshire	1925	Yorkshire	1969	Glamorgan
1884	Nottinghamshire	1926	Lancashire	1970	Kent
1885	Nottinghamshire	1927	Lancashire	1971	Surrey
1886	Nottinghamshire	1928	Lancashire	1972	Warwickshire
1887	Surrey	1929	Nottinghamshire	1973	Hampshire
1888	Surrey	1930	Lancashire	1974	Worcestershire
1889	Surrey / Lancashire / Nottinghamshire	1931	Yorkshire	1975	Leicestershire
		1932	Yorkshire	1976	Middlesex
		1933	Yorkshire	1977	Kent / Middlesex
1890	Surrey	1934	Lancashire		
1891	Surrey	1935	Yorkshire	1978	Kent
1892	Surrey	1936	Derbyshire	1979	Essex
1893	Yorkshire	1937	Yorkshire	1980	Middlesex
1894	Surrey	1938	Yorkshire	1981	Nottinghamshire
1895	Surrey	1939	Yorkshire	1982	Middlesex
1896	Yorkshire	1946	Yorkshire		
1897	Lancashire	1947	Middlesex		

THE COUNTIES AND THEIR PLAYERS

Compiled by Barry McCaully

with the assistance of **Brian Croudy** (averages and first-class records), **Brian Heald** (Test cricket), **Vic Isaacs** (JPL and limited-over records), **Nigel McCaully** (NW and BH) and **Tony Webb** (Universities).

Abbreviations

B	Born	HSGC/	Highest score in
RHB	Right-hand bat	NW	Gillette Cup if higher
LHB	Left-hand bat		than NatWest Trophy
RF	Right-arm fast	HSJPL	Highest score John Player
RFM	Right-arm fast medium		League
RM	Right-arm medium	HSBH	Highest score Benson &
LF	Left-arm fast		Hedges Cup
LFM	Left-arm fast medium	BB	Best bowling figures
LM	Left-arm medium	BBUK	Best bowling figures in this
OB	Off-break		country
LB	Leg-break	BBTC	Best bowling figures in Test
LBG	Leg-break and googly		cricket if different from
SLA	Slow left-arm orthodox		above
SLC	Slow left-arm 'chinaman'	BBC	Best bowling figures for
WK	Wicket-keeper		County if different from
*	Not out or unfinished stand		above
HS	Highest score	BBNW	Best bowling figures
HSUK	Highest score in this		NatWest Trophy
	country	BBGC/	Best bowling figures in
HSTC	Highest score in Test	NW	Gillette Cup if better
	cricket if different from		than NatWest Trophy
	above	BBJPL	Best bowling figures John
HSC	Highest score for County if		Player League
	different from highest	BBBH	Best bowling figures Benson
	first-class score		& Hedges Cup
HSNW	Highest score NatWest		
	Trophy		

When a player is known by a name other than his first name, the name in question has been underlined.

All Test appearances are complete to 1st September 1982.

'Debut' denotes 'first-class debut' and 'Cap' means '1st XI county cap'.

Wisden 1981 indicates that a player was selected as one of *Wisden*'s Five Cricketers of the Year for the year indicated.

Best Young Cricketer of the Year indicates that a player was so elected by the Cricket Writers Club in the year indicated.

All overseas tours on which a player played first-class cricket are listed.

Qualification for best performances: HS: 10. BB: 3 wkts.

DERBYSHIRE

Formation of present club: 1870.
Colours: Chocolate, amber and pale blue.
Badge: Rose and crown.
County Champions: 1936.
Nat West Trophy Winners: 1981.
Gillette Cup Finalists: 1969.
Best final position in John Player League: 3rd in 1970.
Benson & Hedges Cup Finalists: 1978.
NatWest Trophy Man of the Match Awards: 4.
Gillette Man of the Match Awards: 15.
Benson & Hedges Gold Awards: 30.

Secretary: R. Pearman, County Cricket Ground, Nottingham Road, Derby DE2 6DA.
Captain: B. Wood.

Iain Stuart ANDERSON B Derby 24/4/1960. RHB, OB. Debut 1978. HS: 103* v Hants (Derby) 1982. HSJPL: 28 v Sussex (Chesterfield) 1982. BB: 4-35 v Australians (Derby) 1981.

Kim John BARNETT B Stoke-on-Trent 17/7/1960. RHB, LB. Debut 1979. Cap 1982. Tour: D.H. Robins Under-23 in New Zealand 1979-80. NatWest Man of the Match Awards: 1. HS: 120 v Warwicks (Birmingham) 1982. HSNW: 59 v Essex (Derby) 1981. HSJPL: 111 v Lancs (Derby) 1982. HSBH: 34 v Notts (Nottingham) 1980. BB: 4-76 v Warwicks (Birmingham) 1980. BBJPL: 3-39 v Yorks (Chesterfield) 1979.

Michael John DEAKIN B Bury, Lancs 5/5/1957. RHB, WK. Debut 1981 as deputy for R.W. Taylor. Did not play in 1982. HS: 15 v Somerset (Taunton) 1981.

Roger John FINNEY B Darley Dale 2/8/1960. RHB, LM. Debut 1982. HS: 39 v Somerset (Derby) 1982. HSJPL: 10 v Sussex (Chesterfield) 1982.

William Peter FOWLER B St. Helen's, Lancs. RHB, SLA. Debut and played for Northern Districts 1979-80 and 1980-81. Played for Auckland 1981-82. Played in limited overs matches for Derby in 1982. HS: 48 Northern Districts v Auckland (Tauranga) 1979-80. HSJPL: 29 v Kent (Canterbury) 1982.

John Harry HAMPSHIRE B Thurnscoe, Yorks 10/2/1941. Son of J. Hampshire (Yorks 1937). RHB, LB. Played for Yorks 1961-81. Cap 1963. Captain 1979-80. Debut for Derby and cap 1982. Played for Tasmania in 1967-68, 1968-69, 1977-78 and 1978-79. Benefit (£28,425) in 1976. Tests: 8 between 1969 and 1975. Scored 107 on debut v West Indies (Lord's). Tours: Cavaliers in West Indies 1964-65; Commonwealth in Pakistan 1967-68; MCC in Ceylon 1969-70; MCC in Australia and New Zealand 1970-71, D.H. Robins in South Africa 1972-73, and West Indies 1974-75, Leics XI v West Indies 1980-81. 1,000 runs (15): 1,596 (av. 53.20) in 1978 best. Gillette Man of the Match: 4. Benson & Hedges Gold Awards: 3. HS: 183* Yorks v Sussex (Hove) 1971. HSTC: 107 v West Indies (Lord's) 1969. HSGC/NW: 110 Yorks v Durham (Middlesbrough) 1978. HSJPL: 119 Yorks v Leics (Hull) 1971. HSBH: 85 Yorks v Warwicks (Leeds) 1980. BB: 7-52 Yorks v Glamorgan (Cardiff) 1963.

Alan HILL B Buxworth 29/6/1950. RHB, OB. Debut 1972. Cap 1976. Played for Orange Free State in 1976-77. Gillette Man of the Match: 1. Benson & Hedges Gold Award: 1. 1,000 runs (2): 1,303 (av. 34.28) in 1976 best. HS: 160* v Warwicks (Coventry) 1976. HSGC/NW: 72 v Middlesex (Derby) 1978. HSJPL: 120 v Northants (Buxton) 1976. HSBH: 102* v Warwicks (Ilkeston) 1978. BB: 3-5 Orange Free State v Northern Transvaal (Pretoria) 1976-77.

Michael Anthony HOLDING B Kingston, Jamaica 16/2/1954. RHB, RF. Debut for Jamaica in 1972-73. *Wisden* 1976. Debut for Lancs 1981. Did not play in 1982. Tests: 31 for West Indies between 1975-76 and 1981-82. Tours: West Indies to Australia 1975-76, 1981-82, England 1976 and 1980, Australia and New Zealand 1979-80, Pakistan 1980-81, International team to Pakistan 1981-82. HS: 67 International XI v Pakistan (Hyderabad) 1981-82. HSUK: 42 West Indians v MCC (Lord's) 1976. HSC: 32 v Glos (Manchester) 1981. HSTC: 58* West Indians v England (St. John's) 1980-81. HSNW: 12* v Northants (Northampton) 1981. BB: 8-92 (14-149 match) West Indies v England (Oval) 1976. BBC: 6-74 v Glos (Manchester) 1981. BBNW: 3-35 v Hants (Southampton) 1981. Derby 1983.

Peter Noel KIRSTEN B Pietermaritzburg, South Africa 14/5/1955. RHB, OB. Played for Western Province 1973-74 to 1981-82. Played for Sussex v Australians 1975. Debut for Derby and cap 1978. Scored 4 centuries in consecutive innings and 6 in 7 for Western Province in 1976-77 including 173* and 103 v Eastern Province (Cape Town). 1,000 runs (5): 1,941 (av. 64.70) in 1982 best. Also scored 1,074 runs (av. 76.71) in 1976-77. Scored county record of 8 centuries in 1982. Shared 3rd wkt partnership record for county (291) with D.S. Steele v Somerset (Taunton) 1981. NatWest Man of the Match: 2. Benson & Hedges Gold Award: 1. HS: 228 v Somerset (Taunton) 1981. HSNW: 110* v Hants (Southampton) 1982. HSJPL: 102 v Glamorgan (Swansea) 1979. HSBH: 77 v Leics (Leicester) 1982. BB: 4-44 v Middlesex (Derby) 1979. BBJPL: 5-34 v Northants (Long Eaton) 1979.

Bernard Joseph Michael MAHER B Hillingdon, Middlesex 11/2/1958. RHB, WK. Debut 1981. HS: 15* v Lancs (Derby) 1982.

Geoffrey MILLER B Chesterfield 8/9/1952. RHB, OB. Debut 1973. Best Young Cricketer 1976. Cap 1976. Captain 1979-81. Tests: 27 between 1976 and 1982. Tours: India, Sri Lanka and Australia 1976-77, Pakistan and New Zealand 1977-78, Australia 1978-79 and 1979-80, West Indies 1980-81, Australia and New Zealand 1982-83. Most wickets in a season: 87 (av. 17.82) in 1977. Benson & Hedges Gold Awards: 4. HS: 98* v Pakistan (Lahore) 1977-78. HSUK: 98 v India (Manchester) 1982. HSC: 95 v Lancs (Manchester) 1978. HSGC/NW: 59* v Worcs (Worcester) 1978. HSJPL: 84 v Somerset (Chesterfield) 1980. HSBH: 88* v Minor Counties (Derby) 1982. BB: 8-70 v Leics (Cleveland) 1982. BBTC: 5-44 v Australia (Sydney) 1978-79. BBJPL: 4-22 v Yorks (Huddersfield) 1978. BBBH: 3-23 v Surrey (Derby) 1979.

John Edward MORRIS B Crewe, Cheshire 1/4/1964. RHB, RM. Debut 1982. HS: 12 v Pakistanis (Chesterfield) 1982.

Paul Geoffrey NEWMAN B Leicester 10/1/1959. RHB, RFM. Debut 1980. HS: 39* v Glamorgan (Derby) 1982. HSJPL: 19* v Yorks (Derby) 1982. BB: 5-51 v Essex (Derby) 1981. BBBH: 4-48 v Worcs (Worcester) 1982.

Stephen OLDHAM B High Green, Sheffield, Yorks 26/7/1948. RHB, RFM. Played for Yorkshire 1974-79. Debut and cap for Derby 1980. Benson & Hedges

DERBYSHIRE

Gold Award: 1 (for Yorks). HS: 50 Yorks v Sussex (Hove) 1979. HSC: 35* v Warwicks (Birmingham) 1982. HSJPL: 38* Yorks v Glamorgan (Cardiff) 1977. BB: 7-78 v Warwicks (Birmingham) 1982. BBNW: 3-29 v Notts (Derby) 1981. BBJPL: 5-37 v Lancs (Derby) 1982. BBBH: 5-32 Yorks v Minor Counties (North) (Scunthorpe) 1975.

Robert William TAYLOR B Stoke-on-Trent 17/7/1941. RHB, WK, RM. Debut 1960 for Minor Counties v South Africans. Debut for Derby 1961. Cap 1962. Captain 1975-76. Testimonial (£6,672) 1973 and 1981, Wisden 1976. MBE 1981. Tests: 42 between 1970-71 and 1982. Tours: Ceylon and Far East 1969-70, Australia and New Zealand 1970-71, Rest of the World in Australia 1971-72, West Indies 1973-74, Australia and New Zealand 1974-75, International Wanderers in South Africa 1975-76, Pakistan and New Zealand 1977-78, Australia 1978-79, Australia and India 1979-80, India and Sri Lanka 1981-82, Australia and New Zealand 1982-83. Most dismissals in a season: 86 (79 ct 7 st) in 1965. Dismissed 7 batsmen in an innings (equals Test record) and 10 batsmen in match (all caught) for Test record v India (Bombay) 1979-80. Dismissed 10 batsmen in a match (all ct) v Hants (Chesterfield) 1963 and 7 in an innings (all ct) v Glamorgan (Derby) 1966. Gillette Man of the Match: 1. Benson & Hedges Gold Award: 1. HS: 100 v Yorks (Sheffield) 1981. HSTC: 97 v Australia (Adelaide) 1978-79. HSGC/NW: 53* v Middlesex (Lord's) 1975. HSJPL: 43* v Glos (Burton-on-Trent) 1969. HSBH: 31* v Hants (Southampton) 1976. Broke world record for dismissals by a wicket-keeper in 1982-83.

Colin John TUNNICLIFFE B Derby 11/8/1951. RHB, LFM. Debut 1973. Cap 1977. Hat-trick in JPL v Worcs (Derby) 1979. HS: 82* v Middlesex (Ilkeston) 1977. HSNW: 14* v Northants (Lord's) 1981. HSJPL: 51* v Northants (Milton Keynes) 1982. HSBH: 28 v Warwicks (Birmingham) 1979. BB: 7-36 v Essex (Chelmsford) 1980. BBNW: 5-50 v Worcs (Worcester) 1981. BBJPL: 5-24 v Northants (Derby) 1981. BBBH: 5-24 v Yorks (Derby) 1981.

Andrew WATTS B Chapeltown, Yorks 4/10/1960. LHB, RM. Debut 1982.

Barry WOOD B Ossett, Yorks 26/12/1942. RHB, RM. Brother of R. Wood (Yorks 1952-56). Debut for Yorks 1964. Played for Lancs 1966-79. Cap 1968. Played for Eastern Province 1971-72 and 1973-74. Debut for Derby and cap 1980. Captain 1981. Tests: 12 between 1972 and 1978. Tours: India, Pakistan and Sri Lanka 1972-73, New Zealand 1974-75, International Wanderers in Rhodesia 1975-76. 1,000 runs (8): 1,492 (av. 38.25) in 1971 best. Gillette Man of the Match: 6 (for Lancs). Benson & Hedges Gold Awards: 11 (10 for Lancs). HS: 198 Lancs v Glamorgan (Liverpool) 1976. HSC: 153 v Worcs (Chesterfield) 1981. HSTC: 90 v Australia (Oval) 1972. HSGC/NW: 116 Lancs v Kent (Canterbury) 1979. HSJPL: 90* Lancs v Notts (Manchester) 1977 and v Hants (Southampton) 1980. HSBH: 106 v Worcs (Worcester) 1982. BB: 7-52 Lancs v Middlesex (Manchester) 1968. BBC: 3-22 v Sussex (Derby) 1980. BBGC/NW: 4-17 Lancs v Hants (Manchester) 1975. BBJPL: 5-19 Lancs v Kent (Manchester) 1971. BBBH: 5-12 Lancs v Derby (Stockport) 1976.

John Geoffrey WRIGHT B Darfield, New Zealand 5/7/1954. LHB, RM. Debut for Northern Districts 1975-76. Debut for Derby and Cap 1977. Tests: 20 for New Zealand between 1977-78 and 1981-82. Tours: New Zealand to England 1978 and

Australia 1980-81. D.H. Robins in Sri Lanka 1977-78. 1,000 runs (5): 1,830 (av. 55.45) in 1982 best. Benson & Hedges Gold Awards: 3. HS: 190 v Yorks (Derby) 1982. HSTC: 141 New Zealand v Australia (Christchurch) 1981-82. HSGC/NW: 87* v Sussex (Hove) 1977. HSJPL: 103 v Worcs (Worcester) 1982. HSBH: 102 v Worcs (Chesterfield) 1977.

N.B. The following players whose particulars appeared in the 1982 Annual have been omitted: A.J. Borrington, K.G. Brooks, P.J. Hacker, S.T. Jefferies, D.G. Moir and P.E. Russell.

County Averages

Schweppes County Championship: Played 22, won 4, drawn 15, lost 3.
All first-class matches: Played 23, won 4, drawn 15, lost 4.

BATTING AND FIELDING

Cap		M	I	NO	Runs	HS	Avge	100	50	Ct	St
1978	P.N. Kirsten	21	37	7	1941	164*	64.70	8	6	12	—
1977	J.G. Wright	21	39	6	1830	190	55.45	7	5	13	—
1982	J.H. Hampshire	22	36	6	1256	101*	41.86	1	9	14	—
1976	G. Miller	13	22	6	614	72*	38.37	—	5	16	—
1982	K.J. Barnett	18	25	5	642	120	32.10	2	1	11	—
—	I.S. Anderson	17	26	4	671	103*	30.50	1	3	19	—
1980	B. Wood	21	38	4	851	124*	25.02	1	2	20	—
1976	A. Hill	7	14	3	219	54	19.90	—	1	5	—
1980	S. Oldham	21	18	10	156	35*	19.50	—	—	7	—
1977	C.J. Tunnicliffe	16	19	2	273	40	16.05	—	—	8	—
—	P.G. Newman	18	22	4	204	39*	11.33	—	—	4	—
—	P.J. Hacker	8	4	2	22	10*	11.00	—	—	3	—
1962	R.W. Taylor	13	19	2	142	45	8.35	—	—	27	4
—	B.J.M. Maher	10	11	5	49	15*	8.16	—	—	13	—
—	D.G. Moir	23	22	1	136	25	6.47	—	—	24	—

Played in one match: R.J. Finney 39 (1 ct); S.T. Jefferies 14*, 0; J.E. Morris 6, 12; A. Watts 0 (1 ct).

BOWLING

	Type	O	M	R	W	Avge	Best	5 wI	10 wM
S.T. Jefferies	LFM	28	3	109	5	21.80	3-57	—	—
P.J. Hacker	LFM	174.1	25	677	25	27.08	5-51	2	—
D.G. Moir	SLA	811.5	231	2076	76	27.31	6-63	4	—
G. Miller	OB	413.5	125	938	31	30.25	8-70	1	1
S. Oldham	RFM	507.5	98	1544	48	32.16	7-78	2	—
C.J. Tunnicliffe	LFM	383.1	92	1213	37	32.78	5-73	1	—
I.S. Anderson	OB	62.4	22	176	5	35.20	2-43	—	—
P.N. Kirsten	OB	121	28	348	9	38.66	3-25	—	—
P.G. Newman	RFM	440.3	65	1622	38	42.68	4-59	—	—
B. Wood	RM	231.2	54	690	10	69.00	2-0	—	—

Also bowled: K.J. Barnett 43.3-8-147-0; R.J. Finney 14.5-5-40-1; J.H. Hampshire 4-1-26-0; A. Hill 1-0-4-0; A. Watts 9-1-31-0; J.G. Wright 3-0-29-0.

County Records

First-class cricket

Highest innings totals:	For	645 v Hants (Derby)	1898
	Agst	662 by Yorks (Chesterfield)	1898
Lowest innings totals:	For	16 v Notts (Nottingham)	1879
	Agst	23 by Hants (Burton-on-Trent)	1958
Highest individual innings:	For	274 G. Davidson v Lancs (Manchester)	1896
	Agst	343* P.A. Perrin for Essex (Chesterfield)	1904
Best bowling in an innings:	For	10-40 W. Bestwick v Glamorgan (Cardiff)	1921
	Agst	10-47 T.F. Smailes for Yorks (Sheffield)	1939
Best bowling in a match:	For	16-84 C. Gladwin v Worcs (Stourbridge)	1952
	Agst	16-101 G. Giffen for Australians (Derby)	1886
Most runs in a season:		2165 (av. 48.11) D.B. Carr	1959
runs in a career:		20516 (av. 31.41) D. Smith	1927-1952
100s in a season:		8 by P.N. Kirsten	1982
100s in a career:		30 by D. Smith	1927-1952
wickets in a season:		168 (av. 19.55) T.B. Mitchell	1935
wickets in a career:		1670 (av. 17.11) H.L. Jackson	1947-1963

RECORD WICKET STANDS

1st	322	H. Storer & J. Bowden v Essex (Derby)	1929
2nd	349	C.S. Elliot & J.D. Eggar v Notts (Nottingham)	1947
3rd	291	P.N. Kirsten & D.S. Steele v Somerset (Taunton)	1981
4th	328	P. Vaulkhard & D. Smith v Notts (Nottingham)	1946
5th	203	C.P. Wilkins & I.R. Buxton v Lancs (Manchester)	1971
6th	212	G.M. Lee & T.S. Worthington v Essex (Chesterfield)	1932
7th	241*	G.H. Pope & A.E.G. Rhodes v Hants (Portsmouth)	1948
8th	182	A.H.M. Jackson & W. Carter v Leics (Leicester)	1922
9th	283	A.R. Warren & J. Chapman v Warwicks (Blackwell)	1910
10th	93	J. Humphries & J. Horsley v Lancs (Derby)	1914

One-day cricket

Highest innings totals:	NatWest Trophy	270-6 v Suffolk (Bury St. Edmund's)	1981
	John Player League	260-6v Glos (Derby)	1972
	Benson & Hedges Cup	284-6 v Worcs (Worcester)	1982
Lowest innings totals:	Gillette Cup/NatWest Trophy	79 v Surrey (Oval)	1967
	John Player League	70 v Surrey (Derby)	1972
	Benson & Hedges Cup	102 v Yorks (Bradford)	1975
Highest individual innings:	NatWest Trophy	110* P.N. Kirsten v Hants (Southampton)	1982
	John Player League	120 A. Hill v Northants (Buxton)	1976
	Benson & Hedges Cup	111* P.J. Sharpe v Glamorgan (Chesterfield)	1976
Best bowling figures:	Gillette Cup/NatWest Trophy	6-18 T.J.P. Eyre v Sussex (Chesterfield)	1969
	John Player League	6-7 M. Hendrick v Notts (Nottingham)	1972
	Benson & Hedges Cup	6-33 E.J. Barlow v Glos (Bristol)	1978

ESSEX

Formation of present club: 1876.
Colours: Blue, Gold and red.
Badge: Three seaxes with word 'Essex' underneath.
County Champions: 1979.
Gillette Cup semi-finalists: 1978.
NatWest Trophy semi-finalists: 1981.
John Player League Champions: 198
Benson & Hedges Cup winners: 197
Benson & Hedges Cup Finalists: 1980.
Gillette Man of Match Awards: 14.
NatWest Trophy Man of the Match Awards: 4.
Benson & Hedges Gold Awards: 32.

Secretary: P.J. Edwards, The County Ground, New Writtle Street, Chelmsford CM2 0PG.
Captain: K.W.R. Fletcher.
Prospects of Play Telephone No: Chelmsford matches only. Chelmsford (0245) 7921.

David Laurence ACFIELD (Brentwood School and Cambridge) B Chelmsford 24/7/1947. RHB, OB. Debut for Cambridge U and Essex 1966. Blue 1967-68. Cap 1970. Benefit 1981. Best season's bowling: 76 wkts (av. 22.61) in 1981. HS: 42 Cambridge U v Leics (Leicester) 1967. HSC: 38 v Notts (Chelmsford) 1973. BB: 8-55 v Kent (Canterbury) 1981. BBJPL: 5-14 v Northants (Northampton) 1970. Fencing Blue, Olympic International and British Champion (sabre).

David Edward EAST B Clapton 27/7/1959. No relation to R.E. East. RHB, WK. Debut 1981. Cap 1982. NW Man of the Match: 1. HS: 78 v Cambridge U (Cambridge) 1982. HSNW: 18 v Derby (Derby) 1981. HSBH: 30 v Hants (Chelmsford) 1982. HSJPL: 43 v Derby (Derby) 1982.

Raymond Eric EAST B Manningtree 20/6/1947. RHB, SLA. Debut 1965. Cap 1967. Played for Overseas XI v Board President's XI (Calcutta) 1980-81. Benefit 1978 (£29,000). Tour: D.H. Robins to South Africa 1973-74. Hat-trick: The Rest v MCC Tour XI (Hove) 1973. BH Gold Awards: 3. HS: 113 v Hants (Chelmsford) 1976. HSGC/NW: 38* v Glos (Chelmsford) 1973. HSJPL: 25* v Glamorgan (Colchester) 1976. HSBH: 54 v Northants (Chelmsford) 1977. BB: 8-30 v Notts (Ilford) 1977. BBGC/NW: 4-28 v Herts (Hitchin) 1976. BBJPL: 6-18 v Yorks (Hull) 1969. BBBH: 5-33 v Kent (Chelmsford) 1975.

Keith William Robert FLETCHER B Worcester 20/5/1944. RHB, LB. Debut 1962. Cap 1963. County Captain 1974. Benefit 1973 (£13,000). *Wisden* 1973. Testimonial: 1982. Tests: 59 between 1968 and 1981-82. Captain in 7 and played in 4 matches v Rest of the World in 1970. Tours: Cavaliers to West Indies 1964-65, MCC Under-25 to Pakistan 1966-67, International XI to India, Pakistan and Ceylon 1967-68, Ceylon and Pakistan 1968-69, Ceylon 1969-70, Australia and New Zealand 1970-71, India, Pakistan and Sri Lanka 1972-73, West Indies 1973-74, Australia and New Zealand 1974-75, India, Sri Lanka and Australia 1976-77, India and Sri Lanka 1981-82 (captain). 1,000 runs (18) – 1,890 (av. 41.08) in 1968 best. Century in each innings (111 and 102*) v Notts (Nottingham) 1976. GC Man of the Match: 1. NW Man of the Match: 1. BH Gold Awards: 5. HS: 228* v Sussex (Hastings) 1968. HSTC: 216 v New Zealand (Auckland) 1974-75. HSNW: 97 v Kent (Chelmsford)

1982. HSJPL: 99* v Notts (Ilford) 1974. HSBH: 101* v Sussex (Hove) 1982. BB: 5-41 v Middlesex (Colchester) 1979.

Neil Adam FOSTER B Colchester 6/5/1962. RHB, RFM. Debut 1980. HS: 36* v Derby (Chesterfield) 1982. HSJPL: 10 v Middlesex (Lord's) 1982. BB: 3-32 v Derby (Chesterfield) 1982.

Christopher GLADWIN B East Ham 10/5/1962. LHB, RM. Debut 1981. Played one match v Lancs (Southend) and one JPL match in 1982. HS: 53 v Lancs (Southend) 1981.

Graham Alan GOOCH B Leytonstone 23/7/1953. RHB, RM. Debut 1973. Cap 1975. *Wisden* 1979. Tests: 42 between 1975 and 1981-82. Banned for 3 years for going on SAB tour. Tours: Australia 1978-79, Australia and India 1979-80, West Indies 1980-81, India and Sri Lanka 1981-82, SAB in South Africa 1981-82. Shared county record 2nd wicket partnership (321) with K.S. McEwan v Northants (Ilford) 1978. 1,000 runs (6) – 1,632 (av. 44.10) in 1982 best. Scored 1,363 (av. 54.60) in 1981-82. NW Man of the Match: 1. BH Gold Awards: 8. HS: 205 v Cambridge U (Cambridge) 1980. HSTC: 153 v West Indies (Kingston) 1980-81. HSNW: 101 v Herts (Hitchin) 1981. HSJPL: 122 v Lancs (Manchester) 1982. HSBH: 198* v Sussex (Hove) 1982 (Competition Record). BB: 7-14 v Worcs (Ilford) 1982. BBJPL: 3-14 v Derby (Derby) 1978. BBBH: 3-24 v Sussex (Hove) 1982.

Brian Ross HARDIE B Stenhousemuir 14/1/1950. RHB, RM. Debut for Scotland 1970, for Essex 1973. Cap 1974. Benefit 1983. 1,000 runs (7) – 1,522 (av. 43.48) in 1975 best. HS: 162 v Warwicks (Birmingham) 1975. HSGC/NW: 83 v Staffs (Stone) 1976. HSJPL: 108* v Yorks (Chelmsford) 1981. HSBH: 53 v Glos (Bristol) 1980.

Robert James LEIPER (Chigwell School) B Woodford Green 30/8/1961. Son of J.M. Leiper (Essex 1950). LHB, RM. Debut 1981. HS: 49 v Australians (Chelmsford) 1981.

John Kenneth LEVER B Stepney 24/2/1949. RHB, LFM. Debut 1967. Cap 1970. *Wisden* 1978. Benefit: 1980 (£66,110). Tests: 20 between 1976-77 and 1981-82. Banned for 3 years for going on SAB tour. Tours: D.H. Robins to South Africa 1972-73 and 1973-74, India, Sri Lanka and Australia 1976-77, D.H. Robins in Sri Lanka 1977-78, Pakistan and New Zealand 1977-78, Australia 1978-79, Australia and India 1978-79, India and Sri Lanka 1981-82, SAB in South Africa 1981-82. Played for Overseas XI v Board President's XI (Calcutta) 1980-81. 100 wkts (2) – 106 (av. 15.18) in 1978 and (av.17.30) 1979. GC Man of the Match: 3. NW Man of the Match: 1. BH Gold Awards: 1. HS: 91 v Glamorgan (Cardiff) 1970. HSTC: 53 v India (Delhi) 1976-77. HSNW: 10* v Sussex (Hove) 1981. HSJPL: 23 v Worcs (Worcester) 1974. HSBH: 12* v Warwicks (Birmingham) 1975. BB: 8-49 v Warwicks (Birmingham) 1979 and v Yorks (Leeds) 1981. BBTC: 7-46 v India (Delhi) 1976-77 on debut. BBGC/NW: 5-8 v Middlesex (Westcliff) 1972. BBJPL: 5-13 v Glamorgan (Ebbw Vale) 1975. BBBH: 5-16 v Middlesex (Chelmsford) 1976.

Alan William LILLEY B Ilford 8/5/1959. RHB, WK. Debut 1978 scoring 100* in second innings. BH Gold Award: 1. HS: 100* v Notts (Nottingham) 1978. HSNW: 40 v Glos (Bristol) 1981. HSJPL: 60 v Northants (Chelmsford) 1980. HSBH: 119 v Combined Universities (Chelmsford) 1979.

Kenneth Scott McEWAN B Bedford, Cape Province, South Africa 16/7/1952. RHB, OB, WK. Played for Eastern Province 1972-73 to 1977-78 and 1981-82, for T.N. Pearce's XI v West Indians (Scarborough) 1973, and for Western Australia 1979-80 and 1980-81. Debut for county and cap 1974. *Wisden* 1977. Shares 2nd wicket county partnership record with G.A. Gooch, 1,000 runs (9) – 1,821 (av. 49.21) in 1976 best. Scored 4 consecutive hundreds including two in match (102 and 116) v Warwicks (Birmingham) 1977. GC Man of the Match: 1. BH Gold Awards: 5. HS: 218 v Sussex (Chelmsford) 1977. HSGC/NW: 119 v Leics (Leicester) 1980. HSJPL: 156* v Warwicks (Colchester) 1982. HSBH: 133 v Notts (Chelmsford) 1978.

Norbert PHILLIP B Bioche, Dominica 12/6/1948. RHB, RFM. Debut for Windward Islands 1969-70 and has also played for Combined Islands. Debut for county and cap 1978. Tests: 9 for West Indies between 1977-78 and 1978-79. Tour: West Indies in India and Sri Lanka 1978-79. HS: 134 v Glos (Gloucester) 1978. HSTC: 47 West Indies v India (Calcutta) 1978-79. HSGC/NW: 45 v Surrey (Chelmsford) 1980. HSJPL: 84 v Glamorgan (Cardiff) 1982. HSBH: 33* v Surrey (Oval) 1982. BB: 7-33 Windward Is v Leeward Is (Roseau) 1981. BBUK: 6-33 v Pakistanis (Chelmsford) 1978. BBTC: 4-48 West Indies v India (Madras) 1978-79. BBNW: 4-26 v Kent (Chelmsford) 1982. BBJPL: 6-13 v Lancs (Manchester) 1982. BBBH: 4-19 v Hants (Chelmsford) 1982.

Keith Rupert PONT B Wanstead 16/1/1953. RHB, RM. Debut 1970. Cap 1976. BH Gold Awards: 2. HS: 113 v Warwicks (Birmingham) 1973. HSGC/NW: 39 v Somerset (Taunton) 1978. HSJPL: 55* v Warwicks (Birmingham) 1981. HSBH: 60* v Notts (Ilford) 1976. BB: 5-17 v Glamorgan (Cardiff) 1982. BBJPL: 4-22 v Warwicks (Birmingham) 1981. BBBH: 4-60 v Northants (Lord's) 1980.

Paul John PRICHARD B Billericay 7/1/1965. RHB. Played one JPL match in 1982. Has not played first-class cricket.

Derek Raymond PRINGLE (Felsted School and Cambridge) B Nairobi, Kenya 18/9/1958. 6ft 4½in tall. RHB, RM. Debut 1978. Cap 1982. Blue 1979-80-81. University captain 1982 but did not play in University match. Tour: Australia and New Zealand 1982-83. Tests: 4 in 1982. HS: 127* Cambridge U v Worcs (Cambridge) 1981, HSC: 54 v Warwicks (Colchester) 1982. HSTC: 23 v India (Manchester) 1982. HSNW: 17 v Sussex (Hove) 1981. HSJPL: 42* v Derby (Chesterfield) 1981. HSBH: 58 Combined Universities v Essex (Chelmsford) 1979. BB: 6-33 Cambridge U v Lancs (Cambridge) 1982. BBC: 5-59 v Indians (Chelmsford) 1982. BBTC: 2-16 v India (Lord's) 1982. BBNW: 3-12 v Glos (Bristol) 1981. BBJPL: 3-11 v Worcs (Ilford) 1982.

Stuart TURNER B Chester 18/7/1943. RHB, RFM. Debut 1965. Cap 1970. Hat-trick v Surrey (Oval) 1981. Played for Natal 1976-77 and 1977-78. Benefit 1979 (£37,288). Tour: D.H. Robins to South Africa 1974-75. BH Gold Awards: 2. HS: 121 v Somerset (Taunton) 1970. HSNW: 50* v Yorks (Leeds) 1982. HSJPL: 87 v Worcs (Chelmsford) 1975. HSBH: 55* v Hants (Chelmsford) 1982. BB: 6-26 v Northants (Northampton) 1977. BBNW: 4-23 v Kent (Chelmsford) 1982. BBJPL: 5-35 v Hants (Chelmsford) 1978. BBBH: 4-19 v Combined Universities (Chelmsford) 1981.

NB. The following players whose particulars appeared in the 1982 Annual have been omitted: G.E. Sainsbury and N. Smith.

County Averages

Schweppes County Championship: Played 22, won 5, drawn 12, lost 5.
All first-class matches: Played 24, won 6, drawn 13, lost 5.

BATTING AND FIELDING

Cap		M	I	NO	Runs	HS	Avge	100	50	Ct	St
1975	G.A. Gooch	23	38	1	1632	149	44.10	3	12	25	—
1974	B.R. Hardie	24	39	5	1432	161	42.11	1	8	15	—
1974	K.S. McEwan	24	37	3	1421	150*	41.79	3	6	10	—
1976	K.R. Pont	16	24	7	687	89	40.41	—	6	11	—
1963	K.W.R. Fletcher	23	35	4	1238	124	39.93	3	6	12	—
1970	S. Turner	23	28	4	679	83	28.29	—	5	8	—
1978	N. Phillip	24	32	4	783	79	27.00	—	5	6	—
—	D.E. East	24	32	8	525	78	21.87	—	2	65	9
—	A.W. Lilley	10	14	1	276	67	21.23	—	1	4	—
—	N.A. Foster	5	4	1	58	36*	19.33	—	—	—	—
1967	R.E. East	21	23	2	344	58	16.38	—	1	22	—
1982	D.R. Pringle	7	11	1	162	54	16.20	—	2	—	—
1970	D.L. Acfield	21	18	4	23	4*	5.75	—	—	8	—
1970	J.K. Lever	18	19	3	89	22*	5.56	—	—	5	—

Played in one match: R.J. Leiper 3, 0 (2 ct).

BOWLING

	Type	O	M	R	W	Avge	Best	5 wI	10 wM
K.R. Pont	RM	62	11	158	10	15.80	5-17	1	—
D.R. Pringle	RM	185.5	47	460	22	20.90	5-59	1	—
N. Phillip	RFM	584.1	107	1842	82	22.46	6-50	5	1
J.K. Lever	LFM	543.5	112	1683	72	23.37	6-48	5	1
G.A. Gooch	RM	230	72	541	22	24.59	7-14	1	—
R.E. East	SLA	490.5	141	1231	45	27.35	6-80	2	—
D.L. Acfield	OB	565.2	129	1332	45	29.60	4-35	—	—
N.A. Foster	RM	125	29	425	12	35.41	3-32	—	—
S. Turner	RM	453	117	1080	30	36.00	4-59	—	—

Also bowled: K.W.R. Fletcher 20.1-0-156-2; B.R. Hardie 7-1-20-0; A.W. Lilley 3-0-10-0; K.S. McEwan 13-0-120-1.

County Records

First-Class Cricket

Highest innings	For	692 v Somerset (Taunton)	1895
totals:	Agst	803-4 by Kent (Brentwood)	1934
Lowest innings	For	30 v Yorkshire (Leyton)	1901
totals	Agst	31 by Derby (Derby) and by Yorks (Huddersfield)	1914 & 1935
Highest indi-	For	343* P.A. Perrin v Derby (Chesterfield)	1904
vidual innings	Agst	332 W.H. Ashdown for Kent (Brentwood)	1934

Best bowling	For	10-32 H. Pickett v Leics (Leyton)	1895
in an innings	Agst	10-40 E.G. Dennett for Glos (Bristol)	1906
Best bowling	For	17-119 W. Mead v Hants (Southampton)	1895
in a match	Agst	17-56 C.W.L. Parker for Glos (Gloucester)	1925
Most runs in a season:		2,308 (av. 56.29) J. O'Connor	1934
runs in a career		29,162 (av. 36.18) P.A. Perrin	1896-1928
100s in a season:		9 by J. O'Connor and D.J. Insole	1934 & 1955
100s in a career:		71 by J. O'Connor	1921-1939
wickets in a season:		172 (av. 27.13) T.P.B. Smith	1947
wickets in a career		1610 (av. 26.68) T.P.B. Smith	1929-1951

RECORD WICKET STANDS

1st	270	A.V. Avery & T.C. Dodds v Surrey (Oval)	1946
2nd	321	G.A. Gooch & K.S. McEwan v Northants (Ilford)	1978
3rd	343	P.A. Gibb & R. Horsfall v Kent (Blackheath)	1951
4th	298	A.V. Avery & R. Horsfall v Worcs (Clacton)	1948
5th	287	C.T. Ashton & J. O'Connor v Surrey (Brentwood)	1934
6th	206	J.W.H.T. Douglas & J. O'Connor v Glos (Cheltenham)	1923
		B.R. Knight & R.A.G. Luckin v Middlesex (Brentwood)	1962
7th	261	J.W.H.T. Douglas & J. Freeman v Lancs (Leyton)	1914
8th	263	D.R. Wilcox & R.M. Taylor v Warwicks (Southend)	1946
9th	251	J.W.H.T. Douglas & S.N. Hare v Derby (Leyton)	1921
10th	218	F.H. Vigar & T.P.B. Smith v Derby (Chesterfield)	1947

One-day cricket

Highest innings totals:	Gillette Cup/NatWest Trophy	316-6 v Staffs (Stone)	1976
	John Player League	299-4 v Warwicks (Colchester)	1982
	Benson & Hedges Cup	350-3 v Combined Universities (Chelmsford)	1979
Lowest innings totals:	Gillette Cup/NatWest Trophy	100 v Derby (Brentwood)	1965
	John Player League	69 v Derby (Chesterfield)	1974
	Benson & Hedges Cup	123 v Kent (Canterbury)	1973
Highest individual innings:	Gillette Cup/NatWest Trophy	119 K.S. McEwan v Leics (Leicester)	1980
	John Player League	156* K.S. McEwan v Warwicks (Colchester)	1982
	Benson & Hedges Cup	198* G.A. Gooch v Sussex (Hove)	1982
Best bowling figures:	Gillette Cup/NatWest Trophy	5-8 J.K. Lever v Middlesex (Westcliff)	1972
	John Player League	8-26 K.D. Boyce v Lancs (Manchester)	1971
	Benson & Hedges Cup	5-16 J.K. Lever v Middlesex (Chelmsford)	1976

GLAMORGAN

Formation of present club: 1888.
Colours: Blue and gold.
Badge: Gold daffodil.
County Champions (2): 1948 and 1969.
Gillette Cup finalists: 1977.
NatWest Trophy Second Round: 1981.
Best final position in John Player League: 8th in 1977.
Benson & Hedges Cup quarter-finalists (5): 1972, 1973, 1977, 1978 and 1979.
Gillette Man of the Match Awards: 13.
NatWest Man of the Match Awards: Nil.
Benson & Hedges Gold Awards: 23.

Secretary: P.G. Carling, 6 High Street, Cardiff CF1 2PW.
Cricket Manager: T.W. Cartwright.
Captain: M.W.W. Selvey.
Prospects of Play Telephone Nos: Cardiff (0222) 29956 or 387367
Swansea (0792) 466321.

Stephen Royston BARWICK B Neath 6/9/1960. RHB, RM. Debut 1981. HS: 24 v Oxford U (Swansea) 1982. HSJPL: 12* v Sussex (Hastings) 1982. BB: 5-44 v Somerset (Taunton) 1982. BBNW: 4-14 v Hants (Bournemouth) 1981. BBJPL: 3-39 v Sussex (Ebbw Vale) 1981. BBBH: 3-28 v Somerset (Swansea) 1982.

Simon Anthony Brewis DANIELS (Sedbergh School) B Darlington, Co. Durham 23/8/1958. RHB, RFM. Debut 1981. HS: 73 v Glos (Swansea) 1982. BB: 3-33 v Essex (Colchester) 1981. BBJPL: 3-32 v Middlesex (Swansea) 1982.

Terry DAVIES B St. Albans, Herts 25/10/1960. RHB, WK. Debut 1979. HS: 66* v Glos (Swansea) 1982. HSJPL: 10 v Sussex (Hastings) 1982. HSBH: 10 v Somerset (Swansea) 1982.

Winston Walter DAVIS B St Vincent 18/9/1958. RHB, RFM. Played for Windward Islands and Combined Islands 1979-80 to 1981-82. Tour: Young West Indies to Zimbabwe 1981-82. Debut for county 1982. HS: 60 Windward Islands v Leeward Islands (Antigua) 1979-80. HSUK: 20* v Leics (Leicester) 1982. BB: 7-101 v Notts (Swansea) 1982. BBJPL: 4-24 v Derby (Derby) 1982.

David Arthur FRANCIS B Clydach 29/11/1953. RHB, OB. Debut 1973. Cap 1982. 1,000 runs (1) – 1,076 (av. 38.42) in 1982. HS: 142* v Kent (Canterbury) 1982. HSGC/NW: 62* v Worcs (Worcester) 1977. HSJPL: 101* v Warwicks (Birmingham) 1980. HSBH: 59 v Warwicks (Birmingham) 1977.

Geoffrey Clark HOLMES B Newcastle-upon-Tyne 16/9/1958. RHB, RM. Debut 1978. HS: 100* v Glos (Bristol) 1979. HSNW: 11 v Hants (Boournemouth) 1981. HSJPL: 43* v Hants (Portsmouth) 1979. HSBH: 30 v Glos (Bristol) 1980. BB: 5-86 v Surrey (Oval) 1980. BBJPL: 3-17 v Notts (Swansea) 1980.

John Anthony HOPKINS B Maesteg 16/6/1953. RHB, WK. Younger brother of J.D. Hopkins (Glamorgan and Middlesex). Debut 1970. Cap 1977. 1,000 runs (5) – 1,371 (av. 33.43) 1978 best. GC Man of Match: 1. BH Gold Awards: 4. HS: 230 v Worcs (Worcester) 1977. HSGC/NW: 63 v Leics (Swansea) 1977. HSJPL: 75 v Warwicks (Swansea) 1981. HSBH: 103* v Minor Counties (Swansea) 1980.

JAVED MIANDAD KHAN B Karachi 12/6/1957. RHB, LBG. Debut 1973-74 for Karachi Whites aged 16 years 5 months. Has played for various Karachi, Sind and Habib Bank teams in Pakistan. Played for Sussex 1976-79. Cap 1977. Debut for Glamorgan and cap 1980. *Wisden* 1981. Tests: 43 for Pakistan between 1976-77 and 1982, captain in 10 matches. Tours: Pakistan in Sri Lanka 1975-76, Australia and West Indies 1976-77, England 1978, New Zealand and Australia 1978-79, India 1979-80, Australia 1981-82 (captain), England 1982. 1,000 runs (3) 2,083 (av. 69.43) in 1981 best including 8 centuries (both county records). Also scored 1,000 runs in an overseas season 6 times. Scored 163 for Pakistan v New Zealand (Lahore) on Test debut. Century in each innings twice (107 and 123) Habib Bank v National Bank (Lahore) 1980-81 and (137 and 106) v Somerset (Taunton) 1981. GC Man of the Match: 1. BH Gold Awards: 1. HS: 311 Karachi Whites v National Bank (Karachi) 1974-75. HSUK: 200* v Somerset (Taunton) 1981 and v Essex (Colchester) 1981. HSTC: 206 Pakistan v New Zealand (Karachi) 1976-77. HSGC/NW: 75 Sussex v Lancs (Hove) 1978. HSJPL: 107* v Leics (Leicester) 1981. HSBH: 76 Sussex v Surrey (Oval) 1977. BB: 7-39 Habib Bank v IDBP (Lahore) 1980-81. BBUK: 4-10 Sussex v Northants (Northampton) 1977. BBTC: 3-74 Pakistan v New Zealand (Hyderabad) 1976-77.

Alan JONES B Swansea 4/11/1938. LHB, OB. Debut 1957. Cap 1962. Captain 1976 to 1978. *Wisden* 1977. Testimonial 1980 (£35,000). Played 1 match v Rest of the World in 1970. Played for Western Australia 1963-64, Northern Transvaal 1975-76 and Natal 1976-77. Tours: Glamorgan in West Indies and MCC to Ceylon 1969-70. 1,000 runs (22) — 1,865 (av. 34.53) in 1966 best. Hundred in each innings 3 times (187* and 105*) v Somerset (Glastonbury) 1963, (132 and 156*) v York (Middlesbrough) 1976 and (147 and 100) v Hants (Swansea) 1978. Shared county record partnership for any wicket (330 for 1st) with R.C. Fredericks v Northants (Swansea) 1972; also 2nd wicket record (*q.v.*). Holds county record aggregates for runs and centuries. GC Man of the Match: 2. BH Gold Awards: 1. HS: 204* v Hants (Basingstoke) 1980. HSGC/NW: 124* v Warwicks (Birmingham) 1976. HSJPL: 110* v Glos (Cardiff) 1978. HSBH: 89 v Worcs (Cardiff) 1979. BBJPL: 3-21 v Northants (Wellingborough) 1975.

Eifion Wyn JONES B Swansea 25/6/1942. Brother of A. Jones. RHB, WK. Debut 1961. Cap 1967. Benefit 1975 (£17,000). Tour: Glamorgan in West Indies 1969-70. BH Gold Award: 1. HS: 146* v Sussex (Hove) 1968. HSGC/NW: 67* v Herts (Swansea) 1969. HSJPL: 48 v Hants (Cardiff) 1971. HSBH: 39* v Minor Counties (West) (Amersham) 1977.

Alan Lewis JONES B Alltwen 1/6/1957. No relation to A. and E.W. Jones. LHB. Debut 1973 aged 16 years 99 days. HS: 88 v Northants (Swansea) 1982. HSGC/NW: 11 v Hants (Southampton) 1975. HSJPL: 82 v Warwicks (Birmingham) 1982. HSBH: 36 v Worcs (Cardiff) 1979.

Michael John LLEWELLYN B Clydach 27/11/1953. LHB, OB. Debut 1970 aged 16 years 202 days. Cap 1977. GC Man of the Match: 1. BH Gold Awards: 2. HS: 129* v Oxford U (Oxford) 1977. HSGC/NW: 62 v Middlesex (Lord's) 1977. HSJPL: 79* v Glos (Bristol) 1977. HSBH: 63 v Hants (Swansea) 1973. BB: 4-35 v Oxford U (Oxford) 1970.

Barry John LLOYD B Neath 6/9/1953. RHB, OB. Debut 1972. Cap 1982. HS: 48 v Sussex (Cardiff) 1982. HSNW: 12 v Warwicks (Cardiff) 1982. HSJPL: 23 v Sussex (Hastings) 1982. HSBH: 28* v Somerset (Swansea) 1982. BB: 8-70 v Lancs (Cardiff) 1981. BBJPL: 3-22 v Derby (Derby) 1980. BBBH: 4-26 v Combined Universities (Cardiff) 1982.

GLAMORGAN

Hugh MORRIS (Blundell's School) B Cardiff 5/10/1963. LHB. Debut 1981. HS: 63 v Derby (Derby) 1982.

Ezra Alphonse MOSELEY B Christ Church, Barbados 5/1/1958. RHB, RFM. Debut 1980 taking 6-102 v Essex (Swansea) in debut match. Cap 1981. Hat-trick in Benson & Hedges Cup v Kent (Cardiff) 1981. BH Gold Awards: 1. HS: 70* v Kent (Canterbury) 1980. HSJPL: 20 v Worcs (Abergavenny) 1981. BB: 6-23 v Australians (Swansea) 1981. BBJPL: 4-22 v Leics (Leicester) 1981. BBBH: 4-8 v Kent (Cardiff) 1981. Did not play in 1982.

Malcolm Andrew NASH B Abergavenny 9/5/1945. LHB, LM. Debut 1966. Cap 1969. Captain 1980-81. Benefit 1978 (£18,000). BH Gold Awards: 3. Tour: Glamorgan to West Indies 1969-70. Hat-trick in JPL v Worcs (Worcester) 1975. HS: 130 v Surrey (Oval) 1976. HSGC/NW: 51 v Lincs (Swansea) 1974. HSJPL: 68 v Essex (Purfleet) 1972. HSBH: 103* v Hants (Swansea) 1976. BB: 9-56 v Hants (Basingstoke) 1975. BBNW: 5-31 v Oxfordshire (Oxford) 1981. BBJPL: 6-29 v Worcs (Worcester) 1975. BBBH: 4-12 v Surrey (Cardiff) 1975.

Rodney Craig ONTONG B Johannesburg, South Africa 9/9/1955. RHB, RFM. Played for Border 1972-73 to 1975-76, Transvaal 1976-77 and 1977-78, Northern Transvaal 1978-79 to 1981-82. Debut for county 1975. Cap 1979. 1,000 runs (2) – 1,205 (av. 30.89) in 1982 best. Shared 10th wkt county partnership record (140*) with R.N.S. Hobbs v Hants (Swansea) 1981. BH Gold Awards: 1. HS: 152* v Glos (Swansea) 1982. HSGC/NW: 64 v Somerset (Cardiff) 1978. HSJPL: 100 v Northants (Abergavenny) 1982. HSBH: 50* v Glos (Swansea) 1979. BB: 7-60 Border v Northern Transvaal (Pretoria) 1975-76. BBUK: 6-62 v Sri Lankans (Cardiff) 1981. BBJPL: 4-31 v Middlesex (Lord's) 1979. BBBH: 4-28 v Worcs (Cardiff) 1979.

Christopher James Castell ROWE (King's School, Canterbury) B Hong Kong 27/11/1951. RHB, OB. Played for Kent 1974 to 1981. Cap 1977 Joined Glamorgan 1982. 1,000 runs (2) – 1,071 (av. 32.45) in 1982 best. HS: 147* Kent v Sussex (Canterbury) 1979. HSGC/NW: 18* Kent v Somerset (Canterbury) 1980. HSBH: 54 v Somerset (Swansea) 1982. BB: 6-46 Kent v Derby (Dover) 1976. BBJPL: 5-32 Kent v Worcs (Worcester) 1976.

Michael Walter William SELVEY B Chiswick 25/4/1948. RHB, RFM. Played for Surrey 1968 and 1971, Cambridge U (Blue) 1971, Middlesex 1972-82. Cap 1973. Transferred to Glamorgan as captain 1983. Played for Orange Free State 1973-74. Tours: India, Sri Lanka and Australia 1976-77, Middlesex in Zimbabwe 1980-81, International XI in Pakistan 1981-82. 101 wkts (av. 19.09) in 1978. BH Gold Award: 1. HS: 67 Middlesex v Zimbabwe (Bulawayo) 1980-81. HSUK: 57 Middlesex v Essex (Ilford) 1981. HSGC/NW: 14 Middlesex v Derby (Derby) 1978. HSJPL: 38* Middlesex v Essex (Chelmsford) 1979. HSBH: 27* Middlesex v Surrey (Lord's) 1973. BB: 7-20 Middlesex v Glos (Gloucester) 1976. BBGC/NW: 3-32 Middlesex v Somerset (Lord's) 1977. BBJPL: 5-18 Middlesex v Glamorgan (Cardiff) 1975. BBBH: 5-39 Middlesex v Glos (Lord's) 1972.

John Gregory THOMAS B Trebannws 12/8/1960. RHB, RM. Debut 1979. HS: 84 v Surrey (Guildford) 1982. HSJPL: 15* v Essex (Cardiff) 1982. BB: 5-61 v Derby (Derby) 1982. BBJPL: 3-33 v Somerset (Cardiff) 1981.

NB. The following players whose particulars appeared in the 1982 Annual have been omitted: N.G. Featherstone and P.J. Lawlor.

County Averages

Schweppes County Championship: Played 22, won 1, drawn 13, lost 8.
All first-class matches: Played 25, won 1, drawn 15, lost 9.

BATTING AND FIELDING

Cap		M	I	NO	Runs	HS	Avge	100	50	Ct	St
—	H. Morris	4	6	3	213	63	71.00	—	2	1	—
1980	Javed Miandad	8	16	2	601	96*	42.92	—	6	10	—
—	D.A. Francis	19	33	5	1076	142*	38.42	2	7	9	—
1962	A. Jones	25	47	5	1491	146*	35.50	4	6	4	—
—	C.J.C. Rowe	25	39	6	1071	105	32.45	1	6	10	—
1979	R.C. Ontong	24	43	4	1205	152*	30.89	3	4	12	—
1977	J.A. Hopkins	23	41	5	978	124	27.16	1	4	16	—
—	A.L. Jones	22	38	2	900	88	25.00	—	6	13	—
—	T. Davies	10	16	4	283	66*	23.58	—	2	20	1
—	G.C. Holmes	7	10	1	210	68	23.33	—	1	2	—
—	S.A.B. Daniels	11	15	6	197	73	21.88	—	1	3	—
1967	E.W. Jones	15	21	3	268	65	14.88	—	2	37	4
1982	B.J. Lloyd	25	32	8	318	48	13.25	—	—	14	—
—	J.G. Thomas	9	13	0	172	84	13.23	—	1	4	—
—	S.R. Barwick	15	18	7	126	24	11.45	—	—	6	—
1969	M.A. Nash	16	20	1	216	37	11.36	—	—	10	—
—	W.W. Davis	13	13	6	58	20*	8.28	—	1	2	—

Played in two matches: M.N. Davies 0 (1 ct); M.J. Llewellyn 2, 61*, 25, 0 (1 ct).

BOWLING

	Type	O	M	R	W	Avge	Best	5 wI	10 wM
J.G. Thomas	RM	140	25	514	22	23.36	5-61	1	—
S.R. Barwick	RM	326.2	80	981	32	30.65	5-44	1	—
W.W. Davis	RFM	391.5	70	1296	42	30.85	7-101	1	—
R.C. Ontong	RM	638.1	139	2059	64	32.17	6-50	1	1
M.A. Nash	LM	418.2	102	1276	38	33.57	5-35	1	—
B.J. Lloyd	OB	687.2	139	2201	55	40.01	5-58	2	—
S.A.B. Daniels	RFM	223.2	37	836	20	41.80	3-49	—	—
Javed Miandad	LBG	101.4	31	293	7	41.85	3-52	—	—
C.J.C. Rowe	OB	265.2	57	898	19	47.26	3-67	—	—

Also bowled: G.C. Holmes 18-4-60-0; A. Jones 1-1-0-0.

County Records

First-class cricket

Highest innings	For	587-8d v Derby (Cardiff)	1951
totals:	Agst	653-6d by Glos (Bristol)	1928
Lowest innings	For	22 v Lancs (Liverpool)	1924
totals:	Agst	33 by Leics (Ebbw Vale)	1965
Highest indi-	For	287* D.E. Davies v Glos (Newport)	1939
vidual innings:	Agst	302* W.R. Hammond for Glos (Bristol)	1934
		302 W.R. Hammond for Glos (Newport)	1939

GLAMORGAN

Best bowling	For	10-51 J. Mercer v Worcs (Worcester)	1936
in an innings	Agst	10-18 G. Geary for Leics (Pontypridd)	1929
Best bowling	For	17-212 J.C. Clay v Worcs (Swansea)	1937
in a match:	Agst	16-96 G. Geary for Leics (Pontypridd)	1929
Most runs in a season:		2,083 (av. 69.43) Javed Miandad	1981
runs in a career:		32,997 (av. 32.99) A. Jones	1957-1982
100s in a season:		8 by Javed Miandad	1981
100s in a career:		51 by A. Jones	1957-1982
wickets in a season:		176 (av. 17.34) J.C. Clay	1937
wickets in a career:		2,174 (av. 20.95) D.J. Shepherd	1950-1972

RECORD WICKET STANDS

1st	330	A. Jones & R.C. Fredericks v Northants (Swansea)	1972
2nd	238	A. Jones & A.R. Lewis v Sussex (Hastings)	1962
3rd	313	D.E. Davies & W.E. Jones v Essex (Brentwood)	1948
4th	263	G. Lavis & C. Smart v Worcs (Cardiff)	1934
5th	264	M. Robinson & S.W. Montgomery v Hants (Bournemouth)	1949
6th	230	W.E. Jones & B.L. Muncer v Worcs (Worcester)	1953
7th	195*	W. Wooller & W.E. Jones v Lancs (Liverpool)	1947
8th	202	D. Davies & J.J. Hills v Sussex (Eastbourne)	1928
9th	203*	J.J. Hills & J.C. Clay v Worcs (Swansea)	1929
10th	143	T. Davies & S.A.B. Daniels v Glos (Swansea)	1982

One-day cricket

Highest innings totals:	Gillette Cup/ NatWest Trophy	283-3 v Warwicks (Birmingham)	1976
	John Player League	266-6 v Northants (Wellingborough)	1975
	Benson & Hedges Cup	245-7 v Hants (Swansea)	1982
Lowest innings totals:	Gillette Cup/ NatWest Trophy	76 v Northants (Northampton)	1968
	John Player League	42 v Derby (Swansea)	1979
	Benson & Hedges Cup	68 v Lancs (Manchester)	1973
Highest individual innings:	Gillette Cup/ NatWest Trophy	124* A. Jones v Warwicks (Birmingham)	1976
	John Player League	110* A. Jones v Glos (Cardiff)	1978
	Benson & Hedges Cup	103* M.A. Nash v Hants (Swansea)	1976
		103* J.A. Hopkins v Minor Counties (Swansea)	1980
Best bowling figures:	Gillette Cup/ NatWest Trophy	5-21 P.M. Walker v Cornwall (Truro)	1970
	John Player League	6-29 M.A. Nash v Worcs (Worcester)	1975
	Benson & Hedges Cup	5-17 A.H. Wilkins v Worcs (Worcester)	1978

GLOUCESTERSHIRE

Formation of present club: 1871.
Colours: Blue, gold, brown, silver, green and red.
Badge: Coat of Arms of the City and County of Bristol.
County Champions (3): 1874, 1876 and 1877.
Joint Champions: 1873.
Gillette Cup Winners: 1973.
NatWest Trophy Quarter-finals: 1982.
Best position in John Player League: 6th in 1969, 1973 and 1977.
Benson & Hedges Cup Winners: 1977.
Gillette Man of the Match Awards: 17.
NatWest Man of the Match Awards: 3.
Benson & Hedges Gold Awards: 23.

Secretary: County Ground, Nevil Road, Bristol BS7 9EJ.
Captain: D.A. Graveney.
Prospects of Play Telephone Nos: Bristol (0272) 48461
Prospects of Play Telephone Nos: Cheltenham (0242) 22000
Gloucester (0452) 24621

Philip **BAINBRIDGE** B Stoke-on-Trent, Staffordshire 16/4/1958, RHB, RM. Debut 1977. Cap 1981. 1,000 runs (2) – 1,069 (av. 42.76) 1982 best. HS: 105* v Middlesex (Lord's) 1981. HSNW: 61* v Ireland (Dublin) 1981. HSJPL: 35 v Sussex (Moreton-in-Marsh) 1980, v Sussex (Hove) 1981 and v Warwicks (Birmingham) 1982. HSBH: 80 v Somerset (Taunton) 1982. BB: 6-59 v Glamorgan (Swansea) 1982. BBJPL: 4-27 v Middlesex (Cheltenham) 1982. BBBH: 3-21 v Notts (Gloucester) 1981.

Andrew James **BRASSINGTON** B Bagnall, Staffordshire 9/8/1954. RHB, WK. Debut 1974. Cap 1978. HS: 35 v Sussex (Hastings) 1982. HSGC/NW: 20 v Hants (Bristol) 1979. HSJPL: 14* v Northants (Bristol) 1982.

Brian Christopher **BROAD** B Bristol 29/9/1957. 6ft 4ins tall. LHB, RM. Debut 1979. Cap 1981. 1,000 runs (2) – 1,153 (av. 28.12) in 1982 best. NW Man of the Match: 1. HS: 129 v Northants (Bristol) 1979. HSNW: 98 v Middlesex (Bristol) 1982. HSJPL: 59 v Sussex (Gloucester) 1982. HSBH: 53 v Combined Universities (Oxford) 1982.

John Henry **CHILDS** B Plymouth, Devon 15/8/1951. LHB, SLA. Debut 1975. Cap 1977. BH Gold Award: 1. HS: 34* v Notts (Cheltenham) 1982. HSJPL: 16* v Notts (Nottingham) 1981. HSBH: 10 v Somerset (Bristol) 1979. BB: 9-56 v Somerset (Bristol) 1981. BBJPL: 4-15 v Northants (Northampton) 1976. BBBH: 3-36 v Glamorgan (Bristol) 1982.

Edward James **CUNNINGHAM** B Oxford 16/5/1962. LHB. Debut 1982. HS: 11* v Indians (Bristol) 1982. HSJPL: 22 v Surrey (Oval) 1982.

Richard James **DOUGHTY** B Bridlington, Yorkshire 17/11/1960. RHB, RM. Debut 1981. HS: 29 v Glamorgan (Bristol) 1982. HSJPL: 18* v Lancs (Manchester) 1982. BB: 6-43 v Glamorgan (Bristol) 1982. BBJPL: 3-34 v Somerset (Bristol) 1982.

GLOUCESTERSHIRE

David Anthony GRAVENEY (Millfield School) B Bristol 2/1/1953. Son of J.K. Graveney (Glos 1947-64). RHB, SLA. Debut 1972. Cap 1976. Captain 1981. HS: 119 v Oxford University (Oxford) 1980. HSGC/NW: 44 v Surrey (Bristol) 1973. HSJPL: 49 v Notts (Nottingham) 1981. HSBH: 49* v Somerset (Taunton) 1982. BB: 8-85 v Notts (Cheltenham) 1974. BBNW: 5-11 v Ireland (Dublin) 1981. BBJPL: 4-22 v Hants (Lydney) 1974. BBBH: 3-32 v Middlesex (Bristol) 1977.

Alastair James HIGNELL (Denstone College and Cambridge) B Cambridge 4/9/1955. RHB, LB. Debut 1974. Cap 1977. Blue 1975-76-77-78. Captain 1977-78. 1,000 runs (2) – 1,140 (av. 30.81) in 1976. 100 runs in each innings (108 and 145) Cambridge U v Surrey (Cambridge) 1978. BH Gold Award: 1 for Combined Universities. HS: 149* v Northants (Bristol) 1979. HSGC/NW: 85* v Northants (Bristol) 1977. HSJPL: 51 v Northants (Northampton) 1976. HSBH: 63 Combined Universities v Worcs (Worcester) 1978. Rugby Blue and England international (14 caps).

David Valentine LAWRENCE B Gloucester 28/1/1964. RHB, RFM. Debut 1981.

Paul William ROMAINES B Bishop Auckland, Co Durham 25/12/1955. RHB. Played for Northants 1975-76. Debut for Glos 1982. HS: 186 v Warwicks (Nuneaton) 1982. HSGC/NW: 48 Durham v Berks (Durham) 1979. HSJPL: 55 v Leics (Leicester) 1982.

Robert Charles (Jack) RUSSELL B Stroud 15/8/1963. LHB, WK. Debut 1981. HS: 41 v Leics (Gloucester) 1982. HSNW: 10 v Middlesex (Bristol) 1982.

SADIQ MOHAMMAD B Junagadh, India 3/5/1945. LHB, LBG. Youngest brother of Hanif and Mushtaq Mohammad. Debut in Pakistan 1959-60 aged 14 years 9 months and has played since for Karachi, Pakistan International Airways and United Bank, and for Tasmania v MCC in 1974-75. Played for D.H. Robins' XI v Oxford U in 1969 and for Essex v Jamaica XI in 1970. Debut for Glos 1972. Cap 1973. Benefit: 1982. Tests: 41 for Pakistan between 1969-70 and 1980-81. Tours: Pakistan Eaglets to England 1963, PIA to East Africa 1964-65, Pakistan to England 1971, 1974 and 1978, Australia and New Zealand 1972-73, Australia and West Indies 1976-77, India 1979-80. 1,000 runs (7) – 1,759 (av. 47.54) in 1976 best. 1,000 runs overseas twice (1972-73 and 1976-77). 4 centuries in consecutive innings, including two (163* and 150) v Derby (Bristol) 1976. Also scored century in each innings (171 and 103) v Glamorgan (Bristol) 1979. GC Man of the Match: 1. BH Gold Awards: 4. HS: 203 v Sri Lankans (Bristol) 1981. HSTC: 166 Pakistan v New Zealand (Wellington) 1972-73. HSGC/NW: 122 v Lancs (Manchester) 1975. HSJPL: 131 v Somerset (Imperial Ground, Bristol) 1975. HSBH: 128 v Minor Counties (South) (Bristol) 1974. BB: 7-34 United Bank v Universities (Peshawar) 1978-79. BBUK: 5-37 v Kent (Bristol) 1973. BBGC/NW: 3-19 v Oxfordshire (Bristol) 1975. BBJPL: 3-27 v Hants (Bristol) 1972. BBBH: 3-20 v Minor Counties (South) (Bristol) 1972.

Gary Edward SAINSBURY B Wanstead 17/1/1958. RHB, LM. Played for Essex 1979 and 1980. Joined Glos for 1983. BB: 4-85 Essex v Surrey (Oval) 1980.

John Neil SHEPHERD B St Andrew, Barbados 9/11/1943. RHB, RM. Debut 1964-65 for Barbados v Cavaliers and for Barbados in 1967-68, 1968-69 and 1970-71. Debut for Kent 1966. Cap 1967. Played for Rhodesia 1975-76. *Wisden* 1978. Benefit 1979 (£58,537). Debut for Glos 1982. Tests: 5 for West Indies in 1969 and 1970-71. Tours: West Indies to England 1969, D.H. Robins to South Africa

86

1973-74 and 1974-75, International Wanderers to South Africa 1974-75. Scored 1,157 runs (av. 29.66) in 1968 and also took 96 wkts (av. 18.72). GC Man of the Match: 1 (for Kent). BH Gold Awards: 3 (2 for Kent). HS: 170 Kent v Northants (Folkestone) 1968. HSTC: 32 West Indies v England (Lord's) 1969. HSGC/NW: 101 Kent v Middlesex (Canterbury) 1977. HSJPL: 94 Kent v Hants (Southampton) 1978. HSBH: 96 Kent v Middlesex (Lord's) 1975. BB: 8-40 West Indies v Glos (Bristol) 1969. BBC: 6-75 v Sussex (Hastings) 1982. BBTC: 5-104 West Indies v England (Manchester) 1969. BBGC/NW: 4-23 Kent v Essex (Leyton) 1977. BBJPL: 4-17 Kent v Middlesex (Lord's) 1978. BBBH: 4-25 Kent v Derby (Lord's) 1978.

David Paul SIMPKINS B Chippenham, Wiltshire 28/3/1962. RHB, OB. Debut 1982. One match v Middlesex (Cheltenham).

Franklyn DaCosta STEPHENSON B St James, Barbados 8/4/1959. RHB, RF. Debut for Tasmania 1981-82. Also played for Barbados. Debut for Glos 1982. HS: 165 Barbados v Leeward Islands (Basseterre) 1981-82. HSUK: 63 D.B. Close's International XI v Pakistanis (Scarborough) 1982. HSC: 14 v Sussex (Bristol) 1982. HSJPL: 26 v Northants (Bristol) 1982. BB: 6-19 Tasmania v Victoria (Melbourne) 1981-82. BBUK: 5-64 D.B. Close's International XI v Pakistanis (Scarborough) 1982. BBC: 5-69 v Middlesex (Cheltenham) 1982. BBJPL: 3-16 v Notts (Nottingham) 1982. BBBH: 3-37 v Combined Universities (Oxford) 1982.

Andrew Willis STOVOLD B Bristol 19/3/1953. RHB, WK. Debut 1973. Cap 1976. Played for Orange Free State in 1974-75 and 1975-76. 1,000 runs (4) – 1,388 (av. 36.52) in 1979 best. NW Man of the Match: 2. BH Gold Awards: 6. HS: 212* v Northants (Northampton) 1982. HSNW: 76* v Notts (Nottingham) 1982. HSJPL: 98* v Kent (Cheltenham) 1977. HSBH: 123 v Combined Universities (Oxford) 1982.

Christopher Richard TREMBATH B London 27/9/1961. RHB, RM. Debut 1982. BB: 5-91 v Oxford U (Oxford) 1982.

Anthony John WRIGHT B Stevenage, Hertfordshire 27/6/1962. RHB, RM. Debut 1982. HS: 65 v Warwicks (Nuneaton) and v Somerset (Bristol) 1982. HSNW: 14 v Middlesex (Bristol) 1982. HSJPL: 52 v Essex (Cheltenham) 1982.

Syed ZAHEER ABBAS B Sialkot, Pakistan 24/7/1947. RHB, OB. Wears glasses. Debut for Karachi Whites 1965-66 and has also played for Pakistan International Airways. Wisden 1971. Debut for Glos 1972. Cap 1975. Tests: 49 for Pakistan between 1969-70 and 1982 and 5 matches for Rest of the World v Australia 1971-72. Tours: Pakistan to England 1971, 1974 and 1982, Australia and New Zealand 1972-73, Sri Lanka 1975-76, Australia and West Indies 1976-77, New Zealand and Australia 1978-79, India 1979-80, Australia 1981-82, Rest of the World to Australia 1971-72. 1,000 runs (11) – 2,554 (av. 75.11) in 1976 best. Scored 1,597 runs (av. 84.05) in Pakistan in 1973-74. 4 centuries in consecutive innings in 1970-71. Centuries in each innings of a match on 8 occasions (world record and including world record of a double century and century 4 times). GC Man of the Match: 4. HS: 274 Pakistan v England (Birmingham) 1971. HSC: 230* v Kent (Canterbury) 1976. HSGC/NW 131* v Leics (Leicester) 1975. HSJPL: 129* v Middlesex (Lord's) 1981. HSBH: 98 v Surrey (Oval) 1975. BB: 5-15 Dawood Club v Railways (Lahore) 1975-76. BBUK: 3-32 v Warwicks (Gloucester) 1981. Scored 100th century in 1982-83. Benefit 1983.

NB. The following players whose particulars appeared in the 1982 Annual have been omitted: J.H. Dixon, B. Dudleston, M.D. Partridge, M.J. Procter, M.W. Stovold, D. Surridge, M.R. Whitney, A.H. Wilkins and S.J. Windaybank.

County Averages

Schweppes County Championship: Played 22, won 2, drawn 11, lost 9.
All first-class matches: Played 24, won 3, drawn 12, lost 9.

BATTING AND FIELDING

Cap		M	I	NO	Runs	HS	Avge	100	50	Ct	St
1975	Zaheer Abbas	7	13	1	811	162*	67.58	3	4	1	—
1981	P.A. Bainbridge	18	33	8	1069	103	42.76	2	7	9	—
1973	Sadiq Mohammad	15	29	1	998	91	35.64	—	9	8	—
—	B. Dudleston	6	12	1	373	111	33.90	1	1	6	—
1976	A.W. Stovold	23	42	1	1350	212*	32.92	2	7	24	—
1977	A.J. Hignell	15	28	6	664	72	30.18	—	4	9	—
1981	B.C. Broad	22	41	0	1153	97	28.12	—	7	4	—
—	P.W. Romaines	14	24	2	609	186	27.68	1	2	5	—
1976	D.A. Graveney	23	30	11	489	55*	25.73	—	1	14	—
—	J.N. Shepherd	22	34	9	590	67*	23.60	—	3	13	—
—	A.J. Wright	10	19	2	399	65	23.47	—	2	3	—
—	M.W. Stovold	5	9	0	155	52	17.22	—	1	—	—
—	R.C. Russell	4	6	1	81	41	16.20	—	—	4	2
—	R.J. Doughty	5	5	1	58	29	14.50	—	—	2	—
1978	A.J. Brassington	20	20	5	141	35	9.40	—	—	37	8
1977	J.H. Childs	21	21	5	132	34*	8.25	—	—	7	—
—	E.J. Cunningham	4	6	2	26	11*	6.50	—	—	—	—
—	D. Surridge	18	17	7	61	12	6.10	—	—	3	—
—	F.D. Stephenson	9	9	1	42	15	5.25	—	—	1	—

Played in two matches: C.R. Trembath 8* (1 ct).

Played in one match: D.V. Lawrence did not bat; S.J. Windaybank 8, 10*; D. Simpkin 1*, 0.

BOWLING

	Type	O	M	R	W	Avge	Best	5 wI	10 wM
F.D. Stephenson	RF	175.2	37	542	25	21.68	5-69	1	—
D.A. Graveney	SLA	498.4	145	1242	44	28.22	7-37	1	—
D. Surridge	RM	561	159	1507	47	32.06	5-78	1	—
J.N. Shepherd	RM	742.1	177	2026	63	32.15	6-75	2	—
R.J. Doughty	RM	149.1	19	533	15	35.53	6-43	1	—
C.R. Trembath	RM	49.3	7	219	6	36.50	5-91	1	—
Sadiq Mohammad	LBG	101.4	20	305	7	43.57	4-42	—	—
J.H. Childs	SLA	656.3	201	1681	38	44.23	5-112	1	—
P.A. Bainbridge	RM	301	77	915	19	48.15	6-59	1	—

Also bowled: B.C. Broad 39-8-104-2; E.J. Cunningham 4-0-13-0; B. Dudleston 37-10-108-3; D.V. Lawrence 23-3-74-2; P.W. Romaines 5-2-9-0; D. Simpkin 2-0-15-0; M.W. Stovold 1-0-13-0; Zaheer Abbas 2-0-15-0.

County Records

First-class cricket

Highest innings	For	653-6d v Glamorgan (Bristol)	1928
totals:	Agst	774-7d by Australians (Bristol)	1948
Lowest innings	For	17 v Australians (Cheltenham)	1896
totals:	Agst	12 by Northants (Gloucester)	1907

Highest individual innings:	For	318* W.G. Grace v Yorks (Cheltenham)	1876
	Agst	296 A.O. Jones for Notts (Nottingham)	1903
Best bowling in an innings:	For	10-40 E.G. Dennett v Essex (Bristol)	1906
	Agst	10-66 A.A. Mailey for Aust (Cheltenham)	1921
		and K. Smales for Notts (Stroud)	1956
Best bowling in a match:	For	17-56 C.W.L. Parker v Essex (Gloucester)	1925
	Agst	15-87 A.J. Conway for Worcs (Moreton-in-Marsh)	1914
Most runs in a season:		2,860 (av. 69.75) W.R. Hammond	1933
runs in a career:		33,664 (av. 57.05) W.R. Hammond	1920-1951
100s in a season:		13 by W.R. Hammond	1938
100s in a career:		113 by W.R. Hammond	1920-1951
wickets in a season:		222 (av. 16.80 & 16.37) T.W.J. Goddard	1937 & 1947
wickets in a career:		3,170 (av. 19.44) C.W.L. Parker	1903-1935

RECORD WICKET STANDS

1st	395	D.M. Young & R.B. Nicholls v Oxford U (Oxford)	1962
2nd	256	C.T.M. Pugh & T.W. Graveney v Derby (Chesterfield)	1960
3rd	336	W.R. Hammond & B.H. Lyon v Leics (Leicester)	1933
4th	321	W.R. Hammond & W.L. Neale v Leics (Gloucester)	1937
5th	261	W.G. Grace & W.O. Moberley v Yorks (Cheltenham)	1876
6th	320	G.L. Jessop & J.H. Board v Sussex (Hove)	1903
7th	248	W.G. Grace & E.L. Thomas v Sussex (Hove)	1896
8th	239	W.R. Hammond & A.E. Wilson v Lancs (Bristol)	1938
9th	193	W.G. Grace & S.A.P. Kitcat v Sussex (Bristol)	1896
10th	131	W.R. Gouldsworthy & J.G. Bessant v Somerset (Bristol)	1923

One-day cricket

Highest innings totals:	Gillette Cup/NatWest Trophy	327-7 v Berkshire (Reading)	1966
	John Player League	255 v Somerset (Imperial Ground, Bristol)	1975
	Benson & Hedges Cup	300-4 v Combined Universities (Oxford)	1982
Lowest innings totals:	NatWest Trophy	85 v Essex (Bristol)	1981
	John Player League	49 v Middlesex (Bristol)	1978
	Benson & Hedges Cup	62 v Hants (Bristol)	1975
Highest individual innings:	Gillette Cup/NatWest Trophy	131* Zaheer Abbas v Leics (Leicester)	1975
	John Player League	131 Sadiq Mohammad v Somerset (Imperial Ground, Bristol)	1975
	Benson & Hedges Cup	154* M.J. Procter v Somerset (Taunton)	1972
Best bowling figures:	NatWest Trophy	5-11 D.A. Graveney v Ireland (Dublin)	1981
	John Player League	5-8 M.J. Procter v Middlesex (Gloucester)	1977
	Benson & Hedges Cup	6-13 M.J. Procter v Hants (Southampton)	1977

HAMPSHIRE

Formation of present club: 1863.
Colours: Blue, gold and white.
Badge: Tudor rose and crown.
County Champions (2): 1961 and 1973.
Gillette Cup Semi-Finalists (2): 1966 and 1976.
NatWest Trophy Quarter-Finalists: 1982.
John Player League Champions (2): 1975 and 1978.
Benson & Hedges Cup Semi-Finalists (2): 1975 and 1977.
Fenner Trophy Winners (3): 1975, 1976 and 1977.
Gillette Man of the Match Awards: 25.
NatWest Man of the Match Awards: 2.
Benson & Hedges Gold Awards: 24.

Secretary: A.K. James, County Cricket Ground, Northlands Road, Southampton SO9 2TY.
Captain: N.E.J. Pocock.

Nigel Geoffrey COWLEY B Shaftesbury (Dorset) 1/3/1953. RHB, OB. Debut 1974. Cap 1978. HS: 109* v Somerset (Taunton) 1977. HSGC/NW: 63* v Glos (Bristol) 1979. HSJPL: 74 v Warwicks (Birmingham) 1981. HSBH: 59 v Glos (Southampton) 1977. BB: 6-48 v Leics (Southampton) 1982. BBGC/NW: 4-20 v Middlesex (Lord's) 1979. BBJPL: 4-46 v Sussex (Hove) 1980. BBBH: 3-39 v Sussex (Bournemouth) 1982.

Christopher Colin CURZON B Lenton, Nottingham 22/12/1958. RHB, WK. Played for Notts 1978 to 1980. Debut for Hants 1981. One match v Sri Lankans (Bournemouth) 1981. HS: 45 Notts v Glamorgan (Swansea) 1980. HSC: 31* v Sri Lankans (Bournemouth) 1981. HSJPL: 28* Notts v Kent (Nottingham) 1980. HSBH: 15 Notts v Northants (Northampton) 1980. Did not play in 1982.

Kevin St John Dennis EMERY B Swindon, Wiltshire 28/11/1960. RHB, RFM. Debut 1982. HS: 18* v Derby (Derby) 1982. BB: 6-51 v Glamorgan (Portsmouth) 1982. BBJPL: 4-21 v Leics (Leicester) 1982. BBBH: 5-24 v Essex (Chelmsford) 1982.

Christopher Frederick Evelyn GOLDIE (St Paul's School and Cambridge) B Johannesburg, South Africa 2/11/1960. RHB, WK. Debut 1981 for Cambridge U. Blue 1981-82. HS: 77 Cambridge U v Oxford U (Lord's) 1981. Joined Hants for 1983.

Cuthbert Gordon GREENIDGE B St Peter, Barbados 1/5/1951. RHB, RM. Debut 1970. Cap 1972. Has subsequently played for Barbados. Wisden 1976. Tests: 36 for West Indies between 1974-75 and 1981-82. Tours: West Indies to India, Sri Lanka and Pakistan 1974-75, Australia 1975-76 and 1981-82, England 1976 and 1980, Australia and New Zealand 1979-80, Pakistan 1980-81. 1,000 runs (11) – 1,952 runs (av. 55.77) in 1976 best. Scored two centuries in match (134 and 101) West Indies v England (Manchester) 1976 and (136 and 120) v Kent (Bournemouth) 1978. Gillette Man of the Match: 3. NW Man of the Match: 1. BH Gold Awards: 4. HS: 273* D.H. Robins' XI v Pakistanis (Eastbourne) 1974. HSC: 259 v Sussex (Southampton) 1975. HSTC: 134 West Indies v England (Manchester) 1976.

90

HSGC/NW: 177 v Glamorgan (Southampton) 1975 – record for GC competition.
HSJPL: 163* v Warwicks (Birmingham) 1979 – record for competition. HSBH:
173* v Minor Counties (South) (Amersham) 1973 and shared in partnership of 285*
for second wicket with D.R. Turner – the record partnership for all one-day
competitions. BB: 5-49 v Surrey (Southampton) 1971. Benefit 1983.

Trevor Edward JESTY B Gosport 2/6/1948. RHB, RM. Debut 1966. Cap 1971.
Played for Border in 1973-74 and Griqualand West in 1974-75, 1975-76 and 1980-81.
Played for Canterbury in 1979-80. Benefit in 1982. Tour: Australia and New Zealand
1982-83. 1,000 runs (5) – 1,645 (av. 58.75) in 1982 best. Gillette Man of the Match:
3. NW Man of the Match: 1. BH Gold Awards: 6. Took 3 wkts in 4 balls v Somerset
(Portsmouth) 1969. HS: 164* v Indians (Southampton) 1982. HSGC/NW: 118 v
Derby (Derby) 1980. HSJPL: 110* v Yorks (Southampton) 1982. HSBH: 105 v
Glamorgan (Swansea) 1977. BB: 7-75 v Worcs (Southampton) 1976. BBGC/NW:
6-46 v Glos (Bristol) 1979. BBJPL: 6-20 v Glamorgan (Cardiff) 1976. BBBH: 4-28
v Somerset (Taunton) 1974.

Steven John MALONE (King's School, Ely) B Chelmsford 19/10/1953. RHB,
RM. Debut for Essex 1975 playing in one match v Cambridge U (Cambridge).
Reappeared in corresponding match in 1978. Did not play in 1979 and made debut
for Hants in 1980. HS: 23 v Kent (Bournemouth) 1981. BB: 7-55 v Oxford U
(Oxford) 1982. BBNW: 5-34 v Cheshire (Southampton) 1981. BBJPL: 4-39 v Yorks
(Basingstoke) 1980.

Malcolm Denzil MARSHALL B St Michael, Barbados 18/4/1958. RHB, RF.
Played for Barbados 1977-78 to 1980-81. Debut for county 1979. Cap 1981. Tests:
12 between 1978-79 and 1980-81. Tours: West Indies to India and Sri Lanka 1978-
79, Australia and New Zealand 1979-80, England 1980, Pakistan 1980-81, Zimbabwe
1981-82, Australia 1981-82. Hat-trick in John Player League v Surrey (Southampton)
1981. 134 wkts (av. 15.73) in 1982. HS: 116* v Lancs (Southampton) 1982. HSTC:
45 West Indies v England (Oval) 1980. HSGC/NW: 21* v Middlesex (Lord's) 1979.
HSJPL: 46 v Leics (Leicester) 1982. HSBH: 21 v Kent (Canterbury) 1982. BB: 8-71
v Worcs (Southampton) 1982. BBTC: 4-25 West Indies v Pakistan (Faisalabad)
1980-81. BBJPL: 5-13 v Glamorgan (Portsmouth) 1979. BBBH: 3-11 v Sussex
(Hove) 1981.

Mark Charles Jefford NICHOLAS (Bradfield College) B London 29/9/1957.
RHB, RM. Debut 1978. Cap 1982. Scored 1,312 runs (av. 39.75) in 1982. HS: 206*
v Oxford U (Oxford) 1982. HSGC/NW: 28 v Yorks (Southampton) 1980. HSJPL:
76 v Lancs (Portsmouth) 1982. HSBH: 44 v Essex (Chelmsford) 1982. BBBH: 3-29
v Surrey (Oval) 1980.

Robert James PARKS (Eastbourne GS) B Cuckfield, Sussex 15/6/1959. Son of
J.M. Parks and grandson of J.H. Parks. RHB, WK. Debut 1980. Cap 1982. Dismissed
10 batsmen (all ct.) in match v Derby (Portsmouth) 1981. HS: 64* v Essex
(Chelmsford) 1982. HSNW: 19* v Glamorgan (Cardiff) 1981. HSJPL: 36* v Leics
(Leicester) 1982. HSBH: 11 v Middlesex (Lord's) 1981.

Nicholas Edward Julian POCOCK (Shrewsbury School) B Maracaibo, Venezuela
15/12/1951. RHB, LM. Debut 1976. Appointed county captain in 1980. Cap 1980.
HS: 164 v Lancs (Southampton) 1982. HSGC/NW: 73* v Derby (Derby) 1980.
HSJPL: 53* v Northants (Northampton) 1978. HSBH: 41 v Somerset (Bournemouth) 1980.

HAMPSHIRE

Christopher Lyall (Kippy) SMITH (Northlands HS, Durban) B Durban, South Africa 15/10/1958. Older brother of R.A. Smith. RHB, OB. Played for Natal B 1977-78 to 1981-82. Debut for Glamorgan 1979. One match v Sri Lankans (Swansea). Debut for Hants 1980. Cap 1981. Will be regarded as an English player for qualification purposes in May 1983. Scored 1,048 runs (av. 31.75) in 1980. HS: 130 v Kent (Bournemouth) 1980. HSJPL: 66 v Middlesex (Bournemouth) 1980. HSBH: 48 v Kent (Canterbury) 1980.

Robin Arnold SMITH B Durban, South Africa 13/9/1963. Younger brother of C.L. Smith. RHB, LB. Played for Natal in 1980-81 and 1981-82. Debut for Hants 1982. Will be regarded as an English player for qualification purposes in 1983. HS: 91 Natal v Eastern Province (Durban) 1981-82. HSC: 8 v Pakistanis (Bournemouth) 1982.

John William SOUTHERN B King's Cross, London 2/9/1952. RHB, SLA. Debut 1975. Cap 1978. HS: 61* v Yorks (Bradford) 1979. HSBH: 14 v Somerset (Bournemouth) 1980. BB: 6-46 v Glos (Bournemouth) 1975.

Keith STEVENSON B Derby 6/10/1950. RHB, RFM. Played for Derby 1974 to 1977. Debut for Hants 1978. Cap 1979. HS: 33 Derby v Northants (Chesterfield) 1974. HSC: 31 v Derby (Portsmouth) 1980. HSGC/NW: 14 Derby v Surrey (Ilkeston) 1976. HSJPL: 11* v Somerset (Taunton) 1981. BB: 7-22 v Oxford U (Oxford) 1979. BBGC/NW: 4-21 Derby v Surrey (Ilkeston) 1976. BBJPL: 3-22 v Essex (Chelmsford) 1980. BBBH: 4-18 v Middlesex (Lord's) 1981.

Vivian Paul TERRY (Millfield School) B Osnabruck, West Germany 14/1.1959. RHB, RM. Debut 1978. HS: 94* v Northants (Southampton) 1981. HSGC/NW: 11 v Middlesex (Lord's) 1979. HSJPL: 33 v Glos (Basingstoke) 1979. HSBH: 15 v Essex (Chelmsford) 1982.

Timothy Maurice TREMLETT B Wellington, Somerset 26/7/1956. Son of M.F. Tremlett, former Somerset player. RHB, RM. Debut 1976. HS: 88 v Lancs (Manchester) 1981. HSJPL: 28 v Glos (Cheltenham) 1980. HSBH: 29 v Surrey (Bournemouth) 1981. BB: 5-30 v Notts (Nottingham) 1980. BBJPL: 4-22 v Lancs (Manchester) 1981. BBBH: 3-21 v Combined Universities (Cambridge) 1978.

David Roy TURNER B Chippenham, Wilts 5/2/1949. LHB, RM. Debut 1966. Cap 1970. Played for Western Province in 1977-78. Benefit in 1981. Tour: D.H. Robins to South Africa 1972-73. 1,000 runs (6) – 1,269 runs (av. 36.25) in 1976 best. Gillette Man of the Match: 1. BH Gold Awards: 4. HS: 181* v Surrey (Oval) 1969. HSGC/NW: 86 v Northants (Southampton) 1976. HSJPL: 109 v Surrey (Oval) 1980. HSBH: 123* v Minor Counties (South) (Amersham) 1973.

NB. The following players whose particulars appeared in the 1982 Annual have been omitted: M.J. Bailey, J.J.E. Hardy, R.E. Hayward and J.N.C. Massey.

County Averages

Schweppes County Championship: Played 22, won 8, drawn 8, lost 6.
All first-class matches: Played 25, won 10, drawn 8, lost 7.

BATTING AND FIELDING

Cap		M	I	NO	Runs	HS	Avge	100	50	Ct	St
1971	T.E. Jesty	22	36	8	1645	164*	58.75	8	4	13	—
1972	C.G. Greenidge	21	41	8	1526	183*	46.24	3	4	23	—
—	M.C.J. Nicholas	24	42	9	1312	206*	39.75	3	7	14	—
1970	D.R. Turner	15	21	1	459	96	22.95	—	2	6	—
1981	M.D. Marshall	22	31	3	633	116*	22.60	1	2	4	—
1980	N.E.J. Pocock	22	30	2	616	164	22.00	1	3	20	—
1978	N.G. Cowley	23	28	1	584	104	21.62	1	2	9	—
1978	J.W. Southern	19	21	7	300	50*	21.42	—	1	8	—
—	R.E. Hayward	6	9	1	169	59	21.12	—	1	3	—
1975	J.M. Rice	23	44	4	777	69	19.42	—	5	26	—
1982	R.J. Parks	25	30	5	350	44	14.00	—	—	70	6
—	T.M. Tremlett	16	22	3	209	48	11.00	—	—	15	—
—	V.P. Terry	4	6	2	41	16*	10.25	—	—	3	—
—	S.J. Malone	6	5	2	13	4	4.33	—	—	1	—
—	K.S.D. Emery	23	26	15	37	18*	3.36	—	—	3	—

Played in one match: M.J. Bailey 3; C.L. Smith 71 (2 ct); R.A. Smith 8, 1 (2 ct); K. Stephenson did not bat (1 ct).

BOWLING

	Type	O	M	R	W	Avge	Best	5 wI	10 wM
M.D. Marshall	RF	822	225	2108	134	15.73	8-71	12	4
T.E. Jesty	RM	288.1	89	750	35	21.42	6-71	1	—
S.J. Malone	RM	150.5	35	505	22	22.95	7-55	2	1
J.W. Southern	SLA	440.5	118	1314	55	23.89	5-51	2	—
T.M. Tremlett	RM	354.3	114	766	32	23.93	5-59	1	—
K.S.D. Emery	RFM	637	149	1892	79	23.94	6-51	3	1
N.G. Cowley	OB	310.1	86	895	24	37.29	6-48	1	—

Also bowled: M.J. Bailey 18-4-76-2; N.E.J. Pocock 12.5-1-55-0; K. Stephenson 22-10-56-1; D.R. Turner 1-0-1-0; J.M. Rice 61.3-10-240-3; M.C.J. Nicholas 3-0-13-1.

County Records

First-class cricket

Highest innings totals:	For	672-7d v Somerset (Taunton)	1899
	Agst	742 by Surrey (Oval)	1909
Lowest innings totals:	For	15 v Warwicks (Birmingham)	1922
	Agst	23 by Yorks (Middlesbrough)	1965
Highest individual innings:	For	316 R.H. Moore v Warwicks (Bournemouth)	1937
	Agst	302* P. Holmes for Yorks (Portsmouth)	1920
Best bowling in an innings:	For	9-25 R.M.H. Cottam v Lancs (Manchester)	1965
	Agst	9-21 L.B. Richmond for Notts (Nottingham)	1922

HAMPSHIRE

Best bowling	For	16-88 J.A. Newman v Somerset	
in a match:		(Weston-super-Mare)	1927
	Agst	17-119 W. Mead for Essex (Southampton)	1895
Most runs in a season:		2,854 (av. 79.27) C.P. Mead	1928
runs in a career:		48,892 (av. 48.84) C.P. Mead	1905-1936
100s in a season:		12 by C.P. Mead	1928
100s in a career:		138 by C.P. Mead	1905-1936
wickets in a season:		190 (av. 15.61) A.S. Kennedy	1922
wickets in a career:		2,669 (av. 18.22) D. Shackleton	1948-1969

RECORD WICKET STANDS

1st	249	R.E. Marshall & J.R. Gray v Middlesex (Portsmouth)	1960
2nd	321	G. Brown & E.I.M. Barrett v Glos (Southampton)	1920
3rd	344	C.P. Mead & G. Brown v Yorks (Portsmouth)	1927
4th	263	R.E. Marshall & D.A. Livingstone v Middlesex (Lord's)	1970
5th	235	G. Hill & D.F. Walker v Sussex (Portsmouth)	1937
6th	411	R.M. Poore & E.G. Wynyard v Somerset (Taunton)	1899
7th	325	G. Brown & C.H. Abercrombie v Essex (Leyton)	1913
8th	178	C.P. Mead & C.P. Brutton v Worcs (Bournemouth)	1925
9th	230	D.A. Livingstone & A.T. Castell v Surrey (Southampton)	1962
10th	192	A. Bowell & W.H. Livsey v Worcs (Bournemouth)	1921

NB. A partnership of 334 for the first wicket by B.A. Richards, C.G. Greenidge and D.R. Turner occurred against Kent at Southampton in 1973. Richards retired hurt after 241 runs had been scored.

One-day cricket

Highest innings totals:	Gillette Cup/ NatWest Trophy	371-4 v Glamorgan (Southampton)	1975
	John Player League	288-5 v Somerset (Weston-super-Mare)	1975
	Benson & Hedges Cup	321-1 v Minor Counties (South) (Amersham)	1973
Lowest innings totals:	Gillette Cup/ NatWest Trophy	98 v Lancs (Manchester)	1975
	John Player League	43 v Essex (Basingstoke)	1972
	Benson & Hedges Cup	94 v Glamorgan (Swansea)	1973
Highest individual innings:	Gillette Cup/ NatWest Trophy	177 C.G. Greenidge v Glamorgan (Southampton)	1975
	John Player League	163* C.G. Greenidge v Warwicks (Birmingham)	1979
	Benson & Hedges Cup	173* C.G. Greenidge v Minor Counties (South) (Amersham)	1973
Best bowling figures:	Gillette Cup/ NatWest Trophy	7-30 P.J. Sainsbury v Norfolk (Southampton)	1965
	John Player League	6-20 T.E. Jesty v Glamorgan (Cardiff)	1975
	Benson & Hedges Cup	5-24 R.S. Herman v Glos (Bristol)	1975
		5-24 K.S.D. Emery v Essex (Chelmsford)	1982

KENT

Formation of present club: 1859, re-organised 1870.
Colours: Maroon and white.
Badge: White horse.
County Champions (6): 1906, 1909, 1910, 1913, 1970 and 1978.
Joint Champions: 1977.
Gillette Cup Winners (2): 1967 and 1974.
Gillette Cup Finalists: 1971.
NatWest Trophy Second Round: 1981.
John Player League Champions (3): 1972, 1973 and 1976.
Benson & Hedges Cup Winners (3): 1973, 1976 and 1978.
Benson & Hedges Cup Finalists: 1977.
Fenner Trophy Winners (2): 1971 and 1973.
Gillette Man of the Match Awards: 23.
NatWest Trophy Man of the Match Awards: 1.
Benson & Hedges Gold Awards: 32.

Secretary: D. Dalby, St. Lawrence Ground, Canterbury CT1 3NZ.
Cricket Manager: B.W. Luckhurst.
Captain: C.J. Tavaré.
Prospects of Play Telephone No: Canterbury matches only, Canterbury (0227) 57323.

Derek George ASLETT B Dover 12/2/1958. RHB, LB. Debut 1981 scoring 146* in first innings. HS: 146* v Hants (Bournemouth) 1981. HSJPL: 43 v Leics (Canterbury) 1982. HSBH: 19 v Sussex (Hove) 1982. BB: 4-119 v Sussex (Hove) 1982.

Eldine Ashworth Elderfield BAPTISTE B St. John's, Antigua 12/3/1960. RHB, RFM. Debut 1981. HS: 69* v Glamorgan (Canterbury) 1982. HSJPL: 22 v Glos (Cheltenham) 1981. BB: 5-37 v Lancs (Maidstone) 1981. BBJPL: 3-32 v Sussex (Eastbourne) 1981 and v Glos (Folkestone) 1982.

Mark Richard BENSON (Sutton Valence School) B Shoreham, Sussex 6/7/1958. LHB, OB. Debut 1980. Cap 1981. 1,000 runs (1) – 1,100 (av. 44.00) in 1982 best. HS: 137 v Sussex (Hove) 1982. HSNW: 57 v Yorks (Canterbury) 1981. HSJPL: 97 v Surrey (Oval) 1982. HSBH: 65 v Surrey (Canterbury) 1982.

Christopher Stuart COWDREY (Tonbridge School) B Farnborough, Kent 20/10/1957. Eldest son of M.C. Cowdrey. RHB, RM. Played for 2nd XI at age of 15. Played in one John Player League match in 1976. Debut 1977. Cap 1979. BH Gold Awards: 2. HS: 101* v Glamorgan (Swansea) 1977. HSNW: 25 v Notts (Canterbury) 1981. HSJPL: 74 v Worcs (Worcester) 1978. HSBH: 114 v Sussex (Canterbury) 1977. BB: 3-17 v Hants (Bournemouth) 1980. BBNW: 4-41 v Yorks (Canterbury) 1981.

Graham Roy DILLEY B Dartford 18/5/1959. LHB, RFM. Debut 1977. Cap 1980. Best Young Cricketer of the Year in 1980. Tests: 16 between 1979-80 and 1981-82. Tours: Australia and India 1979-80, West Indies 1980-81, India and Sri Lanka 1981-82. HS: 81 v Northants (Northampton) 1979. HSTC: 56 v Australia (Leeds) 1981. HSJPL: 33 v Northants (Northampton) 1982. HSBH: 13* v Hants (Canterbury)

1980. BB: 6-66 v Middlesex (Lord's) 1979. BBTC: 4-24 v Australia (Nottingham) 1981. BBJPL: 4-20 v Glos (Canterbury) 1980. BBBH: 4-14 v Combined Universities (Canterbury) 1981.

Richard Mark ELLISON (Tonbridge School) B Ashford (Kent) 21/9/1959. LHB, RM. Debut 1981. HS: 61* v Somerset (Canterbury) 1981. HSJPL: 24 v Sussex (Maidstone) 1982. BB: 3-12 v Northants (Folkestone) 1982.

Simon Graham HINKS B Northfleet 12/10/1960. LHB, LM, WK. Debut 1982. HS: 18 v Northants (Northampton) 1982.

Kevin Bertram Sidney JARVIS B Dartford 23/4/1953. RHB, RFM. Debut 1975. Cap 1977. BH Gold Awards: 1. HS: 12* v Cambridge U (Canterbury) 1977. BB: 8-97 v Worcs (Worcester) 1978. BBGC/NW: 3-53 v Sussex (Canterbury) 1976. BBJPL: 4-27 v Surrey (Maidstone) 1977. BBBH: 4-34 v Worcs (Lord's) 1976.

Graham William JOHNSON B Beckenham 8/11/1946. RHB, OB. Debut 1965. Cap 1970. 1,000 runs (3) – 1,438 runs (av. 31.26) in 1973 and 1,438 runs (av. 35.95) in 1975 best. Gillette Man of the Match Awards: 1. BH Gold Awards: 3. HS: 168 v Surrey (Oval) 1976. HSGC/NW: 120* v Bucks (Canterbury) 1974. HSJPL: 89 v Sussex (Hove) 1976. HSBH: 85* v Minor Counties (South) (Canterbury) 1975. BB: 6-32 v Surrey (Tunbridge Wells) 1978. BBJPL: 5-26 v Surrey (Oval) 1974. Benefit 1983.

Alan Philip Eric KNOTT B Belvedere 9/4/1946. RHB, WK, OB. Debut 1964. Cap 1965. Best Young Cricketer of the Year in 1965. *Wisden* 1969. Played for Tasmania 1969-70. Benefit (£27,037) in 1976. Tests: 95 between 1967 and 1981. Played in 5 matches against Rest of World in 1970. Tours: Cavaliers to West Indies 1964-65, Pakistan 1966-67, West Indies 1967-68 and 1973-74, Ceylon and Pakistan 1968-69, Australia and New Zealand 1970-71, 1974-75, India, Sri Lanka and Pakistan 1972-73, India, Sri Lanka and Australia 1976-77, SAB to South Africa 1981-82. Banned for 3 years from Test cricket. 1,000 runs (2) – 1,209 runs (av. 41.68) in 1971 best. Scored two centuries in match (127* and 118*) v Surrey (Maidstone) 1972. Gillette Man of the Match Awards: 2. BH Gold Awards: 1. HS: 156 MCC v South Zone (Bangalore) 1972-73. HSUK: 144 v Sussex (Canterbury) 1976. HSTC: 135 v Australia (Nottingham) 1977. HSGC/NW: 46 v Notts (Nottingham) 1975. HSJPL: 60 v Hants (Canterbury) 1969. HSBH: 65 v Combined Universities (Oxford) 1976. Dismissed 84 batsmen (74 ct 10 st) in 1965. 81 batsmen (73 ct 7 st) in 1966, and 98 batsmen (90 ct 8 st) in 1967. Dismissed 7 batsmen (7 ct) on debut in Test cricket v Pakistan (Nottingham) 1967.

Steven MARSH B Westminster 27/1/1961. RHB, WK. Debut 1982. HS: 10* v Warwicks (Dartford) 1982.

Christopher PENN B Dover 19/6/1963. LHB, RFM. Debut 1982. HS: 30 v Somerset (Taunton) 1982. HSJPL: 40 v Sussex (Maidstone) 1982. BBJPL: 3-35 v Yorks (Canterbury) 1982. BBBH: 4-34 v Surrey (Canterbury) 1982.

Laurie POTTER (Kelmscott HS, Perth, Western Australia) B Bexleyheath 7/11/1962. RHB, LM. Emigrated to Australia with parents at age of four. Debut 1981. HS: 118 v Indians (Canterbury) 1982. HSNW: 45 v Essex (Chelmsford) 1982. HSJPL: 45 v Warwicks (Birmingham) 1982. BBJPL: 4-27 v Somerset (Bath) 1981.

Christopher James TAVARÉ (Sevenoaks School and Oxford) B Orpington 27/10/1954. RHB, RM. Debut 1974. Blue 1975-76-77. Cap 1978. Captain for 1983.

Tests: 17 between 1980 and 1982. Tour: India and Sri Lanka 1981-82. 1,000 runs (6) – 1,770 runs (av. 53.63) in 1981 best. NatWest Man of the Match Awards: 1. BH Gold Awards: 4 (2 for Combined Universities). HS: 168* v Essex (Chelmsford) 1982. HSTC: 149 v India (Delhi) 1981-82. HSNW: 118* v Yorks (Canterbury) 1981. HSJPL: 136* v Glos (Canterbury) 1978. HSBH: 95 v Surrey (Oval) 1980.

Neil Royston TAYLOR B Orpington 21/7/1959. RHB, OB. Debut 1979 scoring 110 v Sri Lankans (Canterbury) in debut match. 1,340 runs (av. 34.35) in 1982. BH Gold Awards: 3. HS: 143* v Warwicks (Dartford) 1982. HSNW: 20 v Essex (Chelmsford) 1982. HSJPL: 74 v Glos (Folkestone) 1982. HSBH: 121 v Sussex (Hove) and v Somerset (Canterbury) 1982.

Derek Leslie UNDERWOOD B Bromley 8/6/1945. RHB, LM. Debut 1963, taking 100 wkts and being the youngest player ever to do so in debut season. Cap 1964 (second youngest Kent player to have received this award). Best Young Cricketer of the Year in 1966. *Wisden* 1968. Benefit (£24,114) in 1975. Awarded MBE in 1981 New Year's Honours List. Took 1,000th wkt in first-class cricket in New Zealand 1970-71 at age of 25 years 264 days – only W. Rhodes (in 1902) and G.A. Lohmann (in 1890) have achieved the feat at a younger age – and 2,000th wkt in 1981. Took 200th wkt in Test cricket against Australia in 1975. Tests: 86 between 1966 and 1981-82. Played in 3 matches against Rest of World in 1970. Tours: Pakistan 1966-67, International XI to Africa and Asia 1967-68, Ceylon and Pakistan 1968-69, Duke of Norfolk to West Indies 1969-70, Australia and New Zealand 1970-71, 1974-75, India, Sri Lanka and Pakistan 1972-73, West Indies 1973-74, International Wanderers to South Africa 1975-76, India, Sri Lanka and Australia 1976-77, Australia and India 1979-80, India and Sri Lanka 1981-82, SAB to South Africa 1981-82. Banned from Test cricket for 3 years. BH Gold Award: 1. 100 wkts (9) – 157 wkts (av. 13.80) in 1966 best. Hat-trick v Sussex (Hove) 1977. HS: 80 v Lancs (Manchester) 1969. HSTC: 45* v Australia (Leeds) 1968. HSGC/NW: 28 v Sussex (Tunbridge Wells) 1963. HSJPL: 22 v Worcs (Dudley) 1969. HSBH: 17 v Essex (Canterbury) 1973. BB: 9-28 v Sussex (Hastings) 1964 and 9-32 v Surrey (Oval) 1978. BBTC: 8-51 v Pakistan (Lord's) 1974. BBGC/NW: 4-57 v Leics (Canterbury) 1974. BBJPL: 5-19 v Glos (Maidstone) 1972. BBBH: 5-35 v Surrey (Oval) 1976.

Stuart Nicholas Varney WATERTON B Dartford 6/12/1960. RHB, WK. Debut 1980. HS: 40* v Surrey (Maidstone) 1980.

Lindsay Jonathan WOOD B Ruislip (Middlesex) 12/5/1961. LHB, SLA. Debut 1981. BB: 4-124 v Essex (Chelmsford) 1981.

Robert Andrew WOOLMER B Kanpur, India 14/5/1948. RHB, RM. Debut 1968. Cap 1970. *Wisden* 1975. Played for Natal between 1973-74 and 1975-76 in Currie Cup competition and for Western Province in 1980-81. Tests: 19 between 1975 and 1981. Tours: India, Sri Lanka and Australia 1976-77, SAB to South Africa 1981-82. Banned from Test cricket for 3 years. 1,000 runs (5) – 1,749 (av. 47.27) in 1976 best. Hat-trick for MCC v Australians (Lord's) 1975. Gillette Man of the Match Awards: 2. BH Gold Awards: 5. HS: 203 v Sussex (Tunbridge Wells) 1982. HSTC: 149 England v Australia (Oval) 1975. HSGC/NW: 91 v Yorks (Leeds) 1980. HSJPL: 112* v Notts (Nottingham) 1980. HSBH: 79* v Essex (Dartford) 1981. BB: 7-47 v Sussex (Canterbury) 1969. BBGC/NW: 4-28 v Somerset (Taunton) 1979. BBJPL: 6-9 v Derbyshire (Chesterfield) 1979. BBBH: 4-14 v Sussex (Tunbridge Wells) 1972.

NB. The following players whose particulars appeared in the 1982 Annual have been omitted: Asif Iqbal, A.G.E. Ealham and G.D. Spelman.

County Averages

Schweppes County Championship: Played 22, won 3, drawn 15, lost 4.
All first-class matches: Played 24, won 3, drawn 17, lost 4.

BATTING AND FIELDING

Cap		M	I	NO	Runs	HS	Avge	100	50	Ct	St
1978	C.J. Tavaré	13	23	2	954	168*	45.42	3	4	13	—
1981	M.R. Benson	16	30	5	1100	137	44.00	3	7	7	—
1970	R.A. Woolmer	13	22	3	809	203	42.57	2	4	13	—
—	L. Potter	12	21	2	775	118	40.78	2	5	5	—
1968	Asif Iqbal	11	17	2	558	115*	37.20	1	4	7	—
1965	A.P.E. Knott	21	32	5	942	115*	34.88	1	6	46	7
—	N.R. Taylor	23	41	4	1290	143*	34.86	3	6	14	—
—	E.A. Baptiste	9	12	3	319	69*	35.44	—	2	7	—
—	D.G. Aslett	16	28	3	794	82	31.76	—	7	12	—
1979	C.S. Cowdrey	22	35	4	794	72*	25.61	—	4	26	—
—	R.M. Ellison	7	11	3	179	46*	22.37	—	—	3	—
1970	G.W. Johnson	22	34	7	582	86	21.55	—	2	20	—
—	C. Penn	7	8	4	54	30	13.50	—	—	4	—
1964	D.L. Underwood	22	22	11	129	30	11.72	—	—	3	—
1980	G.R. Dilley	7	17	2	199	33	9.95	—	—	9	—
1977	K.B.S. Jarvis	21	15	4	21	6	1.90	—	—	6	—

Played in two matches: S.G. Hinks 1, 2*, 18, 14 (1 ct); S. Marsh 10* (6 ct).
Played in one match: A.G.E. Ealham 31*, 16; G.D. Spelman did not bat; S.N.V. Waterton did not bat (1 ct); L.J. Wood did not bat.

BOWLING

	Type	O	M	R	W	Avge	Best	5 wI	10 wM
D.L. Underwood	LM	690.4	223	1751	78	22.44	7-79	5	1
R.A. Woolmer	RM	60	20	140	6	23.33	2-13	—	—
R.M. Ellison	RM	153.5	35	433	16	27.06	3-12	—	—
G.R. Dilley	RF	513.2	110	1691	57	29.66	6-71	3	1
G.W. Johnson	OB	330.4	84	892	26	34.30	5-36	2	—
C.S. Cowdrey	RM	166.3	39	533	14	38.07	3-45	—	—
K.B.S. Jarvis	RFM	614	138	2026	52	38.96	5-94	1	—
C. Penn	RFM	93.4	17	327	7	46.71	2-11	—	—
D.G. Aslett	LB	84.1	10	343	7	49.00	4-119	—	—
E.A. Baptiste	RFM	186.4	45	671	12	55.91	3-41	—	—

Also bowled: M.R. Benson 4-0-28-0; S.G. Hinks 1.4-1-5-0; L. Potter 13-4-33-2; G.D. Spelman 23-8-66-3; N.R. Taylor 17-5-83-4; L.J. Wood 12-2-58-0.

County Records

First-class cricket

Highest innings totals:	For	803-4d v Essex (Brentwood)	1934
	Agst	676 by Australians (Canterbury)	1921
Lowest innings totals:	For	18 v Sussex (Gravesend)	1867
	Agst	16 by Warwicks (Tonbridge)	1913

Highest individual innings:	For	332 W.H. Ashdown v Essex (Brentwood)	1934
	Agst	344 W.G. Grace for MCC (Canterbury)	1876
Best bowling in an innings:	For	10-30 C. Blythe v Northants (Northampton)	1907
	Agst	10-48 C.H.G. Bland for Sussex (Tonbridge)	1899
Best bowling in a match:	For	17-47 C. Blythe v Northants (Northampton)	1907
	Agst	17-106 T.W.J. Goddard for Glos (Bristol)	1939
Most runs in a season:		2,894 (av. 59.06) F.E. Woolley	1928
runs in a career:		47,868 (av. 41.77) F.E. Woolley	1906-1938
100s in a season:		10 by F.E. Woolley	1928 & 1934
100s in a career:		122 by F.E. Woolley	1906-1938
wickets in a season:		262 (av. 14.74) A.P. Freeman	1933
wickets in a career:		3,340 (av. 17.64) A.P. Freeman	1914-1936

RECORD WICKET STANDS

1st	283	A.E. Fagg & P.R. Sunnucks v Essex (Colchester)	1938
2nd	352	W.H. Ashdown & F.E. Woolley v Essex (Brentwood)	1934
3rd	321*	A. Hearne & J.R. Mason v Notts (Nottingham)	1899
4th	297	H.T.W. Hardinge & A.P.F. Chapman v Hants (Southampton)	1926
5th	277	F.E. Woolley & L.E.G. Ames v New Zealanders (Canterbury)	1931
6th	284	A.P.F. Chapman & G.B. Legge v Lancs (Maidstone)	1927
7th	248	A.P. Day & E. Humphreys v Somerset (Taunton)	1908
8th	157	A.L. Hilder & C. Wright v Essex (Gravesend)	1924
9th	161	B.R. Edrich & F. Ridgway v Sussex (Tunbridge Wells)	1949
10th	235	F.E. Woolley & A. Fielder v Worcs (Stourbridge)	1909

One-day cricket

Highest innings totals:	Gillette Cup/ NatWest Trophy	297-3 v Worcs (Canterbury)	1970
	John Player League	278-5 v Glos (Maidstone)	1976
	Benson & Hedges Cup	280-3 v Surrey (Oval)	1976
Lowest innings totals:	Gillette Cup/ NatWest Trophy	60 v Somerset (Taunton)	1979
	John Player League	84 v Glos (Folkestone)	1969
	Benson & Hedges Cup	73 v Middlesex (Canterbury)	1979
Highest individual innings:	Gillette Cup/ NatWest Trophy	129 B.W. Luckhurst v Durham (Canterbury)	1974
	John Player League	142 B.W. Luckhurst v Somerset (Weston-super-Mare)	1970
	Benson & Hedges Cup	121 N.R. Taylor v Sussex (Hove)	1982
		121 N.R. Taylor v Somerset (Canterbury)	1982
Best bowling figures:	Gillette Cup/ NatWest Trophy	7-15 A.L. Dixon v Surrey (Oval)	1967
	John Player League	6-9 R.A. Woolmer v Derby (Chesterfield)	1979
	Benson & Hedges Cup	5-21 B.D. Julien v Surrey (Oval)	1973

LANCASHIRE

Formation of present club: 1864.
Colours: Red, green and blue.
Badge: Red rose.
County Champions (8): 1881, 1897, 1904, 1926, 1927, 1928, 1930 and 1934.
Joint Champions (4): 1879, 1882, 1889 and 1950.
Gillette Cup Winners (4): 1970, 1971, 1972 and 1975.
Gillette Cup Finalists (2): 1974 and 1976.
NatWest Trophy Semi-Finalists: 1981.
John Player League Champions (2): 1969 and 1970.
Benson & Hedges Cup Semi-Finalists (3): 1973, 1974 and 1982.
Gillette Man of the Match Awards: 35.
NatWest Man of the Match Awards: 3.
Benson & Hedges Gold Awards: 30.

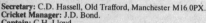

Secretary: C.D. Hassell, Old Trafford, Manchester M16 0PX.
Cricket Manager: J.D. Bond.
Captain: C.H. Lloyd.
Prospects of Play Telephone No: 061-872 0261.

John ABRAHAMS B Cape Town, South Africa 21/7/1952. LHB, OB. Debut 1973. Cap 1982. 1,000 runs (1) – 1,013 (av. 37.51) in 1982. HS: 126 Lancs v Cambridge U (Cambridge) 1978. HSGC/NW: 46 v Northants (Lord's) 1976. HSJPL: 59 v Hants (Manchester) 1979. HSBH: 47 v Leics (Leicester) 1980. BB: 3-27 v Worcs (Manchester) 1981.

Paul John Walter ALLOTT (Durham University) B Altrincham, Cheshire 14/9/1956. RHB, RFM. Debut 1978. Cap 1981. Tests: 5 between 1981 and 1982. Tour: India and Sri Lanka 1981-82. HS: 52* England v Australia (Manchester) 1981. HSC: 30* v Essex (Blackpool) 1980. HSGC/NW: 19* v Worcs (Worcester) 1980. HSJPL: 22* v Middlesex (Manchester) 1979. HSBH: 10 v Notts (Nottingham) 1982. BB: 8-48 v Northants (Northampton) 1981. BBNW: 3-22 v Durham (Manchester) 1981. BBJPL: 3-15 v Warwicks (Birmingham) 1979. BBBH: 3-34 v Derby (Manchester) 1981.

Ian COCKBAIN B Bootle 19/4/1958. RHB, SLA. Debut 1979. HS: 98 v Warwicks (Southport) 1982. HSJPL: 53* v Glos (Manchester) 1982. HSBH: 53 v Worcs (Manchester) 1980.

Neil Harvey FAIRBROTHER B Warrington 9/9/1963. LHB. Debut 1982 in one match v Kent (Manchester) but did not bat or bowl.

Ian FOLLEY B Burnley 9/1/1963. RHB, LM. Debut 1982. HS: 36 v Derby (Manchester) 1982. HSBH: 11* v Notts (Nottingham) 1982. BB: 4-40 v Cambridge U (Cambridge) 1982. BBBH: 4-18 v Middlesex (Lord's) 1982.

Graeme FOWLER B Accrington 20/4/1957. LHB, WK. Debut 1979. Cap 1981. Tour: Australia and New Zealand 1982-83. 1,000 runs (2) – 1,560 runs (av. 39.00) in 1981 best. Tests: 1 in 1982. HS: 150 v Warwicks (Birmingham) 1982. HSTC: 86 England v Pakistan (Leeds) 1982. HSNW: 57 v Northants (Northampton) 1981. HSJPL: 65 v Worcs (Manchester) 1981. HSBH: 59 v Notts (Nottingham) 1982.

Frank Charles HAYES B Preston 6/12/1946. RHB, RM. Debut 1970 scoring 94 and 99 in first two matches. Cap 1972. County Captain 1978 to 1980. Tests: 9 between 1973 and 1976. Tours: D.H. Robins to South Africa 1972-73 and 1975-76, West Indies 1973-74, International Wanderers to South Africa 1975-76, International team to Pakistan 1981-82. Also played for Overseas XI v Board President's XI (Calcutta) 1980-81. 1,000 runs (6) – 1,311 runs (av. 35.43) in 1974 best. Scored 34 in one over (6 4 6 6 6 6) off M.A. Nash v Glamorgan (Swansea) 1977. Gillette Man of the Match Awards: 1. BH Gold Awards: 2. HS: 187 v Indians (Manchester) 1974. HSTC: 106* v West Indies (Oval) 1973 in second innings on Test debut. HSGC/NW: 93 v Warwickshire (Birmingham) 1976. HSJPL: 87 v Essex (Manchester) 1982. HSBH: 102 v Minor Counties (North) (Manchester) 1973. Amateur soccer player. Studied at Sheffield University. Benefit 1983.

Kevin Anthony HAYES (Oxford U) B Mexborough (Yorks) 26/9/1962. No relation to F.C. Hayes. RHB, RM. Debut 1980. Blue 1981. Secretary 1982. HS: 152 Oxford U v Warwicks (Oxford) 1982. HSC: 62 v Somerset (Taunton) 1982. HSBH: 17 Combined Universities v Essex (Chelmsford) 1981. Soccer Blues 1980-81, 1981-82.

David Paul HUGHES B Newton-le-Willows 13/5/1947. RHB, SLA. Debut 1967. Cap 1970. Played for Tasmania in 1975-76 and 1976-77. Testimonial in 1981. Tour: D.H. Robins to South Africa 1972-73. 1,000 runs (2) – 1,303 runs (av. 48.25) in 1982 best. Gillette Man of the Match: 1. BH Gold Awards: 1. HS: 126* v Yorks (Leeds) 1982. HSGC/NW: 42* v Middlesex (Lord's) 1974. HSJPL: 84 v Essex (Leyton) 1973. HSBH: 52 v Derbyshire (Manchester) 1981. BB: 7-24 v Oxford U (Oxford) 1970. BBGC/NW: 4-61 v Somerset (Manchester) 1972. BBJPL: 6-29 v Somerset (Manchester) 1977. BBBH: 5-23 v Minor Counties (West) (Watford) 1978.

Clive Hubert LLOYD B Georgetown, British Guiana 31/8/1944. 6ft 4½ins tall. Cousin of L.R. Gibbs. LHB, RM. Wears glasses. Debut 1963-64 for British Guiana. Played for Rest of World XI in 1967 and 1968. Debut for county 1968. Cap 1969. *Wisden* 1970. Testimonial (£27,199) in 1977. Appointed County Captain in 1981. Tests: 85 for West Indies between 1966-67 and 1981-82, captaining West Indies in 49 Tests, the record for all countries. Played in 5 matches for Rest of World 1970 and 2 in 1971-72. Scored 118 on debut v England (Port of Spain) 1967-68, 129 on debut v Australia (Brisbane) 1968-69, and 82 and 78* on debut v India (Bombay) 1966-67. Tours: West Indies to India and Ceylon 1966-67, Australia and New Zealand 1968-69, 1979–80 (captain), England 1969, 1973, 1976 (captain), and 1980 (captain), Rest of World to Australia 1971-72 (returning early owing to back injury), World XI to Pakistan 1973-74, India, Sri Lanka and Pakistan 1974-75 (captain), Australia 1975-76 (captain), 1981-82 (captain). Pakistan 1980-81 (captain). 1,000 runs (10) – 1,603 runs (av. 47.14) in 1970 best. Also scored 1,000 runs in 1968-69, 1974-75, 1975-76 and 1980-81. Scored 201* in 120 minutes for West Indies v Glamorgan (Swansea) 1976 to equal record for fastest double-century in first-class cricket. Gillette Man of the Match: 6. NW Man of the Match: 1. BH Gold Award: 1. HS: 242* West Indies v India (Bombay) 1974-75. HSUK: 217* v Warwickshire (Manchester) 1971. HSGC/NW: 126 v Warwickshire (Lord's) 1972. HSJPL: 134* v Somerset (Manchester) 1970. HSBH: 124 v Warwicks (Manchester) 1981. BB: 4-48 v Leics (Manchester) 1970. BBGC/NW: 3-39 v Somerset (Taunton) 1970. BBJPL: 4-33 v Middlesex (Lord's) 1971. BBBH: 3-23 v Derby (Manchester) 1974.

David LLOYD B Accrington 18/3/1947. LHB, SLA. Debut 1965. Cap 1968. County Captain from 1973 to 1977. Testimonial (£40,171) in 1978. Tests 9 in 1974 and 1974-75. Tours: Australia and New Zealand 1974-75, D.H. Robins to South

LANCASHIRE

Africa 1975-76. 1,000 runs (11) – 1,510 runs (av. 47.18) in 1972 best. Scored two centuries in match (116 and 104*) v Worcs (Southport) 1979. Gillette Man of the Match: 3. NW Man of the Match: 1. BH Gold Awards: 2. HS: 214* England v India (Birmingham) 1974. HSC: 195 v Glos (Manchester) 1973. HSGC/NW: 121* v Glos (Manchester) 1978. HSJPL: 103* v Northants (Bedford) 1971. HSBH: 113 v Minor Counties (North) (Manchester) 1973 and 113 v Scotland (Manchester) 1980. BB: 7-38 v Glos (Lydney) 1966. BBNW: 3-22 v Durham (Manchester) 1981. BBJPL: 3-23 v Glos (Manchester) 1980. BBBH: 4-17 v Notts (Manchester) 1980.

Leslie Leopold McFARLANE B Portland, Jamaica 19/8/1952. RHB, RM. Played for Northants in 1979. Debut for Lancs 1982. HS: 12 v Cambridge U (Cambridge) 1982. BB: 6-59 v Warwicks (Southport) 1982. BBJPL: 4-18 v Hants (Portsmouth) 1982.

Christopher MAYNARD B Haslemere (Surrey) 8/4/1958. RHB, WK. Played for Warwicks 1978 to 1982. Specially registered for Lancs in middle of 1982 season. Tour: D.H. Robins to New Zealand 1979-80. HS: 85 Warwicks v Kent (Birmingham) 1979. HSJPL: 35 Warwicks v Essex (Birmingham) 1979. HSBH: 60 v Notts (Nottingham) 1982.

Steven Joseph O'SHAUGHNESSY B Bury 9/9/1961. RHB, RM. Debut 1980. HS: 62 v Somerset (Taunton) 1982. HSNW: 13* v Middlesex (Manchester) 1981. HSJPL: 38 v Hants (Southampton) 1980. BB: 4-66 v Notts (Nottingham) 1982. BBJPL: 3-23 v Hants (Southampton) 1980.

Neal Victor RADFORD B Luanshya, Northern Rhodesia (now Zambia) 7/6/1957. RHB, RFM. Debut for Transvaal B 1978-79. Debut for county 1980. Did not play in 1982. HS: 76* v Derbyshire (Blackpool) 1981. HSJPL: 48* v Glamorgan (Cardiff) 1981. BB: 6-41 Transvaal B v Griqualand West (Kimberley) 1980-81. BBUK: 5-107 v Notts (Nottingham) 1981. BBNW: 3-20 v Middlesex (Manchester) 1981. BBJPL: 3-16 v Hants (Manchester) 1981.

Jack SIMMONS B Clayton-le-Moors (Lancs) 28/3/1941. RHB, OB. Debut 1968. Cap 1971. Played for Tasmania from 1972-73 to 1978-79 whilst coaching there and for Overseas XI v Board President's XI (Calcutta) 1980-81. Benefit (£128,000) in 1980. Hat-trick v Notts (Liverpool) 1977. Gillette Man of the Match: 1. BH Gold Awards: 2. HS: 112 v Sussex (Hove) 1970. HSGC/NW: 54* v Essex (Manchester) 1979. HSJPL: 65 v Essex (Manchester) 1980. HSBH: 64 v Derby (Manchester) 1978. BB: 7-59 Tasmania v Queensland (Brisbane) 1978-79. BBUK: 7-64 v Hants (Southport) 1973. BBGC/NW: 5-49 v Worcs (Worcester) 1974. BBJPL: 5-17 v Worcs (Worcester) 1982. BBBH: 4-31 v Yorks (Manchester) 1975. Has played soccer in Lancs Combination.

Gary John SPEAK B Chorley 26/4/1962. RHB, RFM. Debut 1981. HS: 15* v Cambridge U (Cambridge) 1982.

Timothy John TAYLOR (Stockport GS and Oxford) B Romiley (Cheshire) 28/3/1961. RHB, SLA. Debut for both county and university in 1981. Also played for Minor Counties v Sri Lankans (Reading). Blue 1981-82. HS: 28* Oxford U v Kent (Oxford) 1981. BB: 5-81 Oxford U v Middlesex (Oxford) 1981.

Mark Andrew WALLWORK B Urmston 14/12/1960. RHB, WK. Debut in 1982 (one match v Yorks).

Michael WATKINSON B Westhoughton 1/8/1961. RHB, RM. Debut 1982 (one match v Kent).

Roger Graeme WATSON B Rawtenstall 14/1/1964. LHB, OB. Debut 1982. HS: 11 v Somerset (Taunton) 1982.

NB. The following players whose particulars appeared in the 1982 Annual have been omitted: D.K. Beckett, C.E.H. Croft, P.A. Davis, M.A. Holding, A. Kennedy, P.G. Lee, H. Pilling, B.W. Reidy, C.J. Scott.

County Averages

Schweppes County Championship: Played 22, won 4, drawn 15, lost 3.
All first-class matches: Played 24, won 4, drawn 16, lost 4.

BATTING AND FIELDING

Cap		M	I	NO	Runs	HS	Avge	100	50	Ct	St
1971	J. Simmons	18	21	12	487	79*	54.11	—	4	14	—
—	K.A. Hayes	3	3	1	103	90	51.50	—	1	1	—
1970	D.P. Hughes	23	36	9	1303	126*	48.25	3	6	19	—
—	S.J. O'Shaughnessy	11	19	7	560	62	46.66	—	7	1	—
1981	G. Fowler	19	31	2	1246	150	42.96	5	4	5	—
1969	C.H. Lloyd	21	29	2	1135	100	42.03	1	9	19	—
1968	D. Lloyd	22	35	2	1336	114	40.48	5	7	8	—
—	J. Abrahams	23	32	5	1013	124	37.51	1	7	24	—
1972	F.C. Hayes	3	4	1	73	43	24.33	—	—	—	—
1975	A. Kennedy	9	12	1	242	43	22.00	—	—	7	—
—	I. Cockbain	14	25	1	492	98	20.50	—	2	4	—
1980	B.W. Reidy	9	13	2	199	37	18.09	—	—	7	—
—	I. Folley	17	15	4	165	36	15.00	—	—	3	—
1981	P.J.W. Allott	13	11	2	135	30	15.00	—	—	5	—
—	G.J. Speak	3	4	2	27	15*	13.50	—	—	3	—
—	C.E.H. Croft	12	12	3	109	20	12.11	—	—	5	—
—	C. Maynard	16	19	3	187	37	11.68	—	—	18	5
—	C.J. Scott	7	8	1	39	15	5.57	—	—	12	1
—	L.L. McFarlane	13	10	3	39	12	5.57	—	—	3	—
1972	P.G. Lee	3	1	0	0	0	—	—	—	—	—

Played in one match: N.H. Fairbrother did not bat; T.J. Taylor did not bat; M.A. Wallwork did not bat (3 ct); M. Watkinson did not bat; R.G. Watson 11, 4.

BOWLING

	Type	O	M	R	W	Avge	Best	5 wI	10 wM
D.P. Hughes	SLA	292.3	79	789	31	25.45	4-22	—	—
S.J. O'Shaughnessy	RM	209.2	34	710	27	26.29	4-66	—	—
J. Simmons	OB	538.4	152	1284	49	26.20	5-57	2	—
P.J.W. Allott	RFM	330	94	831	30	27.70	5-58	1	—
I. Folley	LFM	309	76	758	27	28.07	4-40	—	—
C.E.H. Croft	RF	303	61	1003	30	33.43	7-88	1	—
L.L. McFarlane	RFM	223.5	44	946	27	35.03	6-59	1	—
D. Lloyd	SLA	297.2	68	801	21	38.14	4-36	—	—
B.W. Reidy	LM	137	32	457	10	45.70	3-33	—	—
J. Abrahams	OB	316.1	59	921	16	57.56	2-19	—	—

Also bowled: I. Cockbain 2-2-0-0; G. Fowler 7-3-13-0; A. Kennedy 9-2-28-1;
P.G. Lee 32-3-101-2; G.J. Speak 53-6-176-1; T.J. Taylor 16-1-72-1; M. Watkinson
13-4-45-1.

County Records

First-class cricket

Highest innings totals:	For	801 v Somerset (Taunton)	1895
	Agst	634 by Surrey (Oval)	1898
Lowest innings totals:	For	25 v Derby (Manchester)	1871
	Agst	22 by Glamorgan (Liverpool)	1924
Highest individual innings:	For	424 A.C. MacLaren v Somerset (Taunton)	1895
	Agst	315* T.W. Hayward for Surrey (Oval)	1898
Best bowling in innings:	For	10-55 J. Briggs v Worcs (Manchester)	1900
	Agst	10-40 G.O.B. Allen for Middlesex (Lord's)	1929
Best bowling in a match:	For	17-91 H. Dean v Yorks (Liverpool)	1913
	Agst	16-65 G. Giffen for Australians (Manchester)	1886
Most runs in a season:		2,633 (av. 56.02) J.T. Tyldesley	1901
runs in a career:		34,222 (av. 45.20) G.E. Tyldesley	1909-1936
100s in a season:		11 by C. Hallows	1928
100s in a career:		90 by G.E. Tyldesley	1909-1936
wickets in a season:		198 (av. 18.55) E.A. McDonald	1925
wickets in a career:		1,816 (av. 15.12) J.B. Statham	1950-1968

RECORD WICKET STANDS

1st	368	A.C. MacLaren & R.H. Spooner v Glos (Liverpool)	1903
2nd	371	F.B. Watson & G.E. Tyldesley v Surrey (Manchester)	1928
3rd	306	E. Paynter & N. Oldfield v Hants (Southampton)	1938
4th	324	A.C. MacLaren & J.T. Tyldesley v Notts (Nottingham)	1904
5th	249	B. Wood & A. Kennedy v Warwicks (Birmingham)	1975
6th	278	J. Iddon & H.R.W. Butterworth v Sussex (Manchester)	1932
7th	245	A.H. Hornby & J. Sharp v Leics (Manchester)	1912
8th	158	J. Lyon & R.M. Ratcliffe v Warwickshire (Manchester)	1979
9th	142	L.O.S. Poidevin & A. Kermode v Sussex (Eastbourne)	1907
10th	173	J. Briggs & R. Pilling v Surrey (Liverpool)	1885

One-day cricket

Highest innings totals:	Gillette Cup/ NatWest Trophy	304-9 v Leics (Manchester)	1963
	John Player League	255-5 v Somerset (Manchester)	1970
	Benson & Hedges Cup	288-9 v Warwicks (Manchester)	1981
Lowest innings totals:	Gillette Cup/ NatWest Trophy	59 v Worcs (Worcester)	1963
	John Player League	76 v Somerset (Manchester)	1972
	Benson & Hedges Cup	82 v Yorks (Bradford)	1972
Highest individual innings:	Gillette Cup/ NatWest Trophy	131 A. Kennedy v Middlesex (Manchester)	1978
	John Player League	134* C.H. Lloyd v Somerset (Manchester)	1970
	Benson & Hedges Cup	124 C.H. Lloyd v Warwicks (Manchester)	1981
Best bowling figures:	Gillette Cup/ NatWest Trophy	5-28 J.B. Statham v Leics (Manchester)	1963
	John Player League	6-29 D.P. Hughes v Somerset (Manchester)	1977
	Benson & Hedges Cup	6-10 C.E.H. Croft v Scotland (Manchester)	1982

LEICESTERSHIRE

Formation of present club: 1879.
Colours: Scarlet and dark green.
Badge: Running fox (gold) on green background.
County Champions: 1975.
Gillette Cup Semi-Finalists: 1977.
NatWest Trophy Third Round: 1981.
John Player League Champions (2): 1974 and 1977.
Benson & Hedges Cup Winners (2): 1972 and 1975.
Benson & Hedges Cup Finalists: 1974.
Fenner Trophy Winners: 1979.
Gillette Man of the Match Awards: 15.
NatWest Man of the Match Awards: 1.
Benson & Hedges Gold Awards: 32.

Secretary/Manager: F.M. Turner, County Ground, Grace Road, Leicester LE2 8AD.
Captain: R.W. Tolchard.
Prospects of Play Telephone No: Leicester (0533) 836236.

Jonathan Philip AGNEW (Uppingham School) B Macclesfield, Cheshire 4/4/1960. RHB, RF. Debut 1978. Tour: Leics in Zimbabwe 1980-81. HS: 56 v Worcs (Worcester) 1982. BB: 6-70 v Zimbabwe (Salisbury) 1980-81. BBUK: 5-72 v Yorks (Bradford) 1981.

John Christopher BALDERSTONE B Huddersfield 16/11/1940. RHB, SLA. Played for Yorks 1961 to 1970. Debut for Leics 1971. Cap 1973. Tests: 2 in 1976. Tour: Leics in Zimbabwe 1980-81. 1,000 runs (8) – 1,482 (av. 39.00) in 1982 best. Shared 2nd wkt partnership record for county (289*) with D.I. Gower v Essex (Leicester) 1981. Hat-trick v Sussex (Eastbourne) 1976. GC Man of the Match: 2. BH Gold Awards: 8. HS: 178* v Notts (Nottingham) 1977. HSTC: 35 v West Indies (Leeds) 1976. HSGC/NW: 119* v Somerset (Taunton) 1973. HSJPL: 96 v Northants (Leicester) 1976. HSBH: 113* v Glos (Leicester) 1977. BB: 6-25 v Hants (Southampton) 1978. BBGC/NW: 4-33 v Herts (Leicester) 1977. BBJPL: 3-29 v Worcs (Leicester) 1971. Soccer for Huddersfield Town, Carlisle United, Doncaster Rovers and Queen of the South.

Timothy James BOON B Doncaster, Yorks 1/11/1961. RHB, RM. Debut 1980. Tour: Leics in Zimbabwe 1980-81. HS: 90 v Pakistanis (Leicester) 1982. HSC: 83 v Warwicks (Coventry) 1981. HSJPL: 39 v Surrey (Leicester) 1981.

Nigel Edwin BRIERS B Leicester 15/1/1955. RHB. Cousin of N. Briers who played once for county in 1967. Debut 1971 at age of 16 years 103 days. Youngest player ever to appear for county. Cap 1981. Tour: Leics to Zimbabwe 1980-81. 1,000 runs (2) – 1,194 runs (av. 36.18) in 1981 best. Shared in 5th wkt partnership record for county, 235 with R.W. Tolchard v Somerset (Leicester) 1979. BH Gold Awards: 1. HS: 119 v Warwicks (Birmingham) 1979. BSGC/NW 20 v Worcs (Leicester) 1979 and v Norfolk (Leicester) 1982. HSJPL: 119* v Hants (Bournemouth) 1981. HSBH: 71* v Hants (Southampton) 1979.

Ian Paul BUTCHER B Farnborough, Kent 1/7/1962. RHB, WK. Brother of A.R. Butcher of Surrey. Debut 1980. HS: 71* v Pakistanis (Leicester) 1982. HSJPL: 71 v Northants (Leicester) 1982. HSBH: 47 v Worcs (Worcester) 1982.

Patrick Bernard (Paddy) CLIFT (St George's College, Salisbury, Rhodesia) B Salisbury, Rhodesia 14/7/1953. RHB, RM. Played for Rhodesia 1971-72 to 1979-80 and Natal 1980-81 and 1981-82. Debut for county 1975. Cap 1976. Hat-trick v Yorks (Leicester) 1976. HS: 88* v Oxford U (Oxford) 1979, HSGC/NW: 48* v Worcs (Leicester) 1979. HSJPL: 51* v Somerset (Leicester) 1979. HSBH: 91 v Notts (Leicester) 1980. BB: 8-17 v MCC (Lord's) 1976. BBGC: 3-36 v Worcs (Leicester) 1979. BBJPL: 4-14 v Lancs (Leicester) 1978. BBBH: 4-13 v Minor Counties (East) (Amersham) 1978.

Russell Alan COBB (Trent College) B Leicester 18/5/1961. RHB, LM. Tours: D.H. Robins to New Zealand 1979-80, Leics to Zimbabwe 1980-81. Debut 1980. HS: 64 v Zimbabwe (Leicester) 1982. HSJPL: 24 v Worcs (Leicester) 1981.

Nicholas Grant Billson COOK B Leicester 17/6/1956. RHB, SLA. Debut 1978. Cap 1982. HS: 75 v Somerset (Taunton) 1980. HSJPL: 13* v Kent (Leicester) 1979 and 13* v Middlesex (Lord's) 1981. BB: 7-63 v Somerset (Taunton) 1982.

Brian Fettes DAVISON B Bulawayo, Rhodesia 21/12/1946. RHB, RM. Played for Rhodesia 1967-68 to 1978-79. Debut for county 1970 after having played for International Cavaliers. Cap 1971. County Captain in 1980. Played for Tasmania from 1979-80 to 1981-82. Is now regarded as an English player for qualification purposes. Benefit in 1982. 1,000 runs (12) – 1,818 runs (av. 56.81) in 1976 best. Gillette Man of the Match: 1. NW Man of the Match: 1. BH Gold Awards: 6. HS: 189 v Australians (Leicester) 1975. HSGC/NW 99 v Essex (Southend) 1977. HSJPL: 85* v Glamorgan (Cardiff) 1974. HSBH: 158* v Warwicks (Coventry) 1972. BB: 5-52 Rhodesia v Griqualand West (Bulawayo) 1967-68. BBUK: 4-99 v Northants (Leicester) 1970. BBJPL: 4-29 v Glamorgan (Neath) 1971. Has played hockey for Rhodesia.

Michael Anthony GARNHAM B Johannesburg 20/8/1960. RHB, WK. Debut for Glos 1979. Debut for Leics in 1980. HS: 74 v Kent (Leicester) 1981. BH Gold Award: 1. HSGC/NW: 25 v Essex (Leicester) 1980. HSJPL: 79* v Lancs (Leicester) 1982. HSBH: 55 v Derby (Leicester) 1982.

David Ivon GOWER (King's School, Canterbury) B Tunbridge Wells 1/4/1957. LHB, OB. Debut 1975. Cap 1977. *Wisden* 1978. Best Young Cricketer of the Year in 1978. Tests: 44 between 1978 and 1982. Tours: D.H. Robins to Sri Lanka 1977-78, Australia 1978-79, Australia and India 1979-80, West Indies 1980-81, India and Sri Lanka 1981-82, Australia and New Zealand 1982-83. 1,000 runs (4) – 1,530 (av. 46.36) in 1982 best. Shared in 2nd wkt partnership record for county, 289* with J.C. Balderstone v Essex (Leicester) 1981. Gillette Man of the Match: 1. BH Gold Awards: 1. HS: 200* England v India (Birmingham) 1979. HSC: 176* v Pakistanis (Leicester) 1982. HSGC/NW: 117* v Herts (Leicester) 1977. HSJPL: 135* v Warwicks (Leicester) 1977. HSBH: 114* v Derby (Derby) 1980. BB: 3-47 v Essex (Leicester) 1977.

Kenneth HIGGS B Sandyford (Staffordshire) 14/1/1937. LHB, RM. Debut for Lancs 1958. Cap 1959. *Wisden* 1967. Benefit (£8,390) in 1968. Retired after 1969 season. Reappeared for Leics in 1972. Cap 1972. Appointed County Vice-Captain in 1973 and County Captain for 1979 relinquishing post at end of season. Is now county coach. Tests: 15 between 1965 and 1968. Shared in 10th wkt partnership of 128 with J.A. Snow v West Indies (Oval) 1966 – 2 runs short of then record 10th wkt partnership in Test cricket. Also shared in 10th wkt partnership record for county, 228 with R. Illingworth v Northants (Leicester) 1977. Tours: Australia and New

LEICESTERSHIRE

Zealand 1965-66, West Indies 1967-68. 100 wkts (5) – 132 wkts (av. 19.42) in 1960 best. Hat-tricks (3) – Lancs v Essex (Blackpool) 1960, Lancs v Yorks (Leeds) 1968 and v Hants (Leicester) 1977. Hat-trick also in Benson & Hedges Cup Final v Surrey (Lord's) 1974. NW Man of the Match: 1. BH Gold Awards: 1. HS: 98 v Northants (Leicester) 1977. HSTC: 63 England v West Indies (Oval) 1966. HSGC/NW: 25 Lancs v Somerset (Taunton) 1966. HSJPL: 17* v Notts (Nottingham) 1975. HSBH: 10 v Surrey (Oval) 1981. BB: 7-19 Lancs v Leics (Manchester) 1965. BBTC: 6-91 v West Indies (Lord's) 1966. BBC: 7-44 v Middlesex (Lord's) 1978. BBGC/NW: 6-20 v Staffs (Longton) 1975. BBJPL: 6-17 v Glamorgan (Leicester) 1973. BBBH: 4-10 v Surrey (Lord's) 1974. Soccer for Port Vale.

Gordon James PARSONS B Slough (Bucks) 17/10/1959. LHB, RM. Debut 1978. Tour: Leics to Zimbabwe 1980-81. HS: 51 v Lancs (Leicester) 1982. HSGC/NW: 22 v Essex (Leicester) 1980. HSBH: 18* v Notts (Trent Bridge) 1982. BB: 5-25 v Essex (Leicester) 1982. BBJPL: 4-19 v Essex (Harlow) 1982. BBBH: 4-33 v Worcs (Leicester) 1981.

Anderson Montgomery Everton (Andy) ROBERTS B Antigua 29/1/1951. RHB, RF. Played for Leeward Islands and Combined Islands from 1969-70 to 1981-82. Debut for Hants 1973. Cap 1974. Wisden 1974. Played for New South Wales in 1976-77. Left Hants in 1978. Debut for Leics 1981. Tests: 40 for West Indies between 1973-74 and 1981-82. Tours: West Indies to India, Sri Lanka and Pakistan 1974-75, Australia 1975-76, 1981-82, England 1976 and 1980, Australia and New Zealand 1979-80. Took 100th wkt in Test cricket in 1976 in then record time of 2 years 142 days. Took 119 wkts (av. 13.62) in 1974. Hat-trick for Combined Islands v Jamaica (St. Kitts) 1980-81. BH Gold Awards: 1 (for Hants). HS: 63 Combined Islands v Guyana (Grenada) 1980-81. HSUK: 57 v Essex (Colchester) 1981. HSTC: 54 West Indies v Australia (Melbourne) 1979-80. HSNW: 46 v Somerset (Taunton) 1982. HSJPL: 59* v Somerset (Leicester) 1981. HSBH: 29 Hants v Glos (Bristol) 1975 and 29 v Surrey (Oval) 1981. BB: 8-47 Hants v Glamorgan (Cardiff) 1974. BBC: 8-56 v Glamorgan (Leicester) 1982. BBTC: 7-54 West Indies v Australia (Perth) 1975-76. BBGC/NW: 3-17 Hants v Glamorgan (Southampton) 1975. BBJPL: 5-13 Hants v Sussex (Hove) 1974. BBBH: 4-12 Hants v Somerset (Bournemouth) 1975.

John Frederick STEELE B Stafford 23/7/1946. Younger brother of D.S. Steele of Northants. RHB, SLA. Debut 1970. Was 12th man for England v Rest of World (Lord's) a month after making debut. Cap 1971. Played for Natal in 1973-74, 1975-76 and 1977-78. Tour: D.H. Robins to South Africa 1974-75. 1,000 runs (6) – 1,347 runs (av. 31.32) in 1972 best. Shared in 1st wkt partnership record for county, 390 with B. Dudleston v Derby (Leicester) 1979. Gillette Man of the Match: 3. BH Gold Awards: 4. HS: 195 v Derby (Leicester) 1971. HSGC/NW: 108* v Staffs (Longton) 1975. HSJPL: 92 v Essex (Leicester) 1973. HSBH: 91 v Somerset (Leicester) 1974. BB: 7-29 Natal B v Griqualand West (Umzinto) 1973-74 and 7-29 v Glos (Leicester) 1980. BBGC/NW: 5-19 v Essex (Southend) 1977. BBJPL: 5-22 v Glamorgan (Leicester) 1979. BBBH: 3-17 v Cambridge U (Leicester) 1972. Benefit 1983.

Leslie Brian TAYLOR B Earl Shilton 25/10/1953. RHB, RFM. Debut 1977. Cap 1981. Tour: Leics to Zimbabwe 1980-81. Played for Natal in 1981-82. Hat-trick v Middlesex (Leicester) 1979. HS: 25 v Notts (Leicester) 1982. HSJPL: 15* v Somerset (Taunton) 1980. BB: 7-28 v Derby (Leicester) 1981. BBNW: 4-34 v Norfolk (Leicester) 1982. BBJPL: 5-23 v Notts (Nottingham) 1978. BBBH: 6-35 v Worcs (Worcester) 1982.

Roger William TOLCHARD (Malvern College) B Torquay 15/6/1946. RHB, WK. Debut 1965. Cap 1966. Appointed County Captain in 1981. Tests: 4 in 1976-77. Tours: International XI in East Africa, Pakistan, India and Ceylon 1967-68, India, Pakistan and Sri Lanka 1972-73, D.H. Robins to South Africa 1973-74, 1974-75 and 1975-76, Sri Lanka 1977-78, International Wanderers to Rhodesia 1974-75, India, Sri Lanka and Australia 1976-77, Australia 1978-79, Leics to Zimbabwe 1980-81. Played for Overseas XI v Board Presidents XI (Calcutta) 1980-81. Scored 998 runs (av. 30.24) in 1970. Shared in 5th-wicket partnership record for county, 235 with N.E. Briers v Somerset (Leicester) 1979. BH Gold Awards: 4. HS: 126* v Cambridge U (Cambridge) 1970. HSGC/NW: 86* v Glos (Leicester) 1975. HSJPL: 103 v Middlesex (Lord's) 1972 and was dismissed obstructing the field. HSBH: 92* v Worcs (Worcester) 1976. Benefit 1979.

NB. The following players whose particulars appeared in the 1982 Annual have been omitted: G. Forster and D.A. Wenlock.

County Averages

Schweppes County Championship: Played 22, won 10, drawn 8, lost 4.
All first-class matches: Played 25, won 10, drawn 11, lost 4.

BATTING AND FIELDING

Cap		M	I	NO	Runs	HS	Avge	100	50	Ct	St
1971	B.F. Davison	22	37	4	1800	172	54.54	7	8	16	—
1977	D.I. Gower	12	21	1	1017	176*	50.85	2	8	4	—
1973	J.C. Balderstone	23	41	3	1482	148	39.00	4	8	17	—
1981	N.E. Briers	23	38	4	1175	106	34.55	1	6	12	—
1976	P.B. Clift	5	6	2	123	45	30.75	—	—	1	—
—	I.P. Butcher	6	9	3	182	71*	30.33	—	1	5	—
1966	R.W. Tolchard	23	38	8	843	93*	28.10	—	7	44	8
—	R.A. Cobb	22	37	1	759	63	21.08	—	4	11	—
—	A.M.E. Roberts	13	20	3	338	47	19.88	—	—	4	—
—	M.A. Garnham	11	17	2	298	57	19.86	—	3	13	4
1971	J.F. Steele	20	31	6	497	64	19.86	—	2	28	—
1982	N.G.B. Cook	24	25	8	284	37	16.70	—	—	19	—
—	T.J. Boon	9	14	1	210	90	16.15	—	1	3	—
—	G.J. Parsons	24	32	7	392	51	15.68	—	1	7	—
—	G. Forster	3	3	1	28	22*	14.00	—	—	2	—
—	J.P. Agnew	10	12	1	122	56	11.09	—	1	1	—
1981	L.B. Taylor	21	23	8	119	25	7.93	—	—	2	—
—	D.A. Wenlock	3	3	0	15	9	5.00	—	—	1	—

Played in one match: K. Higgs did not bat.

BOWLING

	Type	O	M	R	W	Avge	Best	5 wI	10 wM
A.M.E. Roberts	RF	427.2	114	1081	55	19.65	8-56	5	1
J.F. Steele	SLA	470.2	134	1075	52	20.67	5-4	3	—
L.B. Taylor	RFM	582.2	153	1465	67	21.86	5-24	3	—
N.G.B. Cook	SLA	827.1	252	2027	87	23.29	7-63	6	1
J.C. Balderstone	SLA	79	23	187	7	26.71	4-51	—	—
G.J. Parsons	RM	517.5	93	1931	50	38.62	5-25	1	—
P.B. Clift	RM	113	27	294	7	42.00	2-49	—	—
J.P. Agnew	RF	203.5	27	816	19	42.94	4-55	—	—

Also bowled: N.E. Briers 29-4-86-4; R.A. Cobb 4-2-5-0; G. Forster 44-11-125-1;
D.I. Gower 5-2-10-0; K. Higgs 19-5-64-1; D.A. Wenlock 30.1-7-104-4.

County Records

First-class cricket

Highest innings	For	701-4d v Worcs (Worcester)	1906
totals:	Agst	739-7d by Notts (Nottingham)	1903
Lowest innings	For	25 v Kent (Leicester)	1912
totals:	Agst	24 by Glamorgan (Leicester)	1971
Highest indi-	For	252* S. Coe v Northants (Leicester)	1914
vidual innings:	Agst	341 G.H. Hirst for Yorks (Leicester)	1905
Best bowling	For	10-18 G. Geary v Glamorgan (Pontypridd)	1929
in an innings:	Agst	10-32 H. Pickett for Essex (Leyton)	1958
Best bowling	For	16-96 G. Geary v Glamorgan (Pontypridd)	1929
in a match:	Agst	16-102 C. Blythe for Kent (Leicester)	1909
Most runs in a season:		2,446 (av. 52.04) G.L. Berry	1937
runs in a career:		30,143 (av. 30.32) G.L. Berry	1924-1951
100s in a season:		7 by G.L. Berry, W. Watson	1937, 1959
		and B.F. Davison	and 1982
100s in a career:		45 by G.L. Berry	1924-1951
wickets in a season:		170 (av. 18.96) J.E. Walsh	1948
wickets in a career:		2,130 (av. 23.19) W.E. Astill	1906-1939

RECORD WICKET STANDS

1st	390	B. Dudleston & J.F. Steele v Derby (Leicester)	1979
2nd	339*	J.C. Balderstone & D.I. Gower v Essex (Leicester)	1981
3rd	316*	W. Watson & A. Wharton v Somerset (Taunton)	1961
4th	270	C.S. Dempster & G.S. Watson v Yorks (Hull)	1937
5th	233	N.E. Briers & R.W. Tolchard v Somerset (Leicester)	1979
6th	262	A.T. Sharpe & G.H.S. Fowke v Derby (Chesterfield)	1911
7th	206	B. Dudleston & J. Birkenshaw v Kent (Canterbury)	1969
8th	164	M.R. Hallam & C.T. Spencer v Essex (Leicester)	1964
9th	160	W.W. Odell & R.T. Crawford v Worcs (Leicester)	1902
10th	228	R. Illingworth & K. Higgs v Northants (Leicester)	1977

One-day cricket

Highest innings totals:	Gillette Cup/ NatWest Trophy	326-6 v Worcs (Leicester)	1979
	John Player League	262-6 v Somerset (Frome)	1970
	Benson & Hedges Cup	327-4 v Warwicks (Coventry)	1972
Lowest innings totals:	Gillette Cup/ NatWest Trophy	56 v Northants (Leicester)	1964
	John Player League	36 v Sussex (Leicester)	1973
	Benson & Hedges Cup	56 v Minor Counties (Wellington)	1982
Highest individual innings:	Gillette Cup/ NatWest Trophy	125 B. Dudleston v Worcs (Leicester)	1979
	John Player League	152 B. Dudleston v Lancs (Manchester)	1975
	Benson & Hedges Cup	158* B.F. Davison v Warwicks (Coventry)	1972
Best bowling figures:	Gillette Cup/ NatWest Trophy	6-20 K. Higgs v Staffs (Longton)	1975
	John Player League	6-17 K. Higgs v Glamorgan (Leicester)	1973
	Benson & Hedges Cup	6-35 L.B. Taylor v Worcs (Worcester)	1982

MIDDLESEX

Formation of present club: 1863.
Colours: Blue.
Badge: Three seaxes.
County Champions (8): 1866, 1903, 1920, 1921, 1947, 1976, 1980 and 1982.
Joint Champions (2): 1949 and 1977.
Gillette Cup Winners: 1977 and 1980.
Gillette Cup Finalists: 1975.
NatWest Trophy Semi-final: 1982.
Best Position in John Player League: 2nd in 1982.
Benson & Hedges Cup Finalists: 1975.
Gillette Man of the Match Awards: 27.
NatWest Man of the Match Awards: 2.
Benson & Hedges Gold Awards: 25.

Secretary: A.J. Wright, Lord's Cricket Ground, St. John's Wood Road, London NW8 8QN.
Captain: M.W. Gatting.
Prospects of Play Telephone No: 01-286 8011.

Graham Derek BARLOW B Folkestone 26/3/1950. LHB, RM. Debut 1969. Cap 1976. Tests: 3 in 1976-77 and 1977. Tour: India, Sri Lanka and Australia 1976-77. 1,000 runs (5): 1,478 (av. 49.26) in 1976 best. Shared 1st wkt partnership record for county (367*) with W.N. Slack v Kent (Lord's) 1981. GC Man of the Match: 1. BH Gold Awards: 2. HS: 177 v Lancs (Southport) 1981. HSTC: 7* v India (Calcutta) 1976-77. HSGC/NW: 76* v Warwicks (Birmingham) 1975. HSJPL: 114 v Warwicks (Lord's) 1979. HSBH: 129 v Northants (Northampton) 1977.

Roland Orlando BUTCHER B East Point, St. Philip, Barbados 14/10/1953. RHB, RM. Debut 1974. Played for Barbados in 1974-75 Shell Shield competition. Cap 1979. Tests: 3 v West Indies in 1980-81. Tours: Middlesex to Zimbabwe 1981-82, West Indies 1980-81, International XI to Pakistan 1981-82. Scored 1,058 runs (av. 43.32) in 1982. HS: 197 v Yorks (Lord's) 1982. HSTC: 32 v West Indies (Kingston) 1980-81. HSGC/NW: 50* v Surrey (Lord's) 1980. HSJPL: 94 v Surrey (Oval) 1979. HSBH: 50* v Glamorgan (Lord's) 1981.

Colin Roy COOK (Merchant Taylor's School, Northwood) B Edgware 11/1/1960. RHB. Debut 1981. HS: 79 v Lancs (Southport) 1981 in debut match. HSJPL: 73 v Glos (Lord's) 1981.

Norman George COWANS B Enfield St. Mary, Jamaica 17/4/1961. RHB, RFM. Debut 1980. Tours: Middlesex to Zimbabwe 1980-81, Australia and New Zealand 1982-83. NW Man of the Match: 1. HS: 10 v Oxford U (Oxford) 1981. HSJPL: 14* v Sussex (Hove) 1982. BB: 5-58 v Leics (Leicester) 1981. BBNW: 4-26 v Lancs (Lord's) 1982. BBJPL: 4-44 v Sussex (Hove) 1982.

Wayne Wendell DANIEL B St. Philip, Barbados 16/1/1956. RHB, RF. Played for Barbados 1975-76 to date. Debut for county and cap 1977. Tests: 5 for West Indies in 1975-76 and 1976. Tours: West Indies to England 1976, Young West Indies to Zimbabwe 1981-82. Hat-trick v Lancs (Southport) 1981. Gillette Man of the Match: 2. BH Gold Awards: 2. Took 51 wkts (av. 13.72) in limited-overs matches in 1980 to equal record of R.J. Clapp of Somerset in 1974. HS: 53* Barbados v Jamaica

112

(Bridgetown) 1979-80 and 53* v Yorks (Lord's) 1981. HSTC: 11 West Indies v India (Kingston) 1975-76. HSGC/NW: 14 v Lancs (Manchester) 1978. HSJPL: 14 v Kent (Lord's) 1980. HSBH: 20* v Derby (Derby) 1978. BB: 9-61 v Glamorgan (Swansea) 1982. BBTC: 4-53 West Indies v England (Nottingham) 1976. BBGC/NW: 6-15 v Sussex (Hove) 1980. BBJPL: 5-27 v Lancs (Lord's) 1982. BBBH: 7-12 v Minor Counties (East) (Ipswich) 1978 – record for competition.

Paul Rupert DOWNTON (Sevenoaks School) B Farnborough (Kent) 4/4/1957. Son of G. Downton, former Kent player. RHB, WK. Debut for Kent 1977. Cap 1979. Debut for Middlesex in 1980. Cap 1981. Tests: 4 in 1980-81 and 1981. Tours: Pakistan and New Zealand 1977-78, Middlesex to Zimbabwe 1980-81, West Indies 1980-81. HS: 90* v Derby (Uxbridge) 1980. HSTC: 26* v West Indies (Kingston) 1980-81. HSNW: 40* v Glos (Bristol) 1982. HSJPL: 58* v Worcs (Worcester) 1982. HSBH: 11 v Hants (Lord's) 1981.

Phillipe Henri EDMONDS (Cambridge) B Lusaka, Northern Rhodesia (now Zambia) 8/3/1951. RHB, SLA. Debut for Cambridge U and county 1971. Blue 1971-73 (capt in 1973). Cap 1974. Best Young Cricketer of the Year in 1974. Played for Eastern Province in 1975-76. Tests: 21 between 1975 and 1982. Tours: Pakistan and New Zealand 1977-78, Australia 1978-79. Hat-trick v Leics (Leicester) 1981. NW Man of the Match: 1. BH Gold Awards: 2. HS: 141* v Glamorgan (Lord's) 1979. HSTC: 64 v India (Lord's) 1982. HSGC/NW: 63* v Somerset (Lord's) 1979. HSJPL: 52 v Somerset (Taunton) 1980. HSBH: 44* v Notts (Newark) 1976. BB: 8-80 v Sussex (Lord's) 1982. BBTC: 7-66 v Pakistan (Karachi) 1977-78. BBNW: 5-12 v Cheshire (Enfield) 1982. BBJPL: 3-19 v Leics (Lord's) 1973. BBBH: 4-11 v Kent (Lord's) 1975. Also played rugby for University and narrowly missed obtaining Blue. Benefit 1983.

Richard Gary Peter ELLIS (Haileybury College and Oxford) B Paddington 20/2/1960. RHB, OB. Debut for Oxford U 1981. Blue 1981-82. University captain 1982. Debut for Middlesex 1982. HS: 105* v Surrey (Oxford) 1982. HSC: 55 v Sussex (Hove) 1982. HSJPL: 21 v Worcs (Worcester) 1982. HSBH: 32 Combined Universities v Essex (Chelmsford) 1981.

John Ernest EMBUREY B Peckham 20/8/1952. RHB, OB. Debut 1973. Cap 1977. Tests: 22 between 1978 and 1982. Tours: D.H. Robins to Sri Lanka 1977-78, Australia 1978-79, Australia and India 1979-80 (as replacement for G. Miller), Middlesex to Zimbabwe 1980-81, West Indies 1980-81, India and Sri Lanka 1981-82, SAB to South Africa 1981-82. Banned from Test cricket for 3 years. BH Gold Awards: 1. HS: 100* v Northants (Lord's) 1982. HSTC: 57 v Australia (Manchester) 1981. HSGC/NW: 36* v Lancs (Manchester) 1978. HSJPL: 35* v Warwicks (Lord's) 1981. HSBH: 44* v Glos (Bristol) 1982. BB: 7-36 v Cambridge U (Cambridge) 1977. BBTC: 6-33 v Sri Lanka (Colombo) 1981-82. BBJPL: 4-25 v Warwicks (Birmingham) 1982. BBBH: 3-35 v Kent (Lord's) 1980.

Michael William GATTING B Kingsbury 6/6/1957. RHB, RM. Debut 1975. Cap 1977. Best Young Cricketer of the Year in 1981. Captain 1983. Tests: 22 between 1977-78 and 1982. Tours: Pakistan and New Zealand 1977-78, Middlesex to Zimbabwe 1980-81, West Indies 1980-81, India and Sri Lanka 1981-82. 1,000 runs (4) – 1,651 (av. 58.96) in 1982 best. Gillette Man of the Match: 1. BH Gold Awards: 2. HS: 192 v Surrey (Oval) 1982. HSTC: 59 v Australia (Lord's) 1981. HSGC/NW: 95* v Notts (Nottingham) 1980. HSJPL: 85 v Notts (Lord's) 1976. HSBH: 95* v Somerset (Taunton) 1980. BB: 5-34 v Glamorgan (Swansea) 1982. BBJPL: 4-32 v Kent (Lord's) 1978. BBBH: 3-19 v Kent (Lord's) 1980.

MIDDLESEX

Simon Peter HUGHES B Kingston-upon-Thames 20/12/1959. RHB, RFM. Debut 1980. Cap 1981. Gillette Man of the Match: 1. HS: 18 v Kent (Maidstone) 1981 and v Worcs (Worcester) 1982. BB: 6-75 v Lancs (Southport) 1981. BBGC/NW: 3-23 v Worcs (Worcester) 1980.

Kevan David JAMES B Lambeth 18/3/1961. LHB, LM. Debut 1980. HS: 16 v Oxford U (Oxford) 1980. HSJPL: 13 v Kent (Canterbury) 1981. BB: 3-14 v Oxford U (Oxford) 1980.

Rajesh Jaman MARU B Nairobi, Kenya 28/10/1962. RHB, SLA. Debut 1980. Tour: Middlesex to Zimbabwe 1980-81. HS: 25 v Zimbabwe (Bulawayo) 1980-81. HSUK: 18 v Glamorgan (Swansea) 1982. BB: 4-30 v Oxford U (Oxford) 1982.

William Gerald MERRY B Newbury (Berks) 8/8/1955. RHB, RM. Debut 1979. HS: 14* v Oxford U (Oxford) 1981. HSJPL: 13 v Glamorgan (Swansea) 1982. BB: 4-24 v Somerset (Taunton) 1980. BBJPL: 3-29 v Lancs (Manchester) 1979. BBBH: 3-19 Minor Counties (West) v Derby (Derby) 1978.

James Dermot MONTEITH (Royal Belfast Academical Institute) B Lisburn (Co Antrim, Northern Ireland) 2/6/1943. RHB, SLA. Played for Ireland 1965 to 1982. Debut for county 1981. Had match double of 100 runs and 10 wickets (26 and 78, 7-38 and 5-57) Ireland v Scotland (Cork) 1973. HS: 78 Ireland v Scotland (Cork) 1973. HSC: 36 v Hants (Uxbridge) 1982. HSJPL: 10 v Warwicks (Lord's) 1981. BB: 7-38 Ireland v Scotland (Cork) 1973. BBC: 5-68 v Northants (Northampton) 1981.

Clive Thornton RADLEY B Hertford 13/5/1944. RHB, LB. Debut 1964. Cap 1967. Benefit (£26,000) in 1977. *Wisden* 1978. Tests: 8 in 1977-78 and 1978. Tours: D.H. Robins to South Africa 1972-73 and 1974-75, Pakistan and New Zealand 1977-78 (as replacement for J.M. Brearley), Australia 1978-79, Middlesex to Zimbabwe 1980-81. 1,000 runs (14) – 1,491 runs (av. 57.34) in 1980 best. Shared in 6th wicket partnership record for county, 227 with F.J. Titmus v South Africans (Lord's) 1965. Gillette man of the Match: 2. BH Gold Awards: 2. HS: 171 v Cambridge U (Cambridge) 1976. HSTC: 158 v New Zealand (Auckland) 1977-78. HSGC/NW: 105* v Worcs (Worcester) 1975. HSJPL: 133* v Glamorgan (Lord's) 1969. HSBH: 121* v Minor Counties (East) (Lord's) 1976.

Wilfred Norris SLACK B Troumaca, St. Vincent 12/12/1954. LHB, RM. Debut 1977. Cap 1981. 1,000 runs (2) 1,499 (av. 44.08) in 1982 best. Shared 1st wicket partnership record for county, 367* with G.D. Barlow v Kent (Lord's) 1981. HS: 248* v Worcs (Lord's) 1981. HSNW: 54* v Cheshire (Enfield) 1982. HSJPL: 77 v Somerset (Weston-super-Mare) 1982. HSBH: 60* v Combined Universities (Cambridge) 1982. BB: 3-17 v Leics (Uxbridge) 1982.

Keith Patrick TOMLINS B Kingston-upon-Thames 23/10/1957. RHB, RM. Debut 1977. HS: 146 v Oxford U (Oxford) 1982. HSJPL: 58 v Warwicks (Birmingham) 1982. BBJPL: 4-24 v Notts (Lord's) 1978.

Neil Fitzgerald WILLIAMS B Hope Well, St Vincent, WI 2/7/1962. RHB, RFM. Debut 1982. HS: 27* v Essex (Lord's) 1982. BB: 4-38 v Oxford U (Oxford) 1982. BBBH: 3-16 v Combined Universities (Cambridge) 1982.

NB. The following players whose particulars appeared in the 1982 Annual have been omitted: J.M. Brearley, C.P. Metson, M.W.W. Selvey, A.G. Smith, C.R.V. Taylor, J.R. Thomson.

County Averages

Schweppes County Championship: Played 22, won 12, drawn 8, lost 2.
All first-class matches: Played 25, won 14, drawn 9, lost 2.

BATTING AND FIELDING

Cap		M	I	NO	Runs	HS	Avge	100	50	Ct	St
1977	M.W. Gatting	18	25	4	1462	192	69.61	6	5	24	—
1964	J.M. Brearley	20	32	9	1083	165	47.08	3	4	18	—
1981	W.N. Slack	25	40	6	1499	203*	44.08	2	10	20	—
1979	R.O. Butcher	21	28	3	1058	197	42.32	3	2	22	—
—	K.P. Tomlins	13	17	1	607	146	37.93	2	3	8	—
1977	J.E. Emburey	24	27	5	752	100*	34.18	1	4	16	—
—	R.G.P. Ellis	3	5	0	157	55	31.40	—	2	—	—
1967	C.T. Radley	21	28	3	773	141*	30.92	2	2	20	—
—	N.J. Kemp	5	6	2	121	46*	30.25	—	—	5	—
1974	P.H. Edmonds	17	18	4	406	92	29.00	—	3	6	—
1973	M.W.W. Selvey	10	6	1	114	36*	22.80	—	—	2	—
1976	G.D. Barlow	7	12	3	199	37*	22.11	—	—	5	—
—	P.R. Downton	25	25	2	483	65	21.00	—	2	51	10
—	N.F. Williams	12	11	5	112	27*	18.66	—	—	2	—
—	R.J. Maru	4	4	1	45	18	14.75	—	—	2	—
1977	W.W. Daniel	19	15	9	88	21	14.66	—	—	13	—
—	C.R. Cook	3	3	0	38	36	12.66	—	—	2	—
—	N.G. Cowans	11	10	1	63	16	7.00	—	—	8	—
—	S.P. Hughes	10	8	4	27	18	6.75	—	—	—	—
—	W.G. Merry	4								3	—

Played in one match: K.D. James 1; J.D. Monteith 36, 1; F.J. Titmus 1*.

BOWLING

	Type	O	M	R	W	Avge	Best	5 wI	10 wM
R.J. Maru	SLA	54.2	26	88	7	12.57	4-30	—	—
M.W. Gatting	RM	111	32	283	19	14.89	5-34	1	—
W.W. Daniel	RF	468.5	107	1245	71	17.53	9-61	5	1
P.H. Edmonds	SLA	675.4	206	1475	73	20.20	8-80	3	2
N.G. Cowans	RFM	222.3	50	721	33	21.84	5-28	2	—
W.N. Slack ·	RM	81	18	225	10	22.50	3-17	—	—
J.E. Emburey	OB	764.5	198	1787	77	23.20	5-50	2	—
S.P. Hughes	RFM	218.5	30	723	27	26.77	4-28	—	—
M.W.W. Selvey	RFM	254.5	74	597	20	29.85	3-47	—	—
N.F. Williams	RFM	236.4	34	819	23	35.60	4-38	—	—

Also bowled: J.M. Brearley 1-0-3-0; R.O. Butcher 1-0-10-0; K.D. James 6-1-13-1;
N.J. Kemp 66-13-180-4; W.G. Merry 76.2-18-201-3; J.D. Monteith 6-1-18-0;
C.T. Radley 4-0-27-0; F.J. Titmus 25-4-92-3; K.P. Tomlins 12.3-1-73-2.

County Records

First-class cricket

Highest innings totals:	For	642-3d v Hants (Southampton)	1923
	Agst	665 by West Indians (Lord's)	1939
Lowest innings totals:	For	20 v MCC (Lord's)	1864
	Agst	31 by Glos (Bristol)	1924
Highest individual innings:	For	331* J.D.B. Robertson v Worcs (Worcester)	1949
	Agst	316* J.B. Hobbs for Surrey (Lord's)	1926
Best bowling in an innings:	For	10-40 G.O.B. Allen v Lancs (Lord's)	1929
	Agst	9-38 R.C. Robertson-Glasgow for Somerset (Lord's)	1924
Best bowling in a match:	For	16-114 { G. Burton v Yorks (Sheffield)	1888
		{ J.T. Hearne v Lancs (Manchester)	1898
	Agst	16-109 C.W.L. Parker for Glos (Cheltenham)	1930
Most runs in a season:		2,650 (av. 85.48) W.J. Edrich	1947
runs in a career:		40,302 (av. 48.82) E.H. Hendren	1907-1937
100s in a season:		13 by D.C.S. Compton	1947
100s in a career:		119 by E.H. Hendren	1907-1937
wickets in a season:		158 (av. 14.63) F.J. Titmus	1955
wickets in a career:		2,361 (av. 21.27) F.J. Titmus	1949-1982

RECORD WICKET STANDS

1st	367*	G.D. Barlow & W.N. Slack v Kent (Lord's)	1981
2nd	380	F.A. Tarrant & J.W. Hearne v Lancs (Lord's)	1914
3rd	424*	W.J. Edrich & D.C.S. Compton v Somerset (Lord's)	1948
4th	325	J.W. Hearne & E.H. Hendren v Hants (Lord's)	1919
5th	338	R.S. Lucas & T.C. O'Brien v Sussex (Hove)	1895
6th	227	C.T. Radley & F.J. Titmus v South Africans (Lord's)	1965
7th	271*	E.H. Hendren & F.T. Mann v Notts (Nottingham)	1925
8th	182*	M.H.C. Doll & H.R. Murrell v Notts (Lord's)	1913
9th	160*	E.H. Hendren & T.J. Durston v Essex (Leyton)	1927
10th	230	R.W. Nicholls & W. Roche v Kent (Lord's)	1899

One-day cricket

Highest innings totals:	Gillette Cup/ NatWest Trophy	280-8 v Sussex (Lord's)	1965
	John Player League	256-9 v Worcs (Worcester)	1976
	Benson & Hedges Cup	303-7 v Northants (Northampton)	1977
Lowest innings totals:	Gillette Cup/ NatWest Trophy	41 v Essex (Westcliff)	1972
	John Player League	23 v Yorks (Leeds)	1974
	Benson & Hedges Cup	97 v Northants (Lord's)	1976
Highest individual innings:	Gillette Cup/ NatWest Trophy	124* J.M. Brearley v Bucks (Lord's)	1975
	John Player League	133* C.T. Radley v Glamorgan (Lord's)	1969
	Benson & Hedges Cup	129 G.D. Barlow v Northants (Northampton)	1977
Best bowling figures:	Gillette Cup/ NatWest Trophy	6-15 W.W. Daniel v Sussex (Hove)	1980
	John Player League	6-6 R.W. Hooker v Surrey (Lord's)	1969
	Benson & Hedges Cup	7-12 W.W. Daniel v Minor Counties (East) (Ipswich)	1978

NORTHAMPTONSHIRE

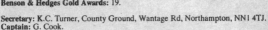

Formation of present club: 1878.
Colours: Maroon.
Badge: Tudor Rose.
County Championship Runners-up (4): 1912, 1957, 1965 and 1976.
Gillette Cup Winners: 1976.
Gillette Cup Finalists: 1979.
NatWest Trophy Finalists: 1981.
Best final position in John Player League: 4th in 1974.
Benson & Hedges Cup Winners: 1980.
Fenner Trophy Winners: 1978.
Gillette Man of the Match Awards: 17.
NatWest Man of the Match Awards: 15.
Benson & Hedges Gold Awards: 19.

Secretary: K.C. Turner, County Ground, Wantage Rd, Northampton, NN1 4TJ.
Captain: G. Cook.
Prospects of Play Telephone No: Northampton (0604) 37040.

Robert John BAILEY B Biddulph, Staffordshire 28/10/1963. RHB, OB. Debut 1982. HS: 10 v Sussex (Eastbourne) 1982.

Martin John BAMBER B Cheam, Surrey 7/1/1961. RHB, RM. Debut 1982. HS: 31 v Cambridge U (Cambridge) 1982.

Robin James BOYD-MOSS (Bedford School and Cambridge) B Hattoh, Ceylon 16/12/1959. RHB, SLA. Debut for Cambridge U and County in 1980. Blue 1980-82. Scored 1,602 runs (av. 44.50) in 1982. HS: 137 v Derby (Northampton) 1982. HSJPL: 62 v Warwicks (Northampton) 1981. HSBH: 58 Combined Universities v Northants (Northampton) 1980. BB: 4-42 Cambridge U v Oxford U (Lord's) 1982. Rugby Blue 1980-81, 1981-82.

David John CAPEL B Northampton 6/2/1963. RHB, RM. Debut 1981. HS: 60* v Somerset (Northampton) 1982. HSJPL: 79 v Kent (Northampton) 1982. HSBH: 25 v Warwicks (Birmingham) 1982. BBJPL: 4-30 v Yorks (Middlesbrough) 1982.

Geoffrey COOK B Middlesbrough 9/10/1951. RHB, SLA. Debut 1971. Cap 1975. Played for Eastern Province from 1978-79 to 1980-81. Appointed County Captain in 1981. Tours: India and Sri Lanka 1981-82, Australia and New Zealand 1982-83. 1,000 runs (7) – 1,759 runs (av. 43.97) in 1981 best. Gillette Man of Match: 2. NatWest Man of the Match: 2. BH Gold Awards: 2. HS: 172 Eastern Province v Northern Transvaal (Port Elizabeth) 1979-80. HSUK: 155 v Derby (Northampton) 1978. HSGC/NW: 114* v Surrey (Northampton) 1979. HSJPL: 85 v Leics (Leicester) 1976. HSBH: 96 v Minor Counties (East) (Northampton) 1978.

Brian James GRIFFITHS B Wellingborough 13/6/1949. RHB, RFM. Debut 1974. Cap 1978. HS: 16 v Glos (Bristol) 1982. HSJPL: 11* v Surrey (Tring) 1982. BB: 8-50 v Glamorgan (Northampton) 1981. BBGC/NW: 3-39 v Leics (Northampton) 1979. BBJPL: 4-22 v Somerset (Weston-super-Mare) 1977. BBBH: 5-43 v Sussex (Eastbourne) 1979.

NORTHAMPTONSHIRE

KAPIL DEV NIKHANJ B Chandigarh, India 6/1/1959. RHB, RFM. Debut for Haryana in Ranji Trophy 1975-76 aged 16 years 10 months taking 6-39 in debut match v Punjab (Rohtak). Debut for county 1981. *Wisden* 1983. Tests: 41 for India between 1978-79 and 1982. Tours: India to England 1979, Australia and New Zealand 1980-81. Is youngest player to take 100 wkts in Test cricket (21 years 25 days) and score 1,000 runs (21 years 27 days). Took 100 wkts in 1 year 107 days to beat record held previously by I.T. Botham. Hat-trick North Zone v West Zone (Delhi) 1978-79. HS: 193 Haryana v Punjab (Chandigarh) 1979-80. HSTC: 126* India v West Indies (Delhi) 1978-79. HSUK: 103 v Sussex (Eastbourne) 1982. HSJPL: 75 v Derby (Milton Keynes) 1982. BB: 8-38 Haryana v Services (Rohtak) 1977-78. BBTC: 7-56 India v Pakistan (Madras) 1979-80. BBUK: 5-39 Indians v Notts (Nottingham) 1982.

Allan Joseph LAMB B Langebaanweg, Cape Province, South Africa 20/6/1954. RHB, RM. Played for Western Province 1972-73 to 1981-82. Debut for county and cap 1978. *Wisden* 1980. Tests: 6 in 1981-82 and 1982. Tour: Australia and New Zealand 1982-83. 1,000 runs (4) – 2,049 runs (av. 60.26) in 1981 best. BH Gold Awards: 3. HS: 178 v Leics (Leicester) 1979. HSGC/NW: 101 v Sussex (Hove) 1979. HSJPL: 127* v Worcs (Worcester) 1981. HSBH: 95 v Notts (Northampton) 1982.

Hon. Timothy Michael LAMB (Shrewsbury School and Oxford) B Hartford (Cheshire) 24/3/1953. RHB, RM. Debut for Oxford U 1973. Blue 1973-74. Debut for Middlesex 1974. Left county and made debut for Northants 1978. Cap 1978. NW Man of the Match: 1. BH Gold Awards: 1. HS: 77 Middlesex v Notts (Lord's) 1976. HSC: 30* v Glos (Northampton) 1982. HSGC/NW: 12 v Surrey (Oval) 1980. HSJPL: 27 Middlesex v Hants (Basingstoke) 1976. HSBH: 10* v Combined Universities (Northampton) 1980. BB: 7-56 v Cambridge U (Cambridge) 1980. BBGC/NW: 4-52 v Sussex (Hove) 1979. BBJPL: 5-13 v Notts (Northampton) 1979. BBBH: 5-44 Middlesex v Yorks (Lord's) 1975.

Wayne LARKINS B Roxton (Beds) 22/11/1953. RHB, RM. Debut 1972. Cap 1976. Tests: 6 between 1979-80 and 1981. Tours: Australia and India 1979-80, SAB to South Africa 1981-82. Banned from Test cricket for 3 years. Played for Overseas XI v Board President's XI (Calcutta) 1980-82. 1,000 runs (5) – 1,863 (av. 45.43) in 1982 best. Shared in 2nd wkt partnership record for county, 322 with R.G. Williams v Leics (Leicester) 1980. Hat-trick in Benson & Hedges Cup v Combined Universities (Northampton) 1980. NW Man of the Match: 1. BH Gold Awards: 4. HS: 186 v Yorks (Middlesbrough) 1980. HSTC: 34 v Australia (Oval) 1981. HSGC/NW: 92* v Leics (Northampton) 1979. HSJPL: 158 v Worcs (Luton) 1982. HSBH: 132 v Warwicks (Birmingham) 1982. BB: 3-34 v Somerset (Northampton) 1976. BBJPL: 5-32 v Essex (Ilford) 1978. BBBH: 4-37 v Combined Universities (Northampton) 1980.

Neil Alan MALLENDER B Kirk Sandall (Yorks) 13/8/1961. RHB, RFM. Debut 1980. HS: 42 v Leics (Leicester) 1982. HSJPL: 22 v Warwicks (Northampton) 1981. BB: 7-41 v Derby (Northampton) 1982. BBNW: 3-35 v Derby (Lord's) 1981. BBJPL: 5-34 v Middlesex (Tring) 1981. BBBH: 3-13 v Worcs (Worcester) 1981.

George SHARP B West Hartlepool 12/3/1959. RHB, WK. Can also bowl SLA. Debut 1968. Cap 1973. Benefit in 1982. HS: 94 v Lancs (Southport) 1980. HSGC/NW: 35* v Durham (Northampton) 1977. HSJPL: 47 v Sussex (Hove) 1974 and 47* v Worcs (Milton Keynes) 1978. HSBH: 43 v Surrey (Northampton) 1979.

David Stanley STEELE B Stoke-on-Trent 29/9/1941. Elder brother of J.F. Steele of Leics and cousin of B.S. Crump, former Northants player. Wears glasses. RHB, SLA. Debut for Northants 1963. Cap 1965. Benefit (£25,500) in 1975. *Wisden* 1975. Transferred to Derbyshire in 1979 as county captain. Relinquished post during season. Cap 1979. Rejoined Northants for 1982. Tests: 8 in 1975 and 1976. 1,000 runs (10) – 1,756 (av. 48.77) in 1975 best. Hat-trick v Glamorgan (Derby) 1980. Had match double of 100 runs and 10 wkts (130, 6-36 and 5-39) v Derbyshire (Northampton) 1978. Gillette Man of the Match: 1. NW Man of the Match: 1 (for Derbyshire). HS: 140* v Worcs (Worcester) 1971. HSTC: 106 v West Indies (Nottingham) 1976. HSGC/NW: 109 v Cambs (March) 1975. HSJPL: 76 v Sussex (Hove) 1974. HSBH: 71 Derby v Notts (Nottingham) 1980. BB: 8-29 v Lancs (Northampton) 1966. BBNW: 3-23 Derby v Suffolk (Bury St. Edmunds) 1981. BBJPL: 4-21 Derby v Notts (Derby) 1979. BBBH: 3-27 v Scotland (Glasgow) 1982.

Duncan James WILD B Northampton 28/11/1962. Son of J. Wild, former Northants player. LHB, RM. Debut 1980. HS: 30 v Essex (Southend) 1981. HSJPL: 18 v Derby (Derby) 1981.

Peter WILLEY B Sedgefield, County Durham 6/12/1949. RHB, OB. Debut 1966 aged 16 years 180 days scoring 78 in second innings of first match v Cambridge U (Cambridge). Cap 1971. Benefit (£31,400) in 1981. Tests: 20 between 1976 and 1981. Tours: D.H. Robins to South Africa 1972-73 and to Sri Lanka 1977-78, Australia and India 1979-80, West Indies 1980-81, SAB to South Africa 1981-82. Banned from Test cricket for 3 years. 1,000 runs (3) – 1,783 (av. 50.94) in 1982 best. Shared in 4th wkt partnership record for county, 370 with R.T. Virgin v Somerset (Northampton) 1976. Gillette Man of the Match: 4. NW Man of the Match: 1. BH Gold Awards: 1. HS: 227 v Somerset (Northampton) 1976. HSTC: 102* v West Indies (St. John's) 1980-81. HSGC/NW: 89 v Sussex (Hove) 1979. HSJPL: 107 v Warwicks (Birmingham) 1975 and 107 v Hants (Tring) 1976. HSBH: 66* v Warwicks (Birmingham) 1980. BB: 7-37 v Oxford U (Oxford) 1975. BBGC/NW: 3-37 v Cambs (March) 1975. BBJPL: 4-38 v Leics (Leicester) 1980. BBBH: 3-12 v Minor Counties (East) (Horton) 1977.

Richard Grenville WILLIAMS B Bangor, Caernarvonshire 10/8/1957. RHB, OB. Debut 1974 aged 16 years 313 days. Cap 1979. 1,000 runs (4) – 1,262 runs (av. 34.10) in 1980 best. Scored two centuries in match (109 and 151*) v Warwicks (Northampton) 1979. Shared in 2nd wkt partnership record for county, 322 with W. Larkins v Leics (Leicester) 1980. Hat-trick v Glos (Northampton) 1980. Gillette Man of the Match: 1. BH Gold Awards: 2. HS: 175* v Leics (Leicester) 1980. HSGC/NW: 51 v Durham (Northampton) 1977. HSJPL: 82 v Glos (Bristol) 1982. HSBH: 83 v Yorks (Bradford) 1980. BB: 7-73 v Cambridge U (Cambridge) 1980. BBGC/NW: 3-15 v Leics (Northampton) 1979. BBJPL: 4-22 v Yorks (Scarborough) 1980.

Thomas James YARDLEY B Chaddesley Corbett, Worcs 27/10/1946. LHB, RM. Occasional WK. Debut for Worcs 1967. Cap 1972. Not re-engaged after 1975 season and made debut for Northants in 1976. Cap 1978. Scored 1,066 runs (av. 30.45) in 1971. HS: 135 Worcs v Notts (Worcester) 1973. HSC: 100* v Glos (Northampton) 1980. HSGC/NW: 52 Worcs v Warwicks (Birmingham) 1972 and 52* Worcs v Warwicks (Birmingham) 1973. HSJPL: 66* v Middlesex (Lord's) 1977. HSBH: 75* Worcs v Warwicks (Worcester) 1972.

NB. The following players whose particulars appeared in the 1982 Annual have been omitted: J.P.C. Mills, N. Priestley and Sarfraz Nawaz.

County Averages

Schweppes County Championship: Played 22, won 5, drawn 14, lost 3.
All first-class matches: Played 25, won 6, drawn 16, lost 3.

BATTING AND FIELDING

Cap		M	I	NO	Runs	HS	Avge	100	50	Ct	St
1978	A.J. Lamb	12	19	1	1047	140	58.16	4	4	5	—
1971	P. Willey	23	41	6	1783	145	50.94	5	8	10	—
—	Kapil Dev	6	9	2	332	103	47.42	2	1	8	—
1976	W. Larkins	24	44	3	1863	186	45.43	5	9	13	—
1982	R.J. Boyd-Moss	14	24	4	885	137	44.25	2	7	10	—
1965	D.S. Steele	25	36	13	853	74*	37.08	—	4	19	—
1975	G. Cook	19	34	2	1067	125	33.34	3	5	21	—
—	R.M. Carter	11	19	6	411	79	31.61	—	1	12	—
1979	R.G. Williams	24	39	4	1087	141	31.05	2	4	3	—
1978	T.M. Lamb	13	13	8	137	39*	27.40	—	—	1	—
—	D.J. Capel	14	22	4	460	60*	25.55	—	1	8	—
—	D.J. Wild	7	7	2	113	29	22.60	—	—	—	—
1973	G. Sharp	25	26	7	401	58*	21.10	—	1	47	7
1978	T.J. Yardley	4	7	1	111	39	18.50	—	—	4	—
1975	Sarfraz Nawaz	8	8	1	108	26	15.42	—	—	4	—
—	N.A. Mallender	24	17	8	121	42	13.44	—	—	10	—
1978	B.J. Griffiths	19	11	4	39	16	5.57	—	—	5	—

Played in two matches: R. Bailey 10, 4, 3 (1 ct).
Played in one match: M. Bamber 27, 31.

BOWLING

	Type	O	M	R	W	Avge	Best	5 wI	10 wM
B.J. Griffiths	RFM	411.1	91	1200	46	26.08	5-71	2	—
D.S. Steele	SLA	754	245	1846	70	26.37	6-59	6	1
P. Willey	OB	670.1	223	1371	51	26.88	6-17	1	—
Sarfraz Nawaz	RFM	200.4	48	569	20	28.95	4-33	—	—
R.G. Williams	OB	274	75	747	21	35.57	4-25	—	—
N.A. Mallender	RFM	563.2	131	1860	51	36.47	7-41	3	1
T.M. Lamb	RM	308.5	76	850	20	42.50	5-37	1	—
Kapil Dev	RFM	139.4	32	404	9	44.88	2-17	—	—
D.J. Capel	RM	98.5	9	432	6	72.00	2-14	—	—

Also bowled: R.J. Boyd-Moss 2-0-26-0; R.M. Carter 38-7-145-2; G. Cook 3-0-14-0; A.J. Lamb 2-1-1-0; W. Larkins 17-2-66-1; G. Sharp 3-0-19-0; D.J. Wild 52.3-10-182-4.

County Records

First-class cricket

Highest innings totals:	For	557-6d v Sussex (Hove)	1914
	Agst	670-9d by Sussex (Hove)	1921
Lowest innings totals:	For	12 v Glos (Gloucester)	1907
	Agst	33 by Lancs (Northampton)	1977
Highest individual innings	For	300 R. Subba Row v Surrey (Oval)	1958
	Agst	333 K.S. Duleepsinhji for Sussex (Hove)	1930
Best bowling in an innings:	For	10-127 V.W.C. Jupp v Kent (Tunbridge Wells)	1932
	Agst	10-30 C. Blythe for Kent (Northampton)	1907
Best bowling in a match:	For	15-31 G.E. Tribe v Yorks (Northampton)	1958
	Agst	17-48 C. Blythe for Kent (Northampton)	1907
Most runs in a season:		2198 (av. 51.11) D. Brookes	1952
runs in a career:		28980 (av. 36.13) D. Brookes	1934-1959
100s in a season:		8 by R.A. Haywood	1921
100s in a career:		67 by D. Brookes	1934-1959
wickets in a season:		175 (av. 18.70) G.E. Tribe	1955
wickets in a career:		1097 (av. 21.31) E.W. Clark	1922-1947

RECORD WICKET STANDS

1st	361	N. Oldfield & V. Broderick v Scotland (Peterborough)	1953
2nd	322	W. Larkins & R.G. Williams v Leics (Leicester)	1980
3rd	320	L. Livingston & F. Jakeman v South Africans (Northampton)	1951
4th	370	R.T. Virgin & P. Willey v Somerset (Northampton)	1976
5th	347	D. Brookes & D.W. Barrick v Essex (Northampton)	1952
6th	376	R. Subba Row & A. Lightfoot v Surrey (Oval)	1958
7th	229	W.W. Timms & F.A. Walden v Warwicks (Northampton)	1926
8th	155	F.R. Brown & A.E. Nutter v Glamorgan (Northampton)	1952
9th	156	R. Subba Row & S. Starkie v Lancs (Northampton)	1955
10th	148	B.W. Bellamy & J.V. Murdin v Glamorgan (Northampton)	1925

One-day cricket

Highest innings totals:	Gillette Cup/ NatWest Trophy	275-5 v Notts (Nottingham)	1976
	John Player League	282-4 v Yorks (Middlesbrough)	1982
	Benson & Hedges Cup	259-5 v Scotland (Glasgow)	1982
Lowest innings totals:	Gillette Cup/ NatWest Trophy	62 v Leics (Leicester)	1974
	John Player League	41 v Middlesex (Northampton)	1972
	Benson & Hedges Cup	85 v Sussex (Northampton)	1978
Highest individual innings:	Gillette Cup/ NatWest Trophy	114* G. Cook v Surrey (Northampton)	1979
	John Player League	158 W. Larkins v Worcs (Luton)	1982
	Benson & Hedges Cup	132 W. Larkins v Warwicks (Birmingham)	1982
Best bowling figures:	Gillette Cup/ NatWest Trophy	5-24 J.D.F. Larter v Leics (Leicester)	1964
	John Player League	7-39 A. Hodgson v Somerset (Northampton)	1976
	Benson & Hedges Cup	5-21 Sarfraz Nawaz v Middlesex (Lord's)	1980

NOTTINGHAMSHIRE

Formation of present club: 1841, reorganised 1866.
Colours: Green and gold.
Badge: County Badge of Nottinghamshire.
County Champions (13): 1865, 1868, 1871, 1872, 1875, 1880, 1883, 1884, 1885, 1886, 1907, 1929 and 1981.
Joint Champions (5): 1869, 1873, 1879, 1882 and 1889.
Gillette Cup Semi-Finalists: 1969.
NatWest Trophy Third Round: 1981.
Best final position in John Player League: 5th in 1975 and 1982.
Benson & Hedges Finalists: 1982.
Gillette Man of the Match Awards: 13.
NatWest Man of the Match Awards: 3.
Benson & Hedges Gold Awards: 28.

Chief Executive: B. Robson, County Cricket Ground, Trent Bridge, Nottingham NG2 6AG.
Cricket Manager: K. Taylor.
Captain: C.E.B. Rice.
Prospects of Play Telephone No: Nottingham (0602) 869681.

John Dennis BIRCH B Nottingham 18/6/1955. RHB, RM. Debut 1973. Cap 1981. 1,000 runs (1) – 1,011 (av. 34.86) in 1982. BH Gold Award: 1. HS: 125 v Leics (Nottingham) 1982. HSGC/NW: 32 v Yorks (Bradford) 1978. HSJPL: 71 v Yorks (Scarborough) 1978. HSBH: 85 v Minor Counties (North) (Nottingham) 1979. BB: 6-64 v Hants (Bournemouth) 1975. BBJPL: 3-29 v Glamorgan (Swansea) 1976.

Michael Kenneth BORE B Hull 2/6/1947. RHB, LM. Played for Yorks 1969 to 1978. Debut for Notts 1979. Cap 1980. BH Gold Award: 1. HS: 37* Yorks v Notts (Bradford) 1973. HSC: 24* v Yorks (Nottingham) 1980. HSJPL: 28* v Northants (Northampton) 1979. BB: 8-89 v Kent (Folkestone) 1979. BBGC/NW: 3-35 Yorks v Kent (Canterbury) 1971. BBJPL: 4-21 Yorks v Sussex (Middlesbrough) 1971 and v Worcs (Worcester) 1970. BBBH: 6-22 v Leics (Leicester) 1980.

Kevin Edward COOPER B Hucknall (Notts) 27/12/1957. LHB, RFM. Debut 1976. Cap 1980. HS: 38* v Cambridge U (Cambridge) 1982. HSNW: 11 v Glos (Nottingham) 1982. HSJPL: 12 v Northants (Northampton) 1982. HSBH: 14 v Leics (Nottingham) 1982. BB: 6-32 v Derby (Derby) 1978. BBJPL: 4-25 v Hants (Nottingham) 1976. BBBH: 4-23 v Kent (Canterbury) 1979.

Mark Andrew FELL B Newark 17/11/1960. RHB, SLA. Debut 1982. HS: 108 v Essex (Nottingham) 1982. HSJPL: 28 v Warwicks (Nottingham) 1982. HSBH: 26 v Lancs (Nottingham) 1982.

Bruce Nicholas FRENCH B Warsop 13/8/1959. RHB, WK. Debut 1976 aged 16 years 287 days. Cap 1980. HS: 79 v Leics (Leicester) 1982. HSNW: 33* v Kent (Canterbury) 1981. HSJPL: 25 v Northants (Nottingham) 1978. HSBH: 16 v Surrey (Nottingham) 1981.

Richard John HADLEE B Christchurch, New Zealand 3/7/1951. Youngest son of W.A. Hadlee, former New Zealand Test cricketer, and brother of D.R. Hadlee. LHB, RFM. Played for Canterbury 1971-72 to 1981-82. Debut for county and cap 1978. Played for Tasmania in 1979-80. *Wisden* 1981. Tests: 38 for New Zealand between 1972-73 and 1981-82. Tours: New Zealand to England 1973 and 1978. Australia 1972-73, 1973-74 and 1980-81, Pakistan and India 1976-77. Took 105 wkts (av. 14.89) in 1981. NW Man of the Match Awards: 1. BH Gold Awards: 4. HS: 142* v Yorks (Bradford) 1981. HSTC: 103 New Zealand v West Indies (Christchurch) 1979-80. HSNW: 38* v Kent (Canterbury) 1981. HSJPL: 100* v Glos (Cheltenham) 1982. HSBH: 70 v Warwicks (Nottingham) 1982. BB: 7-23 New Zealand v India (Wellington) 1975-76 and 7-23 v Sussex (Nottingham) 1979. BBJPL: 6-12 v Lancs (Nottingham) 1980. BBBH: 4-13 Derby (Nottingham) 1980.

Sheikh Basharat HASSAN B Nairobi, Kenya 24/3/1944. RHB, RM, occasional WK. Debut for East Africa Invitation XI v MCC 1963-64. Played for Coast Invitation XI v Pakistan International Airways 1964. Also played for Kenya against these and other touring sides. Debut for county 1966. Cap 1970. Benefit in 1978. BH Award: 1. 1,000 runs (5) – 1,395 runs (av. 32.44) in 1970 best. Scored century with aid of a runner v Kent (Canterbury) 1977. HS: 182* v Glos (Nottingham) 1977. HSGC/NW: 79 v Hants (Southampton) 1977. HSJPL: 120* v Warwicks (Birmingham) 1981. HSBH: 99* v Warwicks (Nottingham) 1982. BB: 3-33 v Lancs (Manchester) 1976. BBGC/NW: 3-20 v Durham (Chester-le-Street) 1967.

Edward Ernest HEMMINGS B Leamington Spa 20/2/1949. RHB, OB. Debut for Warwicks 1966. Cap 1974. Left staff after 1978 season and made debut for Notts in 1979. Cap 1980. Hat-trick Warwicks v Worcs (Birmingham) 1977. Tour: Australia and New Zealand 1982-83. HS: 127 v Yorks (Worksop) 1982. HSGC/NW: 20 Warwicks v Worcs (Birmingham) 1973. HSJPL: 44* Warwicks v Kent (Birmingham) 1971. HSBH: 61* Warwicks v Leics (Birmingham) 1974. BB: 7-33 Warwicks v Cambridge U (Cambridge) 1975. BBC: 7-59 (13-129 match) v Derby (Nottingham) 1981. BBJPL: 5-22 Warwicks v Northants (Birmingham) 1974. BBBH: 3-18 Warwicks v Oxford and Cambridge Universities (Coventry) 1975. Took all 10 wickets for 175 for International XI v West Indies XI (Kingston) 1982-83.

Michael HENDRICK B Darley Dale (Derbyshire) 22/10/1948. RHB, RFM. Debut for Derbyshire 1969. Cap 1972. Best Young Cricketer of the Year in 1973. *Wisden* 1977. Benefit (£36,050) in 1980. Left county after 1981 season and made debut for Notts 1982. Tests: 30 between 1974 and 1981. Tours: West Indies 1973-74, Australia and New Zealand 1974-75, D.H. Robins to South Africa 1975-76, Pakistan and New Zealand 1977-78, Australia 1978-79, Australia (returned home early through injury) 1979-80, SAB to South Africa 1981-82. Banned from Test cricket for 3 years. Hat-trick Derby v West Indians (Derby) 1980. Gillette Man of the Match: 1 (for Derby). BH Gold Awards: 3 (for Derby). HS: 46 Derby v Essex (Chelmsford) 1973. HSTC: 15 v Australia (Oval) 1977. HSGC/NW: 17 Derby v Middlesex (Derby) 1978. HSJPL: 21 Derby v Warwicks (Buxton) 1974. HSBH: 32 Derby v Notts (Chesterfield) 1973. BB: 8-45 Derby v Warwicks (Chesterfield) 1973. BBTC: 4-28 v India (Birmingham) 1974. BBGC/NW: 4-15 Derby v Middlesex (Chesterfield) 1975. BBJPL: 6-7 Derbyshire v Notts (Nottingham) 1972. BBBH: 6-33 v Northants (Northampton) 1982.

Nigel John Bertie ILLINGWORTH (Denstone College) B Chesterfield 23/11/1960. RHB, RM. Debut 1981. HS: 49 v Cambridge U (Cambridge) 1982. BB: 5-89 v Middlesex (Lord's) 1982. BBJPL: 4-15 v Leics (Nottingham) 1982.

NOTTINGHAMSHIRE

Paul JOHNSON B Newark 24/4/1965. RHB, RM. Debut 1982. HS: 37* v Derby (Nottingham) 1982. HSJPL: 16 v Lancs (Nottingham) 1982.

Derek William RANDALL B Retford 24/2/1951. RHB, RM. Debut 1972. Cap 1973. *Wisden* 1979. Tests: 33 between 1976-77 and 1982. Tours: D.H. Robins to South Africa 1975-76, India, Sri Lanka and Australia 1976-77, Pakistan and New Zealand 1977-78, Australia 1978-79, Australia and India 1979-80, Australia and New Zealand 1982-83. 1,000 runs (8) – 1,546 runs (av. 42.94) in 1976 best. Scored two centuries in match (209 and 146) v Middlesex (Nottingham) 1979. Gillette Man of Match: 1. BH Gold Awards: 3. HS: 209 v Middlesex (Nottingham) 1979. HSTC: 174 v Australia (Melbourne) 1976-77. HSGC/NW: 75 v Sussex (Hove) 1979. HSJPL: 107* v Middlesex (Lord's) 1976. HSBH: 103* v Minor Counties (North) (Nottingham) 1979. BB: 3-15 v MCC (Lord's) 1982. Benefit 1983.

Clive Edward Butler RICE B Johannesburg 23/7/1949. RHB, RFM. Played for Transvaal 1969-70 to 1981-82. Played for D.H. Robins XI v West Indians 1973 and Pakistanis 1974. Debut for county and cap 1975. Appointed county captain for 1978, but was relieved of appointment when his signing for World Series Cricket was announced. Re-appointed county captain during 1979 season. *Wisden* 1980. 1,000 runs (8) – 1,871 runs (av. 66.82) in 1978 best. Scored two centuries in match (131* and 114*) v Somerset (Nottingham) 1980. Scored 105* out of innings total of 143 v Hants (Bournemouth) 1981 – lowest innings total in first-class cricket to contain a century. BH Gold Awards: 5. HS: 246 v Sussex (Hove) 1976. HSGC/NW: 71 v Yorks (Bradford) 1978. Scored 157 for Transvaal v Orange Free State (Bloemfontein) 1975-76 in South African Gillette Cup competition. HSJPL: 120* v Glamorgan (Swansea) 1978. HSBH: 130* v Scotland (Glasgow) 1982. BB: 7-62 Transvaal v Western Province (Johannesburg) 1975-76. BBUK: 6-16 v Worcs (Worcester) 1977. BBNW: 6-18 v Sussex (Hove) 1982. BBJPL: 4-15 v Hants (Nottingham) 1980. BBBH: 6-22 v Northants (Northampton) 1981.

Robert Timothy ROBINSON B Sutton-in-Ashfield (Notts) 21/11/1958. RHB, RM. Debut 1978. BH Gold Awards: 1. HS: 138 v Leics (Nottingham) 1980. HSNW: 44* v Sussex (Hove) 1982. HSJPL: 56 v Essex (Chelmsford) 1982. HSBH: 77* v Worcs (Nottingham) 1981.

Kevin SAXELBY B Worksop 23/2/1959. RHB, RM. Debut 1978. HS: 59* v Derby (Chesterfield) 1982. HSJPL: 10* v Sussex (Hove) 1982. HSBH: 13* v Lancs (Nottingham) 1982. BB: 4-18 v Hants (Nottingham) 1982. BBJPL: 4-37 v Yorks (Nottingham) 1981.

Christopher William SCOTT B Thorpe-on-the-Hill (Lincs) 23/1/1964. RHB, WK. Debut 1981. HS: 17* v Indians (Nottingham) 1982.

Peter Mark SUCH B Helensburgh, Scotland 12/6/1964. RHB, OB. Debut 1982. BB: 5-112 v Glos (Cheltenham) 1982).

NB. The following players whose particulars appeared in the 1982 Annual have been omitted: M.J. Harris, I.L. Pont, P.A. Todd, N.I. Weightman, R.A. White and P.G. Wood.

County Averages

Schweppes County Championship: Played 22, won 8, drawn 6, lost 7, abandoned 1.
All first-class matches: Played 25, won 8, drawn 9, lost 7, abandoned 1.

BATTING AND FIELDING

Cap		M	I	NO	Runs	HS	Avge	100	50	Ct	St
1973	D.W. Randall	13	22	3	846	122	44.53	1	7	14	—
1981	J.D. Birch	22	35	6	1011	125	34.86	2	6	11	—
1975	C.E.D. Rice	22	36	3	1095	144	33.18	1	5	25	—
1970	S.B. Hassan	19	34	4	970	89*	32.33	—	7	18	—
1978	R.J. Hadlee	18	28	2	807	131	31.04	2	4	16	—
1980	E.E. Hemmings	18	21	8	391	127*	30.08	1	—	14	—
—	R.T. Robinson	21	38	3	984	109	28.11	1	5	13	—
1980	B.N. French	23	34	6	721	79	25.75	—	5	61	3
1977	P.A. Todd	12	21	2	461	117*	24.26	2	1	13	—
—	M.A. Fell	10	18	0	315	108	17.50	1	—	9	—
—	K. Saxelby	14	15	5	160	59*	16.00	—	1	2	—
—	N.J.B. Illingworth	11	14	4	158	49	15.80	—	1	4	—
—	P.A. Johnson	4	7	1	90	37*	15.00	—	—	1	—
1980	M.K. Bore	8	8	5	44	23*	14.67	—	—	4	—
1980	K.E. Cooper	23	26	5	247	38*	11.76	—	—	8	—
—	M. Hendrick	10	10	4	54	29	9.00	—	—	6	—
—	I.L. Pont	4	7	1	32	16	5.33	—	—	1	—
—	P.M. Such	8	9	3	3	2	0.50	—	—	7	—

Played in two matches: M.J. Harris 41, 43*, 31* (1 ct).
Played in one match: C.W. Scott 17*, 14 (2 ct); N.I. Weightman 36.

BOWLING

	Type	O	M	R	W	Avge	Best	5 wI	10 wM
R.J. Hadlee	RF	403.5	123	889	61	14.57	7-25	4	—
M. Hendrick	RFM	244.2	86	473	26	18.19	5-21	1	—
K. Saxelby	RM	291.4	68	799	37	21.59	4-18	—	—
M.K. Bore	LM	279.4	104	609	28	21.75	6-134	1	—
E.E. Hemmings	OB	606	190	1462	61	23.97	6-76	3	—
K.E. Cooper	RFM	685	192	1719	68	25.28	6-46	2	—
P.M. Such	OB	232.1	51	737	25	29.48	5-112	1	—
C.E.B. Rice	RFM	78.5	25	206	6	34.33	2-10	—	—
N.J.B. Illingworth	RM	164.1	29	565	14	40.36	5-89	1	—

Also bowled: J.D. Birch 2.3-0-19-1; M.A. Fell 45-7-146-1; I.L. Pont 78.5-13-302-3;
D.W. Randall 3.5-1-15-3; R.T. Robinson 7-0-41-1; N.I. Weightman 1-0-4-0.

County Records

First-class cricket

Highest innings totals:	For	739-7d v Leics (Nottingham)	1903
	Agst	706-4d by Surrey (Nottingham)	1947
Lowest innings totals:	For	13 v Yorks (Nottingham)	1901
	Agst	16 by Derby (Nottingham) and Surrey (Oval)	1879 & 1880

NOTTINGHAMSHIRE

Highest indi-	For	312* W.W. Keeton v Middlesex (Oval)
vidual innings:	Agst	345 C.G. Macartney for Australians (Nottingham)
Best bowling	For	10-66 K. Smales v Glos (Stroud)
in an innings:	Agst	10-10 H. Verity for Yorks (Leeds)
Best bowling	For	17-89 F.C.L. Matthews v Northants (Nottingham)
in a match:	Agst	17-89 W.G. Grace for Glos (Cheltenham)
Most runs in a season:		2,620 (av. 53.46) W.W. Whysall
runs in a career:		31,592 (av. 35.70) G. Gunn
100s in a season:		9 by W.W. Whysall
		and M.J. Harris
100s in a career:		65 by J. Hardstaff
wickets in a season:		181 (av. 14.96) B. Dooland
wickets in a career:		1,653 (av. 20.34) T. Wass

1939	
1921	
1956	
1932	
1923	
1877	
1929	
1902-1932	
1928	
1971	
1930-1955	
1954	
1896-1920	

RECORD WICKET STANDS

1st	391	A.O. Jones & A. Shrewsbury v Glos (Bristol)	1899
2nd	398	W. Gunn & A. Shrewsbury v Sussex (Nottingham)	1890
3rd	369	J.R. Gunn & W. Gunn v Leics (Nottingham)	1903
4th	361	A.O. Jones & J.R. Gunn v Essex (Leyton)	1905
5th	266	A. Shrewsbury & W. Gunn v Sussex (Hove)	1884
6th	303*	F.H. Winrow & P.F. Harvey v Derby (Nottingham)	1947
7th	204	M.J. Smedley & R.A. White v Surrey (Oval)	1967
8th	220	G.F.H. Heane & R. Winrow v Somerset (Nottingham)	1935
9th	165	W. McIntyre & G. Wootton v Kent (Nottingham)	1869
10th	152	E. Alletson & W. Riley v Sussex (Hove)	1911

One-day cricket

Highest innings totals:	Gillette Cup/ NatWest Trophy	271 v Glos (Nottingham)	1968
	John Player League	260-5 v Warwicks (Birmingham)	1976
	Benson & Hedges Cup	269-5 v Derby (Nottingham)	1980
Lowest innings totals:	Gillette Cup/ NatWest Trophy	123 v Yorks (Scarborough)	1969
	John Player League	66 v Yorks (Bradford)	1969
	Benson & Hedges Cup	94 v Lancs (Nottingham)	1975
Highest indi- vidual innings:	Gillette Cup/ NatWest Trophy	107 M. Hill v Somerset (Taunton)	1964
	John Player League	120* C.E.B. Rice v Glamorgan (Swansea)	1978
		120* S.B. Hassan v Warwicks (Birmingham)	1981
	Benson & Hedges Cup	130* C.E.B. Rice v Scotland (Glasgow)	1982
Best bowling figures:	Gillette Cup/ NatWest Trophy	6-18 C.E.B. Rice v Sussex (Hove)	1982
	John Player League	6-12 R.J. Hadlee v Lancs (Nottingham)	1980
	Benson & Hedges Cup	6-22 M.K. Bore v Leics (Leicester)	1980
		6-22 C.E.B. Rice v Northants (Northampton)	1981

SOMERSET

Formation of present club: 1875, reorganised 1885.
Colours: Black, silver and maroon.
Badge: Wessex Wyvern.
Best final position in Championship: Third (5): 1892, 1958, 1963, 1966 and 1981.
Gillette Cup Winners: 1979.
Gillette Cup Finalists (2): 1967 and 1978.
NatWest Trophy Quarter-final: 1982.
John Player League Champions: 1979.
Benson & Hedges Cup Winners (2): 1981 and 1982.
Gillette Man of the Match Awards: 26.
NatWest Man of the Match Awards: 1.
Benson & Hedges Gold Awards: 33.

Secretary and Chief Executive: D. Brown, County Cricket Ground, St. James's Street, Taunton TA1 1JT.
Captain: B.C. Rose.
Prospects of Play Telephone No: Taunton (0823) 70007.

Ian Terrence BOTHAM B Haswell (Cheshire) 24/11/1955. RHB, RFM. Debut 1974. Cap 1976. Best Young Cricketer of the Year in 1977. *Wisden* 1977. Tests: 54 between 1977 and 1982, captaining England in 12 Tests. Tours: Pakistan and New Zealand 1977-78, Australia 1978-79, Australia and India 1979-80, West Indies 1980-81 (Captain), India and Sri Lanka 1981-82, Australia and New Zealand 1982-83. 1,000 runs (3) – 1,241 (av. 44.32) in 1982 best. Took 100 wkts (av. 16.40) in 1978. Became first player ever to score a century and take 8 wkts in innings in a Test match v Pakistan (Lord's) 1978, and to score a century and take 10 wkts in a Test, v India (Bombay) 1979-80. Took 100th wkt in Test cricket in 1979 in record time of 2 years 9 days. Achieved double of 1,000 runs and 100 wkts in Tests in 1979 to create record of fewest Tests (21). Took 200th wkt in 1981 in record time of 4 years 34 days and at youngest age of 25 years 280 days. Became third player in Test cricket to achieve double of 2,000 runs and 200 wkts in 1981-82 in fewest Tests (42), shortest time (4 years 126 days) and youngest age (26 years 7 days). Scored centuries against Australia in 1981 off 87 balls (Leeds) and 86 balls (Manchester). Hat-trick for MCC v Middlesex (Lord's) 1978. Gillette Man of Match: 1. BH Gold Awards: 5. HS: 228 v Glos (Taunton) 1980 in 184 minutes with 10 6's and 27 4's, scoring 182 between lunch and tea, and sharing in 4th wkt partnership record for county, 310 with P.W. Denning. HSTC: 208 v India (Oval) 1982. HSGC/NW: 91* v Northumberland (Taunton) 1977. HSJPL: 106 v Hants (Taunton) 1981. HSBH: 57* v Kent (Taunton) 1981. BB: 8-34 v Pakistan (Lord's) 1978. BBC: 7-61 v Glamorgan (Cardiff) 1978. BBGC/NW: 3-15 v Kent (Taunton) 1979. BBJPL: 4-10 v Yorks (Scarborough) 1979. BBBH: 4-16 v Combined Universities (Taunton) 1978. Soccer for Scunthorpe United.

Mark Richard DAVIS B Kilve (Somerset) 26/2/1962. LHB, LFM. Debut 1982. HS: 21* v Leics (Taunton) 1982. HSJPL: 11 v Middlesex (Weston-super-Mare) 1982. BB: 3-36 v Glamorgan (Swansea) 1982.

Peter William DENNING (Millfield School) B Chewton Mendip (Somerset) 16/12/1949. LHB, OB. Debut 1969. Cap 1973. 1,000 runs (6) – 1,222 runs (av. 42.13) in 1979 best. Scored two centuries in match (122 and 107) v Glos (Taunton)

127

SOMERSET

1977. Shared in 4th wkt partnership record for county, 310 with I.T. Botham v Glos (Taunton) 1980. Gillette Man of Match: 4. BH Gold Awards: 3. HS: 184 v Notts (Nottingham) 1980. HSGC/NW: 145 v Glamorgan (Cardiff) 1978. HSJPL: 112* v Warwicks (Birmingham) 1982. HSBH: 129 v Glos (Taunton) 1982. Benefit 1981.

Colin Herbert DREDGE B Frome 4/8/1954. LHB, RM. 6ft 5ins tall. Debut 1976. Cap 1978. Gillette Man of Match: 1 HS: 56* v Yorks (Harrogate) 1977. HSJPL: 25* v Middlesex (Weston-super-Mare) 1982. HSBH: 10* v Worcs (Taunton) 1978 and v Glamorgan (Swansea) 1982. BB: 6-37 v Glos (Bristol) 1981. BBGC/NW: 4-23 v Kent (Canterbury) 1978. BBJPL: 5-35 v Middlesex (Lord's) 1981. BBBH: 4-10 v Hants (Bournemouth) 1980.

Nigel Alfred FELTON B Guildford, Surrey 24/10/1960. LHB. Debut 1982. HS: 71 v Yorks (Weston-super-Mare) 1982.

Trevor GARD B West Lambrook, near South Petheron 2/6/1957. RHB, WK. Debut 1976. HS: 51* v Indians (Taunton) 1979.

Joel GARNER B Barbados 16/12/1952. RHB, RF. 6ft 8ins tall. Played for Barbados 1975-76 to 1981-82. Debut for county 1977. Cap 1979. Wisden 1979. Tests: 28 for West Indies between 1976-77 and 1981-82. Tours: West Indies to Australia and New Zealand 1979-80, England 1980, Pakistan 1980-81, Australia 1981-82. Gillette Man of Match: 1. BH Gold Awards: 2. HS: 104 West Indians v Glos (Bristol) 1980. HSTC: 60 West Indies v Australia (Brisbane) 1979-80. HSC: 90 v Glos (Bath) 1981. HSGC/NW: 38* v Glamorgan (Cardiff) 1978. HSJPL: 59* v Surrey (Bath) 1982. HSBH: 17 v Sussex (Hove) 1978. BB: 8-31 v Glamorgan (Cardiff) 1977. BBTC: 6-56 West Indies v New Zealand (Auckland) 1979-80. BBGC/NW: 6-29 v Northants (Lord's) 1979. BBJPL: 4-6 v Notts (Bath) 1982. BBBH: 5-14 v Surrey (Lord's) 1981.

Jeremy William LLOYDS (Blundell's School) B Penang, Malaya 17/11/1954. LHB, OB. Debut 1979. Cap 1982. HS: 132* v Northants (Northampton) 1982. HSJPL: 33 v Surrey (Oval) 1981. HSBH: 28 v Glamorgan (Swansea) 1982. BB: 7-88 v Essex (Chelmsford) 1982.

Victor James MARKS (Blundell's School and Oxford) B Middle Chinnock 25/6/1955. RHB, OB. Debut for Oxford U and county 1975. Blue 1975-76-77-78 (Captain in 1976-77). Cap 1979. NW Man of the Match: 1. BH Gold Awards: 3. HS: 105 Oxford U v Worcs (Oxford) 1976. HSC: 98 v Essex (Leyton) 1976. HSNW: 55 v Warwicks (Taunton) 1982. HSJPL: 71* v Surrey (Taunton) 1980. HSBH: 81* v Hants (Bournemouth) 1980. BB: 7-51 v Notts (Nottingham) 1982. BBJPL: 3-19 v Derby (Taunton) 1979, v Glos (Bristol) 1980 and v Warwicks (Birmingham) 1982. Half-blue for Rugby Fives.

Hallam Reynold MOSELEY B Christ Church, Barbados 28/5/1948. RHB, RFM. Toured England with Barbados team in 1969 and made debut v Notts (Nottingham). Played for Barbados in 1971-72. Debut for county in 1971. Cap 1972. Testimonial (£24,085) in 1979. Is now regarded as an English player for qualification purposes. HS: 67 v Leics (Taunton) 1972. HSGC/NW: 15 v Lancs (Manchester) 1972. HSJPL: 24 v Notts (Torquay) 1972 and 24 v Hants (Weston-super-Mare) 1975. HSBH: 33 v Hants (Bournemouth) 1973. BB: 6-34 v Derby (Bath) 1975 and 6-35 v Glos (Taunton) 1978. BBGC/NW: 4-31 v Surrey (Taunton) 1974. BBJPL: 5-30 v Middlesex (Lord's) 1973. BBBH: 3-13 v Combined Universities (Taunton) 1982.

Richard Leslie OLLIS B Clifton (Glos) 14/1/1961. LHB, RM. Debut 1981. HS: 22 v Warwicks (Birmingham) 1981.

Gary Vincent PALMER B Taunton 11/1/1965. RHB, RM. Debut 1982. HS: 27 v Leics (Taunton) 1982.

Nigel Francis Mark POPPLEWELL (Radley College and Cambridge) B Chislehurst (Kent) 8/8/1957. Son of O.B. Popplewell, Q.C., former Cambridge Blue. RHB, RM. Debut for Cambridge U 1977. Blue 1977-78-79 (secretary). Debut for county 1979. BH Gold Awards: 1. HS: 135* v Kent (Taunton) 1980. HSNW: 57 v Northants (Northampton) 1981. HSJPL: 55 v Surrey (Taunton) 1980. HSBH: 42 v Kent (Taunton) 1981. BB: 5-33 v Northants (Weston-super-Mare) 1981.

Isaac Vivian Alexander RICHARDS B St. John's, Antigua 7/3/1952. RHB, OB. Played for Leeward Islands and Combined Islands 1971-72 to 1981-82. Debut for county and cap 1974. *Wisden* 1976. Played for Queensland in 1976-77. Benefit in 1982. Tests: 47 for West Indies between 1974-75 and 1981-82, captaining West Indies in 1 Test in 1980. Tours: West Indies to India, Sri Lanka and Pakistan 1974-75, Australia 1975-76, 1979-80 1981-82, England 1976 and 1980, Pakistan 1980-81. 1,000 runs (9) – 2,161 runs (av. 65.48) in 1977 best. Also scored 1,267 runs (av. 60.33) on 1974-75 tour and 1,107 runs (av. 58.26) on 1975-76 tour. Has also scored 1,000 runs overseas 3 times (1974-75, 1975-76 and 1980-81). Scored 1,710 in 11 Test matches in 1976 including 829 runs in 4 Tests against England – record aggregate for a year. Scored 99 and 110 in Leics (Taunton) 1978. Gillette Man of Match: 3. BH Gold Awards: 5. HS: 291 West Indies v England (Oval) 1976. HSC: 241* v Glos (Bristol) 1977. HSGC/NW: 139* v Warwicks (Taunton) 1978. HSJPL: 126* v Glos (Bristol, Imperial Ground) 1975. HSBH: 132* v Surrey (Lord's) 1981. BB: 5-88 West Indians v Queensland (Brisbane) 1981-82. BBUK: 4-55 v Glamorgan (Taunton) 1981. BBJPL: 4-9 v Essex (Chelmsford) 1982 including a hat-trick.

Peter Michael ROEBUCK (Millfield School and Cambridge) B Oxford 6/3/1956. RHB, OB. Debut 1974. Blue 1975-76-77. Cap 1978. 1,000 runs (2) – 1,273 runs (av. 47.14) in 1979 best. BH Gold Awards: 1. HS: 158 Cambridge U v Oxford U (Lord's) 1975. HSC: 131* v New Zealanders (Taunton) 1978. HSGC/NW: 57 v Essex (Taunton) 1978. HSJPL: 83 v Worcs (Taunton) 1982. HSBH: 53* v Notts (Lord's) 1982. BB: 6-50 Cambridge U v Kent (Canterbury) 1977.

Brian Charles ROSE B Dartford (Kent) 4/6/1950. LHB, LM. Wears spectacles. Debut 1969. Cap 1975. Appointed county captain in 1978. *Wisden* 1979. Tests: 9 between 1977-78 and 1980-81. Tours: Pakistan and New Zealand 1977-78, West Indies 1980-81 (returned through eyesight problem). 1,000 runs (8) – 1,624 runs (av. 46.40) in 1976 best. Scored two centuries in match (124 and 150*) v Worcs (Worcester) 1980. Gillette Man of Match: 2. BH Gold Awards: 2. HS: 205 v Northants (Weston-super-Mare) 1977. HSTC: 70 v West Indies (Manchester) 1980. HSGC/NW: 128 v Derby (Ilkeston) 1977. HSJPL: 112* v Essex (Ilford) 1980. HSBH: 137* v Kent (Canterbury) 1980. BB: 3-9 v Glos (Taunton) 1975. BBJPL: 3-25 v Lancs (Manchester) 1978. Benefit 1983.

Neil RUSSOM (Cambridge) B Finchley (London) 3/12/1958. RHB, RM. Debut for Cambridge U 1979. Blues 1980-81. Debut for county 1980. BH Gold Awards: 1 (for Combined Universities). HS: 79* Cambridge U v Northants (Cambridge) 1980. HSBH: 22 Combined Universities v Kent (Canterbury) 1981. BB: 4-84 Cambridge U v Leics (Cambridge) 1980. BBBH: 5-40 Combined Universities v Northants (Northampton) 1980.

SOMERSET

Philip Anthony SLOCOMBE (Millfield School) B Weston-super-Mare 6/9/1954. RHB, RM. Debut 1975. Cap 1978. 1,000 runs (2) – 1,221 runs (av. 38.15) in 1978 best. Scored 106* & 98 v Worcs (Worcester) 1978. HS: 132 v Notts (Taunton) 1975. HSGC/NW: 42 v Surrey (Oval) 1975. HSJPL: 42 v Leics (Leicester) 1981. HSBH: 42 v Middlesex (Taunton) 1980. Plays soccer for Weston-super-Mare in Western League.

Derek John Somerset TAYLOR B Amersham (Bucks) 12/11/1942. Twin brother of M.N.S. Taylor of Hants. RHB, WK. Debut for Surrey 1966. Cap 1969. Left staff after 1969 season and made debut for Somerset in 1970. Cap 1971. Testimonial (£20,764) in 1978. Played for Griqualand West in Currie Cup competition 1970-71 and 1971-72. Scored 1,121 runs (av. 28.02) in 1975. Was dismissed obstructing the field in John Player League match v Warwicks (Birmingham) 1980. BH Gold Award: 1. HS: 179 v Glamorgan (Swansea) 1974. HSGC/NW: 49 v Kent (Canterbury) 1974. HSJPL: 93 v Surrey (Guildford) 1975. HSBH: 83* v Glos (Street) 1975. Has played soccer for Corinthian Casuals.

Peter Hugh L'Estrange WILSON (Wellington College) B Guildford 17/8/1958. 6ft 5in tall. RHB, Played for Surrey 1978 to 1982. Joined Somerset for 1983. Played for Northern Transvaal in 1979-80. HS: 29 Northern Transvaal v Transvaal (Pretoria) 1979-80. HSUK: 15 Surrey v Worcs (Guildford) 1979. HSJPL: 18* Surrey v Worcs (Oval) 1979. BB: 5-36 Northern Transvaal v Eastern Province (Pretoria) 1979-80. BBUK: 4-39 Surrey v Warwicks (Oval) 1979. BBGC/NW: 3-59 Surrey v Essex (Colchester) 1978. BBJPL: 4-32 Surrey v Middlesex (Oval) 1979. BBBH: 5-21 Surrey v Combined Universities (Oval) 1979.

NB. The following player whose particulars appeared in the 1982 Annual has been omitted: M. Olive.

County Averages

Schweppes County Championship: Played 22, won 6, drawn 10, lost 6.
All first-class matches: Played 24, won 6, drawn 12, lost 6.

BATTING AND FIELDING

Cap		M	I	NO	Runs	HS	Avge	100	50	Ct	St
1974	I.V.A. Richards	20	31	2	1324	181*	45.65	4	5	11	—
1975	B.C. Rose	21	32	8	1090	173*	45.41	2	5	10	—
1976	I.T. Botham	11	20	1	675	131*	35.52	1	4	5	—
—	N.R. Felton	8	12	0	346	71	28.83	—	3	4	—
1982	J.W. Lloyds	23	39	3	981	132*	27.25	2	3	30	—
1978	P.A. Slocombe	13	23	1	579	78	26.31	—	6	9	—
1973	P.W. Denning	14	22	1	541	91*	25.76	—	3	6	—
1978	P.M. Roebuck	22	38	2	914	90	25.38	—	10	7	—
—	N.F.M. Popplewell	16	24	5	451	55	23.73	—	1	8	—
1979	V.J. Marks	19	30	3	509	67	18.85	—	4	11	—
1972	H.R. Moseley	18	19	13	113	24*	18.83	—	—	6	—
1978	C.H. Dredge	20	26	8	317	54*	17.61	—	1	9	—
1979	J. Garner	10	11	5	98	40*	16.33	—	—	4	—
1971	D.J.S. Taylor	17	26	5	334	67	15.90	—	2	41	4
—	T. Gard	6	5	1	37	31	9.25	—	—	8	3
—	M.R. Davis	9	12	2	65	21*	6.50	—	—	4	—

Played in two matches: M. Bryant 6, 0 (1 ct).
Played in one match: R.J. McCool 7, 12 (1 ct); R.L. Ollis 1, 1 (1 ct); G.V. Palmer 6, 27; N. Russom did not bat (1 ct).

BOWLING

	Type	O	M	R	W	Avge	Best	5 wI	10 wM
J. Garner	RF	259.1	76	583	33	17.66	6-23	4	1
I.T. Botham	RFM	247.2	65	719	39	18.43	5-48	2	—
H.R. Moseley	RFM	320	68	985	35	28.14	5-40	2	—
V.J. Marks	OB	661.2	193	1840	65	28.30	7-51	4	—
J.W. Lloyds	OB	468.3	96	1463	46	31.80	7-88	3	—
C.H. Dredge	RM	446.5	108	1214	35	34.68	3-33	—	—
M.R. Davis	LFM	144	19	481	12	40.08	3-36	—	—
I.V.A. Richards	OB	265.3	75	671	16	41.93	3-6	—	—
N.F.M. Popplewell	RM	94	17	320	6	53.33	2-23	—	—

Also bowled: M. Bryant 17-3-158-2; R.J. McCool 27-2-63-0; G.V. Palmer 17-3-57-0; P.M. Roebuck 39-4-109-1; B.C. Rose 1-0-5-0; N. Russom 16-2-64-3; P.A. Slocombe 3.2-0-10-1; D.J.S. Taylor 3-2-1-0.

County Records

First-class cricket

Highest innings totals:	For	675-9d v Hants (Bath)	1924
	Agst	811 by Surrey (Oval)	1899
Lowest innings totals:	For	25 v Glos (Bristol)	1947
	Agst	22 by Glos (Bristol)	1920
Highest individual innings:	For	310 H. Gimblett v Sussex (Eastbourne)	1948
	Agst	424 A.C. MacLaren for Lancs (Taunton)	1895
Best bowling in an innings:	For	10-49 E.J. Tyler v Surrey (Taunton)	1895
	Agst	10-35 A. Drake for Yorks (Weston-s-Mare)	1914
Best bowling in a match:	For	16-83 J.C. White v Worcs (Bath)	1919
	Agst	17-137 W. Brearley for Lancs (Manchester)	1905
Most runs in a season:		2,761 (av. 58.74) W.E. Alley	1961
runs in a career:		21,142 (av. 36.96) H. Gimblett	1935-1954
100s in a season:		10 by W.E. Alley	1961
100s in a career:		49 by H. Gimblett	1935-1954
wickets in a season:		169 (av. 19.24) A.W. Wellard	1938
wickets in a career:		2,166 (av. 18.02) J.C. White	1909-1937

RECORD WICKET STANDS

1st	346	H.T. Hewett & L.C.H. Palairet v Yorks (Taunton)	1892
2nd	290	J.C.W. MacBryan & M.D. Lyon v Derby (Buxton)	1924
3rd	300	G. Atkinson & P.B. Wight v Glamorgan (Bath)	1960
4th	310	P.W. Denning & I.T. Botham v Glos (Taunton)	1980
5th	235	J.C. White & C.C.C. Case v Glos (Taunton)	1927
6th	265	W.E. Alley & K.E. Palmer v Northants (Northampton)	1961
7th	240	S.M.J. Woods & V.T. Hill v Kent (Taunton)	1898
8th	143*	E.F. Longrigg & C.J.P. Barnwell v Glos (Bristol)	1938
9th	183	C. Greetham & H.W. Stephenson v Leics (Weston-super-Mare)	1963
10th	143	J.J. Bridges & H. Gibbs v Surrey (Weston-super-Mare)	1919

One-day cricket

Highest innings totals:	Gillette Cup/ NatWest Trophy	330-4 v Glamorgan (Cardiff)	1978
	John Player League	286-7 v Hants (Taunton)	1981
	Benson & Hedges Cup	307-6 v Glos (Taunton)	1982
Lowest innings totals:	Gillette Cup/ NatWest Trophy	59 v Middlesex (Lord's)	1977
	John Player League	58 v Essex (Chelmsford)	1977
	Benson & Hedges Cup	98 v Middlesex (Lord's)	1982
Highest individual innings:	Gillette Cup/ NatWest Trophy	145 P.W. Denning v Glamorgan (Cardiff)	1978
	John Player League	131 D.B. Close v Yorks (Bath)	1974
	Benson & Hedges Cup	137* B.C. Rose v Kent (Canterbury)	1980
Best bowling figures:	Gillette Cup/ NatWest Trophy	6-29 J. Garner v Northants (Lord's)	1979
	John Player League	6-25 G.I. Burgess v Glamorgan (Glastonbury)	1972
	Benson & Hedges Cup	5-14 J. Garner v Surrey (Lord's)	1981

SURREY

Formation of present club: 1845.
Colours: Chocolate.
Badge: Prince of Wales' Feathers.
County Champions (18): 1864, 1887, 1888, 1890, 1891,
1892, 1894, 1895, 1899, 1914, 1952, 1953, 1954, 1955,
1956, 1957, 1958 and 1971.
Joint Champions (2): 1889 and 1950.
Gillette Cup Finalists (2): 1965 and 1980.
NatWest Trophy Winners: 1982.
Best final position in John Player League: 5th in 1969
and 1980.
Benson & Hedges Cup Winners: 1974.
Benson & Hedges Cup Finalists (2): 1979 and 1981.
Gillette Man of the Match Awards: 18.
NatWest Trophy Man of the Match Awards: 5.
Benson & Hedges Gold Awards: 31.

Secretary: I.F.B. Scott-Browne, Kennington Oval, London, SE11 5SS.
Cricket manager: M. J. Stewart.
Captain: R. D. V. Knight.
Prospects of Play Telephone No: (01) 735 4911.

Christopher Keith BULLEN B Clapham 5/11/1962. RHB, OB. Debut 1982. One
match v Oxford U (Oxford).

Alan Raymond BUTCHER B Croydon 7/1/1954. LHB, SLA. Debut 1972. Cap
1975. Tests: 1 in 1979. 1,000 runs (4) – 1,713 runs (av. 46.29) in 1980 best. BH
Gold Awards: 4. HS: 216 v Cambridge U (Cambridge) 1980. HSTC: 20 v India
(Oval) 1979. HSNW: 86* v Warwicks (Lord's) 1982. HSJPL: 113* v Warwicks
(Birmingham) 1978. HSBH: 80 v Sussex (Oval) 1982. BB: 6-48 v Hants (Guildford)
1972. BBJPL: 5-19 Glos (Bristol) 1975. BBBH: 3-11 v Lancs (Manchester) 1974.

Martin Simon BUTCHER B Thornton Heath 17/5/1958. Brother of A. R.
Butcher (Surrey) and I. P. Butcher (Leics). RHB. One match v Oxford U (Oxford)
1982.

Robert Giles Lenthall CHEATLE (Stowe School) B London 31/7/1953. LHB,
SLA. Debut for Sussex 1974. Debut for Surrey 1980. HS: 49 Sussex v Kent
(Tunbridge Wells) 1978. HSC: 27* v Sussex (Hove) 1982. HSJPL: 18* Sussex v
Warwicks (Hove) 1979. HSBH: 16 Sussex v Somerset (Hove) 1978. BB: 6-32 Sussex
v Yorks (Hove) 1979. BBC: 5-28 v Sussex (Oval) 1982. BBJPL: 4-33 Sussex v
Glamorgan (Eastbourne) 1977. BBBH: 3-26 v Hants (Oval) 1980.

Sylvester Theophilus CLARKE B Christ Church, Barbados 11/12/1954. RHB,
RF. Debut for Barbados 1977-78. Debut for county 1979. Cap 1980. Tests: 11 for
West Indies between 1977-78 and 1981-82. Tours: West Indies to India and Sri
Lanka 1978-79, Pakistan 1980-81, Australia 1981-82. Hat-tricks (2): Barbados v
Trinidad (Bridgetown) 1977-78, v Notts (Oval) 1980. NW Man of the Match: 1. BH
Gold Awards: 1. HS 100* (in 62 minutes) v Glamorgan (Swansea) 1981. HSTC: 35*
West Indies v Pakistan (Faialabad) 1980-81. HSNW: 45* v Leics (Oval) 1981.
HSJPL: 34* v Hants (Oval) 1980. HSBH: 39 v Hants (Southampton) 1982. BB: 6-

133

39 Barbados v Trinidad (Bridgetown) 1977-78. BBUK: 6-61 v Glamorgan (Cardiff) 1979. BBTC: 5-126 West Indies v India (Bangalore) 1978-79. BBGC/NW: 4-38 v Yorks (Oval) 1980. BBJPL: 3-26 v Lancs (Oval) 1979. BBBH: 5-23 v Kent (Oval) 1980.

Grahame Selvey CLINTON B Sidcup 5/5/1953. LHB, RM. Debut for Kent 1974. Debut for Surrey in 1979. Played for Zimbabwe/Rhodesia in 1979-80. Cap 1980. 1,000 runs (3) – 1,240 runs (av. 37.57) in 1980 best. BH Gold Awards: 2 (1 for Kent). HS: 172* v Oxford U (Oxford) 1982. HSGC/NW: 58 v Essex (Chelmsford) 1980. HSJPL: 105* v Yorks (Scarborough) 1981. HSBH: 79 v Essex (Oval) 1982.

Ian James CURTIS (Whitgift School and Oxford) B Purley 13/5/1959. LHB, SLA/SLC. Debut for Oxford U 1980. Blue 1980 and 1982. Joined Surrey for 1983. HS: 20* Oxford U v Warwicks (Oxford) 1982. BB: 5-140 Oxford U v Glamorgan (Swansea) 1982.

Geoffrey Philip HOWARTH B Auckland 29/3/1951. Younger brother of H. J. Howarth, New Zealand Test cricketer. RHB, OB. Debut for New Zealand under-23 XI v Auckland (Auckland) 1968-69 and has played for Auckland 1972-73 and 1973-74 and Northern Districts 1974-75 to 1981-82. Debut for Surrey 1971. Cap 1974. Awarded M.B.E. in 1981 Birthday Honours List. Tests: 28 for New Zealand between 1974-75 and 1981-82 captaining New Zealand in 11 tests. Tours: D. H. Robins to South Africa 1975-76 and to India 1977-78. New Zealand to Pakistan and India 1976-77, England 1978, Australia 1980-81 (Captain). 1,000 runs (4) – 1,554 runs (av. 37.90) in 1976 best. Scored two centuries in match (122 and 102) New Zealand v England (Auckland) 1977-78. BH Gold Awards: 1. HS: 183 v Hants (Oval) 1979. HSTC: 147 New Zealand v West Indies (Christchurch) 1979-80. HSGC/NW: 34 v Lancs (Manchester) 1977 and 34 v Northants (Northampton) 1979. HSJPL: 122 v Glos (Oval) 1976. HSBH: 80 v Yorks (Oval) 1974. BB: 5-32 Auckland v Central Districts (Auckland) 1973-74. BBUK: 3-20 v Northants (Northampton) 1976. BBJPL: 4-16 v Warwicks (Byfleet) 1979. Benefit 1983.

Roger David Verdon KNIGHT (Dulwich College and Cambridge) B Streatham 6/9/1946. LHB, RM. Debut for Cambridge U 1967. Blue 1967-68-69-70. Debut for Surrey 1968. Debut for Glos by special registration 1971. Cap 1971. Debut for Sussex in 1976. Cap 1976. Rejoined Surrey for 1978 as county captain. Cap 1978. 1,000 runs (11) – 1,350 runs (av. 38.57) in 1974 best. Gillette Man of the Match: 5 (3 for Glos). BH Gold Awards: 5 (1 for Sussex, 2 for Glos). HS: 165* Sussex v Middlesex (Hove) 1976. HSC: 132 v Lancs (Oval) 1980. HSGC/NW: 75 Glos v Glamorgan (Cardiff) 1973. HSJPL: 127 Sussex v Hants (Hove) 1976. HSBH: 117 Sussex v Surrey (Oval) 1977. BB: 6-44 Glos v Northants (Northampton) 1974. BBC: 5-44 v Glos (Cheltenham) 1979. BBGC/NW: 5-39 Glos v Surrey (Bristol) 1971. BBJPL: 5-42 Sussex v Notts (Nottingham) 1977. BBBH: 3-19 Sussex v Surrey (Oval) 1977.

Monte Alan LYNCH B Georgetown, British Guiana 21/5/1958. RHB, RM/OB. Debut 1977. Cap 1982. NW Man of the Match: 1. HS: 141* v Glamorgan (Guildford) 1982. HSNW: 129 v Durham (Oval) 1982. HSJPL: 80* v Warwicks (Oval) 1981. HSBH: 67 v Worcs (Worcester) 1979. BB: 3-6 v Glamorgan (Swansea) 1981.

Kevin Scott MACKINTOSH (Kingston-upon-Thames GS) B Surbiton (Surrey) 30/8/1957. RHB, RM. Debut for Notts in 1978. Rejoined Surrey in 1981. HS: 31 v Somerset (Oval) 1982. HSJPL: 12* Notts v Lancs (Nottingham) 1982. BB: 6-61 v Middlesex (Lord's) 1982. BBNW: 3-27 v Durham (Oval) 1982. BBJPL: 4-26 Notts v Glos (Nottingham) 1979.

Graham MONKHOUSE B Carlisle 26/4/1955. RHB, RM. Debut 1981. HS: 63* v Somerset (Oval) 1982. BB: 3-40 v Pakistanis (Oval) 1982. BBJPL: 3-22 v Hants (Oval) 1982. HSJPL: 55 v Essex (Southend) 1982. Has played soccer for Carlisle United and Workington.

Andrew NEEDHAM B Calow (Derbyshire) 23/3/1957. RHB, OB. Debut 1977. HS: 134* v Lancs (Manchester) 1982. BB: 5-91 v Lancs (Manchester) 1982. BBJPL: 3-41 v Lancs (Manchester) 1982.

Duncan Brian PAULINE B Aberdeen 15/12/1960. RHB, RM. Debut 1979. HS: 46 v Leics (Leicester) 1980. HSNW: 10 v Durham (Oval) 1982. HSJPL: 92 v Worcs (Oval) 1981.

Ian Roger PAYNE (Emanuel School) B Lambeth Hospital, Kennington 9/5/1958. RHB, RM. Debut 1977. BH Gold Awards: 1. HS: 29 v Kent (Oval) 1977. HSJPL: 33 v Notts (Oval) 1981. BBJPL: 5-21 v Derby (Derby) 1982. BBBH: 3-20 v Leics (Oval) 1981.

Patrick Ian POCOCK B Bangor, Caernarvonshire 24/9/1946. RHB, OB. Debut 1964. Cap 1967. Benefit (£18,500) in 1977. Played for Northern Transvaal in 1971-72. Tests: 17 between 1967-68 and 1976. Tours: Pakistan 1966-67, West Indies 1967-68 and 1973-74, Ceylon and Pakistan 1968-69, Ceylon 1969-70, India, Pakistan and Sri Lanka 1972-73. Played for Rest of the World XI v Pakistan XI (Karachi) 1970-71. Took 112 wkts (av. 18.22) in 1967. Took 4 wkts in 4 balls, 5 in 6, 6 in 9, and 7 in 11 (the last two being first-class records) v Sussex (Eastbourne) 1972. Hattricks (2): as above and v Worcs (Guildford) 1971. BH Gold Awards: 2. HS: 75* v Notts (Oval) 1968. HSTC: 33 v Pakistan (Hyderabad) 1972-73. HSGC/NW: 14 v Essex (Colchester) 1978. HSJPL: 22 v Notts (Nottingham) 1971. HSBH: 19 v Middlesex (Oval) 1972. BB: 9-57 v Glamorgan (Cardiff) 1979. BBTC: 6-79 v Australia (Manchester) 1968: BBGC/NW: 3-34 v Somerset (Oval) 1975. BBJPL: 4-27 v Essex (Chelmsford) 1974. BBBH: 4-11 v Yorks (Barnsley) 1978.

Clifton James RICHARDS B Penzance 10/8/1958. RHB, WK. Debut 1976. Cap 1978. Tour: D.H. Robins to New Zealand 1979-80, India and Sri Lanka 1981-82. HS: 117* v Notts (Oval) 1982. HSNW: 20* v Durham (Oval) 1982. HSJPL: 52 v Lancs (Manchester) 1982. HSBH: 32 v Leics (Oval) 1981.

David Mark SMITH B Balham 9/1/1956. LHB, RM. Debut 1973 aged 17 years 4 months whilst still at school. Cap 1980. Scored 1065 (av. 50.71) in 1982. NW Man of the Match: 1. BH Gold Awards: 1. HS: 160 v Worcs (Worcester) 1982. HSNW: 103* v Northants (Oval) 1982. HSJPL: 87* v Hants (Oval) 1980. HSBH: 45* v Northants (Northampton) 1979 and 45* v Hants (Oval) 1980. BB: 3-40 v Sussex (Oval) 1976. BBGC/NW: 3-39 v Derby (Ilkeston) 1976. BBBH: 4-29 v Kent (Oval) 1980.

Alec James STEWART (Tiffin School) B Merton 8/4/1963. Son of M.J. Stewart, RHB, WK. Debut 1981. HS: 16 v Northants (Northampton) 1982.

David James THOMAS B Solihull (Warwicks) 30/6/1959. LHB, LM. Debut 1977. Cap 1982. Played for Northern Transvaal in 1980-81. HS: 64 v Kent (Maidstone) 1982. HSNW: 27 v Middlesex (Oval) 1982. HSJPL: 56* v Leics (Oval) 1980. HSBH: 13 v Kent (Oval) 1980 and 13 v Notts (Nottingham) 1981. BB: 6-84 v Derby (Oval) 1979. BBNW: 3-16 v Durham (Oval) 1982. BBJPL: 4-13 v Sussex (Oval) 1978. BBBH: 3-30 v Leics (Oval) 1981.

NB. The following players whose particulars appeared in the 1982 Annual have been omitted: Intikhab Alam, R.D. Jackman, G.R.J. Roope and P.H.L. Wilson.

County Averages

Schweppes County Championship: Played 22, won 6, drawn 10, lost 6.
All first-class matches: Played 24, won 6, drawn 12, lost 6.

BATTING AND FIELDING

Cap		M	I	NO	Runs	HS	Avge	100	50	Ct	St
1980	D.M. Smith	14	25	4	1065	160	50.71	3	5	13	—
1975	A.R. Butcher	22	41	5	1452	187*	40.33	4	6	12	—
1974	G.P. Howarth	19	32	3	1158	156*	39.93	4	2	16	—
1970	R.D. Jackman	18	19	8	402	68	36.54	—	3	4	—
1980	G.S. Clinton	14	23	4	622	172*	32.73	2	1	4	—
1982	M.A. Lynch	23	38	2	1155	141*	32.08	3	4	18	—
—	K.S. McIntosh	12	10	7	94	31	31.33	—	—	5	—
1969	G.R.J. Roope	14	25	7	560	108	31.11	1	1	13	—
1978	R.D.V. Knight	24	40	4	1114	111	30.94	2	7	10	—
—	G.A. Monkhouse	8	10	5	137	63*	27.40	—	1	3	—
1978	C.J. Richards	23	36	9	700	117*	25.92	1	4	50	3
—	D.J. Thomas	17	20	3	409	64	24.05	—	3	6	—
—	A. Needham	13	20	6	319	134*	22.78	1	—	7	—
1980	S.T. Clarke	22	25	0	408	52	16.32	—	1	11	—
—	D.B. Pauline	3	6	0	69	26	11.50	—	—	—	—
—	F.H.L. Wilson	4	4	2	20	13	10.00	—	—	—	—
1967	P.I. Pocock	7	8	2	32	10*	5.33	—	—	1	—
—	R.G.L. Cheatle	4	2	2	28	27*	—	—	—	1	—

Played in one match: C. Bullen did not bat; M. Butcher did not bat (1 ct); A.J.
Stewart 9, 16 (4 ct).

BOWLING

	Type	O	M	R	W	Avge	Best	5 wI	10 wM
S.T. Clarke	RF	659.3	159	1696	85	19.95	6-63	6	1
R.D. Jackman	RFM	571.1	164	1504	65	23.13	6–28	2	—
K.S. McIntosh	RM	304.2	59	1023	34	30.08	6-61	1	—
P.I. Pocock	OB	233	64	632	21	30.09	5-73	1	—
G.A. Monkhouse	RM	131.3	27	395	12	32.91	3-40	—	—
D.J. Thomas	LM	426.4	109	1284	36	35.66	4-39	—	—
F.H.L. Wilson	RFM	103.4	26	283	6	47.16	2-57	—	—
R.D.V. Knight	RM	266.2	61	762	15	50.80	3-34	—	—
A. Needham	OB	359	73	1170	22	53.18	5-91	1	—
A.R. Butcher	SLA	98	16	411	5	82.20	1-23	—	—

Also bowled: C. Bullen 9-0-29-0; M. Butcher 1-0-2-0; R.G.L. Cheatle 49-8-183-3;
G.S. Clinton 1-0-11-0; M.A. Lynch 51.5-8-208-4; D.B. Pauline 1-0-3-0; C.J.
Richards 5-0-19-0; G.R.J. Roope 32-12-81-3.

County Records

First-class cricket

Highest innings totals:	For	811 v Somerset (Oval)	1899
	Agst	705-8d by Sussex (Hastings)	1902
Lowest innings totals:	For	16 v Notts (Oval)	1880
	Agst	16 by MCC (Lord's)	1872
Highest Individual innings:	For	357* R. Abel v Somerset (Oval)	1899
	Agst	300* F. B. Watson for Lancs (Manchester)	1928
		300 R. Subba Row for Northants (Oval)	1958
Best bowling in an innings:	For	10-43 T. Rushby v Somerset (Taunton)	1921
	Agst	10-28 W. P. Howell for Australians (Oval)	1899
Best bowling in a match:	For	16-83 G. A. R. Lock v Kent (Blackheath)	1956
	Agst	15-57 W. P. Howell for Australians (Oval)	1899
Most runs in a season:		3,246 (av. 72.13) T. W. Hayward	1906
runs in a career:		43,554 (av. 49.72) J. B. Hobbs	1905-1934
100s in a season:		13 by T. W. Hayward and	1906
		J. B. Hobbs	1925
100s in a career:		144 by J. B. Hobbs	1905-1934
wickets in a season:		252 (av. 17.87) T. Richardson	1895
wickets in a career:		1,775 (av. 17.88) T. Richardson	1892-1904

RECORD WICKET STANDS

1st	428	J. B. Hobbs & A. Sandham v Oxford U (Oval)	1926
2nd	371	J. B. Hobbs & E. G. Hayes v Hants (Oval)	1909
3rd	353	A. Ducat & E. G. Hayes v Hants (Southampton)	1919
4th	448	R. Abel & T. W. Hayward v Yorks (Oval)	1899
5th	308	J. N. Crawford & F. C. Holland v Somerset (Oval)	1908
6th	298	A. Sandham & H. S. Harrison v Sussex (Oval)	1913
7th	200	T. F. Shepherd & J. W. Hitch v Kent (Blackheath)	1921
8th	204	T. W. Hayward & L. C. Braund v Lancs (Oval)	1898
9th	168	E. R. T. Holmes & E. W. J. Brooks v Hants (Oval)	1936
10th	173	A. Ducat & A. Sandham v Essex (Leyton)	1921

One-day cricket

Highest innings totals:	GC/Natwest Trophy	280-5 v Middlesex (Oval)	1970
	John Player League	248-2 v Glos (Oval)	1976
	Benson & Hedges Cup	276-6 v Essex (Oval)	1982
Lowest innings totals:	GC/NatWest Trophy	74 v Kent (Oval)	1967
	John Player League	64 v Worcs (Worcester)	1978
	Benson & Hedges Cup	125 v Sussex (Hove)	1972
Highest individual innings:	Gillette Cup/ NatWest Trophy	129 M.A. Lynch v Durham (Oval)	1982
	John Player League	122 G.P. Howarth v Glos (Oval)	1976
	Benson & Hedges Cup	115 G.R.J. Roope v Essex (Chelmsford)	1973
Best bowling figures:	Gillette Cup/ NatWest Trophy	7-33 R.D. Jackman v Yorks (Harrogate)	1970
	John Player League	6-25 Intikhab Alam v Derby (Oval)	1974
	Benson & Hedges Cup	5-21 P.H.L. Wilson v Combined U. (Oval)	1979

SUSSEX

Formation of present club: 1839, reorganised 1857.
Colours: Dark blue, light blue, and gold.
Badge: County Arms of six martlets (in shape of inverted pyramid).
County Championship Runners-up (7): 1902, 1903, 1932, 1933, 1934, 1953 and 1981.
Gillette Cup Winners (3): 1963, 1964 and 1978.
Gillette Cup Finalists (3): 1968, 1970 and 1973.
NatWest Trophy third round: 1981.
John Player League Winners: 1982.
Benson & Hedges Cup Semi-finalists: 1982.
Gillette Man of the Match Awards: 30.
NatWest Man of the Match Awards: 1.
Benson & Hedges Gold Awards: 28.

Secretary: R. Stevens, County Ground, Eaton Road, Hove, BN3 3AN.
Captain: J.R.T. Barclay.
Prospects of Play Telephone No: Brighton (0273) 772766.

John Robert Troutbeck **BARCLAY** (Eton College) B Bonn, West Germany 22/1/1954. RHB, OB. Debut 1970 aged 16 years 205 days. Cap 1976. Captain 1981. Played for Orange Free State in 1978-79. 1,000 runs (4) – 1,093 (av. 32.14) in 1979 best. Gillette Man of the Match: 1. BH Gold Awards: 2. HS: 119 v Leics (Hove) 1980. HSGC/NW: 44 v Derby (Hove) 1977 and v Somerset (Lord's) 1978. HSJPL: 48 v Derby (Derby) 1974. HSBH: 93* v Surrey (Oval) 1976. BB: 6-61 v Sri Lankans (Hove) 1979. BBGC/NW: 3-27 v Lancs (Hove) 1978. BBJPL: 3-11 v Worcs (Eastbourne) 1978. BBBH: 5-43 v Combined Universities (Oxford) 1979.

Ian James **GOULD** B Slough (Bucks) 19/8/1957. LHB, WK. Debut for Middlesex 1975. Cap 1977. Played for Auckland in 1979-80. Debut for Sussex in 1981. Cap 1981. Tour: Australia and New Zealand 1982-83. HS: 128 Middlesex v Worcs (Worcester) 1978. HSC: 94 v Somerset (Hove) 1982. HSGC/NW: 58 Middlesex v Derby (Derby) 1978. HSJPL: 69* v Hants (Basingstoke) 1981. HSBH: 72 v Kent (Hove) 1982.

Allan Michael **GREEN** B Pulborough 28/5/1960. RHB, RM. Debut 1980. HS: 99 v Middlesex (Hove) 1982. HSNW: 41 v Notts (Hove) 1982. HSJPL: 19 v Notts (Hove) 1982.

Ian Alexander **GREIG** (Queen's College, Queenstown and Cambridge) B Queenstown, South Africa 8/12/1955. RHB, RM. Younger brother of A.W. Greig. Played for Border in 1974-75 and 1979-80 and for Griqualand West in 1975-76. Debut for Cambridge U 1977. Blue 1977-78-79 (captain). Debut for county 1980. Cap 1981. Tests: 2 in 1982. Had match double of 100 runs and 10 wkts (118*, 6-75, 4-57) v Hants (Hove) 1981. NW Man of the Match: 1. BH Gold Awards: 1. HS: 118* v Hants (Hove) 1981. HSTC: 14 v Pakistan (Birmingham) 1982. HSNW: 82 v Warwicks (Birmingham) 1981. HSJPL: 54 v Warwicks (Horsham) 1981. HSBH: 51 v Hants (Hove) 1981. BB: 7-43 v Cambridge U (Cambridge) 1981. BBTC: 4-53 v Pakistan (Birmingham) 1982. BBNW: 4-31 v Warwicks (Birmingham) 1981. BBJPL: 5-42 v Leics (Hove) 1982. BBBH: 5-35 v Hants (Hove) 1981. Blues for rugby 1977-78.

Jerry Richard Percy HEATH B Turner's Hill 26/4/1959. LHB. Debut 1980. HS: 101* v Sri Lankans (Hastings) 1981. HSJPL: 35 v Hants (Hove) 1980.

IMRAN KHAN NIAZI (Aitchison College, Lahore and Oxford) B Lahore, Pakistan 25/11/1952. RHB, RF. Cousin of Majid Jahangir Khan. Debut for Lahore A 1969-70 and has played subsequently for various Lahore teams and Pakistan International Airways. Debut for Worcs 1971. Blue 1973-74-75 (capt. in 1974). Cap 1976. Debut for Sussex by special registration 1977. Cap 1978. Tests: 40 for Pakistan between 1971 and 1982. Captain in 3 Tests. Tours: Pakistan to England 1971, 1974 and 1982, Pakistan to Sri Lanka 1975-76, Australia and West Indies 1976-77, New Zealand and Australia 1978-79, India 1979-80, Australia 1981-82. 1,000 runs (3) – 1,339 runs (av. 41.84) in 1978 best. Scored two centuries in match (117* and 106), Oxford U v Notts (Oxford) 1974. Had match double of 111* and 13-99 (7-53 and 6-46) v Lancs (Worcester) 1976. Gillette Man of Match award: 4. (1 for Worcs). BH Gold Awards: 6, (1 for Oxford and Cambridge Universities, 1 for Worcs). HS: 170 Oxford U v Northants (Oxford) 1974. HSC: 167 v Glos (Hove) 1978. HSTC: 123 Pakistan v West Indies (Lahore) 1980-81. HSGC/NW: 63* v Suffolk (Hove) 1980. HSJPL: 75 Worcs v Warwicks (Worcester) 1976. HSBH: 72 Worcs v Warwicks (Birmingham) 1976. BB: 8-58 Pakistan v Sri Lanka (Faisalabad) 1981-82. BBUK: 7-52 v Glos (Bristol) 1978 and for Pakistan v England (Birmingham) 1982. BBGC/NW: 4-27 v Staffs (Stone) 1978. BBJPL: 5-29 Worcs v Leics (Leicester) 1973. BBBH: 5-8 v Northants (Northampton) 1978.

Adrian Nicholas JONES B Woking (Surrey) 22/7/1961. LHB, RFM. Debut 1981. Played for Border 1981-82. HS: 29 v Kent (Hove) 1982. BB: 4-33 v Yorks (Hove) 1981.

Garth Stirling LE ROUX B Cape Town 4/9/1955. RHB, RF. Played for Western Province 1975-76 to 1981-82. Debut for county 1978. One match v New Zealanders (Hove). Cap 1981. Hat-trick v Warwicks (Hove) 1981. HS: 83 v Surrey (Hove) 1982. HSNW: 10 v Notts (Hove) 1982. HSJPL: 88 v Glamorgan (Hastings) 1982. HSBH: 46 v Somerset (Taunton) 1982. BB: 8-107 v Somerset (Taunton) 1981. BBNW: 5-35 v Essex (Hove) 1981. BBJPL: 4-18 v Notts (Hove) 1982. BBBH: 4-59 v Kent (Hove) 1982.

Gehan Dixon MENDIS (St Thomas College, Colombo) B Colombo, Ceylon 20/4/1955. RHB, occasional WK. Debut 1974. Cap 1980. Tour: International team to Pakistan 1981-82. 1,000 runs (3) – 1,522 runs (av. 41.13) in 1981 best. Gillette Man of Match: 2. BH Gold Awards: 2. HS: 204 v Northants (Eastbourne) 1980. HSGC/NW: 141* v Warwicks (Hove) 1980. HSJPL: 125* v Glos (Hove) 1981. HSBH: 109 v Glos (Hove) 1980.

Paul William Giles PARKER (Cambridge U). B Bulawayo, Rhodesia 15/1/1956. RHB, RM. Debut for both Cambridge U and county 1976. Blue 1976-77-78. University Secretary for 1977 and 1978. Cap 1979. Best Young Cricketer for the Year in 1979. Tests: 1 in 1981. 1,000 runs (5) – 1,412 runs (av. 45.54) in 1981 best. Gillette Man of Match: 2. BH Gold Awards: 3. HS: 215 Cambridge U v Essex (Cambridge) 1976. HSC: 136 v Lancs (Hove) 1981. HSGC/NW: 69 v Lancs (Hove) 1978. HSJPL: 106* v Worcs (Horsham) 1980. HSBH: 77 v Hants (Bournemouth) 1982. Selected for University rugby match in 1977, but had to withdraw through injury.

SUSSEX

Christopher Paul PHILLIPSON (Ardingly College) B Vrindaban, India 10/2/1952. RHB, RM. Debut 1970. Cap 1980. BH Gold Awards: 2. HS: 87 v Hants (Hove) 1980. HSGC/NW: 70* v Suffolk (Hove) 1980. HSJPL: 71 v Lancs (Hastings) 1979. HSBH: 66* v Surrey (Oval) 1982. BB: 6-56 v Notts (Hove) 1972. BBJPL: 4-25 v Middlesex (Eastbourne) 1972. BBBH: 5-32 v Combined Universities (Oxford) 1977.

Anthony Charles Shackleton PIGOTT (Harrow School) B London 4/6/1958. RHB, RFM. Debut 1978. Cap 1982. Tour: D.H. Robins to New Zealand 1979-80. Hat-trick v Surrey (Hove) 1978. HS: 55 v Yorks (Hove) 1979. HSGC/NW: 30 v Northants (Hove) 1979. HSJPL: 49 v Warwicks (Hove) 1979. BB: 7-74 v Northants (Eastbourne) 1982. BBGC/NW: 3-43 v Notts (Hove) 1979. BBJPL: 5-28 v Surrey (Guildford) 1982. BBBH: 3-33 v Hants (Bournemouth) 1982.

David James SMITH B Brighton 28/4/1962. LHB, WK. Debut 1981.

Christopher Edward WALLER B Guildford 3/10/1948. RHB, SLA. Debut for Surrey 1967. Cap 1972. Debut for Sussex in 1974. Cap 1976. HS: 51* v Cambridge U (Cambridge) 1981. HSGC/NW: 14* v Notts (Nottingham) 1975. HSJPL: 18* v Glamorgan (Hove) 1975. HSBH: 11* v Essex (Chelmsford) 1975. BB: 7-64 Surrey v Sussex (Oval) 1971. BBC: 6-40 v Surrey (Hove) 1975. BBJPL: 4-28 v Essex (Hove) 1976. BBBH: 4-25 v Minor Counties (South) (Hove) 1975.

Alan Peter WELLS B Newhaven 2/10/1961. Younger brother of C.M. Wells. RHB, RM. Debut 1981. Played for Border 1981-82. HS: 70 v Notts (Hove) 1982. HSJPL: 47* v Northants (Hastings) 1981.

Colin Mark WELLS B Newhaven 3/3/1960. Older brother of A.P. Wells. Debut 1979. Cap 1982. RHB, RM. 1,000 runs (2) – 1,248 (av. 32.84) in 1982 best. HS: 135 v Glamorgan (Swansea) 1980. HSNW: 28 v Warwicks (Birmingham) 1981. HSJPL: 81* v Glamorgan (Hastings) 1982. HSBH: 80 v Kent (Hove) 1982. BB: 4-23 v Oxford U (Pagham) 1979. BBJPL: 3-18 v Essex (Hove) 1982. BBBH: 4-21 v Middlesex (Lord's) 1980.

Alan WILLOWS B Portslade 24/4/1961. RHB, SLA. Debut 1980. BB: 4-33 v Hants (Southampton) 1980.

NB. The following player whose particulars appeared in the 1982 Annual has been omitted: G.G. Arnold.

County Averages

Schweppes County Championship: Played 22, won 6, drawn 9, lost 7.
All first-class matches: Played 23, won 6, drawn 9, lost 8.

BATTING AND FIELDING

Cap		M	I	NO	Runs	HS	Avge	100	50	Ct	St
	A.P. Wells	5	9	3	233	70	38.83	—	1	1	—
1978	Imran Khan	7	12	3	297	85	33.00	—	1	2	—
1982	C.M. Wells	23	41	3	1248	126	32.84	3	5	6	—
1981	G.S. Le Roux	20	28	5	737	83	32.04	—	6	15	—
—	A.M. Green	14	26	1	776	99	31.04	—	6	7	—
1980	G.D. Mendis	23	42	2	1240	114	31.00	2	5	7	5
1976	J.R.T. Barclay	22	33	6	761	95	28.18	—	6	25	—
1979	P.W.G. Parker	23	39	7	845	106	26.40	1	5	20	—
1981	I.J. Gould	19	32	3	695	94	23.96	—	5	40	5
1981	I.A. Greig	10	23	1	477	109	21.68	1	3	18	—
1980	C.P. Phillipson	16	22	3	274	64	14.42	—	1	24	—
—	J.R.P. Heath	3	5	0	61	19	12.20	—	—	—	—
1976	C.E. Waller	23	27	12	181	50	12.06	—	1	17	—
1979	G.G. Arnold	3	5	4	11	8*	11.00	—	—	—	—
1982	A.C.S. Pigott	23	23	7	167	40	10.43	—	—	9	—
—	A.N. Jones	4	4	0	39	29	9.75	—	—	—	—

Played in one match: R.S. Cowan 0, 18* (1 ct); A. Willows 0*, 4.

BOWLING

	Type	O	M	R	W	Avge	Best	5 wI	10 wM
G.G. Arnold	RFM	59	23	89	6	14.83	2-9	—	—
Imran Khan	RF	194.1	58	458	29	15.79	4-26	—	—
G.S. Le Roux	RF	467	116	1210	65	18.61	5-15	3	—
I.A. Greig	RM	525.5	123	1578	63	25.04	5-46	2	—
A.C.S. Pigott	RFM	477	92	1684	61	27.60	7-74	4	—
C.E. Waller	SLA	605	171	1627	55	29.58	7-67	1	—
C.M. Wells	RM	69.4	12	195	5	39.00	2-15	—	—
A.M. Green	RM	60	6	274	6	45.66	2-48	—	—
J.R.T. Barclay	OB	230.2	58	702	11	63.81	3-44	—	—

Also bowled: R.S. Cowan 9-0-34-0; I.J. Gould 9.3-2-23-0; A.N. Jones 29-5-100-4; P.W.G. Parker 5-0-16-0; C.P. Phillipson 14-0-57-1; A.P. Wells 12-1-42-0; A. Willows 17-4-39-0.

County Records

First-class cricket

Highest innings totals:	For	705-8d v Surrey (Hastings)	1902
	Agst	726 by Notts (Nottingham)	1895
Lowest innings totals:	For	19 v Surrey (Godalming)	1830
		19 v Notts (Hove)	1873
	Agst	18 by Kent (Gravesend)	1867
Highest individual innings:	For	333 by K.S. Duleepsinhji v Northants (Hove)	1930
	Agst	322 E. Paynter for Lancs (Hove)	1937
Best bowling in an innings:	For	10-48 C.H.G. Bland v Kent (Tonbridge)	1899
	Agst	9-11 A.P. Freeman for Kent (Hove)	1922
Best bowling in a match:	For	17-106 G.R. Cox v Warwicks (Horsham)	1926
	Agst	17-67 A.P. Freeman for Kent (Hove)	1922
Most runs in a season:		2850 (av. 64.77) John Langridge	1949
runs in a career:		34152 (av. 37.69) John Langridge	1928-1955
100s in a season:		12 by John Langridge	1949
100s in a career:		76 by John Langridge	1928-1955
wickets in a season:		198 (av. 13.45) M.W. Tate	1925
wickets in a career:		2223 (av. 16.34) M.W. Tate	1912-1937

RECORD WICKET STANDS

1st	490	E.H. Bowley & John Langridge v Middlesex (Hove)	1933
2nd	385	E.H. Bowley & M.W. Tate v Northants (Hove)	1921
3rd	298	K.S. Ranjitsinhji & E.H. Killick v Lancs (Hove)	1901
4th	326*	G. Cox & James Langridge v Yorks (Leeds)	1949
5th	297	J.H. Parks & H.W. Parks v Hants (Portsmouth)	1937
6th	255	K.S. Duleepsinhji & M.W. Tate v Northants (Hove)	1930
7th	344	K.S. Ranjitsinhji & W. Newham v Essex (Leyton)	1902
8th	229*	C.L.A. Smith & G. Brann v Kent (Hove)	1902
9th	178	H.W. Parks & A.F. Wensley v Derby (Horsham)	1930
10th	156	G.R. Cox & H.R. Butt v Cambridge U (Cambridge)	1908

One-day cricket

Highest innings totals:	Gillette Cup/ NatWest Trophy	314-7 v Kent (Tunbridge Wells)	1963
	John Player League	293-4 v Worcs (Horsham)	1980
	Benson & Hedges Cup	305-6 v Kent (Hove)	1982
Lowest innings totals:	Gillette Cup/ NatWest Trophy	49 v Derby (Chesterfield)	1969
	John Player League	61 v Derby (Derby)	1978
	Benson & Hedges Cup	61 v Middlesex (Hove)	1978
Highest individual innings:	Gillette Cup/ NatWest Trophy	141* G.D. Mendis v Warwicks (Hove)	1980
	John Player League	129 A.W. Greig v Yorks (Scarborough)	1976
	Benson & Hedges Cup	117 R.D.V. Knight v Surrey (Oval)	1977
Best bowling figures:	Gillette Cup/ NatWest Trophy	6-30 D.L. Bates v Glos (Hove)	1968
	John Player League	6-14 M.A. Buss v Lancs (Hove)	1973
	Benson & Hedges Cup	5-8 Imran Khan v Northants (Northampton)	1978

WARWICKSHIRE

Formation of club: 1882.
Colours: Blue, gold and silver.
Badge: Bear and ragged staff.
County Champions (3): 1911, 1951 and 1972.
Gillette Cup Winners (2): 1966 and 1968.
Gillette Cup Finalists (2): 1964 and 1972.
NatWest Trophy Finalists: 1982.
John Player League Champions: 1980.
Benson & Hedges Cup Semi-Finalists (4): 1972, 1975, 1976 and 1978.
Gillette Man of the Match Awards: 21.
NatWest Man of the Match Awards: 4.
Benson & Hedges Gold Awards: 27.

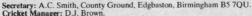

Secretary: A.C. Smith, County Ground, Edgbaston, Birmingham B5 7QU.
Cricket Manager: D.J. Brown.
Captain: R.G.D. Willis, MBE.
Prospects of Play Telephone No: (021) 440 3624.

Dennis Leslie AMISS B Birmingham 7/4/1943. RHB, SLC. Debut 1960. Cap 1965. Benefit 1975 (£34,947). Tests: 50 between 1966 and 1977 and 1 match v Rest of the World in 1970. Tours: Pakistan 1966-67, India, Pakistan and Sri Lanka 1972-73, West Indies 1973-74, Australia and New Zealand 1974-75, India, Sri Lanka and Australia 1976-77, International XI in India and Pakistan 1967-68, SAB XI in South Africa 1981-82. Also played for Rest of the World XI v Pakistan XI in Pakistan 1970-71. 1,000 runs (18) – 2,110 (av. 65.93) in 1976 best. Scored 1,120 runs (av. 74.66) in West Indies in 1973-74. Two centuries in a match twice: 155* and 112 v Worcs (Birmingham) 1978 and 109 and 127 v Derby (Derby) 1981. NW Man of the Match: 1. Gillette Man of the Match: 3. BH Gold Awards: 3. HS: 262* England v West Indies (Kingston) 1973-74. HSUK: 232* v Glos (Bristol) 1979. HSNW: 135 v Cambs (Birmingham) 1982. HSJPL: 117* v Sussex (Horsham) 1981. HSBH: 105* v Scotland (Birmingham) 1982. BB: 3-21 v Middlesex (Lord's) 1970.

Mohamed ASIF DIN B Kampala, Uganda 21/9/1960. RHB, LB. Debut 1981. HS: 102 v Middlesex (Coventry) 1982. HSNW: 45 v Surrey (Lord's) 1982. HSJPL: 56* v Hants (Bournemouth) 1982. HSBH: 61 v Notts (Nottingham) 1982. BB: 5-100 v Glamorgan (Birmingham) 1982.

Robin Ian Henry Benbow DYER (Wellington College) B Hertford 22/12/1958. 6ft 4ins tall. RHB, RM. Debut 1981. HS: 31* v Somerset (Birmingham) 1982. HSJPL: 10 v Lancs (Manchester) 1982.

Anthonie Michal (Yogi) FERREIRA (Hillview High School, Pretoria) B Pretoria, South Africa 13/4/1955. RHB, RM. Played for Northern Transvaal 1974-75 to 1981-82. Played for D.H. Robin's XI v both Oxford and Cambridge Universities at Eastbourne in 1978. Debut for county 1979. HS: 112* v Indians (Birmingham) 1982. HSGC/NW: 14 v Oxfordshire (Birmingham) 1980. HSJPL: 43 v Northants (Northampton) 1981. HSBH: 45 v Lancs (Manchester) 1982. BB: 8-38 Northern Transvaal v Transvaal B (Pretoria) 1977-78. BBUK: 5-66 v Somerset (Birmingham) 1979. BBGC/NW: 4-50 v Notts (Birmingham) 1979. BBJPL: 4-26 v Sussex (Horsham) 1981. BBBH: 4-42 v Scotland (Birmingham) 1982.

WARWICKSHIRE

Norman GIFFORD B Ulverston (Lancs) 30/3/1940. LHB, SLA. Played for Worcs 1960-82. Cap 1961. County captain 1971 to 1980. Benefit (£11,047) in 1974. *Wisden* 1974. Awarded MBE in 1978. Second benefit in 1981. Joined Warwicks for 1983. England selector. Tests: 15 between 1964 and 1973. Played in one match for Rest of World v Australia 1971-72. Tours: International team to South Africa and Pakistan 1961-62, Worcs to South Africa 1964-65, Commonwealth to Pakistan 1970-71, Rest of World to Australia 1971-72, International Wanderers to South Africa 1972-73, India, Pakistan and Sri Lanka 1972-73. 100 wkts: (3) – 133 wkts (av. 19.66) in 1961 best. Hat-trick v Derby (Chesterfield) 1965. Took 4 wkts in 6 balls v Cambridge U (Cambridge) 1972. Gillette Man of Match Awards: 1. BH Gold Awards: 2. HS: 89 Worcs v Oxford U (Oxford) 1963. HSTC: 25* v New Zealand (Nottingham) 1973. HSGC/NW: 38 Worcs v Warwicks (Lord's) 1966. HSJPL: 31 Worcs v Kent (Worcester) 1982. HSBH: 33 Worcs v Kent (Lords's) 1973. BB: 8-28 Worcs v Yorks (Sheffield) 1968. BBTC: 5-55 v Pakistan (Karachi) 1972-73. BBGC/NW: 4-7 Worcs v Surrey (Worcester) 1972. BBJPL: 5-28 Worcs v Northants (Worcester) 1979. BBBH: 6-8 Worcs v Minor Counties (South) (High Wycombe) 1979.

William HOGG B Ulverston (Lancs) 12/7/1955. RHB, RFM. Debut for Lancs 1976. Debut for Warwicks 1981. HS: 31 v Hants (Birmingham) 1981. BB: 7-84 Lancs v Warwicks (Manchester) 1978. BBC: 4:46 v Northants (Northampton) 1981. BBJPL: 4-23 Lancs v Essex (Ilford) 1979. BBBH: 4-35 Lancs v Hants (Manchester) 1979.

Geoffrey William HUMPAGE B Birmingham 24/4/1954. RHB, WK, RM. Debut 1974. Cap 1976. 1,000 runs (5) – 1,701 runs (av. 50.02) in 1981 best. Scored two centuries in match (146 and 110) v Glos (Gloucester) 1981. BH Gold Awards: 2. HS: 254 v Lancs (Southport) 1982 sharing in English record 4th wkt partnership of 470 with A.I. Kallicharran. HSGC/NW: 58 v Somerset (Taunton) 1978. HSJPL: 108* v Middlesex (Birmingham) 1980. HSBH: 93 v Yorks (Birmingham) 1981. BBJPL: 4-53 v Glos (Moreton-in-Marsh) 1979.

Alvin Isaac KALLICHARRAN B Port Mourant, Berbice, British Guiana 21/3/1949. LHB, OB. 5ft 4ins tall. Played for Guyana 1966–67 to 1980–81. Debut for county 1971. Cap 1972. Played for Queensland in 1977–78 and for Transvaal in 1981-82. Tests: 66 for West Indies between 1971-72 and 1980-81 scoring 100* and 101 in first two innings in Tests v New Zealand and captaining country in 9 Tests. Tours: West Indies to England 1973, 1976 and 1980, World XI in Pakistan 1973-74, India, Sri Lanka and Pakistan 1974-75, Australia 1975-76, India and Sri Lanka 1978-79 (captain), Australia and New Zealand 1979-80, Pakistan 1980-81, 1,000 runs (8) – 2,120 (av. 66.25) in 1982 best. Also scored 1,249 runs (av. 56.77) on 1974-75 tour. NW Man of the Match: 1. BH Gold Awards: 2. HS: 235 v Worcs (Worcester) 1982. HSTC: 187 West Indies v India (Bombay) 1978-79. HSNW: 141* v Somerset (Taunton) 1982. HSJPL: 102* v Notts (Birmingham) 1981. HSBH: 109 v Glos (Bristol) 1978. BB: 4-48 v Derby (Birmingham) 1978. Benefit 1983.

Christopher LETHBRIDGE B Castleford (Yorks) 23/6/1961. RHB, RM. Debut 1981 taking wicket of G. Boycott with his first ball in first-class cricket. HS: 87* v Somerset (Taunton) 1982. HSJPL: 57* v Somerset (Birmingham) 1982. BB: 5-68 v Glamorgan (Cardiff) 1982. BBJPL: 5-47 v Northants (Birmingham) 1982. BBBH: 3-49 v Northants (Birmingham) 1982.

144

Timothy Andrew (Andy) LLOYD B Oswestry (Shropshire) 5/11/1956. LHB, RM. Debut 1977. Played for Orange Free State in 1978-79 and 1979-80. Cap 1980. NW Man of the Match: 1. 1,000 runs (3) – 1,445 runs (av. 34.40) in 1981 best. HS: 138 v Somerset (Birmingham) 1981. HSGC/NW: 81 v Devon (Birmingham) 1980. HSJPL: 90 v Kent (Birmingham) 1980. HSBH: 60 v Kent (Oval) 1981.

Michael Stephen Anthony McEVOY B Jorhat, Assam 25/1/1956. RHB, RM. Played for Essex 1976 to 1981. Joined Warwicks for 1983. HS: 67* Essex v Yorks (Middlesbrough) 1977. HSJPL: 15 Essex v Leics (Chelmsford) 1980. HSBH: 13 Essex v Kent (Dartford) 1981.

Christopher Middleton OLD B Middlesbrough 22/12/1948. LHB, RFM. Debut for Yorks 1966. Cap 1969. Best Young Cricketer of the Year in 1970. *Wisden* 1978. Benefit (£32,916) in 1979. County Captain 1981. Replaced in 1982 and joined Warwicks for 1983. Played for Northern Transvaal in 1981-82. Tests: 46 between 1972-73 and 1981. Played in 2 matches against Rest of World 1970. Tours: Duke of Norfolk to West Indies 1969-70, India, Pakistan and Sri Lanka 1972-73, West Indies 1973-74 and 1980-81, Australia and New Zealand 1974-75, International Wanderers to South Africa 1975-76, India, Sri Lanka and Australia 1976-77, Pakistan and New Zealand 1977-78, Australia 1978-79. Scored century in 37 minutes v Warwickshire (Birmingham) 1977 – second fastest ever in first-class cricket. Took 4 wickets in 5 balls, England v Pakistan (Birmingham) 1978. BH Gold Awards: 3 for Yorks. HS: 116 Yorks v Indians (Bradford) 1974. HSTC: 65 v Pakistan (Oval) 1974. HSNW: 55* Yorks v Worcs (Leeds) 1982. HSJPL: 82 Yorks v Somerset (Bath) 1974 and 82* v Somerset (Glastonbury) 1976. HSBH: 78* Yorks v Scotland (Bradford) 1981. BB: 7-20 Yorks v Glos (Middlesbrough) 1969. BBTC: 7-50 v Pakistan (Birmingham) 1978. BBGC/NW: 4-9 Yorks v Durham (Middlesbrough) 1978. BBJPL: 5-53 Yorks v Sussex (Hove) 1971. BBBH: 4-17 Yorks v Derby (Bradford) 1973.

Philip Robert OLIVER B West Bromwich (Staffs) 9/5/1956. RHB, OB. Debut 1975. HS: 171* v Northants (Northampton) 1981. HSGC/NW: 32* v Oxfordshire (Birmingham) 1980. HSJPL: 78* v Hants (Southampton) 1978. HSBH: 46 v Essex (Chelmsford) 1979. BBJPL: 3-36 v Middlesex (Lord's) 1977. Has played soccer for Telford in Southern League.

Gladstone Cleopthas SMALL (Moseley School, Birmingham) B St. George, Barbados 18/10/1961. RHB, RFM. Toured New Zealand with D.H. Robins' XI in 1979-80 and made debut v Northern Districts (Hamilton). Debut for county 1980. Toured Pakistan with International XI 1981-82. Cap 1982. HS: 57* v Oxford U (Oxford) 1982. HSNW: 33 v Surrey (Lord's) 1982. HSJPL: 17 v Notts (Birmingham) 1980. HSBH: 19* v Yorks (Birmingham) 1981. BB: 7-68 v Yorks (Birmingham) 1982. BBNW: 3-22 v Glamorgan (Cardiff) 1982. BBJPL: 5-29 v Surrey (Birmingham) 1980.

David Martin SMITH B Coventry 21/1/1962. No relation to K.D. Smith. LHB, SLA. Debut 1981. HS: 27 v Oxford U (Oxford) 1982.

Kenneth David SMITH B Jesmond, Newcastle-upon-Tyne 9/7/1956. RHB. Son of Kenneth D. Smith, former Leics player. Debut 1973. Cap 1978. 1,000 runs (3) – 1,582 runs (av. 36.79) in 1980 best. NW Man of the Match: 1. BH Gold Awards: 1. HS: 140 v Worcs (Worcester) 1980. HSNW: 113 v Yorks (Birmingham) 1982. HSJPL: 60 v Glamorgan (Swansea) 1979. HSBH: 84 v Worcs (Worcester) 1980.

WARWICKSHIRE

Paul Andrew SMITH B Newcastle-upon-Tyne 15/4/1964. Youngest brother of K.D. Smith. RHB, RM. Debut 1982. HS: 68 v Essex (Colchester) 1982. HSJPL: 36 v Somerset (Birmingham) 1982. BBJPL: 3-21 v Middlesex (Birmingham) 1982.

Simon Paul SUTCLIFFE (King George V GS, Southport and Oxford) B Watford 22/5/1960. Son of Peter W. Sutcliffe, former national coach. RHB, OB. Debut for Oxford U 1980. Blues 1980-81. University Secretary in 1981. Debut for county 1981. HS: 20 v Glos (Nuneaton) 1982. BB: 6-19 Oxford U v Warwickshire (Oxford) 1980. BBNW: 3-40 v Cambridgeshire (Birmingham) 1982.

Geoffrey Alan TEDSTONE B Southport, Lancs 19/1/1961. RHB, WK. Debut 1982. HS: 18* v Northants (Birmingham) 1982. HSJPL: 23 v Middlesex (Birmingham) 1982.

Robert George Dylan WILLIS (Guildford RGS) B Sunderland 30/5/1949. RHB, RF. Debut for Surrey 1969. Debut for Warwickshire in 1972. Cap 1972. *Wisden* 1977. Appointed County Captain in 1980. Benefit in 1981. Awarded MBE in 1982 New Year Honours List. Tests: 74 between 1970-71 and 1981-82, captain in 6 Tests. Tours: Australia and New Zealand 1970-71 (flown out as replacement for A. Ward) and 1974-75, D.H. Robins to South Africa 1972-73, West Indies 1973-74 and 1980-81 (vice-captain) – returned early through injury, India, Sri Lanka and Australia 1976-77, Pakistan and New Zealand 1977-78, Australia 1978-79 (vice-captain), Australia and India 1979-80 (vice-captain), India and Sri Lanka 1981-82 (vice-captain), Australia and New Zealand 1982-83 (captain). Hat-tricks (2) v Derby (Birmingham) 1972 and West Indies (Birmingham) 1976. Also in John Player League v Yorks (Birmingham) 1973. Gillette man of the Match: 1 (for Surrey). BH Gold Awards: 4. HS: 72 v Indians (Birmingham) 1982. HSTC: 28* v Pakistan (Birmingham) 1982. HSGC/NW: 12* Surrey v Sussex (Oval) 1970. HSJPL: 52* v Derby (Birmingham) 1975. HSBH: 37 v Notts (Nottingham) 1982. BB: 8-32 v Glos (Bristol) 1977. BBTC: 8-43 v Australia (Leeds) 1981. BBGC/NW: 6-49 Surrey v Middlesex (Oval) 1970. BBJPL: 4-12 v Middlesex (Lord's) 1973. BBBH: 7-32 v Yorkshire (Birmingham) 1981. Played soccer (goalkeeper) for Guildford City.

Simon Howard WOOTTON B Perivale (Middlesex) 24/2/1959. LHB, SLA. Debut 1981. HS: 77 v Sir Lankans (Birmingham) 1981. HSJPL: 28* v Lancs (Manchester) 1982. HSBH: 33 v Kent (Oval) 1981.

NB. The following players whose particulars appeared in the 1982 Annual have been omitted: J. Cumbes, P.J. Lewington, G.J. Lord, R.K. Maguire, D. Marsh, C. Maynard, S.P. Perryman.

County Averages

Schweppes County Championship: Played 22, won 0, drawn 14, lost 8.
All first-class matches: Played 25, won 0, drawn 17, lost 8.

BATTING AND FIELDING

Cap		M	I	NO	Runs	HS	Avge	100	50	Ct	St
1972	A.I. Kallicharan	23	37	5	2120	235	66.25	8	5	8	—
1976	G.W. Humpage	24	41	4	1407	254	38.02	4	5	49	1
1965	D.L. Amiss	21	38	1	1404	156	37.94	1	9	12	—
—	A.M. Ferreira	8	10	2	303	112*	37.87	1	—	5	—
1980	T.A. Lloyd	25	45	5	1432	122	35.80	2	9	12	—
—	P.J. Lewington	4	5	4	35	15*	35.00	—	—	—	—
—	Asif Din	24	34	2	855	102	26.71	1	2	14	—
1972	R.G.D. Willis	13	16	5	287	72	26.09	—	2	4	—
—	P.A. Smith	10	16	1	383	68	25.53	—	2	7	—
1978	K.D. Smith	20	34	6	691	67	24.67	—	5	16	—
—	C. Lethbridge	16	21	5	369	87*	23.06	—	1	7	—
—	G.A. Tedstone	3	5	2	45	18*	15.00	—	—	4	1
—	R.I.H.B. Dyer	5	5	1	58	31*	14.50	—	—	1	—
—	P.J. Oliver	7	9	—	143	46	15.88	—	—	4	—
1982	G.C. Small	25	29	5	309	57*	12.87	—	1	6	—
—	P.J. Hartley	3	4	1	31	16	10.33	—	—	1	—
—	J. Cumbes	14	14	7	33	7*	4.71	—	—	8	—
—	W. Hogg	5	4	2	9	8	4.50	—	—	2	—
—	S.P. Sutcliffe	14	17	7	52	20	5.20	—	—	2	—
—	S.H. Wootton	3	2	0	3	3	1.50	—	—	—	—
—	K.R. Maguire	3	3	0	3	2	1.00	—	—	1	—
1964	D.J. Brown	3	1	1	7	7*	—	—	—	1	—

Played in two matches: D.M. Smith 27, 0.
Played in one match: C. Maynard 40 (2 ct).

BOWLING

	Type	O	M	R	W	Avge	Best	5 wI	10 wM
A.M. Ferreira	RM	243.3	49	789	26	30.34	5-109	1	—
G.C. Small	RFM	589.1	107	1925	63	30.55	7-68	1	—
C. Lethbridge	RM	304.3	68	977	29	33.68	5-68	1	—
R.G.D. Willis	RF	284	64	892	26	34.30	6-45	1	—
A.I. Kallicharan	OB	154.2	21	578	14	41.28	3-32	—	—
W. Hogg	RFM	105.3	18	339	8	42.37	2-45	—	—
J. Cumbes	RM	349.1	71	993	21	47.28	4-47	—	—
S.P. Sutcliffe	OB	554.3	114	1799	37	48.62	5-151	1	—
P.A. Smith	RM	136	21	536	10	53.60	2-12	—	—
Asif Din	LB	284.1	61	1128	20	56.40	5-100	1	—
T.A. Lloyd	RM	95	24	344	5	68.80	2-29	—	—

Also bowled: D.L. Amiss 2.1-0-18-0; R.I.H.B. Dyer 1-0-2-0; G.W. Humpage 30-6-79-2; P.J. Hartley 57-11-215-2; P.J. Lewington 89.1-19-294-3; K.R. Maguire 35-7-123-1; D.M. Smith 16-2-59-0; D.J. Brown 51-8-204-4.

County Records

First-class cricket

Highest innings totals:	For	657-6d v Hants (Birmingham)	1899
	Agst	887 by Yorks (Birmingham)	1896
Lowest innings totals:	For	16 v Kent (Tonbridge)	1913
	Agst	15 by Hants (Birmingham)	1922
Highest individual innings:	For	305* F.R. Foster v Worcs (Dudley)	1914
	Agst	316 R.H. Moore for Hants (Bournemouth)	1937
Best bowling in an innings:	For	10-41 J.D. Bannister v Combined Services (Birmingham)	1959
	Agst	10-36 H. Verity for Yorks (Leeds)	1931
Best bowling in a match:	For	15-76 S. Hargreave v Surrey (Oval)	1903
	Agst	17-92 A.P. Freeman for Kent (Folkestone)	1932
Most runs in a season:		2,417 (av. 60.42) M.J.K. Smith	1959
runs in a career:		33,862 (av. 36.18) William Quaife	1894-1928
100s in a season:		8 by R.E.S. Wyatt	1937
		R.B. Kanhai	1972
		and A.I. Kallicharran	1982
100s in a career:		71 by William Quaife	1894-1928
wickets in a season:		180 (av. 15.13) W.E. Hollies	1946
wickets in a career:		2,201 (av. 20.45) W.E. Hollies	1932-1957

RECORD WICKET STANDS

1st	377*	N.F. Horner & K. Ibadulla v Surrey (Oval)	1960
2nd	465*	J.A. Jameson & R.B. Kanhai v Glos (Birmingham)	1974
3rd	327	S. Kinneir & William Quaife v Lancs (Birmingham)	1901
4th	470	A.I. Kallicharran & G.W. Humpage v Lancs (Southport)	1982
5th	268	Walter Quaife & William Quaife v Essex (Leyton)	1900
6th	220	H.E. Dollery & J. Buckingham v Derby (Derby)	1938
7th	250	H.E. Dollery & J.S. Ord v Kent (Maidstone)	1953
8th	228	A.J.W. Croom & R.E.S. Wyatt v Worcs (Dudley)	1925
9th	154	G.W. Stephens & A.J.W. Croom v Derby (Birmingham)	1925
10th	128	F.R. Santall & W. Sanders v Yorks (Birmingham)	1930

One-day cricket

Highest innings totals:	Gillette Cup/ NatWest Trophy	314-6 v Oxfordshire (Birmingham)	1980
	John Player League	265-5 v Northants (Northampton)	1979
	Benson & Hedges Cup	291-5 v Lancs (Manchester)	1981
Lowest innings totals:	Gillette Cup/ NatWest Trophy	109 v Kent (Canterbury)	1971
	John Player League	65 v Kent (Maidstone)	1979
	Benson & Hedges Cup	96 v Leics (Leicester)	1972
Highest individual innings	Gillette Cup/ NatWest Trophy	141* A.I. Kallicharran v Somerset (Taunton)	1982
	John Player League	123* J.A. Jameson v Notts (Nottingham)	1973
	Benson & Hedges Cup	119* R.B. Kanhai v Northants (Northampton)	1975

Best bowling figures:	Gillette Cup/ NatWest Trophy	6-32 **K.** Ibadulla v Hants (Birmingham)	1965
	John Player League	5-13 D.J. Brown v Worcs (Birmingham)	1970
	Benson & Hedges Cup	7-32 R.G.D. Willis v Yorks (Birmingham)	1981

WORCESTERSHIRE

Formation of present club: 1865.
Colours: Dark Green and Black.
Badge: Shield, *Argent*, bearing *Fess* between three *Pears Sable*.
County Champions (3): 1964, 1965, and 1974.
Gillette Cup Finalists (2): 1963 and 1966.
NatWest Trophy Second Round: 1981 and 1982.
John Player League Champions: 1971.
Benson & Hedges Cup Finalists (2): 1973 and 1976.
Gillette Man of the Match Awards: 18.
NatWest Man of the Match Awards: Nil.
Benson & Hedges Gold Awards: 25.

Secretary: M.D. Vockins, County Ground, New Road, Worcester WR2 4QQ.
Captain: P.A. Neale.
Prospects of Play Telephone No: (0905) 422011.

David Andrew BANKS B Brierley Hill, Staffordshire 11/1/1965. RHB, RM. Played in one JPL match v Hants (Southampton) in 1982. Has yet to appear in first-class cricket.

Timothy Stephen CURTIS B Chislehurst (Kent) 15/1/1960. RHB, LB. Debut 1979:̄HS: 59* v Warwicks (Birmingham) 1980 and v Glamorgan (Worcester) 1982. HSNW: 29 v Derby (Derby) 1981. HSJPL: 33* v Middlesex (Lord's) 1981.

Damian Basil D'OLIVEIRA B Cape Town, South Africa 19/10/1960. RHB, RM/OB. Son of Basil D'Oliveira (England and Worcs). Debut 1982. HS: 21 v Zimbabwe (Worcester) 1982. HSJPL: 33 v Somerset (Taunton) 1982.

Ricardo McDonald ELLCOCK B Bridgetown, Barbados 17/6/1965. RHB, RFM. Debut 1982 aged 17 years 86 days. HS: 13* v Middlesex (Worcester) 1982. BB: 3-80 in same match.

David John HUMPHRIES B Alveley (Shropshire) 6/8/1953. LHB, WK. Debut for Leics 1974. Debut for Worcs in 1977. Cap 1978. Gillette Man of Match: 1. HS: 111* v Warwicks (Worcester) 1978. HSGC/NW: 58 v Glamorgan (Worcester) 1977. HSJPL: 62 v Notts (Dudley) 1977. HSBH: 41 v Yorks (Leeds) 1982.

Richard Keith ILLINGWORTH B Bradford, Yorks 23/8/1963. RHB, SLA. Debut 1982. HS: 47* v Glamorgan (Worcester) 1982. HSJPL: 21 v Middlesex (Worcester) 1982. BB: 4-85 v Warwicks (Worcester) 1982.

John Darling INCHMORE B Ashington (Northumberland) 22/2/1949. RHB, RFM. Debut 1973. Cap 1976. Played for Northern Transvaal in 1976-77. BH Gold Awards: 2. HS: 113 v Essex (Worcester) 1974. HSNW: 32* v Yorks (Leeds) 1982. HSJPL: 45 v Northants (Worcester) 1981 and 45 v Derby (Chesterfield) 1981. HSBH: 49* v Somerset (Taunton) 1976. BB: 8-58 v Yorks (Worcester) 1977. BBNW: 4-47 v Yorks (Leeds) 1982. BBJPL: 4-9 v Northants (Dudley) 1975. BBBH: 4-21 v Combined Universities (Cambridge) 1980.

Philip Anthony NEALE B Scunthorpe (Lincs) 5/6/1954. RHB, RM. Debut 1975. Cap 1978. Captain 1983. 1,000 runs: (4) – 1,305 runs (av. 42.09) in 1979 best. HS: 163* v Notts (Worcester) 1979. HSGC/NW: 68 v Glos (Bristol) 1976. HSJPL: 102 v Northants (Luton) 1982. HSBH: 128 v Lancs (Manchester) 1980. Soccer for Lincoln City.

Philip John NEWPORT B High Wycombe, Buckinghamshire 11/10/1962. RHB, RFM. Debut 1982. HS: 11 v Notts (Worcester) 1982. BB: 4-76 v Notts (Worcester) 1982.

Joseph Alan ORMROD (Kirkaldy HS) B Ramsbottom (Lancs) 22/12/1942. RHB, OB. Debut 1962. Cap 1966. Benefit (£19,000) in 1977. Tours: Worcs to Jamaica 1965-66, Pakistan 1966-67. 1,000 runs: (12) – 1,535 runs (av. 45.14) in 1978 best. Scored two centuries in match (101 and 131*) v Somerset (Worcester) 1980. Shared in 4th wkt partnership record for county, 281 with Younis Ahmed v Notts (Nottingham) 1979. BH Gold Awards: 4. HS: 204* v Kent (Dartford) 1973. HSGC/NW: 59 v Essex (Worcester) 1975. HSJPL: 110* v Kent (Canterbury) 1975. HSBH: 124* v Glos (Worcester) 1976. BB: 5-27 v Glos (Bristol) 1972. BBJPL: 3-51 v Hants (Worcester) 1972.

Dipak Narshibhai PATEL B Nairobi, Kenya 25/10/1958. Has lived in UK since 1967. RHB, OB. Debut 1976. Cap 1979. 1,000 runs (2) – 1,155 runs (av. 32.08) in 1981 best. Shared in 6th wkt partnership record for county, 227 with E.J.O. Hemsley v Oxford U (Oxford) 1976. HS: 138 v Warwicks (Worcester) 1981. HSNW: 42 v Derby (Derby) 1981. HSJPL: 125 v Hants (Southampton) 1982. HSBH: 90 v Leics (Worcester) 1982. BB: 7-46 v Lancs (Worcester) 1982. BBJPL: 4-39 v Hants (Southampton) 1982. BBBH: 3-42 v Yorks (Worcester) 1980.

Stephen Peter PERRYMAN B Yardley, Birmingham 22/10/1955. RHB, RM. Debut 1974 for Warwicks. Cap 1977. Debut for Worcs 1982. BH Gold Award: 1 (for Warwicks). HS: 42 Warwicks v Somerset (Birmingham) 1977. HSJPL: 19* v Kent (Worcester) 1980. HSBH: 18 Warwicks v Essex (Chelmsford) 1979. BB: 7-49 Warwicks v Hants (Bournemouth) 1978. BBGC/NW: 3-35 Warwicks v Middlesex (Lord's) 1977. BBJPL: 4-19 Warwicks v Surrey (Oval) 1975. BBBH: 4-17 Warwicks v Minor Counties (West) (Birmingham) 1978.

Alan Paul PRIDGEON B Wall Heath (Staffs) 22/2/1954. RHB, RM. Debut 1972. Cap 1980. HS: 34 v Glamorgan (Swansea) 1981. HSGC/NW: 13* v Somerset (Taunton) 1980. HSJPL: 17 v Kent (Worcester) 1982. HSBH: 13* v Leics (Worcester) 1982. BB: 7-35 v Oxford U (Oxford) 1976. BBGC/NW: 3-25 v Somerset (Taunton) 1980. BBJPL: 6-26 v Surrey (Worcester) 1978. BBBH: 3-57 v Warwicks (Birmingham) 1976. Soccer for Ledbury Town in West Midland League.

Mark Stephen SCOTT B Muswell Hill (Middlesex) 10/3/1959. RHB. Debut 1981, scoring 968 runs (av. 26.88). HS: 109 v Glos (Bristol) 1981. HSJPL: 42 v Glos (Worcester) 1981.

Alan Esmond WARNER B Birmingham 12/5/1957. RHB, RFM. Debut 1982. HS: 67 v Warwicks (Birmingham) 1982. HSBH: 24* v Derby (Worcester) 1982. BB: 4-73 v Derby (Worcester) 1982.

Andrew John WEBSTER B Burton-on-Trent (Staffs) 5/3/1959. 6ft 4ins tall. LHB, RM. Debut 1981. HS: 25 v Warwicks (Birmingham) 1982. BB: 5-87 v Hants (Southampton) 1982.

WORCESTERSHIRE

Martin John WESTON B Worcester 8/4/1959. RHB, RM. Debut 1979. HS: 93 v Pakistanis (Worcester) 1982. HSNW: 23 v Yorks (Leeds) 1982. HSJPL: 109 v Somerset (Taunton) 1982. HSBH: 40 v Yorks (Leeds) 1982. BB: 3-42 v Middlesex (Worcester) 1982.

Mohammad YOUNIS AHMED (Moslem HS, Lahore) B Jullunder, Pakistan 20/10/1947. LHB, LM/SLA. Younger brother of Saeed Ahmed, Pakistan Test cricketer. Debut 1961-62 for Pakistan Inter Board Schools XI v South Zone at age of 14 years 4 months. Debut for Surrey 1965. Cap 1969. Played for South Australia in 1972-73 Sheffield Shield competition. Tours: Cavaliers to Jamaica 1969-70, Commonwealth to Pakistan 1970-71, D.H. Robins to South Africa 1973-74 and 1974-75, International Wanderers to South Africa 1974-75 and 1975-76. Debut for Worcs and cap 1979. Is regarded as an English player for qualification purposes. Tests: 2 for Pakistan v New Zealand 1969-70. 1,000 runs (11) – 1,760 runs (av. 47.56) in 1969 best. Shared in 4th wkt partnership record for county, 281 with J.A. Ormrod v Notts (Nottingham) 1979. BH Gold Awards: 3 (1 for Surrey). HS: 221* v Notts (Nottingham) 1979. HSTC: 62 Pakistan v New Zealand (Karachi) 1969-70. HSGC/NW: 87 Surrey v Middlesex (Oval) 1970. HSJPL: 113 Surrey v Warwicks (Birmingham) 1976 and 113 v Yorks (Worcester) 1979. HSBH: 115 v Yorks (Worcester) 1980. BB: 4-10 Surrey v Cambridge U (Cambridge) 1975. BBC: 3-33 v Oxford U (Oxford) 1979. BBJPL: 3-26 v Surrey (Oval) 1979. BBBH: 4-37 v Northants (Northampton) 1980.

NB. The following players whose particulars appeared in the 1982 Annual have been omitted: H.L. Alleyne, N. Gifford, E.J.O. Hemsley, W.R.K. Thomas and G.M. Turner.

County Averages

Schweppes County Championship: Played 22, won 3, drawn 14, lost 5.
All first-class matches: Played 25, won 3, drawn 16, lost 6.

BATTING AND FIELDING

Cap		M	I	NO	Runs	HS	Avge	100	50	Ct	St
1968	G.M. Turner	9	16	3	1171	311*	90.07	5	3	9	—
1979	Younis Ahmed	18	29	6	1247	122	54.21	4	7	11	—
1978	P.A. Neale	25	42	6	992	79*	27.55	—	6	8	—
—	T.S. Curtis	10	17	4	359	59*	27.61	—	2	5	—
1966	J.A. Ormrod	21	38	2	981	200*	27.25	1	4	8	—
1979	D.N. Patel	25	42	1	1104	133	26.92	1	4	20	—
1978	D.J. Humphries	25	37	5	852	98	26.62	—	7	41	5
—	M.J. Weston	17	31	1	704	93	23.46	—	6	4	—
1981	H.L. Alleyne	8	9	3	130	32	21.66	—	—	1	—
1961	N. Gifford	13	15	7	155	31*	19.37	—	—	9	—
—	A.E. Warner	11	17	2	287	67	19.13	—	1	2	—
1976	J.D. Inchmore	15	19	3	294	68	18.37	—	2	5	—
1969	E.J.O. Hemsley	16	24	1	393	49	17.08	—	—	8	—
—	A.J. Warner	8	10	5	75	25	15.00	—	—	3	—
—	R.K. Illingworth	11	16	4	191	47*	14.69	—	—	5	—
—	D.B. D'Oliviera	4	7	1	65	21	10.83	—	—	2	—
—	M.S. Scott	6	11	0	118	37	10.72	—	—	1	—
—	P.J. Newport	3	5	1	38	11	9.50	—	—	1	—
1980	A.P. Pridgeon	15	16	4	110	21	9.16	—	—	4	—
—	S.P. Perryman	14	18	10	58	14	7.25	—	—	5	—

Played in one match: R.M. Ellcock 0, 13*.

BOWLING

	Type	O	M	R	W	Avge	Best	5 wI	10 wM
J.D. Inchmore	RFM	326.2	68	841	35	24.02	7-53	2	—
D.N. Patel	OB	572.2	146	1531	50	30.62	7-46	2	—
S.P. Perryman	RM	430.1	111	1216	35	34.74	6-49	3	—
A.P. Pridgeon	RM	463	103	1184	32	37.00	4-39	—	—
A.E. Warner	RFM	202.1	34	707	19	37.21	4-73	—	—
H.L. Alleyne	RF	207.3	44	599	16	37.43	4-92	—	—
N. Gifford	SLA	482	154	1030	26	39.61	6-48	1	—
P.J. Newport	RFM	47	1	238	6	39.66	4-76	—	—
R.K. Illingworth	SLA	260.4	59	811	18	45.04	4-85	—	—
M.J. Weston	RM	85.1	11	286	6	47.66	3-42	—	—
A.J. Webster	RM	202.1	36	716	15	47.73	5-87	1	—

Also bowled: T.S. Curtis 2-0-7-0; R.M. Ellcock 26.1-2-90-3; E.J.O. Hemsley 20.4-1-80-1 P.A. Neale 6-2-16-0; J.A. Ormrod 1-0-5-0; Younis Ahmed 5-1-14-0.

County Records

First-class Cricket

Highest innings totals:	For	633 v Warwicks (Worcester)	1906
	Agst	701-4d by Leics (Worcester)	1906
Lowest innings totals:	For	24 v Yorks (Huddersfield)	1903
	Agst	30 by Hants (Worcester)	1903
Highest individual innings:	For	311* by G.M. Turner v Warwicks (Worcester)	1982
	Agst	331* J.D.B. Robertson for Middlesex (Worcester)	1949
Best bowling in an innings:	For	9-23 C.F. Root v Lancs (Worcester)	1931
	Agst	10-51 J. Mercer for Glamorgan (Worcester)	1936
Best bowling in a match:	For	15-87 A.J. Conway v Glos (Moreton-in-Marsh)	1914
	Agst	17-212 J.C. Clay for Glamorgan (Swansea)	1937
Most runs in a season:		2654 (av. 52.03) H.H.I. Gibbons	1934
runs in a career:		34490 (av. 34.04) D. Kenyon	1946-1967
100s in a season:		10 by G.M. Turner	1970
100s in a career:		72 by G.M. Turner	1967-1982
wickets in a season:		207 (av. 17.52) C.F. Root	1925
wickets in a career:		2143 (av. 23.73) R.T.D. Perks	1930-1955

RECORD WICKET STANDS

1st	309	F.L. Bowley & H.K. Foster v Derby (Derby)	1901
2nd	274	H.H.I. Gibbons & Nawab of Pataudi v Kent (Worcester)	1933
		H.H.I. Gibbons & Nawab of Pataudi v Glam (Worcester)	1934
3rd	314	M.J. Horton & T.W. Graveney v Somerset (Worcester)	1962
4th	281	J.A. Ormrod & Younis Ahmed v Notts (Nottingham)	1979
5th	393	E.G. Arnold & W.B. Burns v Warwicks (Birmingham)	1909
6th	227	E.J.O. Hemsley & D.N. Patel v Oxford U (Oxford)	1976
7th	197	H.H.I. Gibbons & R. Howorth v Surrey (Oval)	1938
8th	145*	F. Chester & W.H. Taylor v Essex (Worcester)	1914
9th	181	J.A. Cuffe & R.D. Burrows v Glos (Worcester)	1907
10th	119	W.B. Burns & G.A. Wilson v Somerset (Worcester)	1906

One-day Cricket

Highest innings:	GC/NatWest Trophy	286-5 v Yorks (Leeds)	1982
	John Player League	307-4 v Derby (Worcester)	1975
	Benson & Hedges Cup	314-5 v Lancs (Manchester)	1980
Lowest innings totals:	Gillette Cup/ NatWest Trophy	98 v Durham (Chester-le-Street)	1968
	John Player League	86 v Yorks (Leeds)	1969
	Benson & Hedges Cup	92 v Oxford & Cambridge Universities (Cambridge)	1975
Highest individual innings:	Gillette Cup/ NatWest Trophy	117* G.M. Turner v Lancs (Worcester)	1971
	John Player League	147 G.M. Turner v Sussex (Horsham)	1980
	Benson & Hedges Cup	143* G.M. Turner v Warwicks (Birmingham)	1976
Best bowling figures:	Gillette Cup/ NatWest Trophy	6-14 J.A. Flavell v Lancs (Worcester)	1963
	John Player League	6-26 A.P. Pridgeon v Surrey (Worcester)	1978
	Benson & Hedges Cup	6-8 N. Gifford v Minor Cos. (South) (High Wycombe)	1979

YORKSHIRE

Formation of present club: 1863, reorganised 1891.
Colours: Oxford blue, Cambridge blue, and gold.
Badge: White rose.
County Champions (31): 1867, 1870, 1893, 1896, 1898, 1900, 1901, 1902, 1905, 1908, 1912, 1919, 1922, 1923, 1924, 1925, 1931, 1932, 1933, 1935, 1937, 1938, 1939, 1946, 1959, 1960, 1962, 1963, 1966, 1967, and 1968.
Joint Champions (2): 1869 and 1949.
Gillette Cup Winners (2): 1965 and 1969.
NatWest Trophy Semi-Final: 1982.
John Player League runners-up: 1973.
Benson & Hedges Cup Finalists: 1972.
Fenner Trophy Winners: 1972, 1974 and 1981.
Gillette Man of the Match Awards: 14.
NatWest Man of the Match Awards: 2.
Benson & Hedges Gold Awards: 27.

Secretary: J. Lister, Headingley Cricket Ground, Leeds LS6 3BU.
Cricket Manager and Captain: R. Illingworth, CBE.

Charles **William** Jeffrey ATHEY B Middlesbrough 27/9/1957. RHB, RM. Debut 1976. Cap 1980. Tests: 3 in 1980 and 1980-81. Tours: West Indies 1980-81, D.H. Robins' Under-23 to New Zealand 1979-80. 1,000 runs (2) – 1,339 (av. 43.19) in 1982 best. GC Man of the Match: 2. BH Gold Awards: 2. HS: 134 v Derby (Derby) 1982. HSTC: 9 v Australia (Lord's) 1980. HSGC/NW: 115 v Kent (Leeds) 1980. HSJPL: 118 v Leics (Leicester) 1978. HSBH: 74* v Combined Universities (Oxford) 1980. BB: 3-38 v Surrey (Oval) 1978. BBJPL: 5-35 v Derby (Chesterfield) 1981. BBBH: 3-32 v Middlesex (Lord's) 1979.

David Leslie BAIRSTOW B Bradford 1/9/1951. RHB, WK, RM. Debut 1970. Cap 1973. Played for Griqualand West 1976-77 and 1977-78 (captain). Benefit 1982. Tests: 4 between 1979 and 1980-81. Tours: Australia 1979-80, West Indies 1980-81. 1,000 runs (1) – 1,083 (av. 40.11) in 1981. Dismissed 11 batsmen (all ct) for Yorks v Derby (Scarborough) 1982 equalling world record for most catches in a match. NW Man of the Match: 1. BH Gold Awards: 4. HS: 145 v Middlesex (Scarborough) 1980. HSTC: 59 v India (Oval) 1979. HSNW: 92 v Worcs (Leeds) 1982. HSJPL: 78 v Surrey (Scarborough) 1981. HSBH: 103* v Derby (Derby) 1981. BB: 3-82 Griqualand West v Transvaal B (Johannesburg) 1976-77. Soccer for Bradford City.

Paul Anthony BOOTH B Huddersfield 5/9/1965. LHB, SLA. Debut 1982 aged 17 years 3 days. Scored 0* and took 0-22 in only match v Derby (Scarborough).

Geoffrey BOYCOTT B Fitzwilliam (Yorks) 21/10/1940. RHB, RM. Plays in contact lenses. Debut 1962. Cap 1963. Best Young Cricketer of the Year in 1963. *Wisden* 1964. County captain from 1971 to 1978. Played for Northern Transvaal in 1971-72. Benefit (£20,639) in 1974. Awarded OBE in 1980 Birthday Honours List. Tests: 108 between 1964 and 1981-82 captaining England in 4 Tests in 1977-78. Played in 2 matches against Rest of World in 1970. Tours: South Africa 1964-65, Australia and New Zealand 1965-66 and 1970-71 (returned home early through broken arm injury), West Indies 1967-68, 1973-74 and 1980-81, Ceylon 1969-70, Pakistan and New Zealand 1977-78 (vice-captain), Australia 1978-79, Australia and

India 1979-80, India and Sri Lanka 1981-82, SAB to South Africa 1981-82. Banned for 3 years from Test cricket. 1,000 runs (20) – 2,503 runs (av. 100.12) in 1971 best. Only English batsman ever to have an average of 100 for season and repeated the feat in 1979 with 1,538 runs (av. 102.53). Also scored 1,000 runs in South Africa 1964-65 (1,135 runs, av. 56.75), West Indies 1967-68 (1,154, av. 82.42), Australia 1970-71 (1,535 runs, av 95.93). Scored two centuries in match (103 and 105) v Notts (Sheffield) 1966 and (160* and 116) England v The Rest (Worcester) 1974. Completed 30,000 runs in 1977 and scored his 100th century in Leeds Test of that year – only player to have done so in a Test match. Scored 155 v India (Birmingham) 1979 to become the second batsman to have scored a century in a Test on all six grounds in this country. Gillette Man of Match: 2. BH Gold Awards: 8. HS: 261* MCC v President's XI (Bridgetown) 1973-74. HSUK: 260* v Essex (Colchester) 1970. HSTC: 246* v India (Leeds) 1967. HSGC/NW: 146 v Surrey (Lord's) 1965. HSJPL: 108* v Northants (Huddersfield) 1974. HSBH: 142 v Worcs (Worcester) 1980. BB: 4-14 v Lancs (Leeds) 1979. BBTC: 3-47 England v South Africa (Cape Town) 1964-65.

Phillip CARRICK B Armley, Leeds 16/7/1952. RHB, SLA. Debut 1970. Cap 1976. Played for Eastern Province in 1976-77. Tours: D.H. Robins to South Africa 1975-76 and Sri Lanka 1977-78. HS: 131* v Northants (Northampton) 1980. HSNW: 33 v Warwicks (Birmingham) 1982. HSJPL: 39 v Hants (Southampton) 1982. HSBH: 19* v Notts (Bradford) 1979. BB: 8-33 v Cambridge U (Cambridge) 1973. BBJPL: 3-32 v Hants (Bournemouth) 1976 and 3-32 v Notts (Nottingham) 1979.

Simon John DENNIS B Scarborough 18/10/1960. Nephew of Sir Leonard Hutton and F. Dennis, former Yorkshire player. RHB, LFM. Debut 1980. BB: 5-35 v Somerset (Sheffield) 1981. BBJPL: 3-19 v Hants (Middlesbrough) 1981.

Stuart Neil HARTLEY B Shipley (Yorks) 18/3/1956. RHB, RM. Debut 1978. Acted as captain in a number of matches in 1981. Cap 1981. HS: 114 v Glos (Bradford) 1982. HSNW: 58 v Worcs (Leeds) 1982. HSJPL: 67 v Middlesex (Lord's) 1982. HSBH: 17 v Warwickshire (Birmingham) 1981. BB: 3-40 v Glos (Sheffield) 1980. BBJPL: 3-31 v Notts (Scarborough) 1980.

Raymond ILLINGWORTH B Pudsey 8/6/1932. RHB, OB. Debut for Yorks 1951. Cap 1955. Wisden 1959. Benefit (£6,604) in 1965. Joined Leics by special registration in 1969 being appointed county captain. Cap 1969. Awarded CBE in 1973 New Years Honours list. Benefit in 1977. Rejoined Yorks as cricket manager in 1979 and took over captaincy in middle of 1982 season from C.M. Old. Tests: 61 between 1958 and 1973 captaining England in 31 Test matches between 1969 and 1973. Played in 5 matches as captain against Rest of World in 1970. Tours: West Indies 1959-60, Commonwealth to South Africa 1960-61, Australia and New Zealand 1962-63, 1970-71 (captain). 1,000 runs (8) – 1,726 runs (av. 46.64) in 1959 best. Shared in 10th wkt partnership record for county, 228 with K. Higgs v Northants (Leicester) 1977. 100 wkts (10) – 131 wkts (av. 14.36) in 1968 best. Hat-trick v Surrey (Oval) 1975. Doubles (6): 1957, 1959-62 and 1964. Had match double of 100 runs and 10 wkts Yorks v Kent (Dover) 1964 (135 and 14-101). Gillette Man of Match: 1 (for Yorks). BH Gold Awards: 3. HS: 162 Yorks v Indians (Sheffield) 1959. HSTC: 113 v West Indies (Lord's) 1969. HSC: 153* v Essex (Leicester) 1969. HSGC: 59 v Notts (Leicester) 1970. HSJPL: 79 v Yorks (Leicester) 1970. HSBH: 43* v Worcs (Worcester) 1975. BB: 9-42 Yorks v Worcs (Worcester) 1957. BBTC: 6-29 v India (Lord's) 1967. BBC: 8-38 v Glamorgan (Swansea) 1976. BBGC: 5-29 Yorks v Surrey (Lord's) 1965. BBJPL: 5-31 v Yorks (Bradford) 1977. BBBH: 5-20 v Somerset (Leicester) 1974.

Paul William JARVIS B Redcar 29/6/1965. RHB, RFM. Debut 1981 aged 16 years 75 days. BBJPL: 3-24 v Kent (Canterbury) 1982.

James Derek LOVE B Leeds 22/4/1955. RHB, RM. Debut 1975. Cap 1980. Scored 1,203 runs (av. 33.41) in 1981. BH Gold Awards: 1. HS: 170* v Worcs (Worcester) 1979. HSGC/NW: 61* v Hants (Southampton) 1980. HSJPL: 90* v Derby (Chesterfield) 1979. HSBH: 118* v Scotland (Bradford) 1981.

Richard Graham LUMB B Doncaster 27/2/1950. RHB, RM. Debut 1970. Cap 1974. Benefit 1983. 1,000 runs (5) – 1,532 runs (av. 41.40) in 1975 best. HS: 159 v Somerset (Harrogate) 1979. HSGC/NW: 56 v Shropshire (Wellington) 1976. HSJPL: 101 v Notts (Scarborough) 1976. HSBH: 90 v Northants (Bradford) 1980.

Ashley Anthony METCALFE B Horsforth 25/12/1963. RHB, OB. Has not yet played first-class cricket.

Martyn Douglas MOXON B Barnsley 4/5/1960. RHB, RM. Debut 1981 scoring 116 in second innings of debut match. NW Man of the Match: 1. HS: 116 v Essex (Leeds) 1981. HSNW: 78* v Essex (Leeds) 1982. HSJPL: 22 v Surrey (Oval) 1982. HSBH: 22 v Somerset (Leeds) 1981.

Alan RAMAGE B Guisborough 29/11/1957. LHB, RFM. Debut 1979. HS: 52 v Glos (Bristol) 1981. HSJPL: 32* v Middlesex (Lord's) 1982. HSBH: 17* v Combined Universities (Barnsley) 1976. BB: 5-65 v Surrey (Harrogate) 1981. BBGC/NW: 3-33 v Hants (Southampton) 1980. BBJPL: 3-51 v Kent (Canterbury) 1977. BBBH: 3-63 v Warwicks (Leeds) 1980. Has played soccer for Middlesbrough.

Steven John RHODES (Carlton-Bolling School, Bradford) B Bradford 17/6/1964. Son of W.E. Rhodes who played for Nottinghamshire from 1961 to 1964. RHB, WK. Played for 2nd XI 1980. Debut 1981 aged 17 years 35 days. One match v Sri Lankans (Sheffield). Did not play in 1982.

Kevin SHARP B Leeds 6/4/1959. LHB, OB. Debut 1976. Cap 1982. HS: 116 v Sri Lankans (Sheffield) 1981. HSGC/NW: 25 v Middlesex (Lord's) 1979. HSJPL: 62 v Hants (Southampton) 1982. HSBH: 71 v Worcs (Leeds) 1982.

Arnold SIDEBOTTOM B Barnsley 1/4/1954. RHB, RFM. Debut 1973. Cap 1980. HS: 124 v Glamorgan (Cardiff) 1977. HSGC/NW: 45 v Hants (Bournemouth) 1977. HSJPL: 52* v Northants (Middlesbrough) 1982. HSBH: 15 v Notts (Bradford) 1979. BB: 7-18 v Oxford U (Oxford) 1980. BBGC/NW: 4-35 v Kent (Leeds) 1980. BBJPL: 4-24 v Surrey (Scarborough) 1975. BBBH: 3-21 v Minor Counties (North) (Jesmond) 1979. Soccer for Manchester United, Huddersfield Town and Halifax Town.

Graham Barry STEVENSON B Ackworth 16/12/1955. RHB, RM. Debut 1973. Cap 1978. Tests: 2 in 1979-80 and 1980-81. BH Gold Award: 1. Tours: Australia and India 1979-80 (flown out as a replacement for M. Hendrick), West Indies 1980-81. HSTC: 27* v India (Bombay) 1979-80. HSNW: 28* v Worcs (Leeds) 1982. HSJPL: 56 v Somerset (Scarborough) 1981. HSBH: 16 v Middlesex (Lord's) 1977. BB: 8-57 v Northants (Leeds) 1980. BBTC: 3-111 v West Indies (St. John's) 1980-81. BBGC/NW: 4-57 v Lancs (Leeds) 1974. BBJPL: 5-41 v Leics (Leicester) 1976. BBBH: 5-28 v Kent (Canterbury) 1978.

YORKSHIRE

Stephen STUCHBURY B Sheffield 22/6/1954. LHB, LFM. Debut 1978. Did not play in 1979 or 1980. Re-appeared in 1981. Played in limited-over matches only in 1982. BBJPL: 5-16 v Leics (Leicester) 1982. BB: 3-82 v Lancs (Leeds) 1981.

Nicholas Simon TAYLOR B Holmfirth 2/6/1963. RHB, RFM. Son of K. Taylor (England, Yorks and Auckland). Debut 1982.

NB. The following players whose particulars appeared in the 1982 Annual have been omitted: S.P. Coverdale, P.R. Hart, P.G. Ingham, P.A. Jackson, M. Johnson, C.M. Old and J.P. Whiteley.

County Averages

Schweppes County Championship: Played 22, won 5, drawn 15, lost 1, abandoned 1.
All first-class matches: Played 23, won 5, drawn 16, lost 1, abandoned 1.

BATTING AND FIELDING

Cap		M	I	NO	Runs	HS	Avge	100	50	Ct	St
1963	G. Boycott	21	37	6	1913	159	61.70	6	10	10	—
1980	C.W.J. Athey	22	38	7	1339	134	43.19	4	8	21	—
1980	J.D. Love	18	29	6	773	123	33.60	2	4	7	—
—	S.N. Hartley	20	30	9	635	114	30.23	1	4	6	—
1973	D.L. Bairstow	22	29	9	603	77	30.15	—	4	53	3
—	K. Sharp	10	18	2	478	115	29.87	1	1	2	—
1974	R.G. Lumb	20	33	1	844	81	26.37	—	7	9	—
1978	G.B. Stevenson	17	19	4	356	115*	23.73	1	—	6	—
1976	P. Carrick	20	21	3	423	93	23.50	—	2	8	—
1980	A. Sidebottom	19	18	8	233	44*	23.30	—	—	4	—
1955	R. Illingworth	13	6	2	86	33	21.50	—	—	3	—
1969	C.M. Old	16	18	3	207	32	13.80	—	—	9	—
—	J.P. Whiteley	4	2	1	6	5*	6.00	—	—	3	—
—	P.W. Jarvis	6	3	1	7	7	3.50	—	—	5	—
—	A. Ramage	4	2	1	4	4*	2.00	—	—	1	—
—	N.S. Taylor	3	1	1	0	0*	—	—	—	—	—
—	S.J. Dennis	3	1	1	5	5*	—	—	—	1	—

Played in two matches: M.D. Moxon 67, 36, 40, 54.
Played in one match: P.A. Booth 0*.

BOWLING

	Type	O	M	R	W	Avge	Best	5 wI	10 wM
G. Boycott	RM	57.2	13	120	8	15.00	2-14	—	—
A. Sidebottom	RFM	495.2	95	1538	62	24.80	6-31	3	—
C.M. Old	RFM	458.2	125	1229	47	26.14	6-76	1	—
S.J. Dennis	LFM	95	16	365	12	30.41	5-42	1	—
G.B. Stevenson	RM	443.4	88	1474	45	32.75	5-72	1	—
P. Carrick	SLA	568.5	144	1425	40	35.62	6-90	1	—
N.S. Taylor	RFM	84.1	16	293	8	36.62	2-42	—	—
P.W. Jarvis	RFM	132	25	434	8	54.25	2-24	—	—
S.N. Hartley	RM	118	27	388	6	64.66	1-11	—	—
R. Illingworth	OB	223.4	65	587	9	65.22	2-32	—	—
A. Ramage	RFM	90	14	381	5	76.20	2-69	—	—

Also bowled: C.W.J. Athey 27.1-1-98-0; P.A. Booth 10-3-22-0; J.D. Love 3-3-0-0; J.P. Whiteley 48-1-223-4.

County Records

First-class cricket

Highest innings totals:	For	887 v Warwicks (Birmingham)	1896
	Agst	630 by Somerset (Leeds)	1901
Lowest innings totals:	For	23 v Hants (Middlesbrough)	1965
	Agst	13 by Notts (Nottingham)	1901
Highest individual innings:	For	341 G.H. Hirst v Leics (Leicester)	1905
	Agst	318* W.G. Grace for Glos (Cheltenham)	1876
Best bowling in an innings:	For	10-10 H. Verity v Notts (Leeds)	1932
	Agst	10-37 C.V. Grimmett for Australians (Sheffield)	1930
Best bowling in a match:	For	17-91 H. Verity v Essex (Leyton)	1933
	Agst	17-91 H. Dean for Lancs (Liverpool)	1913
Most runs in a season:		2883 (av. 80.08) H. Sutcliffe	1932
Most runs in a career:		38561 (av. 50.21) H. Sutcliffe	1919-1945
100s in a season:		12 by H. Sutcliffe	1932
100s in a career:		112 by H. Sutcliffe	1919-1945
wickets in a season:		240 (av. 12.72) W. Rhodes	1900
wickets in a career:		3608 (av. 16.00) W. Rhodes	1898-1930

RECORD WICKET STANDS

1st	555	P. Holmes & H. Sutcliffe v Essex (Leyton)	1932
2nd	346	W. Barber & M. Leyland v Middlesex (Sheffield)	1932
3rd	323*	H. Sutcliffe & M. Leyland v Glamorgan (Huddersfield)	1928
4th	312	G.H. Hirst & D. Denton v Hants (Southampton)	1914
5th	340	E. Wainwright & G.H. Hirst v Surrey (Oval)	1899
6th	276	M. Leyland & E. Robinson v Glamorgan (Swansea)	1926
7th	254	D.C.F. Burton & W. Rhodes v Hants (Dewsbury)	1919
8th	292	Lord Hawke & R. Peel v Warwicks (Birmingham)	1896
9th	192	G.H. Hirst & S. Haigh v Surrey (Bradford)	1898
10th	149	G. Boycott & G.B. Stevenson v Warwicks (Birmingham)	1982

One-day cricket

Highest innings totals:	Gillette Cup/ NatWest Trophy	317-4 v Surrey (Lord's)	1965
	John Player League	248-5 v Derby (Chesterfield)	1979
	Benson & Hedges Cup	269-6 v Worcs (Worcester)	1980
Lowest innings totals:	Gillette Cup/ NatWest Trophy	76 v Surrey (Harrogate)	1970
	John Player League	74 v Warwicks (Birmingham)	1972
	Benson & Hedges Cup	114 v Kent (Canterbury)	1978
Highest individual innings:	Gillette Cup/ NatWest Trophy	146 G. Boycott v Surrey (Lord's)	1965
	John Player League	119 J.H. Hampshire v Leicestershire (Hull)	1971
	Benson & Hedges Cup	142 G. Boycott v Worcs (Worcester)	1980
Best bowling figures:	Gillette Cup/ NatWest Trophy	6-15 F.S. Trueman v Somerset (Taunton)	1965
	John Player League	7-15 R.A. Hutton v Worcs (Leeds)	1969
	Benson & Hedges Cup	6-27 A.G. Nicholson v Minor Counties (North) (Middlesbrough)	1972

CAMBRIDGE UNIVERSITY

Captain: S.P. Henderson.
Secretary: D.W. Varey.

William Edward James BARRINGTON (Lancing College and St. Catharine's College) B Carshalton, Surrey 4/1/1960. 6ft 4ins tall. RHB. Debut 1982. Blue 1982. HS: 59 v Essex (Cambridge) on debut.

Robin James BOYD-MOSS (Bedford School and Magdalene College) B Hattoh, Ceylon 16/12/1959. RHB, SLA. Debut for University and Northamptonshire 1980. Blue 1980-81-82. HS: 137 Northants v Derby (Northampton) 1982. HSCU: 123 v Warwicks (Cambridge) 1982. BB: 4-42 v Oxford (Lord's) 1982. Commercial Union Under-23 Batting Prize 1982. Two centuries in match 123 and 119 v Warwicks (Cambridge) 1982. Rugby Football Blue 1980-81, 1981-82, 1982-83. Fourth year student with Degree in Land Economy and studying for Certificate of Education.

Andrew George DAVIES (Birkenhead School and Robinson College) B Altrincham, Cheshire 5/5/1962. RHB, WK. Debut 1982. HS: 13 v Essex (Cambridge) in only match. Second year student reading Economics.

Simon Jonathon Graham DOGGART (Winchester College and Magdalene College) B Winchester, Hants 8/2/1961. LHB, OB. Debut 1980. Blue 1980-81-82. Secretary 1982. HS: 69* v Lancs (Cambridge) 1981. BB: 3-54 v Oxford (Lord's) 1980. Son of G.H.G. Doggart and grandson of A.G. Doggart, both former Cambridge Blues. Father also played for Sussex and England.

Richard Stuart DUTTON (Wrekin College and Fitzwilliam College) B Liverpool 24/11/1959. RHB, RM. Debut 1981.

Charles Christopher ELLISON (Tonbridge School and Homerton College) B Pembury, Kent 11/2/1962. RHB, RM. Debut 1982. Blue 1982. HS: 16 v Warwicks (Cambridge). BB: 3-30 v Lancs (Cambridge). Brother of R.M. Ellison of Kent. Second year student studying History and Education.

Christopher Frederick Evelyn GOLDIE (St. Paul's School and Pembroke College) B Johannesburg, South Africa 2/11/1960. RHB, WK. Debut 1981. Blue 1981-82. HS: 77 v Oxford (Lord's) 1981. On Middlesex staff 1979-80. Toured America with MCC team 1982. Joined Hants for 1983.

Peter David GRIFFITHS B Bulawayo, Southern Rhodesia 13/7/1961. RHB, SLA. Debut 1982. HS: 1 v Northants (Cambridge) in only match.

Stephen Peter HENDERSON (Downside School, Durham University and Magdalene College) B Oxford 24/9/1958. LHB, RM. Debut for Worcs 1977. Debut for University 1982. Blue 1982. Captain 1982. HS: 209* v Middlesex (Cambridge) 1982. HSC: 69 v Lancs (Stourport on Severn) 1980. On Worcs staff 1977-81. Second year student.

Kenneth Ian HODGSON (Oundle School and Downing College) B Port Elizabeth, South Africa 24/2/1960. RHB, RM. Debut 1981. Blue 1982. HS: 50 v Lancs (Cambridge) 1982. BB: 8-68 v Glamorgan (Cambridge) 1982. Half-Blue for Squash Rackets.

John Peter Crispin MILLS (Oundle School and Corpus Christi College) B Kettering, Northants 6/12/1958. RHB, RM. Debut 1979. Debut for Northants 1981. Blue 1979-80-81-82. Secretary 1981. Captained University v Oxford 1982 in absence of D.R. Pringle playing in Second Test v India. HS: 111 Combined Universities v Sri Lankans (Oxford) 1981. HSCU: 98 v Middlesex (Cambridge) 1982. Son of J.M. Mills, former Cambridge Blue (captain 1948) and Warwickshire player.

Robert William Michael PALMER (Bedford School and St Catharine's College) B Hong Kong 4/6/1960. RHB, LM. Debut 1981. Blue 1982. HS: 12 v Essex (Cambridge) 1982. BB: 4-96 v Notts (Cambridge) 1982. Third year student reading Law.

Angus John POLLOCK (Shrewsbury School and Trinity College) B Liversedge, Yorks 19/4/1962. RHB, RM. Debut 1982. Blue 1982. HS: 19 v Lancs (Cambridge). BB: 5-108 v Essex (Cambridge). Soccer Blue 1981-82 (Substitute), 1982-83. Second year student reading Economics.

Derek Raymond PRINGLE (Felsted School and Fitzwilliam College) B Nairobi, Kenya 18/9/1958. 6ft 4½ins tall. RHB, RM. Debut for Essex 1978. Debut for University 1979. Blue 1979-80-81. Captain 1982 but did not play v Oxford as playing for England in Second Test v India. HS: 127* v Worcs (Cambridge) 1981. HSC: 54 v Warwicks (Colchester) 1982. BB: 6-33 v Lancs (Cambridge) 1982. BBC: 5-59 v Indians (Chelmsford) 1982. Tests: 4. Tour: Australia and New Zealand 1982-83. Son of late Donald Pringle who played for East Africa in 1975 Prudential Cup.

David William VAREY (Birkenhead School and Pembroke College) B Darlington, Co Durham 15/10/1961. RHB. Debut for Cheshire 1977. Debut for Lancs 2nd XI 1980. Debut 1981. Blue 1982. Secretary 1983. HS: 156* v Northants (Cambridge) 1982. Third year student reading French and German.

NB. The following players whose particulars appeared in the 1982 Annual have been omitted as they did not play in 1982 or are no longer in residence: A.R. Clark, R.J. Compton-Burnett, T.D.W. Edwards, R.J.A. Huxter, A.J. Murley, A. Odendaal and H.F. Torkington.

Averages

All first-class matches: Played 9, won 2, drawn 3, lost 4.

BATTING AND FIELDING

	M	I	NO	Runs	HS	Avge	100	50	Ct	St
D.R. Pringle	6	10	3	521	127	74.42	1	4	1	—
†R.J. Boyd-Moss	9	17	1	717	123	44.81	3	3	3	—
†S.P. Henderson	9	16	3	531	209*	40.84	1	2	12	—
†D.W. Varey	9	17	3	548	156*	39.14	1	3	6	—
†W.E.J. Barrington	4	6	1	174	59	34.80	—	1	1	—
†K.I. Hodgson	8	10	1	213	50	23.66	—	1	—	—
†J.P.C. Mills	9	17	—	389	98	22.88	—	3	3	—
†S.J.G. Doggart	9	13	1	242	64	20.16	—	1	3	—
†C.C. Ellison	7	7	4	56	16	18.66	—	—	1	—
†C.F.E. Goldie	9	9	—	115	31	12.77	—	—	19	4
†A.J. Pollock	7	8	2	63	19	10.50	—	—	—	—
†R.W.M. Palmer	9	8	5	20	12	6.66	—	—	2	—

Played in two matches: R.S. Dutton 0, 0*, 0.

Played in one match: A.G. Davies 13, 4 (3 ct); P.D. Griffiths 1, 0.

† denotes played in Varsity match

BOWLING

	Type	O	M	R	W	Avge	Best	5 wI	10 wM
D.R. Pringle	RM	117.2	37	288	13	22.15	6-33	1	—
R.J. Boyd-Moss	SLA	64	15	233	9	25.88	4-42	—	—
K.I. Hodgson	RM	198.1	42	625	23	27.17	8-68	1	1
A.J. Pollock	RM	115.5	18	483	14	34.50	5-108	1	—
R.W.M. Palmer	LM	219.4	34	849	14	60.64	4-96	—	—
C.C. Ellison	RM	96.5	20	314	5	62.80	3-30	—	—
S.J.G. Doggart	OB	182.4	29	623	7	89.00	2-30	—	—

Also bowled: R.S. Dutton 19-1-130-0; P.D. Griffiths 9-2-39-0; S.P. Henderson 6-3-8-0; D.W. Varey 1-0-4-0.

University Records

Highest Innings	For	703-9d v Sussex (Hove)	1890
Totals:	Agst	703-3 by West Indians (Cambridge)	1950
Lowest Innings	For	30 v Yorks (Cambridge)	1928
Totals:	Agst	32 by Oxford U (Lord's)	1878
Highest Individual Innings:	For	254* K.S. Duleepsinhji v Middlesex (Cambridge)	1927
	Agst	304* E.D. Weekes for West Indies (Cambridge)	1950
Best Bowling in an Innings:	For	10-69 S.M.J. Woods v C.I. Thornton's XI (Cambridge)	1890
	Agst	10-38 S.E. Butler for Oxford U (Lord's)	1871
Best Bowling in a Match:	For	15-88 S.M.J. Woods v C.I. Thornton's XI (Cambridge)	1890
	Agst	15-95 S.E. Butler for Oxford U (Lord's)	1871
Most runs in a season:		1581 (av. 79.05) D.S. Sheppard	1952
runs in a career:		4310 (av.38.48) J.M. Brearley	1961-1968
100s in a season:		7 by D.S. Sheppard	1952
100s in a career:		14 by D.S. Sheppard	1950-1952
wickets in a season:		80 (av. 17.63) O.S. Wheatley	1958
wickets in a career:		208 (av. 21.82) G. Goonesena	1954-1957

RECORD WICKET STANDS

1st	349	J.G. Dewes & D.S. Sheppard v Sussex (Hove)	1950
2nd	429*	J.G. Dewes & G.H.G. Doggart v Essex (Cambridge)	1949
3rd	284	E.T. Killick & G.C. Grant v Essex (Cambridge)	1929
4th	275	R. de W.K. Winlaw & J.H. Human v Essex (Cambridge)	1934
5th	220	R. Subba Row & F.C.M. Alexander v Notts (Nottingham)	1953
6th	245	J.L. Bryan & C.T. Ashton v Surrey (Oval)	1921
7th	289	G. Goonesena & G.W. Cook v Oxford U (Lord's)	1957
8th	145	H. Ashton & A.E.R. Gilligan v Free Foresters (Cambridge)	1920
9th	200	G.W. Cook & C.S. Smith v Lancs (Liverpool)	1957
10th	177	A.E.R. Gilligan & J.H. Naumann v Sussex (Hove)	1919

OXFORD UNIVERSITY

Captain: G.J. Toogood.
Secretary: A.J.T. Miller.

Philip Alexander Nikolas ARMSTRONG (Eastbourne College) B Lambeth, London 23/1/1962. RHB. Debut 1982. HS: 34 v Glam (Swansea) in only match. Second year student reading English.

John Joseph CASSIDY B Leeds 31/1/1963. RHB, RM. Debut 1982. HS: 0 v Glam (Swansea) in only match. Second year student.

John Robert CHESSHER (Ipswich School and Lincoln College) B Banstead, Surrey 21/8/1962. RHB. Debut 1982. HS: 47 v Northants (Oxford) on debut. Second year student reading Engineering.

Philip John CROWE (The Scots College, Sydney, Sydney University and University College) B London 27/10/1955. LHB, LM. Debut 1982. HS: 11 v Glos (Oxford). Rugby Football Blue 1981-82, 1982-83 (captain). Capped six times for Australia at rugby. Third year Post-Doctorate Research in Medicine.

Roger Michael EDBROOKE (Queen Elizabeth's Hospital, Bristol and Hertford College) B Bristol 30/12/1960. RHB. Debut 1982. HS: 84* v Glamorgan (Swansea) in only match. Third year student reading Physics.

Richard Gary Peter ELLIS (Haileybury College and St. Edmund Hall) B Paddington, London 20/12/1960. RHB, OB. Debut for University 1981. Debut for Middlesex 1982. Blue 1981, 1982 (captain). HS: 105* v Surrey (Oxford) 1982. Half-Blue for Squash Rackets. Third year student reading History.

Andrew Douglas GILFILLAN (Hilton College, Natal, Cape Town University and Worcester College) B Johannesburg, South Africa 21/8/1959. RHB, LB. Debut 1982. HS: 31 v Glos (Oxford).

Kevin Anthony HAYES (Queen Elizabeth's GS, Blackburn and Merton College) B Mexborough, Yorks 26/9/1962. RHB, RM. Debut for Lancs 1980. Debut for University 1981. Blue 1981-82. HS: 152 v Warwicks (Oxford) 1982. Secretary 1982. Soccer Blue 1980-81, 1981-82 and 1982-83 (captain). Third year student reading Chemistry.

Mark Philip LAWRENCE (Manchester GS and Merton College) B Warrington, Cheshire 6/5/1962. LHB, SLA. Debut 1962. HS: 18 v Middlesex (Oxford). Third year student reading Chemistry.

Richard Simon LUDDINGTON (King's College School, Wimbledon and St. Edmund Hall) B Kingston-upon-Thames, Surrey 8/4/1960. RHB, WK. Debut 1982. Blue 1982. HS: 65 v Glamorgan (Swansea). Rugby Football Blue 1980-81, 1981-82 and 1982-83. Hockey Blue 1979-80 and 1980-81. Fifth year student with Degree in History and reading M.Phil in Management Studies.

Andrew John Trevor MILLER (Haileybury College and St. Edmund Hall) B Chesham, Bucks 30/5/1963. LHB. Debut 1982. Secretary 1983. HS: 20 v Middlesex (Oxford). Rugby for University but not Blue. Second year student reading Biochemistry.

OXFORD UNIVERSITY

Roger Peter MOULDING (Haberdashers Ashe School, Elstree and Christ Church College) B Enfield, Middlesex 3/1/1958. RHB. Debut for Middlesex 1977 (one match). Debut for University 1978. Blue 1978-79-80-81-82. Secretary in 1979 and Captain in 1981. HS: 77* v Worcs (Worcester) 1978. Obtained First Class Honours Degree in Chemistry and is now in sixth year studying for D.Phil.

Henry Thomas RAWLINSON (Eton College and Christ Church College) B Edgware, Middlesex 21/1/1963. RHB, RM. Debut 1982. HS: 21 v Kent (Oxford). Brother of J.L. Rawlinson who played for University 1979-80. Second year student reading Politics, Philosophy and Economics.

Stuart Peter RIDGE (Dr Challenor's GS, Amersham and Worcester College) B Beaconsfield, Bucks 23/11/1961. RHB, RM. Debut 1981, Blue 1982. HS: 22 v Hants (Oxford) 1982. BB: 4-128 v Glos (Oxford) 1982. Soccer Blue (goalkeeper) 1981-82 and 1982-83. Third year student reading Physics.

Giles John TOOGOOD (North Bromsgrove HS and Lincoln College) B West Bromwich, Staffs 19/11/1961. RHB, OB. Debut 1982. Blue 1982. HS: 83 v Worcs (Oxford). Captain 1983. Rugby Football for University but not Blue. Third year student reading Medicine.

Jonathan Guy VAREY (Birkenhead School and St. Edmund School) B Darlington, Co Durham 15/10/1961. RHB, RM. Debut 1982. Blue 1982. HS: 68 v Hants (Oxford). Twin brother of D.W. Varey (Cambridge). Third year student reading History.

NB. The following players whose particulars appeared in the 1982 Annual have been omitted as they did not play in 1982 or are no longer in residence: I.J. Curtis, R.S. Cowan, R.A. Gordon-Walker, S.J. Halliday, P.N. Huxford, R. Marsden and T.J. Taylor.

Averages

All first-class matches: Played 10, won 0, drawn 5, lost 5.

BATTING AND FIELDING

	M	I	NO	Runs	HS	Avge	100	50	Ct	St
†R.S. Cowan	7	14	3	515	143*	46.81	2	2	3	—
S.J. Halliday	4	7	1	213	113*	35.50	1	—	—	—
†R.G.P. Ellis	10	20	1	666	105*	35.05	1	3	7	—
†J.G. Varey	7	12	5	239	68	34.14	—	1	2	—
†R. Marsden	5	10	1	264	60	29.33	—	1	1	—
K.A. Hayes	10	19	2	491	152	28.88	1	2	4	—
†G.J. Toogood	9	18	4	392	83	28.00	—	2	4	—
J.R. Chessher	3	4	1	67	47	22.33	—	—	—	—
†R.S. Luddington	10	14	1	290	65	22.30	—	2	5	1
I.J. Curtis	5	3	2	20	20*	20.00	—	—	1	—
†T.J. Taylor	4	3	1	37	20	18.50	—	—	—	—
†R.P. Moulding	10	20	2	242	67	13.44	—	1	3	—
A.D. Gillfillan	3	4	1	40	31	13.33	—	—	—	—
†S.P. Ridge	10	13	5	64	22	8.00	—	—	3	—
M.P. Lawrence	4	5	2	20	18	6.66	—	—	—	—
H.T. Rawlinson	4	6	—	30	21	5.00	—	—	1	—

Played in one match: P.A.N. Armstrong 34, 0; J.J. Cassidy 0; P.J. Crowe 11, 0; R. Edbrooke 84*, 16; A.J.T. Miller 0, 20.
† denotes played in Varsity match

BOWLING

	Type	O	M	R	W	Avge	Best	5 wI	10 wM
I.J. Curtis	SLA	214.4	45	659	15	43.93	5-140	1	—
T.J. Taylor	SLA	149	26	469	9	52.11	5-118	1	—
S.P. Ridge	RM	240.1	32	829	13	63.76	4-128	—	—
H.T. Rawlinson	RM	96.1	9	435	5	87.00	2-102	—	—
R.S. Cowan	RM	131	18	559	6	93.16	2-75	—	—

Also bowled: J.J. Cassidy 4-2-12-0; P.J. Crowe 36-4-121-1; R.G.P. Ellis 61-14-182-4; A.D. Gillfillan 51-5-218-2; K.A. Hayes 21-1-96-0; M.P. Lawrence 99-20-366-2; G.J. Toogood 3-0-22-0; J.G. Varey 132-15-550-3.

University Records

Highest Innings	For	651 v Sussex (Hove)	1895
Totals:	Agst	679-7d by Australians (Oxford)	1938
Lowest Innings	For	12 v MCC (Oxford)	1877
Totals:	Agst	24 by MCC (Oxford)	1846
Highest Indi-	For	281 K.J. Key v Middlesex (Chiswick Park)	1887
vidual Innings:	Agst	338 W.W. Read for Surrey (Oval)	1888
Best Bowling	For	10-38 S.E. Butler v Cambridge U (Lord's)	1871
in an Innings:	Agst	10-49 W.G. Grace for MCC (Oxford)	1886

OXFORD UNIVERSITY

Best Bowling	For	15-95 S.E. Butler v Cambridge U (Lord's)	1871
in a Match:	Agst	16-225 J.E. Walsh for Leics (Oxford)	1953
Most runs in a season:		1307 (av. 93.35) Nawab of Pataudi (Snr.)	1931
runs in a career:		3319 (av. 47.41) N.S. Mitchell-Innes	1934-1937
100s in a season:		6 by Nawab of Pataudi (Snr.)	1931
100s in a career:		9 by A.M. Crawley	1927-1930
		Nawab of Pataudi (Snr.)	1928-31
		N.S. Mitchell-Innes	1934-37
		M.P. Donnelly	1946-47
wickets in a season:		70 (av. 18.15) I.A.R. Peebles	1930
wickets in a career:		182 (av. 19.38) R.H.B. Bettington	1920-1923

RECORD WICKET STANDS

1st	338	T. Bowring & H. Teesdale v Gents of England (Oxford)	1908
2nd	226	W.G. Keighley & H.A. Pawson v Cambridge U (Lord's)	1947
3rd	273	F.C. de Saram & N.S. Mitchell-Innes v Glos (Oxford)	1934
4th	276	P.G.T. Kingsley & N.M. Ford v Surrey (Oval)	1930
5th	256*	A.A. Baig & C.A. Fry v Free Foresters (Oxford)	1959
6th	270	D.R. Walsh & S.A. Westley v Warwicks (Oxford)	1969
7th	340	K.J. Key & H. Philipson v Middlesex (Chiswick Park)	1887
8th	160	H. Philipson & A.C.M. Croome v MCC (Lord's)	1889
9th	157	H.M. Garland-Wells & C.K.H. Hill-Wood v Kent (Oxford)	1928
10th	149	F.H. Hollins & B.A. Collins v MCC (Oxford)	1901

BENSON & HEDGES

ZONAL POINTS TABLE

Group A	P	W	L	NR	Pts	Group C	P	W	L	NR	Pts
Derbyshire	4	3	1	0	6	Kent	4	3	1	0	6
Leicestershire	4	3	1	0	6	Sussex	4	3	1	0	6
Worcestershire	4	2	2	0	4	Essex	4	2	2	0	4
Minor Counties	4	1	3	0	2	Surrey	4	2	2	0	4
Yorkshire	4	1	3	0	2	Hampshire	4	0	4	0	0

Group B	P	W	L	NR	Pts	Group D	P	W	L	NR	Pts
Nottinghamshire	4	4	0	0	8	Middlesex	4	4	0	0	8
Lancashire	4	3	1	0	6	Somerset	4	3	1	0	6
Warwickshire	4	2	2	0	4	Gloucestershire	4	2	2	0	4
Northamptonshire	4	1	3	0	2	Glamorgan	4	1	3	0	2
Scotland	4	0	4	0	0	Combined Universities	4	0	4	0	0

NatWest are looking for farmers looking for money.

Buying land? Replacing machinery? Refurbishing buildings? It's better done with a NatWest Farm Development Loan. NatWest offer you:

- **Fixed interest.**
- **Fixed repayments.**
- **Fixed term for easier cash flow.**

You can borrow up to £250,000 and repay it over a period of up to 20 years.

And you don't need to be a current NatWest customer, either.

Simply contact your nearest NatWest branch for details.

 **NatWest** *Agricultural Services*

ZAHEER ABBAS'S 100 CENTURIES

On December 11, 1982, at Lahore, Zaheer Abbas, Gloucestershire's Pakistani batsman, scored 215 for Pakistan against India. This was Zaheer's 100th century in first-class cricket. He became the twentieth player to perform this feat, the third non-Englishman (after Bradman and Turner), the first Pakistani, and the second (after Boycott) in a Test match.

The following is a progressive list of his centuries:

1.	197	Karachi v East Pakistan	(Karachi)	1968-69
2.	103*	Pakistan International Airlines v Bahawalpur	(Bahawalpur)	1969-70
3.	136*	Pakistan International Airlines v Karachi B	(Karachi)	1969-70
4.	136	Pakistan International Airlines v Karachi A	(Karachi)	1969-70
5.	118	Pakistan International Airlines A v East Pakistan Greens	(Dacca)	1970-71
6.	196	Pakistan International Airlines A v East Pakistan Whites	(Dacca)	1970-71
7.	161	Pakistan International Airlines A v Bahawalpur	(Karachi)	1970-71
8.	111	Pakistan International Airlines A v Punjab University	(Lahore)	1970-71
9.	202	Pakistan International Airlines A v Karachi Blues	(Karachi)	1970-71
10.	110	Pakistanis v Worcestershire	(Worcester)	1971
11.	138	Pakistanis v Kent	(Gravesend)	1971
12.	274	Pakistan v England	(Birmingham)	1971
13.	100*	Pakistanis v Lancashire	(Manchester)	1971
14.	112	World XI v Western Australia	(Perth)	1971-72
15.	106	World XI v Tasmania Combined XI	(Hobart)	1971-72
16.	143	Pakistanis v Western Australia	(Perth)	1972-73
17.	113	Pakistanis v Tasmania	(Hobart)	1972-73
18.	105	Pakistanis v Central Districts	(Wanganui)	1972-73
19.	170	Pakistanis v Wellington	(Wellington)	1972-73
20.	110	Pakistan International Airlines v Karachi	(Karachi)	1972-73
21.	153*	Gloucestershire v Surrey	(The Oval)	1973
22.	103	Gloucestershire v Somerset	(Bristol)	1973
23.	145	Pakistan XI v World XI	(Karachi)	1973-74
24.	129	Pakistan XI v World XI	(Lahore)	1973-74
25.	112	Pakistan International Airlines v Pakistan Railways	(Lahore)	1973-74
26.	112	Pakistan International Airlines v Punjab	(Lahore)	1973-74
27.	174	Pakistan International Airlines v Sind	(Lahore)	1973-74
28.	112	Gloucestershire v Cambridge University	(Cambridge)	1974
29.	137	Pakistanis v Minor Counties	(Jesmond)	1974
30.	104	Pakistanis v Glamorgan	(Swansea)	1974
31.	240	Pakistan v England	(The Oval)	1974
32.	117	Pakistanis v Sussex	(Hove)	1974
33.	131	Pakistan International Airlines v Pakistan Railways	(Lahore)	1974-75
34.	157	Pakistan International Airlines v National Bank	(Lahore)	1974-75

35.	111	Gloucestershire v Kent	(Cheltenham)	1975
36.	123	Gloucestershire v Nottinghamshire	(Nottingham)	1975
37.	170	Dawood Industries v Pakistan International Airlines	(Lahore)	1975-76
38.	155	Sind A v Pakistan Universities	(Lahore)	1975-76
39.	188	Gloucestershire v Yorkshire	(Leeds)	1976
40.	141	Gloucestershire v Somerset	(Taunton)	1976
41.	216* }	Gloucestershire v Surrey	(The Oval)	1976
42.	156*			
43.	104	Gloucestershire v Sussex	(Gloucester)	1976
44.	153	Gloucestershire v Essex	(Cheltenham)	1976
45.	177	Gloucestershire v Glamorgan	(Cardiff)	1976
46.	177	Gloucestershire v Leicestershire	(Leicester)	1976
47.	230* }	Gloucestershire v Kent	(Canterbury)	1976
48.	104*			
49.	106	Gloucestershire v Worcestershire	(Worcester)	1976
50.	101	Pakistan v Australia	(Adelaide)	1976-77
51.	104	Gloucestershire v Sussex	(Hove)	1977
52.	105	Gloucestershire v Somerset	(Bristol)	1977
53.	205* }	Gloucestershire v Sussex	(Cheltenham)	1977
54.	108*			
55.	100*	Gloucestershire v Hampshire	(Southampton)	1977
56.	100	Gloucestershire v Cambridge University	(Cambridge)	1978
57.	140	Gloucestershire v Somerset	(Taunton)	1978
58.	213	Gloucestershire v Sussex	(Hove)	1978
59.	104	Gloucestershire v Derbyshire	(Gloucester)	1978
60.	121	Gloucestershire v New Zealanders	(Bristol)	1978
61.	132	Gloucestershire v Hampshire	(Basingstoke)	1978
62.	176	Pakistan v India	(Faisalabad)	1978-79
63.	235*	Pakistan v India	(Lahore)	1978-79
64.	135	Pakistan v New Zealand	(Auckland)	1978-79
65.	126	Pakistanis v South Australia	(Adelaide)	1978-79
66.	101	Gloucestershire v Glamorgan	(Cardiff)	1979
67.	147	Gloucestershire v Somerset	(Taunton)	1979
68.	151*	Gloucestershire v Warwickshire	(Brisbane)	1979
69.	111	Pakistan International Airlines v Lahore	(Lahore)	1979-80
70.	170	Pakistan International Airlines v Pakistan Railways	(Lahore)	1979-80
71.	114	Pakistanis v West Zone	(Pune)	1979-80
72.	104	Gloucestershire v Northamptonshire	(Bristol)	1980
73.	173	Gloucestershire v Somerset	(Taunton)	1980
74.	110*	Pakistan International Airlines v Karachi	(Karachi)	1980-81
75.	138	Pakistan International Airlines v Muslim Commercial Bank	(Karachi)	1980-81
76.	154*	Pakistan International Airlines v National Bank	(Lahore)	1980-81
77.	100* }	Pakistan International Airlines v Pakistan Railways	(Lahore)	1980-81
78.	100*			
79.	215* }	Gloucestershire v Somerset	(Bath)	1981
80.	150*			
81.	101*	Gloucestershire v Hampshire	(Southampton)	1981
82.	100	Gloucestershire v Warwickshire	(Gloucester)	1981
83.	135* }	Gloucestershire v Northamptonshire	(Northampton)	1981
84.	128			
85.	145	Gloucestershire v Sussex	(Hove)	1981

86. 159	Gloucestershire v Glamorgan	(Bristol)	1981
87. 136*	Gloucestershire v Kent	(Cheltenham)	1981
88. 103*	Gloucestershire v Worcestershire	(Worcester)	1981
89. 117	Pakistanis v South Australia	(Adelaide)	1981-82
90. 134	Pakistan v Sri Lanka	(Lahore)	1981-82
91. 144	Gloucestershire v Oxford University	(Oxford)	1982
92. 162* } 93. 107 }	Gloucestershire v Lancashire	(Gloucester)	1982
94. 147	Pakistanis v Worcestershire	(Worcester)	1982
95. 148*	Pakistanis v Derbyshire	(Chesterfield)	1982
96. 126	Pakistan v Australia	(Faisalabad)	1982-83
97. 125 } 98. 101 }	Pakistan International Airlines v Karachi	(Karachi)	1982-83
99. 108	BCCP Patron's XI v Indians	(Rawalpindi)	1982-83
100. 215	Pakistan v India	(Lahore)	1982-83

Of his 100 centuries, 47 have been scored for Gloucestershire, of which 43 have been made in the County Championship. Apart from his own county, Zaheer has scored centuries against all other counties, except Middlesex. He has scored nine Test centuries, 13 for Pakistan on tour, and two for the touring World XI in Australia. 27 centuries (23 for PIA) were scored in Pakistan domestic cricket, two for Pakistan against a World XI and one against the touring Indians.

One hundred small businesses will receive Business Development Loans from NatWest today.

And tomorrow. And the next day. And the day after. And the

THE FIRST-CLASS
UMPIRES FOR 1983

N.B. The abbreviations used below are as for 'The Counties and their Players'.

William Edward ALLEY B Sydney, Australia 3/2/1919. LHB, RM. Played for New South Wales 1945-46 to 1947-48. Subsequently came to England to play League cricket and then for Somerset from 1957 to 1968. *Wisden* 1961. Testimonial (£2,700) in 1961. Tours: India and Pakistan 1949-50, Pakistan 1963-64 with Commonwealth team. Scored 3,019 runs (av. 56.96) in 1961 including 2,761 runs and 10 centuries for county, both being records. Gillette Man of Match Awards: 3. HS: 221* v Warwickshire (Nuneaton) 1961. BB: 8-65 v Surrey (Oval) 1962. Career record: 19,612 runs (av. 31.88), 31 centuries, 768 wkts (av. 22.68). Appointed 1969. Umpired in 10 Tests between 1974 and 1981.

Harold Denis BIRD B Barnsley 19/4/1933. RHB, RM. Played for Yorks from 1956 to 1959 and for Leics from 1960 to 1964. Was subsequently professional at Paignton CC. HS: 181* Yorks v Glamorgan (Bradford) 1959. Career record: 3,315 runs (av. 20.71), 2 centuries. Appointed 1970. Umpired in 24 Tests between 1973 and 1982.

Jack BIRKENSHAW B Rothwell (Yorks) 13/11/1940. LHB, OB. Played for Yorks from 1958 to 1960, for Leics from 1961 to 1980 and for Worcs in 1981. Benefit (£13,000) in 1974. Tests: 5 in 1972-73 and 1973-74. Tours: India, Pakistan and Sri Lanka 1972-73, West Indies 1973-74. Gillette Man of Match Awards: 1 (for Leics). HS: 131 Leics v Surrey (Guildford) 1969. BB: 8-94 Leics v Somerset (Taunton) 1972. Career Record: 12,780 runs (av. 23.57), 4 centuries, 1,073 wkts (av. 27.28). Appointed 1982.

David John CONSTANT B Bradford-on-Avon (Wilts) 9/11/1941. LHB, SLA. Played for Kent from 1961 to 1963 and for Leics from 1965 to 1968. HS: 80 v Glos (Bristol) 1966. Career record: 1,517 runs (av. 19.20), 1 wkt (36.00). Appointed 1969. Umpired in 24 Tests between 1971 and 1982.

Cecil (Sam) COOK B Tetbury (Glos) 23/8/1921. RHB, SLA. Played for Gloucestershire from 1946 to 1964. Benefit (£3,067) in 1957. Took wicket with first ball in first-class cricket. Tests: 1 v SA 1947. HS: 35* v Sussex (Hove) 1957. BB: 9-42 v Yorks (Bristol) 1947. Career record: 1,964 runs (av. 5.39), 1,782 wkts (av. 20.52). Appointed 1971, after having withdrawn from appointment in 1966.

Peter James EELE B Taunton 27/1/1935. LHB, WK. Played for Somerset between 1958 and 1966. HS: 103* v Pakistan Eaglets (Taunton) 1963. Career record: 612 runs (av. 12.24), 1 century, 106 dismissals (87 ct, 19 st). Appointed 1981.

David Gwilliam Lloyd EVANS B Lambeth, London 27/7/1933. RHB, WK. Played for Glamorgan from 1956 to 1969. Benefit (£3,500) in 1969. HS: 46* v Oxford U (Oxford) 1961. Career record: 2,875 runs (av. 10.53), 558 dismissals (502 ct, 56 st). Appointed 1971. Umpired in 3 Tests in 1981 and 1982.

John Humphrey HARRIS B Taunton 13/2/1936. LHB, RFM. Played for Somerset from 1952 to 1959. HS: 41 v Worcs (Taunton) 1957. Career record: 154 runs (av. 11.00), 19 wkts (av. 32.05). Appointed 1983.

172

John Wakefield HOLDER B St George Barbados 19/3/1945. RHB, RFM. Played for Hants from 1968 to 1972. HS: 33 v Sussex (Hove) 1971. BB: 7-79 v Glos (Gloucester) 1972. Career record: 374 runs (av. 10.68), 139 wkts (av. 24.56). Appointed 1983.

Khalid (Billy) IBADULLA B Lahore 20/12/1935. RHB, RM/OB. Played for Warwickshire from 1954 to 1972, having made first-class debut for Pakistan touring team in India 1952-53. Also played for Otago and Tasmania whilst coaching there. Benefit (£7,797) in 1969. Has coached in this country and New Zealand since retirement. Tests: 4 for Pakistan between 1964-65 and 1967. Gillette Man of Match Awards: 2. HS: 171 v Oxford U (Oxford) 1961. BB: 7-22 v Derbyshire (Chesterfield) 1967. Career record: 17,039 runs (av. 27.30), 22 centuries, 462 wkts (av. 30.87). Appointed 1982.

Arthur JEPSON B Selston (Notts) 12/7/1915. RHB, RFM. Played for Notts from 1938 to 1959. Benefit (£2,000) in 1951. HS: 130 v Worcs (Nottingham) 1950. BB: 8-45 v Leics (Nottingham) 1958. Career record: 6,369 runs (av. 14.31), 1 century, 1,051 wkts (av. 29.08). Soccer (goalkeeper) for Port Vale, Stoke City and Lincoln City. Appointed 1960 and is longest-serving umpire on list. Umpired in 4 Tests between 1966 and 1969.

Raymond JULIEN B Cosby (Leics) 23/8/1936. RHB, WK. Played for Leicestershire from 1953 (debut at age of 16) to 1971, but lost regular place in side to R.W. Tolchard in 1966. HS: 51 v Worcs (Worcester) 1962. Career record: 2,581 runs (av. 9.73), 421 dismissals (382 ct, 39 st). Appointed 1972.

Mervyn John KITCHEN B Nailsea (Somerset) 1/8/1940. LHB, RM. Played for Somerset from 1960 to 1979. Testimonial (£6,000) in 1973. Gillette Man of Match Awards: 2. Benson & Hedges Gold Awards: 1. HS: 189 v Pakistanis (Taunton) 1967. Career record: 15,230 runs (av. 26.25), 17 centuries, 2 wkts (av. 54.50). Appointed 1982.

Barrie LEADBEATER B Harehills, Leeds 14/8/1943. RHB, RM. Played for Yorkshire from 1966 to 1979. Joint benefit in 1980 with G.A. Cope. Gillette Man of Match Awards: 1 (in 1969 Cup Final). HS: 140* v Hants (Portsmouth) 1976. Career record: 5,373 runs (av. 25.34), 1 century, 1 wkt (av. 5.00). Appointed 1981.

Barrie John MEYER B Bournemouth 21/8/1932. RHB, WK. Played for Gloucestershire from 1957 to 1971. Benefit 1971. HS: 63 v Indians (Cheltenham) 1959, v Oxford U (Bristol) 1962 and v Sussex (Bristol) 1964. Career record: 5,367 runs (av. 14.19), 826 dismissals (707 ct, 119 st). Soccer for Bristol Rovers, Plymouth Argyle, Newport County and Bristol City. Appointed 1973. Umpired in 11 Tests between 1978 and 1982.

Donald Osmund OSLEAR B Cleethorpes (Lincs) 3/3/1929. Has not played first-class cricket. Played soccer for Grimsby Town, Hull City and Oldham Athletic. Also played ice hockey. Has umpired in county second XI matches since 1972. Appointed in 1975. Umpired in 4 Tests in 1980 and 1981.

Kenneth Ernest PALMER B Winchester 22/4/1937. RHB, RFM. Played for Somerset from 1955 to 1969. Testimonial (£4,000) in 1968. Tour: Pakistan with Commonwealth team 1963-64. Coached in Johannesburg 1964-65 and was called upon by MCC to play in final Test v South Africa owing to injuries to other bowlers. Tests: 1 v South Africa 1964-65. HS: 125* v Northants (Northampton) 1961. BB: 9-57 v Notts (Nottingham) 1963. Career record: 7,771 runs (av. 20.66), 2 centuries, 866 wkts (av. 21.34). Appointed 1972. Umpired in 8 Tests between 1978 and 1981.

Roy PALMER B Devizes (Wilts) 12/7/1942. RHB, RFM. Younger brother of K.E. Palmer. Played for Somerset from 1965 to 1970. Gillette Man of Match Awards: 2. HS: 84 v Leics (Taunton) 1967. BB: 6-45 v Middlesex (Lord's) 1967. Career record: 1,037 runs (av. 13.29). 172 wkts (av. 31.62). Appointed 1980.

Nigel Trevor PLEWIS B Nottingham 5/9/1934. Former policeman. Has not played first-class cricket. Umpired in 2nd XI games since 1968. On Minor Counties reserve list 1980, and on list 1981. Appointed 1982.

David Robert SHEPHERD B Bideford (Devon) 27/12/1940. RHB, RM. Played for Gloucestershire from 1965 to 1979, scoring 108 in debut match v Oxford U. Joint benefit in 1978 with J. Davey. Gillette Man of Match Awards: 1. Benson & Hedges Gold Awards: 1. HS: 153 v Middlesex (Bristol) 1968. Career record: 10,672 runs (av. 24.47), 12 centuries, 2 wkts (av. 53.00). Appointed 1981.

Charles Terry SPENCER B Leicester 18/8/1931. RHB, RFM. Played for Leicestershire from 1952 to 1974. Benefit (£3,500) in 1964. HS: 90 v Essex (Leicester) 1964. BB: 9-63 v Yorks (Huddersfield) 1954. Career record: 5,871 runs (av. 10.77), 1,367 wkts (av. 26.69). Appointed 1979.

Jack VAN GELOVEN B Leeds 4/1/1934. RHB, RM. Played for Yorkshire in 1955 and for Leicestershire from 1956 to 1965. Subsequently played for Northumberland in Minor Counties competition from 1966 to 1973. HS: 157* v Somerset (Leicester) 1960. BB: 7-56 v Hants (Leicester) 1959. Career record: 7,522 runs (av. 19.43), 5 centuries, 486 wkts (av. 28.62). Appointed 1977.

Alan Geoffrey Thomas WHITEHEAD B Butleigh (Somerset) 28/10/1940. LHB, SLA. Played for Somerset from 1957 to 1961. HS: 15 v Hants (Southampton) 1959 and 15 v Leics (Leicester) 1960. BB: 6-74 v Sussex (Eastbourne) 1959. Career record: 137 runs (av. 5.70), 67 wkts (av. 34.41). Served on Minor Counties list in 1969. Appointed 1970. Tests: 1 in 1982.

Peter Bernard WIGHT B Georgetown, British Guiana 25/6/1930. RHB, OB. Played for British Guiana in 1950-51 and for Somerset from 1953 to 1965. Benefit (£5,000) in 1963. HS: 222* v Kent (Taunton) 1959. BB: 6-29 v Derbyshire (Chesterfield) 1957. Career record: 17,773 runs (av. 33.09), 28 centuries, 68 wkts (av. 32.26). Appointed 1966.

Robert Arthur WHITE B Fulham 6/10/1936. LHB, OB. Played for Middlesex 1958 to 1965. Played for Notts 1966 to 1980. Benefit (£11,000) in 1974. HS: 116* Notts v Surrey (Oval) 1967. BB: 7-41 Notts v Derby (Ilkeston) 1971. Career record: 12,452 runs (av. 23.18), 5 centuries, 693 wkts (av. 30.50).

Test Match Panel for 1983: H.D. Bird, D.J. Constant, D.G.L. Evans and B.J. Meyer.

Prudential World Cup Panel: H.D. Bird, J. Birkenshaw, D.J. Constant, D.G.L. Evans, M.J. Kitchen, B. Leadbeater, B.J. Meyer, D.O. Oslear, K.E. Palmer, R. Palmer, D.R. Shepherd and A.G.T. Whitehead.

FIRST CLASS AVERAGES 1982

Compiled by Brian Croudy

The following are the averages for all players who appeared in first-class matches played in England in 1982.
†*Indicates left-handed batsman*

BATTING AND FIELDING

	Cap	M	I	NO	Runs	HS	Avge	100	50	Ct	St
Abdul Qadir (Pak)	—	12	9	3	93	21*	15.50	—	—	3	—
†Abrahams, J. (La)	—	23	32	5	1013	124	37.51	1	7	24	—
Acfield, D.L. (Ex)	1970	21	18	14	23	4*	5.75	—	—	8	—
Agnew, J.P. (Le)	—	10	12	1	122	56	11.09	—	1	1	—
Alleyne, H.L. (Wo)	1981	8	9	3	130	32	21.66	—	—	1	—
Allott, P.J.W. (E/La/MCC/DBC)	1981	18	15	5	220	41*	22.00	—	—	8	—
Amiss, D.L. (Wa)	1965	21	38	1	1404	156	37.94	1	9	12	—
Anderson, I.J. (Ire)	—	1	2	0	12	9	6.00	—	—	—	—
Anderson, I.S. (D)	—	17	26	4	671	103*	30.50	1	3	19	—
Armstrong, P.A.N. (OU)	—	1	2	0	34	34	17.00	—	—	—	—
Arnold, G.G. (Sx)	1979	3	5	4	11	8*	11.00	—	—	—	—
Asif Din, (Wa)	—	24	34	2	855	102	26.71	1	2	14	—
Asif Iqbal (K)	1968	11	17	2	558	115*	37.20	1	4	7	—
Aslett, D.G. (K)	—	16	28	3	794	82	31.76	—	7	12	—
Athey, C.W.J. (Y)	1980	22	38	7	1339	134	43.19	4	8	21	—
†Bailey, M.J. (H)	—	1	1	0	3	3	3.00	—	—	—	—
Bailey, R.J. (No)	—	2	3	0	17	10	5.66	—	—	1	—
Bainbridge, P. (Gs)	1981	18	33	8	1069	103*	42.76	2	7	9	—
Bairstow, D.L. (Y/DBC)	1973	23	30	9	603	77	28.71	—	4	57	4
Balderstone, J.C. (Le)	1973	23	41	3	1482	148	39.00	4	8	17	—
Bamber, M.J. (No)	—	1	2	0	58	31	29.00	—	—	—	—
Baptiste, E.A.E. (K)	—	9	12	3	319	69*	35.44	—	2	7	—
Barclay, J.R.T. (Sx)	1976	22	33	6	761	95	28.18	—	6	25	—
†Barlow, G.D. (M)	1976	7	12	3	199	37*	22.11	—	—	5	—
Barnett, K.J. (D)	1982	18	25	5	642	120	32.10	2	1	11	—
Barrington, W.E.J. (CU)	—	4	6	1	174	59	34.80	—	1	1	—
Barwick, S.R. (Gm)	—	15	18	7	126	24	11.45	—	—	6	—
†Benson, M.R. (K)	1981	16	30	5	1100	137	44.00	3	7	7	—
Birch, J.D. (Nt)	1981	22	35	6	1011	125	34.86	2	6	11	—
Boon, T.J. (Le)	—	9	14	1	210	90	16.15	—	1	3	—
†Booth, P.A. (Y)	—	1	1	1	0	0*	—	—	—	—	—
Bore, M.K. (Nt)	1980	8	8	5	44	23*	14.66	—	—	4	—
Botham, I.T. (E/So)	1976	17	29	1	1241	208	44.32	3	7	7	—
Boycott, G. (Y)	1963	21	37	6	1913	159	61.70	6	10	10	—
Boyd-Moss, R.J. (No/OU)	—	23	41	5	1602	137	44.50	5	10	13	—
Brassington, A.J. (Gs)	1978	20	20	5	141	35	9.40	—	—	37	8
Brearley, J.M. (M)	1964	20	32	9	1083	165	47.08	3	4	18	—
Briers, N.E. (Le)	1981	23	38	4	1175	106	34.55	1	6	12	—

175

	Cap	M	I	NO	Runs	HS	Avge	100	50	Ct	St
†Broad, B.C. (Gs)	1981	22	41	0	1153	97	28.12	—	7	4	—
Brown, A. (Sc)	—	1	1	0	1	1	1.00	—	—	4	—
Brown, D.J. (Wa)	1964	3	1	1	7	7*	—	—	—	1	—
Brown, R.D. (Zim)	—	2	4	0	76	51	19.00	—	1	2	—
Bryant, M. (So)	—	2	2	0	6	6	3.00	—	—	1	—
Bullen, C.K. (Sy)	—	1	—	—	—	—	—	—	—	—	—
Butchart, I.P. (Zim)	—	1	2	0	68	54	34.00	—	1	—	—
†Butcher, A.R. (Sy/MCC)	1975	23	43	5	1514	187*	39.84	4	6	13	—
Butcher, I.P. (Le)	—	6	9	3	182	71*	30.33	—	1	5	—
Butcher, M.S. (Sy)	—	1	—	—	—	—	—	—	—	1	—
Butcher, R.O. (M)	1979	21	28	3	1058	197	42.32	3	2	22	—
Capel, D.J. (No)	—	14	22	4	460	60*	25.55	—	1	8	—
Carrick, P. (Y)	1976	20	21	3	423	93	23.50	—	2	8	—
Carter, R.M. (No)	—	11	19	6	411	79	31.61	—	1	12	—
Cassidy, J.J. (OU)	—	1	1	0	0	0	—	—	—	—	—
†Cheatle, R.G.L. (Sy)	—	4	2	2	28	27*	—	—	—	1	—
Chessher, J.R. (OU)	—	3	4	1	67	47	22.33	—	—	—	—
†Childs, J.H. (Gs)	1977	21	21	5	132	34*	8.25	—	—	7	—
Clark, J. (Sc)	—	1	1	0	3	3	3.00	—	—	1	—
Clarke, S.T. (Sy)	1980	22	25	0	408	52	16.32	—	1	11	—
Clift, P.B. (Le)	1976	5	6	2	123	45	30.75	—	—	1	—
†Clinton, G.S. (Sy)	1980	14	23	4	622	172*	32.73	2	1	4	—
†Close, D.B. (DBC)	—	1	1	1	26	26*	—	—	—	1	—
Cobb, R.A. (Le)	—	22	37	1	759	63	21.08	—	4	11	—
Cockbain, I. (La)	—	14	25	1	492	98	20.50	—	2	4	—
Cook, C.R. (M)	—	3	3	0	38	36	12.66	—	—	2	—
Cook, G. (E/No/MCC)	1975	24	43	2	1285	125	31.34	3	7	27	—
Cook, N.G.B. (Le/EB)	1982	25	25	8	284	37	16.70	—	—	20	—
†Cooper, K.E. (Nt)	1980	23	26	5	247	38*	11.76	—	—	10	—
Corlett, S.C. (Ire)	—	1	2	1	43	39*	43.00	—	—	1	—
Cowan, R.S. (Sx/OU)	—	8	16	4	533	143*	44.41	2	2	4	—
Cowans, N.G. (M)	—	11	10	1	63	16	7.00	—	—	8	—
Cowdrey, C.S. (K)	1979	22	35	4	794	72*	25.61	—	4	26	—
Cowley, N.G. (H)	1978	23	28	1	584	104	21.62	1	2	9	—
Croft, C.E.H. (La)	—	12	12	3	109	20	12.11	—	—	5	—
Crowe, M.D. (DBC)	—	1	1	0	104	104	104.00	1	—	1	—
†Crowe, P.J. (OU)	—	1	2	0	11	11	5.50	—	—	—	—
Cumbes, J. (Wa)	—	14	14	7	33	7*	4.71	—	—	8	—
†Cunningham, E.J. (Gs)	—	4	6	2	26	11*	6.50	—	—	—	—
Curran, K.M. (Zim)	—	1	1	—	0	0*	—	—	—	—	—
Curtis, I.J. (OU)	—	5	3	2	20	20*	20.00	—	—	1	—
Curtis, T.S. (Wo)	—	10	17	4	359	59*	27.61	—	2	5	—
Daniel, W.W. (M)	1977	19	15	9	88	21	14.66	—	—	13	—
Daniels, S.A.B. (Gm)	—	11	15	6	197	73	21.88	—	1	3	—
Davies, A.G. (CU)	—	1	2	0	17	13	8.50	—	—	3	—
†Davies, M.N. (Gm)	—	2	1	0	0	0	—	—	—	—	—
Davies, T. (Gm)	—	10	16	4	283	66*	23.58	—	2	20	1
†Davis, M.R. (So)	—	9	12	2	65	21*	6.50	—	—	4	—
Davis, W.W. (Gm)	—	13	13	6	58	20*	8.28	—	—	3	—
Davison, B.F. (Le)	1971	22	37	4	1800	172	54.54	7	8	16	—
†Denning, P.W. (So)	1973	14	22	1	541	91*	25.76	—	3	6	—
Dennis, S.J. (Y)	—	3	1	1	5	5*	—	—	—	1	—

176

	Cap	M	I	NO	Runs	HS	Avge	100	50	Ct	St
†Dilley, G.R. (K/MCC/EB)	1980	23	27	7	199	33	9.95	—	—	9	—
†Doggart, S.J.G. (CU)	—	9	13	1	242	64	20.16	—	1	3	—
D'Oliveira, D.B. (Wo)	—	4	7	1	65	21	10.83	—	—	2	—
Donald, W.A. (Sc)	—	1	2	1	40	34*	40.00	—	—	—	—
†Doshi, D.R. (Ind)	—	9	4	2	11	5*	5.50	—	—	—	—
Doughty, R.J. (Gs)	—	5	5	1	58	29	14.50	—	—	2	—
Downton, P.R. (M)	1981	25	25	2	483	65	21.00	—	2	51	10
†Dredge, C.H. (So)	1978	20	26	8	317	54*	17.61	—	1	9	—
Dudhia, M.H.E.M. (Zim)	—	1	—	—	—	—	—	—	—	—	—
Dudleston, B. (Gs)	—	6	12	1	373	111	33.90	1	1	6	—
Dutton, R.S. (CU)	—	2	3	1	0	0*	—	—	—	—	—
Dyer, R.I.H.B. (Wa)	—	5	5	1	58	31*	14.50	—	—	1	—
Ealham, A.G.E. (K)	1970	1	2	1	47	31*	47.00	—	—	—	—
East, D.E. (Ex)	—	24	32	8	525	78	21.87	—	2	65	9
East, R.E. (Ex)	1967	21	23	2	344	58	16.38	—	1	22	—
Edbrooke, R.M. (OU)	—	1	2	1	100	84*	100.00	—	1	—	—
Edmonds, P.H. (E/M/MCC)	1974	21	22	4	505	92	28.05	—	4	7	—
Ehtesham-Ud-Din (Pak)	—	2	2	1	0	0*	—	—	—	—	—
Ellcock, R.M. (Wo)	—	1	2	1	13	13*	13.00	—	—	—	—
Ellis, R.G.P. (M/OU)	—	13	25	1	823	105*	34.29	1	5	7	—
Ellison, C.C. (CU)	—	7	7	4	56	16	18.66	—	—	1	—
†Ellison, R.M. (K)	—	7	11	3	179	46*	22.37	—	—	3	—
Emburey, J.E. (M)	1977	24	27	5	752	100*	34.18	1	4	16	—
Emery, K.S.D. (H/EB)	—	24	26	15	37	18*	3.36	—	—	3	—
†Fairbrother, N.H. (La)	—	1	—	—	—	—	—	—	—	—	—
Fell, M.A. (Nt)	—	10	18	0	315	108	17.50	1	—	3	—
†Felton, N.A. (So)	—	8	12	0	346	71	28.83	—	3	4	—
Ferreira, A.M. (Wa)	—	8	10	2	303	112*	37.87	1	—	5	—
Finney, R.J. (D)	—	1	1	0	39	39	39.00	—	—	1	—
†Fletcher, D.A.G. (Zim)	—	2	3	1	97	56*	48.50	—	1	1	—
Fletcher, K.W.R. (Ex/MCC)	1963	24	36	4	1249	124	39.03	3	6	12	—
Folley, I. (La)	—	17	15	4	165	36	15.00	—	—	3	—
†Forster, G. (Le)	—	3	3	1	28	22*	14.00	—	—	2	—
Foster, N.A. (Ex)	—	5	4	1	58	36*	19.33	—	—	—	—
†Fowler, G. (E/La/EB)	1981	21	35	2	1387	150	42.03	5	5	6	—
Francis, D.A. (Gm)	—	19	33	5	1076	142*	38.42	2	7	9	—
French, B.N. (Nt)	1980	23	34	6	721	79	25.75	—	5	60	3
Gard, T. (So)	—	6	5	1	37	31	9.25	—	—	8	3
Garner, J. (So)	1979	10	11	5	98	40*	16.33	—	—	4	—
Garnham, M.A. (Le)	—	11	17	2	298	57	19.86	—	3	13	4
Gatting, M.W. (E/M/MCC/DBC)	1977	23	34	6	1651	192	58.96	6	5	28	—
Gavaskar, S.M. (Ind)	—	8	10	0	438	172	43.80	1	1	9	—
†Gifford, N. (Wo/DBC)	1961	14	15	7	155	31*	19.37	—	—	9	—
Gilfillan, A.D. (OU)	—	3	4	1	40	31	13.33	—	—	—	—
Goldie, C.F.E. (CU)	—	9	9	0	115	31	12.77	—	—	19	4
Gooch, G.A. (Ex)	1975	23	38	1	1632	149	44.10	3	12	25	—
†Gould, I.J. (Sx/EB)	1981	20	32	3	695	94	23.96	—	5	43	5

Congratulations, Surrey, on winning the 1982 NatWest Bank Trophy.

	Cap	M	I	NO	Runs	HS	Avge	100	50	Ct	St
†Gower, D.I. (E/Le/MCC)	1977	20	35	2	1530	176*	46.36	2	12	10	—
Graveney, D.A. (Gs)	1976	23	30	11	489	55*	25.73	—	1	14	—
Green, A.M. (Sx)	—	14	26	1	776	99	31.04	—	*6	7	—
Greenidge, C.G. (H)	1972	21	41	8	1526	183*	46.24	3	4	23	—
Greig, I.A. (E/Sx/MCC)	1981	21	28	1	507	109	18.77	1	3	18	—
Griffiths, B.J. (No)	1978	19	11	4	39	16	5.57	—	—	5	—
Griffiths, P.D. (CU)	—	1	2	0	1	1	0.50	—	—	—	—
Hacker, P.J. (D)	—	8	4	2	22	10*	11.00	—	—	3	—
†Hadlee, R.J. (Nt)	1978	18	28	2	807	131	31.03	2	4	16	—
Halliday, M. (Ire)	—	1	2	0	36	30	18.00	—	—	1	—
Halliday, S.J. (OU)	—	4	7	1	213	113*	35.50	1	—	—	—
Hampshire, J.H. (D)	1982	22	36	6	1256	101*	41.86	1	9	14	—
Hardie, B.R. (Ex)	1974	24	39	5	1432	161	42.11	1	8	15	—
Haroon Rashid (Pak)	—	10	13	3	331	90	33.10	—	2	8	—
Harris, M.J. (Nt)	1970	2	3	2	115	43*	115.00	—	—	1	—
Hartley, P.J. (Wa)	—	3	4	1	31	16	10.33	—	—	1	—
Hartley, S.N. (Y)	—	20	30	9	635	114	30.23	1	4	6	—
Hassan, S.B. (Nt)	1970	19	34	4	970	89*	32.33	—	7	18	—
Hayes, F.C. (La)	1972	3	4	1	73	43	24.33	—	—	—	—
Hayes, K.A. (La/OU)	—	13	22	3	594	152	31.26	1	3	5	—
Haynes, D.L. (DBC)	—	1	1	0	4	4	4.00	—	—	2	—
†Hayward, R.E. (H)	—	6	9	1	169	59	21.12	—	1	3	—
†Heath, J.R.P. (Sx)	—	3	5	0	61	19	12.20	—	—	—	—
Hemmings, E.E. (E/Nt)	1980	20	25	8	432	127*	25.41	1	—	16	—
Hemsley, E.J.O. (Wo)	1969	16	24	1	393	49	17.08	—	—	8	—
†Henderson, S.P. (CU)	—	9	16	3	531	209*	40.84	1	2	12	—
Hendrick, M. (Nt)	—	10	10	4	54	29	9.00	—	—	6	—
Heron, J.G. (Zim)	—	2	4	0	116	83	29.00	—	1	—	—
†Higgs, K. (Le)	1972	1	—	—	—	—	—	—	—	—	—
Hignell, A.J. (Gs)	1977	15	28	6	664	72	30.18	—	4	9	—
Hill, A. (D)	1976	7	14	3	219	54	19.90	—	1	5	—
†Hinks, S.G. (K)	—	2	4	1	35	18	11.66	—	1	—	—
Hodgson, C.A.P. (Zim)	—	1	2	0	80	47	40.00	—	—	—	—
Hodgson, K.I. (CU)	—	8	10	1	213	50	23.66	—	1	—	—
Hogg, V.R. (Zim)	—	1	—	—	—	—	—	—	—	—	—
Hogg, W. (Wa)	—	5	4	2	9	8	4.50	—	—	2	—
Holmes, G.C. (Gm)	—	7	10	1	210	68	22.33	—	1	2	—
Hopkins, J.A. (Gm)	1977	23	41	5	978	124	27.16	1	4	16	—
Hough, E.J. (Zim)	—	1	1	1	0	0*	—	—	—	—	—
Houghton, D.L. (Zim)	—	2	4	1	36	24*	12.00	—	—	4	2
Howarth, G.P. (Sy)	1974	19	32	3	1158	150	39.93	4	2	16	—
Hughes, D.P. (La)	1970	23	36	9	1303	126*	48.25	3	6	19	—
Hughes, S.P. (M)	1981	10	8	4	27	18	6.75	—	—	—	—
Humpage, G.W. (Wa)	1976	24	41	4	1407	254	38.02	4	5	49	5
†Humphries, D.J. (Wo)	1978	25	37	5	852	98	26.62	—	7	41	5
Illingworth, N.J.B. (Nt)	—	11	14	4	158	49	15.80	—	—	4	—
Illingworth, R. (Y)	1955	16	3	2	86	33	21.50	—	—	3	—
Illingworth, R.K. (Wo)	—	11	16	4	191	47*	15.91	—	—	5	—
Imran Khan (Pak/Sx)	1978	16	20	7	588	85	45.23	—	3	2	—
Inchmore, J.D. (Wo)	1976	15	19	3	294	68	18.37	—	1	2	—
Intikhab Alam (Pak)	—	1	2	0	4	4	2.00	—	—	5	—
†Iqbal Qasim (Pak)	—	7	4	1	9	5	3.00	—	—	2	—

	Cap	M	I	NO	Runs	HS	Avge	100	50	Ct	St
Jackman, R.D. (E/Sy)	1970	20	22	8	430	68	30.71	—	3	4	—
Jackson, P.B. (Ire)	—	1	2	0	53	46	26.50	—	—	2	—
Jalauddin (Pak)	—	3	2	0	10	10	5.00	—	—	—	—
†James, K.D. (M)	—	1	1	—	1	1	1.00	—	—	—	—
Jarvis, K.B.S. (K/EB)	1977	22	15	4	21	6	1.90	—	—	6	—
Jarvis, P.W. (Y)	—	6	3	1	7	7	3.50	—	—	5	—
Javed Miandad (Pak/Gm)	1980	18	29	8	1051	105*	50.04	1	9	24	—
†Jefferies, S.T. (D)	—	1	2	1	14	14*	14.00	—	—	1	—
Jesty, T.E. (H)	1971	22	36	8	1645	164*	58.75	8	4	13	—
Johnson, G.W. (K)	1970	22	34	7	582	86	21.55	—	2	20	—
Johnson, P. (Nt)	—	4	7	1	90	37*	15.00	—	—	—	—
†Jones, A. (Gm)	1962	25	47	5	1491	146*	35.50	4	6	4	—
†Jones, A.L. (Gm)	—	22	38	2	900	88	25.00	—	6	13	—
†Jones, A.N. (Sx)	—	4	4	0	39	29	9.75	—	—	—	—
Jones, E.W. (Gm)	1967	15	21	3	268	65	14.88	—	2	37	4
†Kallicharran, A.I. (Wa)	1972	23	37	5	2120	235	66.25	8	5	8	—
Kapil Dev (Ind/No)	1982	14	20	2	770	103	42.77	2	4	13	—
Kemp, N.J. (M)	—	5	6	2	121	46*	30.25	—	—	5	—
†Kennedy, A. (La)	1975	9	12	1	242	43	22.00	—	—	7	—
Ker, A.B.M. (Sc)	—	1	1	0	58	58	58.00	—	1	2	—
King, C.L. (DBC)	—	1	1	0	22	22	22.00	—	—	—	—
Kirmani, S.M.H. (Ind)	—	9	12	3	265	65	29.44	—	2	11	4
Kirsten, P.N. (D)	1978	21	37	1	1941	164*	64.70	8	6	12	—
†Knight, R.D.V. (Sy)	1978	24	40	4	1114	111	30.94	2	7	10	—
Knott, A.P.E. (K)	1965	21	32	5	942	115*	34.88	1	6	46	7
Lamb, A.J. (E/No)	1978	18	30	2	1302	140	46.50	5	4	6	—
Lamb, T.M. (No)	1978	13	13	8	137	39*	27.40	—	—	1	—
Larkins, W. (No)	1976	24	44	3	1863	186	45.43	5	9	13	—
Lawrence, D.V. (Gs)	—	1	—	—	—	—	—	—	—	—	—
†Lawrence, M.P. (OU)	—	4	5	2	20	18	6.66	—	—	—	—
Lee, P.G. (La)	1972	3	1	0	0	0	—	—	—	2	—
†Leiper, R.J. (Ex)	—	1	2	0	3	2	1.50	—	—	2	—
Le Roux, G.S. (Sx)	1981	20	28	5	737	83	32.04	—	6	15	—
Lethbridge, C. (Wa)	—	16	21	5	369	87*	23.06	—	1	7	—
Lever, J.K. (Ex)	1970	18	19	3	89	22*	5.56	—	—	5	—
Lewington, P.J. (Wa)	—	4	5	4	35	15*	35.00	—	—	—	—
Lilley, A.W. (Ex)	—	10	14	1	276	67	21.23	—	1	4	—
†Llewellyn, M.J. (Gm)	1977	2	4	1	88	61*	29.33	—	1	1	—
Lloyd, B.J. (Gm)	1982	25	32	8	318	48	13.25	—	—	14	—
†Lloyd, C.H. (La)	1969	21	29	2	1135	100	42.03	1	9	19	—
†Lloyd, D. (La/DBC)	1968	23	36	2	1371	114	40.32	5	7	10	—
†Lloyd, T.A. (Wa)	1980	25	45	5	1432	122	35.80	2	9	12	—
†Lloyds, J.W. (So)	—	23	39	3	981	132*	27.25	2	3	30	—
Louden, W.D.G. (Sc)	—	1	1	0	21	21	21.00	—	—	1	—
Love, J.D. (Y)	1980	18	29	6	773	123	33.60	2	4	7	—
Luddington, R.S. (OU)	—	10	14	1	290	65	22.30	—	2	5	1
Lumb, R.G. (Y)	1974	20	33	1	844	81	26.37	—	7	9	—
Lynch, M.A. (Sy)	1982	23	38	2	1155	141*	32.08	3	4	18	—
McCool, R.J. (So)	—	1	2	0	19	12	9.50	—	—	1	—
†McDermott, E.A. (Ire)	—	1	2	0	18	18	9.00	—	—	1	—
McEwan, K.S. (Ex)	1974	24	37	3	1421	150*	41.79	3	6	10	—
McFarlane, L. (La)	—	13	10	3	39	12	5.57	—	—	3	—

180

	Cap	M	I	NO	Runs	HS	Avge	100	50	Ct	St
Mackintosh, K.S. (Sy)	—	12	10	7	94	31	31.33	—	—	5	—
Madan Lal, S. (Ind)	—	9	15	10	309	58*	61.80	—	2	1	—
Maguire, K.R. (Wa)	—	3	3	0	3	2	1.00	—	—	4	—
Maher, B.J.M. (D)	—	10	11	5	49	15*	8.16	—	—	13	—
Majid Khan (Pak)	—	11	17	3	403	88	28.78	—	1	8	—
Malhotra, A. (Ind)	—	8	15	1	462	154*	33.00	1	2	5	—
Mallender, N.A. (No)	—	24	17	8	121	42	13.44	—	—	10	—
Malone, S.J. (H)	—	6	5	2	13	4	4.33	—	—	1	—
Mansoor Akhtar (Pak)	—	11	17	2	595	153	39.66	1	5	5	—
Marks, V.J. (E/So/MCC/EB)	1979	23	33	5	599	71*	21.39	—	5	11	—
Marsden, R. (OU)	—	5	10	1	264	60	29.33	—	1	1	—
Marsh, S. (K)	—	2	1	1	10	10*	—	—	—	6	—
Marshall, M.D. (H)	1981	22	31	3	633	116*	22.60	1	1	4	—
Maru, R.J. (M)	—	4	4	1	45	18	15.00	—	—	2	—
Maynard, C. (La/Wa)	—	17	20	3	227	40	13.35	—	—	20	5
Mendis, G.D. (Sx)	1980	23	42	2	1240	114	31.00	2	7	5	—
Merry, W.G. (M)	—	4	—	—	—	—	—	—	—	3	—
†Miller, A.J.T. (OU)	—	1	2	0	20	20	10.00	—	—	—	—
Miller, G. (E/D/MCC)	1976	16	26	7	772	98	40.63	—	6	19	—
Mills, J.P.C. (OU)	—	9	17	0	389	98	22.88	—	3	3	—
Mohsin Khan (Pak)	—	13	20	3	1248	203*	73.41	4	4	5	—
Moir, D.G. (D)	—	23	22	1	136	25	6.47	—	—	24	—
Monkhouse, G. (Sy)	—	8	10	5	137	63*	27.40	—	1	3	—
Monteith, J.D. (M/Ire)	—	2	4	0	97	45	24.25	—	—	1	—
†Morris, H. (Gm)	—	4	6	3	213	63	71.00	—	2	1	—
Morris, J.E. (D)	—	1	2	0	18	12	9.00	—	—	—	—
Morton, W.A. (Sc)	—	1	1	0	3	3	3.00	—	—	—	—
Moseley, H.R. (So)	1972	18	19	13	113	24*	18.83	—	—	6	—
Moulding, R.P. (OU)	—	10	20	2	242	67	13.44	—	1	3	—
Moxon, M.D. (Y)	—	2	4	0	197	67	49.25	—	2	—	—
Mudassar Nazar (Pak)	—	11	16	6	825	211*	82.50	4	2	4	—
Mushtaq Mohammad (DBC)	—	1	1	0	23	23	23.00	—	—	—	—
†Nash, M.A. (Gm)	1969	16	20	1	216	37	11.36	—	—	10	—
†Nayak, S.V. (Ind)	—	10	13	6	253	67*	36.14	—	1	3	—
Neale, P.A. (Wo/EB)	1978	26	44	8	1006	79*	27.94	—	6	10	—
Needham, A. (Sy)	—	13	20	6	319	134*	22.78	1	—	7	—
Newman, P.G. (D/MCC)	—	19	22	4	204	39*	11.33	—	—	4	—
Newport, P.J. (Wo)	—	3	5	1	38	11	9.50	—	—	1	—
Nicholas, M.C.J. (H)	1982	24	42	9	1312	206*	39.75	3	7	14	—
†Old, C.M. (Y)	1969	16	18	3	207	32	13.80	—	—	9	—
Oldham, S. (D)	1980	21	18	10	156	35*	19.50	—	—	7	—
Oliver, P.R. (Wa)	—	7	9	0	143	46	15.88	—	—	4	—
†Ollis, R.L. (So)	—	1	2	0	2	1	1.00	—	—	1	—
Ontong, R.C. (Gm)	1979	24	43	4	1205	152*	30.89	3	4	12	—
O'Reilly, P.M. (Ire)	—	1	2	1	1	1*	1.00	—	—	—	—
Ormrod, J.A. (Wo)	1966	21	38	2	981	200*	27.25	1	4	8	—
O'Shaughnessy, S.J. (La)	—	11	19	7	560	62	46.66	—	7	1	—
Palmer, G.V. (So)	—	1	2	0	33	27.	16.50	—	—	—	—
Palmer, R.W.M. (CU)	—	9	8	5	20	12	6.66	—	—	2	—

181

	Cap	M	I	NO	Runs	HS	Avge	100	50	Ct	St
Parkar, G.A. (Ind)	—	7	14	2	433	146	36.08	1	2	7	1
Parker, P.W.G. (Sx/MCC/EB)	1979	25	43	9	896	106	26.35	1	5	21	—
Parks, R.J. (H)	1982	25	30	5	350	44	14.00	—	—	70	6
†Parsons, G.J. (Le)	—	24	32	7	392	51	15.68	—	1	7	—
Patel, D.N. (Wo)	1979	25	42	1	1104	133	26.92	1	4	20	—
Patil, S.M. (Ind)	—	9	16	1	390	129*	26.00	1	1	1	—
Pauline, D.B. (Sy)	—	3	6	0	69	26	11.50	—	—	—	—
†Penn, C. (K)	—	7	8	4	54	30	13.50	—	—	4	—
Perryman, S.P. (Wo)	—	14	18	10	58	14	7.25	—	—	5	—
Phillip, N. (Ex)	1978	24	32	3	783	79	27.00	—	5	6	—
Phillipson, C.P. (Sx)	1980	16	22	3	274	64	14.42	—	1	24	—
Pigott, A.C.S. (Sx)	1982	23	23	7	167	40	10.43	—	—	9	—
Pocock, N.E.J. (H)	1980	22	30	2	616	164	22.00	1	3	20	—
Pocock, P.I. (Sy)	1967	7	8	2	32	10*	5.33	—	—	1	—
Pollock, A.J. (CU)	—	7	8	2	63	19	10.50	—	—	1	—
Pont, I.L. (Nt)	—	4	7	1	32	16	5.33	—	1	1	—
Pont, K.R. (Ex)	1976	16	24	7	687	89	40.41	—	6	11	—
Popplewell, N.F.M. (So)	—	16	24	5	451	55	23.73	—	1	8	—
Potter, L. (K)	—	12	21	2	775	118	40.78	2	5	5	—
Pridgeon, A.P. (Wo)	1980	15	16	4	110	21	9.16	—	—	4	—
Pringle, D.R. (E/Ex/CU/MCC)	1982	18	26	4	741	127	33.68	1	6	1	—
Prior, J.A. (Ire)	—	1	2	0	24	13	12.00	—	—	1	—
Pycroft, A.J. (Zim)	—	2	3	1	118	62*	59.00	—	2	1	—
Radley, C.T. (M)	1967	21	28	3	773	141*	30.92	2	2	20	—
†Ramage, A. (Y)	—	4	2	1	4	4*	4.00	—	—	—	—
Randall, D.W. (E/Nt/MCC)	1973	20	33	4	1369	130*	47.20	4	8	18	—
Randhir Singh (Ind)	—	5	3	0	0	0	0	—	—	—	—
Rawlinson, H.T. (OU)	—	4	6	0	30	21	5.00	—	—	1	—
Rawson, P.W.E. (Zim)	—	2	2	1	15	13	15.00	—	—	1	—
†Reidy, B.W. (La)	1980	9	13	2	199	37	18.09	—	—	7	—
Rhind, P.A. (Sc)	—	1	1	1	2	2*		—	—	—	—
Rice, C.E.B. (Nt)	1975	22	36	3	1095	144	33.18	1	5	25	—
Rice, J.M. (H)	1975	23	44	4	777	69	19.42	—	5	26	—
Richards, C.J. (Sy/MCC)	1978	25	38	9	716	117*	24.68	1	4	52	3
Richards, I.V.A. (So)	1974	20	31	2	1324	181*	45.65	4	5	11	—
Ridge, S.P. (OU)	—	10	13	5	64	22	8.00	—	—	3	—
Roberts, A.M.E. (Le)	—	13	20	3	338	47	19.88	—	—	4	—
Robinson, R.T. (Nt)	—	21	38	3	984	109	28.11	1	5	13	—
Roebuck, P.M. (So/EB)	1978	23	40	3	958	90	25.38	—	10	8	—
Romaines, P.W. (Gs)	—	14	24	2	609	186	27.68	1	2	5	—
Roope, G.R.J. (Sy)	1969	14	25	7	560	108	31.11	1	1	13	—
†Rose, B.C. (So)	1975	21	32	8	1090	173*	45.41	2	5	10	—
Rowe, C.J.C. (Gm)	—	25	39	6	1071	105	32.45	1	6	10	—
Roy, P. (Ind)	—	7	12	0	174	51	14.50	—	1	1	—
†Russell, R.C. (Gs)	—	4	6	1	81	41	16.20	—	—	4	2
Russom, N. (So)	—	—	1	—						1	—
†Sadiq Mohammad (Gs)	1973	15	29	1	998	91	35.64	—	9	8	—
Saleem Yousuf (Pak)	—	4	4	1	38	15*	12.66	—	—	5	2
Salim Malik (Pak)	—	5	7	1	68	25*	11.33	—	—	4	—

	Cap	M	I	NO	Runs	HS	Avge	100	50	Ct	St
Sarfraz Nawaz (Pak/No)	1975	14	9	1	115	26	14.37	—	—	5	—
Saxelby, K. (Nt)	—	14	15	5	160	59*	16.00	—	1	2	—
†Scott, C.J. (La)	—	7	8	1	39	15	5.57	—	—	12	1
Scott, C.W. (Nt)	—	1	2	1	31	17*	31.00	—	—	2	—
Scott, G.M. (Zim)	—	1	—	—	—	—	—	—	—	—	—
Scott, M.S. (Wo)	—	6	11	0	118	37	10.72	—	—	1	—
Selvey, M.W.W. (M)	1973	10	6	1	114	36*	22.80	—	—	2	—
Sharp, G. (No)	1973	25	26	7	401	58*	21.10	—	1	47	7
Sharp, K. (Y)	—	10	18	2	478	115	29.87	1	3	4	—
Shastri, R.J. (Ind)	—	9	15	2	359	74	27.61	—	3	6	—
Shepherd, J.N. (Gs)	—	22	34	9	590	67*	23.60	—	3	13	—
Short, J.F. (Ire)	—	1	2	0	40	30	20.00	—	—	3	—
Sidebottom, A. (Y)	1980	19	18	8	233	44*	23.30	—	—	4	—
Sikander Bakht (Pak)	—	12	7	2	29	9	5.80	—	—	3	—
Simmons, J. (La)	1971	18	21	12	487	79*	54.11	—	4	14	—
Simpkins, D.P. (Gs)	—	1	2	1	1	1*	1.00	—	—	—	—
†Slack, W.N. (M)	1981	25	40	6	1499	203*	44.08	2	10	20	—
Slocombe, P.A. (So)	1978	13	23	1	579	78	26.31	—	6	9	—
Small, G.C. (Wa)	1982	25	29	5	309	57*	12.87	—	1	6	—
Smith, C.L. (H)	1981	1	1	0	71	71	71.00	—	1	2	—
†Smith, D.J. (Sx)	—	5	3	0	1	1	0.33	—	—	6	—
†Smith, D.M. (Sy)	1980	14	25	4	1065	160	50.71	3	5	13	—
†Smith, D.M. (Wa)	—	2	2	0	27	27	13.50	—	—	—	—
Smith, K.D. (Wa)	1978	20	34	6	691	67	24.67	—	5	16	—
Smith, P.A. (Wa)	—	10	16	1	383	68	25.53	—	2	7	—
Smith, R.A. (H)	—	1	2	0	9	8	4.50	—	—	2	—
Snodgrass, D.L. (Sc)	—	1	1	0	6	6	6.00	—	—	1	—
Southern, J.W. (H)	1978	19	21	7	300	50*	21.42	—	1	8	—
Speak, G.J. (La)	—	3	4	2	27	15*	13.50	—	—	3	—
†Spelman, G.D. (K)	—	1	—	—	—	—	—	—	—	—	—
Steele, D.S. (No)	1965	25	36	13	853	74*	37.08	—	4	19	—
Steele, J.F. (Le)	1971	20	31	6	497	64	19.88	—	2	28	—
Stephenson, F.D. (Gs/DBC)	—	8	10	1	105	63	11.66	—	1	2	—
Stevenson, G.B. (Y)	1978	17	19	4	356	115*	23.73	1	—	6	—
Stevenson, K. (H)	1979	1	—	—	—	—	—	—	—	1	—
Stewart, A.J. (Sy)	—	1	2	0	25	16	12.25	—	—	4	—
Stovold, A.W. (Gs)	1976	23	42	1	1350	212*	32.92	2	7	24	—
†Stovold, M.W. (Gs)	—	5	9	0	155	52	17.22	—	1	6	—
Such, P.M. (Nt)	—	8	9	3	3	2	0.50	—	—	7	—
Surridge, D. (Gs)	—	18	17	7	61	12	6.10	—	—	3	—
Sutcliffe, S.P. (Wa)	—	14	17	7	52	20	5.20	—	—	2	—
Swan, R.G. (Sc)	—	1	2	0	68	66	34.00	—	1	—	—
Tahir Naqqash (Pak)	—	6	4	0	65	39	16.25	—	—	3	—
Tavaré, C.J. (E/K/MCC)	1978	20	36	4	1522	168*	47.56	3	10	18	—
Taylor, D.J.S. (So)	1971	17	26	5	334	67	15.90	—	2	41	4
Taylor, L.B. (Le)	1981	21	23	8	119	25	7.93	—	—	2	—
Taylor, N.R. (K/EB)	—	24	43	4	1340	143*	34.35	3	7	7	—
Taylor, N.S. (Y)	—	1	1	0	0*		—	—	—	1	—
Taylor, R.W. (E/D)	1962	19	29	5	286	54	11.91	—	1	48	4
Taylor, T.J. (La/OU)	—	5	3	1	37	20	18.50	—	—	—	—
Tedstone, G.A. (Wa)	—	3	5	2	45	18*	15.00	—	—	4	1
Terry, V.P. (H)	—	4	6	2	41	16*	10.25	—	—	3	—

183

	Cap	M	I	NO	Runs	HS	Avge	100	50	Ct	St
†Thomas, D.J. (Sy)	—	17	20	3	409	64	24.05	—	3	6	—
Thomas, J.G. (Gm)	—	9	13	0	172	84	13.23	—	1	4	—
Titmus, F.J. (M)	1953	1	1	1	1	1*	—	—	—	—	—
Todd, P.A. (Nt)	1977	12	21	2	461	117*	24.26	2	1	12	—
Tolchard, R.W. (Le)	1966	23	38	8	843	93*	28.10	—	7	44	8
Tomlins, K.P. (M)	—	13	17	1	607	146	37.93	2	3	8	—
Toogood, G.J. (OU)	—	9	18	4	392	83	28.00	—	2	4	—
Torrens, R.W. (Ire)	—	1	2	0	17	17	8.50	—	—	—	—
Traicos, A.J. (Zim)	—	2	2	1	12	12*	12.00	—	—	4	—
Trembath, C.R. (Gs)	—	2	1	1	8	8*	—	—	—	1	—
Tremlett, T.M. (H)	—	16	22	3	209	48	11.00	—	—	15	—
Tunnicliffe, C.J. (D)	1977	16	19	2	273	40	16.05	—	—	8	—
†Turner, D.R. (H)	1970	15	21	1	459	96	22.95	—	2	6	—
Turner, G.M. (Wo)	1968	9	16	3	1171	311*	90.07	5	3	9	—
Turner, S. (Ex)	1970	23	28	4	679	83	28.29	—	5	8	—
Underwood, D.L. (K)	1964	22	22	11	129	30	11.72	—	—	3	—
Varey, D.W. (CU)	—	9	17	3	548	156*	39.14	1	3	6	—
Varey, J.G. (OU)	—	7	12	5	239	68	34.14	—	1	2	—
Vengsarkar, D.B. (Ind)	—	9	13	2	610	157	55.45	1	4	9	—
Viswanath, G.R. (Ind)	—	9	12	3	561	106*	62.33	2	4	8	—
†Wallace, G.C. (Zim)	—	1	2	0	77	43	38.50	—	—	1	—
Waller, C.E. (Sx)	1976	23	27	12	181	50	12.06	—	1	17	—
Wallwork, M.A. (La)	—	1	—	—	—	—	—	—	—	3	—
Warner, A.E. (Wo)	—	11	17	2	287	67	19.13	—	1	2	—
Warner, C.J. (Sc)	—	1	2	0	55	55	27.50	—	1	2	—
†Wasim Bari (Pak)	—	11	7	2	162	45	32.40	—	—	22	7
†Wasim Raja (Pak)	—	12	12	2	247	50*	24.70	—	1	5	—
Waterton, S.N.V. (K)	—	1	—	—	—	—	—	—	—	1	—
Watkinson, M. (La)	—	1	—	—	—	—	—	—	—	—	—
Watson, R.G. (La)	—	1	2	0	15	11	7.50	—	—	—	—
†Watts, A. (D)	—	1	1	0	0	0	—	—	—	1	—
†Webster, A.J. (Wo)	—	8	10	5	75	25	15.00	—	—	3	—
†Weightman, N.I. (Nt)	—	1	1	0	36	36	36.00	—	—	—	—
Weir, R.S. (Sc)	—	1	2	1	79	65	79.00	—	1	—	—
Wells, A.P. (Sx)	—	5	9	3	233	70	38.83	—	1	1	—
Wells, C.M. (Sx)	1982	23	41	3	1248	126	32.84	3	5	6	—
Wenlock, D.A. (Le)	—	3	3	0	15	9	5.00	—	—	1	—
Weston, M.J. (Wo)	—	17	31	1	704	93	23.46	—	6	4	—
Whiteley, J.P. (Y)	—	4	2	1	6	5*	6.00	—	—	3	—
†Wild, D.J. (No)	—	7	7	2	113	29	22.60	—	—	—	—
Willey, P. (No)	1971	23	41	6	1783	145	50.94	5	8	10	—
Williams, N.F. (M)	—	12	11	5	112	27*	18.66	—	—	2	—
Williams, R.G. (No)	1979	24	39	4	1087	141	31.05	2	4	3	—
Willis, R.G.D. (E/Wa)	1972	18	22	9	351	72	27.00	—	2	7	—
Willows, A. (Sx)	—	1	2	1	4	4	4.00	—	—	—	—
Wills, R.T. (Ire)	—	1	2	0	43	43	21.50	—	—	—	—
Wilson, P.H.L. (Sy)	—	4	4	2	20	13	10.00	—	—	1	—
Windaybank, S.J. (Gs)	—	2	1	1	18	10*	18.00	—	—	—	—
Wood, B. (D)	1980	21	38	4	851	124*	25.02	1	2	20	—
†Wood, L.J. (K)	—	1	—	—	—	—	—	—	—	—	—
Woolmer, R.A. (K)	1970	13	22	3	809	203	42.57	2	4	13	—
†Wootton, S.H. (Wa)	—	3	2	0	3	3	1.50	—	—	—	—

	Cap	M	I	NO	Runs	HS	Avge	100	50	Ct	St
Wright, A.J. (Gs)	—	10	19	2	399	65	23.47	—	2	3	—
†Wright, J.G. (D)	1977	21	39	6	1830	190	55.45	7	5	13	—
Yadav, N.S. (Ind)	—	7	2	1	1	1*	1.00	—	—	—	—
†Yardley, T.J. (No)	1978	4	7	1	111	39	18.50	—	—	4	—
Yashpal Sharma (Ind)	—	9	15	5	418	77*	41.80	—	3	6	—
†Younis Ahmed (Wo)	1979	18	29	6	1247	122	54.21	4	7	11	—
Zaheer Abbas (Pak/Gs)	1975	16	25	4	1475	162*	70.23	5	8	3	—

BOWLING

	Type	O	M	R	W	Avge	Best	5 wI	10 wM
Abdul Qadir (Pak)	LBG	542.4	123	1187	57	20.82	7-44	4	1
Abrahams, J. (La)	OB	316.1	59	921	16	57.56	2-19	—	—
Acfield, D.L. (Ex)	OB	565.2	129	1332	45	29.60	4-35	—	—
Agnew, J.P. (Le)	RF	203.5	27	816	19	42.94	4-55	—	—
Alleyne, H.L. (Wo)	RF	207.3	44	599	16	37.43	4-92	—	—
Allott, P.J.W. (E/La/MCC/DBC)	RFM	453	128	1172	36	32.55	5-58	1	—
Amiss, D.L. (Wa)	SLC	2.1	0	18	0	—	—	—	—
Anderson, I.S. (D)	OB	62.4	22	176	5	35.20	2-43	—	—
Arnold, G.G. (Sx)	RFM	59	23	89	6	14.83	2-9	—	—
Asif Din (Wa)	LB	284.1	61	1128	20	56.40	5-100	1	—
Aslett, D.G. (K)	LB	84.1	10	343	7	49.00	4-119	—	—
Athey, C.W.J. (Y)	RM	27.1	1	98	0	—	—	—	—
Bailey, M.J. (H)	OB	18	4	76	2	38.00	2-27	—	—
Bainbridge, P. (Gs)	RM	301	77	915	19	48.15	6-59	1	—
Balderstone, J.C. (Le)	SLA	79	23	187	7	26.71	4-51	—	—
Baptiste, E.A.E. (K)	RFM	186.4	45	671	12	55.91	3-41	—	—
Barclay, J.R.T. (Sx)	OB	230.2	58	702	11	63.81	3-44	—	—
Barnett, K.J. (D)	LB	43.3	8	147	0	—	—	—	—
Barwick, S.R. (Gm)	RM	326.2	80	981	32	30.65	5-44	1	—
Benson, M.R. (K)	OB	4	0	28	0	—	—	—	—
Birch, J.D. (Nt)	RM	2.3	0	19	1	19.00	1-19	—	—
Booth, P.A. (Y)	SLA	10	3	22	0	—	—	—	—
Bore, M.K. (Nt)	LM	279.4	104	609	28	21.75	6-134	1	—
Botham, I.T. (E/So)	RFM	491.4	114	1517	66	22.98	5-46	4	—
Boycott, G. (Y)	RM	57.2	13	120	8	15.00	2-14	—	—
Boyd-Moss, R.J. (No/CU)	SLA	66	15	259	9	28.77	4-42	—	—
Brearley, J.M. (M)	RM	1	0	3	0	—	—	—	—
Briers, N.E. (Le)	RM	24	4	86	4	21.50	2-11	—	—
Broad, B.C. (Gs)	RM	39	8	104	2	52.00	1-13	—	—
Brown, D.J. (Wa)	RFM	51	8	204	4	51.00	2-37	—	—
Bryant, M. (So)	RFM	27	3	158	2	79.00	1-29	—	—
Bullen, C.K. (Sy)	OB	9	0	29	0	—	—	—	—
Butchart, I.P. (Zim)	RM	11	3	33	3	11.00	2-22	—	—
Butcher, A.R. (Sy/MCC)	SLA	98	16	411	5	82.20	1-23	—	—
Butcher, M.S. (Sy)	RM	1	0	2	0	—	—	—	—
Butcher, R.O. (M)	RM	1	0	10	0	—	—	—	—

185

	Type	O	M	R	W	Avge	Best	5 wI	10 wM
Capel, D.J. (No)	RM	98.5	9	432	6	72.00	2-14	—	—
Carrick, P. (Y)	SLA	568.5	144	1425	40	35.62	6-90	1	—
Carter, R.M. (No)	RM	38	7	145	2	72.50	2-26	—	—
Cassidy, J.J. (OU)	RM	4	2	12	0	—	—	—	—
Cheatle, R.G.L. (Sy)	SLA	49	8	183	3	61.00	1-37	—	—
Childs, J.H. (Gs)	SLA	656.3	201	1681	38	44.23	5-112	1	—
Clark, J. (Sc)	RM	42.1	12	79	8	9.87	4-24	—	—
Clarke, S.T. (Sy)	RF	659.3	159	1696	85	19.95	6-63	6	1
Clift, P.B. (Le)	RM	113	27	294	7	42.00	2-49	—	—
Clinton, G.S. (Sy)	RM	1	0	11	0	—	—	—	—
Cobb, R.A. (Le)	LM	4	2	5	0	—	—	—	—
Cockbain, I. (La)	SLA	2	2	0	0	—	—	—	—
Cook, G. (E/No/MCC)	SLA	6	0	36	1	36.00	1-18	—	—
Cook, N.G.B. (Le/EB)	SLA	857.1	257	2093	90	23.25	7-63	6	1
Cooper, K.E. (Nt)	RFM	685	192	1719	68	25.27	6-46	2	—
Corlett, S.C. (Ire)	RM	48	13	101	7	14.42	7-82	1	—
Cowan, R.S. (Sx/OU)	RM	140	18	593	6	98.83	2-75	—	—
Cowans, N.G. (K)	RF	222.3	50	721	33	21.84	5-28	2	—
Cowdrey, C.S. (K)	RM	166.3	39	533	14	38.07	3-45	—	—
Cowley, N.G. (H)	OB	310.1	85	895	24	37.29	6-48	1	—
Croft, C.E.H. (La)	RF	303	61	1003	33	30.39	7-88	1	—
Crowe, P.J. (OU)	LM	36	4	121	1	121.00	1-105	—	—
Cumbes, J. (Wa)	RM	349.1	71	993	21	47.28	4-47	—	—
Cunningham, E.J. (Gs)	OB	4	0	13	0	—	—	—	—
Curran, K.M. (Zim)	RFM	8	0	47	1	47.00	1-31	—	—
Curtis, I.J. (OU)	SLA	214.4	45	659	15	43.93	5-140	1	—
Curtis, T.S. (Wo)	LB	2	0	7	0	—	—	—	—
Daniel, W.W. (M)	RF	468.5	107	1245	71	17.53	9-61	5	1
Daniels, S.A.B. (Gm)	RFM	223.2	37	836	20	41.80	3-49	—	—
Davis, M.R. (So)	LFM	144	19	481	12	40.08	3-36	—	—
Davis, W.W. (Gm)	RFM	391.5	70	1296	42	30.85	7-101	1	—
Dennis, S.J. (Y)	LFM	95	16	365	12	30.41	5-42	1	—
Dilley, G.R. (K/MCC/EB)	RF	563.2	124	1839	64	28.73	6-71	4	1
Doggart, S.J.G. (CU)	OB	182.4	29	623	7	89.00	2-30	—	—
Donald, W.A. (Sc)	RM	2	0	10	0	—	—	—	—
Doshi, D.R. (Ind)	SLA	345.3	78	1003	25	40.12	6-102	1	—
Doughty, R.J. (Gs)	RM	149.1	19	533	15	35.53	6-43	1	—
Dredge, C.H. (So)	RM	446.5	108	1214	35	34.68	3-33	—	—
Dudhia, M.H.E.M. (Zim)	RM	14	5	29	3	9.66	2-13	—	—
Dudleston, B. (Gs)	SLA	37	10	108	3	36.00	3-36	—	—
Dutton, R.S. (CU)	RM	19	1	130	0	—	—	—	—
Dyer, R.I.H.B. (Wa)	RM	1	0	2	0	—	—	—	—
East, R.E. (Ex)	SLA	490.5	141	1231	45	27.35	6-80	2	—
Edmonds, P.H. (E/M/MCC)	SLA	789	242	1768	80	22.10	8-80	3	2
Ehtesham-ud-Din (Pak)	RFM	28	9	81	1	81.00	1-46	—	—
Ellcock, R.M. (Wo)	RF	26.1	2	90	3	30.00	3-80	—	—
Ellis, R.G.P. (M/OU)	OB	61	14	182	4	45.50	2-40	—	—
Ellison, C.C. (CU)	RM	96.5	20	314	5	62.80	3-30	—	—
Ellison, R.M. (K)	RM	153.5	35	433	16	27.06	3-12	—	—
Emburey, J.E. (M)	OB	764.5	198	1787	77	23.20	5-50	2	—

	Type	O	M	R	W	Avge	Best	5 wI	10 wM
Emery, K.S.D. (H/EB)	RFM	659	152	1969	83	23.72	6-51	3	1
Fell, M.A. (Nt)	SLA	45	7	146	1	146.00	1-20	—	—
Ferreira, A.M. (Wa)	RM	243.3	49	789	26	30.34	5-109	1	—
Finney, R.J. (D)	LM	14	5	40	1	40.00	1-37	—	—
Fletcher, D.A.G. (Zim)	RM	30	6	80	1	80.00	1-26	—	—
Fletcher, K.W.R. (Ex/MCC)	LB	20.1	0	156	2	78.00	2-103	—	—
Folley, I. (La)	LFM	309	76	758	27	28.07	4-40	—	—
Forster, G. (Le)	OB	44	11	125	1	125.00	1-29	—	—
Foster, N.A. (Ex)	RM	125	29	425	12	35.41	3-32	—	—
Fowler, G. (E/La/EB)	—	7	3	13	0	—	—	—	—
Garner, J. (So)	RF	259.1	76	583	33	17.66	6-23	4	1
Gatting, M.W. (E/M/MCC/DBC)	RM	135	40	343	21	16.33	5-34	1	—
Gavaskar, S.M. (Ind)	RM	5	0	23	0	—	—	—	—
Gifford, N. (Wo/DBC)	SLA	500	157	1080	31	34.83	6-48	1	—
Gilfillan, A.D. (OU)	LB	51	5	218	2	109.00	2-177	—	—
Gooch, G.A. (Ex)	RM	230	72	541	22	24.59	7-14	1	—
Gould, I.J. (Sx/EB)	RM	9.3	2	23	0	—	—	—	—
Gower, D.I. (E/Le/MCC)	OB	5	2	10	0	—	—	—	—
Graveney, D.A. (Gs)	SLA	498.4	145	1242	44	28.22	7-37	1	—
Green, A.M. (Sx)	RM	60	6	274	6	45.66	2-48	—	—
Greig, I.A. (E/Sx/MCC)	RM	571.1	132	1723	68	25.33	5-46	2	—
Griffiths, B.J. (No)	RFM	411.1	91	1200	46	26.08	5-71	2	—
Griffiths, P.D. (CU)	SLA	9	2	39	0	—	—	—	—
Hacker, P.J. (D)	LFM	174.1	25	677	25	27.08	5-51	2	—
Hadlee, R.J. (Nt)	RF	403.5	123	889	61	14.57	7-25	4	—
Halliday, M. (Ire)	OB	16.4	6	36	2	18.00	2-32	—	—
Hampshire, J.H. (D)	LB	4	1	26	0	—	—	—	—
Hardie, B.R. (Ex)	RM	7	1	20	0	—	—	—	—
Hartley, P.J. (Wa)	RM	57	11	215	2	107.50	2-45	—	—
Hartley, S.N. (Y)	RM	118	27	388	6	64.66	1-11	—	—
Hayes, K.A. (La/OU)	RM	21	1	96	0	—	—	—	—
Hemmings, E.E. (E/Nt)	OB	666.1	202	1611	64	25.17	6-76	3	—
Hemsley, E.J.O. (Wo)	RM	20.4	1	80	1	80.00	1-2	—	—
Henderson, S.P. (CU)	RM	6	3	8	0	—	—	—	—
Hendrick, M. (Nt)	RFM	244.2	86	473	26	18.19	5-21	1	—
Higgs, K. (Le)	RM	19	5	64	1	64.00	1-18	—	—
Hill, A. (D)	OB	1	0	4	0	—	—	—	—
Hinks, S.G. (K)	LM	1.4	1	5	0	—	—	—	—
Hodgson, K.I. (CU)	RM	198.1	42	625	23	27.17	8-68	1	1
Hogg, V.R. (Zim)	RFM	23	4	73	0	—	—	—	—
Hogg, W. (Wa)	RFM	105.3	18	339	8	42.37	2-45	—	—
Holmes, G.C. (Gm)	RM	18	4	60	0	—	—	—	—
Hough, E.J. (Zim)	RFM	27	8	73	2	36.50	1-24	—	—
Hughes, D.P. (La)	SLA	292.3	79	789	31	25.45	4-22	—	—
Hughes, S.P. (M)	RFM	218.5	30	723	27	26.77	4-28	—	—
Humpage, G.W. (Wa)	RM	30	6	79	2	39.50	1-17	—	—
Illingworth, N.J.B. (Nt)	RM	164.1	29	565	14	40.35	5-89	1	—
Illingworth, R. (Y)	OB	223.4	65	587	9	65.22	2-32	—	—
Illingworth, R.K. (Wo)	SLA	260.4	59	811	18	45.05	4-85	—	—

187

Wisden Anthology 1963-1982 Vol IV

Edited by Benny Green

This final volume takes the reader from the introduction of one day, limited-over and prize money cricket to the present day.   **£25.00**

Available from booksellers or in case of difficulty direct from Queen Anne Press Sales, 9 Partridge Drive, Orpington, Kent: cash with order plus 14p in the £ p&p. Please make cheques payable to Macdonald & Company (Publishers) Ltd. Allow 28 days for delivery.

Queen Anne Press
A division of Macdonald & Company

	Type	O	M	R	W	Avge	Best	5 wI	10 wM
Imran Khan (Pak/Sx)	RF	414.4	134	1079	64	16.85	7-52	2	—
Inchmore, J.D. (Wo)	RFM	326.2	68	841	35	24.02	7-53	2	—
Intikhab Alam (Pak)	LBG	6	0	17	1	17.00	1-17	—	—
Iqbal Qasim (Pak)	SLA	161.1	36	434	12	36.16	5-52	1	—
Jackman, R.D. (E/Sy)	RFM	676.1	194	1751	73	23.98	6-28	2	—
Jalauddin (Pak)	RFM	56	19	123	4	30.75	1-16	—	—
James, K.D. (M)	LM	6	1	13	1	13.00	1-13	—	—
Jarvis, K.B.S. (K/EB)	RFM	636	145	2078	54	38.48	5-94	1	—
Jarvis, P.W. (Y)	RFM	132	25	434	8	54.25	2-24	—	—
Javed Miandad (Pak/Gm)	LBG	104.4	31	309	7	44.14	3-52	—	—
Jefferies, S.T. (D)	LFM	28	3	109	5	21.80	3-57	—	—
Jesty, T.E. (H)	RM	288.1	89	750	35	21.42	6-71	1	—
Johnson, G.W. (K)	OB	330.4	84	892	26	34.30	5-36	2	—
Jones, A. (Gm)	OB	1	1	0	0	—	—	—	—
Jones, A.N. (Sx)	RFM	29	5	100	4	25.00	3-59	—	—
Kallicharran, A.I. (Wa)	OB	154.2	21	578	14	41.28	3-32	—	—
Kapil Dev (Ind/No)	RFM	395.2	77	1214	29	41.86	5-39	2	—
Kemp, N.J. (M)	RM	66	13	180	4	45.00	2-53	—	—
Kennedy, A. (La)	RM	9	2	28	1	28.00	1-17	—	—
King, C.L. (DBC)	RM	4	1	11	0	—	—	—	—
Kirsten, P.N. (D)	OB	121	28	348	9	38.66	3-25	—	—
Knight, R.D.V. (Sy)	RM	266.2	61	762	15	50.80	3-34	—	—
Lamb, A.J. (E/No)	RM	2	1	1	0	—	—	—	—
Lamb, T.M. (No)	RM	308.5	76	850	20	42.50	5-37	1	—
Larkins, W. (No)	RM	17	2	66	1	66.00	1-38	—	—
Lawrence, D.V. (Gs)	RFM	23	3	74	2	37.00	1-24	—	—
Lawrence, M.P. (OU)	SLA	99	20	366	2	183.00	1-32	—	—
Lee, P.G. (La)	RFM	32	3	101	2	50.50	1-19	—	—
Le Roux, G.S. (Sx)	RF	467	116	1210	65	18.61	5-15	3	—
Lethbridge, C. (Wa)	RM	304.3	68	977	29	33.68	5-68	1	—
Lever, J.K. (Ex)	LFM	543.5	112	1683	72	23.37	6-48	5	1
Lewington, P.J. (Wa)	OB	89.1	19	294	3	98.00	1-4	—	—
Lilley, A.W. (Ex)	RM	3	0	10	0	—	—	—	—
Lloyd, B.J. (Gm)	OB	687.2	139	2201	55	40.01	5-58	2	—
Lloyd, D. (La/DBC)	SLA	297.2	68	801	21	38.14	4-36	—	—
Lloyd, T.A. (Wa)	RM	95	24	344	5	68.80	2-29	—	—
Lloyds, J.W. (So)	OB	468.3	96	1463	46	31.80	7-88	3	—
Louden, W.D.G. (Sc)	RFM	10.1	8	11	3	3.66	3-4	—	—
Love, J.D. (Y)	RM	3	3	0	0	—	—	—	—
Lynch, M.A. (Sy)	RM/OB	51.5	8	208	4	52.00	2-23	—	—
McCool, R.J. (So)	LB	27	2	63	0	—	—	—	—
McEwan, K.S. (Ex)	OB	13	0	120	1	120.00	1-64	—	—
McFarlane, L. (La)	RFM	223.5	44	946	27	35.03	6-59	1	—
Mackintosh, K.S. (Sy)	RM	304.2	59	1023	34	30.08	6-61	1	—
Madan Lal, S. (Ind)	RFM	246.1	49	763	22	34.68	4-28	—	—
Maguire, K.R. (Wa)	RFM	35	6	123	1	123.00	1-32	—	—
Majid Khan (Pak)	OB	22	9	57	2	28.50	2-24	—	—
Malhotra, A. (Ind)	RM	9	1	37	1	37.00	1-37	—	—
Mallender, N.A. (No)	RFM	563.2	131	1860	51	36.47	7-41	3	1
Malone, S.J. (H)	RM	150.5	35	505	22	22.95	7-55	2	1

189

	Type	O	M	R	W	Avge	Best	5 wI	10 wM
Mansoor Akhtar (Pak)	RM	16.3	6	43	1	43.00	1-16	—	—
Marks, V.J. (E/So/MCC/EB)	OB	700.4	199	1951	68	28.60	7-51	4	—
Marshall, M.D. (H)	RF	822	225	2108	134	15.73	8-71	12	4
Maru, R.J. (M)	SLA	54.2	26	88	7	12.57	4-30	—	—
Merry, W.G. (M)	RM	76.2	18	201	3	67.00	2-54	—	—
Miller, G. (E/D/MCC)	OB	455.3	135	1058	35	30.22	8-70	1	1
Mohsin Khan (Pak)	RM	5	0	32	1	32.00	1-32	—	—
Moir, D.G. (D)	SLA	811.5	231	2076	76	27.31	6-63	4	—
Monkhouse, G. (Sy)	RM	131.3	27	395	12	32.91	3-40	—	—
Monteith, J.D. (M/Ire)	SLA	35.2	7	82	0	—	—	—	—
Morton, W.A. (Sc)	SLA	32	10	82	2	41.00	1-38	—	—
Moseley, H.R. (So)	RFM	320	68	985	35	28.14	5-40	2	—
Mudassar Nazar (Pak)	RM	139	35	368	21	17.52	6-32	1	—
Mushtaq Mohammad (DBC)	LBG	114	2	48	3	16.00	3-34	—	—
Nash, M.A. (Gm)	LM	418.2	102	1276	38	33.57	5-35	1	—
Nayak, S.V. (Ind)	RM/LB	205.3	39	645	14	46.07	5-54	1	—
Neale, P.A. (Wo/EB)	RM	6	2	16	0	—	—	—	—
Needham, A. (Sy)	OB	359	73	1170	22	53.18	5-91	1	—
Newman, P.G. (D/MCC)	RFM	458.3	73	1661	40	41.52	4-59	—	—
Newport, P.J. (Wo)	RFM	47	1	238	6	39.66	4-76	—	—
Nicholas, M.C.J. (H)	RM	3	0	13	1	13.00	1-13	—	—
Old, C.M. (Y)	RFM	458.2	125	1229	47	26.14	6-76	1	—
Oldham, S. (D)	RFM	507.5	98	1544	48	32.16	7-78	2	—
Ontong, R.C. (Gm)	RM	638.1	139	2059	64	32.17	6-50	1	1
O'Reilly, P.M. (Ire)	RFM	6	1	14	1	14.00	1-14	—	—
Ormrod, J.A. (Wo)	OB	1	0	5	0	—	—	—	—
O'Shaughnessy, S.J. (La)	RM	209.2	34	710	27	26.29	4-66	—	—
Palmer, G.V. (So)	RM	17	3	57	0	—	—	—	—
Palmer, R.W.M. (CU)	LM	219.4	34	849	14	60.64	4-96	—	—
Parker, P.W.G. (Sx/MCC/EB)	RM	5	0	16	0	—	—	—	—
Parsons, G.J. (Le)	RM	517.5	93	1931	50	38.62	5-25	1	—
Patel, D.N. (Wo)	OB	572.2	146	1531	50	30.62	7-46	2	—
Patil, S.M. (Ind)	RM	60	9	155	4	38.75	2-26	—	—
Pauline, D.B. (Sy)	RM	1	0	3	0	—	—	—	—
Penn, C. (K)	RFM	93.4	17	327	7	46.71	2-11	—	—
Perryman, S.P. (Wo)	RM	430.1	111	1216	35	34.74	6-49	3	—
Phillip, N. (Ex)	RFM	584.1	107	1842	82	22.46	6-50	5	1
Phillipson, C.P. (Sx)	RM	14	0	57	1	57.00	1-57	—	—
Pigott, A.C.S. (Sx)	RFM	477	92	1684	61	27.60	7-74	4	—
Pocock, N.E.J. (H)	LM	12.5	1	55	0	—	—	—	—
Pocock, P.I. (Sy)	OB	233	64	632	21	30.09	5-73	1	—
Pollock, A.J. (CU)	RM	115.5	18	483	14	34.50	5-108	1	—
Pont, I.L. (Nt)	RFM	78.5	13	302	3	100.66	2-107	—	—
Pont, K.R. (Ex)	RM	62	10	158	10	15.80	5-17	1	—
Popplewell, N.F.M. (So)	RM	94	17	320	6	53.33	2-23	—	—
Potter, L. (K)	LM	13	4	33	2	16.50	1-9	—	—
Pridgeon, A.P. (Wo)	RM	463	103	1184	32	37.00	4-39	—	—
Pringle, D.R. (E/Ex/CU/MCC)	RM	433.1	122	1087	46	23.63	6-33	2	—
Prior, J.A. (Ire)	RM	6	0	19	0	—	—	—	—

	Type	O	M	R	W	Avge	Best	5 wI	10 wM
Radley, C.T. (M)	LB	4	0	27	0	—	—	—	—
Ramage, A. (Y)	RFM	90	14	381	5	76.20	2-69	—	—
Randall, D.W. (E/Nt/MCC)	RM	4.5	1	19	3	6.33	3-15	—	—
Randhir Singh (Ind)	RM	131	24	418	7	59.71	2-50	—	—
Rawlinson, H.T. (OU)	RM	96.1	9	435	5	87.00	2-102	—	—
Rawson, P.W.E. (Zim)	RFM	62	12	177	7	25.28	5-42	1	—
Reidy, B.W. (La)	LM	137	32	457	10	45.70	3-33	—	—
Rhind, P.A. (Sc)	RFM	37	15	85	3	28.33	3-62	—	—
Rice, C.E.B. (Nt)	RFM	78.5	25	206	6	34.33	2-10	—	—
Rice, J.M. (H)	RM	61.3	10	240	3	80.00	1-8	—	—
Richards, C.J. (Sy/MCC)	RM	5	0	19	0	—	—	—	—
Richards, I.V.A. (So)	OB	265.3	75	671	16	41.93	3-6	—	—
Ridge, S.P. (OU)	RM	240.1	33	829	13	63.76	4-128	—	—
Roberts, A.M.E. (Le)	RF	427.2	114	1081	55	19.65	8-56	5	1
Robinson, R.T. (Nt)	RM	7	0	41	1	41.00	1-22	—	—
Roebuck, P.M. (So/EB)	OB	39	4	109	1	109.00	1-40	—	—
Romaines, P.W. (Gs)		5	2	9	0	—	—	—	—
Roope, G.R.J. (Sy)	RM	32	12	81	3	27.00	2-30	—	—
Rose, B.C. (So)	LM	1	0	5	0	—	—	—	—
Rowe, C.J.C. (Gm)	OB	265.2	57	898	19	47.26	3-67	—	—
Roy, P. (Ind)	RM	1	0	14	0	—	—	—	—
Russom, N. (So)	RM	16	2	64	3	21.33	2-49	—	—
Sadiq Mohammad (Gs)	LBG	101.4	20	305	7	43.57	4-42	—	—
Salim Malik (Pak)		1	0	5	0	—	—	—	—
Sarfraz Nawaz (Pak/No)	RFM	327.4	72	920	36	25.55	6-92	1	—
Saxelby, K. (Nt)	RM	291.4	68	799	37	21.59	4-18	—	—
Selvey, M.W.W. (M)	RFM	254.5	74	597	20	29.85	3-47	—	—
Sharp, G. (No)	SLA	3	0	19	0	—	—	—	—
Shastri, R.J. (Ind)	SLA	269.5	69	634	15	42.26	3-109	—	—
Shepherd, J.N. (Gs)	RM	742.1	177	2026	61	32.15	6-75	2	—
Sidebottom, A. (Y)	RFM	495.2	95	1538	62	24.80	6-31	3	—
Sikander Bakht (Pak)	RFM	326	86	959	27	35.51	4-68	—	—
Simmons, J. (La)	OB	538.4	152	1284	49	26.20	5-57	2	—
Simpkins, D.P. (Gs)	OB	2	0	15	0	—	—	—	—
Slack, W.N. (M)	RM	81	18	225	10	22.50	3-17	—	—
Slocombe, P.A. (So)	RM	3.2	0	10	1	10.00	1-2	—	—
Small, G.C. (Wa)	RFM	589.1	107	1925	63	30.55	7-68	1	—
Smith, D.M. (Wa)	SLA	16	2	59	0	—	—	—	—
Smith, P.A. (Wa)	RM	136	21	536	10	53.60	2-12	—	—
Snodgrass, D.L. (Sc)	RFM	36	15	80	3	26.66	2-30	—	—
Southern, J.W. (H)	SLA	439.5	119	1314	55	23.89	5-51	2	—
Speak, G.J. (La)	RFM	53	6	176	1	176.00	1-78	—	—
Spelman, G.D. (K)	RM	23	8	66	3	22.00	2-44	—	—
Steele, D.S. (No)	SLA	754	245	1846	70	26.37	6-59	6	1
Steele, J.F. (Le)	SLA	470.2	134	1075	52	20.67	5-4	3	—
Stephenson, F.D. (Gs/DBC)	RF	197.2	40	632	32	19.75	5-64	2	—
Stevenson, G.B. (Y)	RM	443.4	88	1474	45	32.75	5-72	1	—
Stevenson, K. (H)	RFM	22	10	56	1	56.00	1-35	—	—
Stovold, M.W. (Gs)	RM	1	0	13	0	—	—	—	—
Such, P.M. (Nt)	OB	232.1	51	737	25	29.48	5-112	1	—
Surridge, D. (Gs)	RM	561	159	1507	47	32.06	5-78	1	—
Sutcliffe, S.P. (Wa)	OB	554.3	114	1799	37	48.62	5-151	1	—

191

	Type	O	M	R	W	Avge	Best	5 wI	10 wM
Tahir Naqqash (Pak)	RFM	160	44	537	15	35.80	5-40	1	—
Taylor, D.J.S. (So)	RM	3	2	1	0	—	—	—	—
Taylor, L.B. (Le)	RFM	582.1	153	1465	67	21.86	5-24	3	—
Taylor, N.R. (K/EB)	OB	17	5	83	4	20.75	2-58	—	—
Taylor, N.S. (Y)	RFM	84.1	16	293	8	36.62	2-42	—	—
Taylor, T.J. (La/OU)	SLA	165	27	541	10	54.10	5-118	1	—
Thomas, D.J. (Sy)	LFM	426.4	109	1284	36	35.66	4-39	—	—
Thomas, J.G. (Gm)	RM	140	25	514	22	23.36	5-61	1	—
Titmus, F.J. (M)	OB	25	4	92	3	30.66	3-43	—	—
Tomlins, K.P. (M)	RM	12.3	1	73	2	36.50	2-28	—	—
Toogood, G.J. (OU)	OB	3	0	22	0	—	—	—	—
Torrens, R.W. (Ire)	RFM	37	9	102	2	51.00	2-21	—	—
Traicos, A.J. (Zim)	OB	86	28	186	11	16.90	5-56	2	—
Trembath, C.R. (Gs)	RM	49.3	7	219	6	36.50	5-91	1	—
Tremlett, T.M. (H)	RM	354.3	114	766	32	23.93	5-59	1	—
Tunnicliffe, C.J. (D)	LFM	383.1	92	1213	37	32.78	5-73	1	—
Turner, D.R. (H)	RM	1	0	1	0	—	—	—	—
Turner, S. (Ex)	RM	453	117	1080	30	36.00	4-53	—	—
Underwood, D.L. (K)	LM	690.3	223	1751	78	22.44	7-79	5	1
Varey, D.W. (CU)		1	0	4	0	—	—	—	—
Varey, J.G. (OU)	RM	132	15	550	3	183.33	1-13	—	—
Vengsarkar, D.B. (Ind)	RM	0.2	0	2	0	—	—	—	—
Wallace, G.C. (Zim)	SLA	3	1	8	0	—	—	—	—
Waller, C.E. (Sx)	SLA	605	171	1627	55	29.58	7-67	1	—
Warner, A.E. (Wo)	RFM	202.1	34	707	19	37.21	4-73	—	—
Wasim Raja (Pak)	LBG	117.4	30	346	9	38.44	3-44	—	—
Watkinson, M. (La)	RM	13	4	45	1	45.00	1-24	—	—
Watts, A. (D)	RM	9	1	31	0	—	—	—	—
Webster, A.J. (Wo)	RM	202.1	36	716	15	47.73	5-87	1	—
Weightman, N.I. (Nt)	OB	1	0	4	0	—	—	—	—
Wells, A.P. (Sx)	RM	12	1	42	0	—	—	—	—
Wells, C.M. (Sx)	RM	69.4	12	195	5	39.00	2-15	—	—
Wenlock, D.A. (Le)	RM	30.1	7	104	4	26.00	3-50	—	—
Weston, M.J. (Wo)	RM	85.1	11	286	6	47.66	3-42	—	—
Whiteley, J.P. (Y)	OB	48	1	223	4	55.75	2-59	—	—
Wild, D.J. (No)	RM	52.3	10	182	4	45.50	2-15	—	—
Willey, P. (No)	OB	670.1	223	1371	51	26.88	6-17	1	—
Williams, N.F. (M)	RFM	236.4	34	819	23	35.60	4-38	—	—
Williams, R.G. (No)	OB	274	75	747	21	35.57	4-25	—	—
Willis, R.G.D. (E/Wa)	RF	446	89	1444	51	28.31	6-45	2	—
Willows, A. (Sx)	SLA	17	4	39	0	—	—	—	—
Wilson, P.H.L. (Sy)	RFM	103.4	26	283	6	47.16	2-57	—	—
Wood, B. (D)	RM	231.2	54	690	10	69.00	2-0	—	—
Wood, L.J. (K)	SLA	12	2	58	0	—	—	—	—
Woolmer, R.A. (K)	RM	60	20	140	6	23.33	2-13	—	—
Wright, J.G. (D)	RM	3	0	29	0	—	—	—	—
Yadav, N.S. (Ind)	OB	195	33	604	7	86.28	3-77	—	—
Yashpal Sharma (Ind)	RM	10	2	32	0	—	—	—	—
Younis Ahmed (Wo)	LM	5	1	14	0	—	—	—	—
Zaheer Abbas (Pak/Gs)	OB	2.1	0	15	0	—	—	—	—

CAREER FIGURES FOR THE LEADING PLAYERS

The following are the abbreviated figures of the leading batsmen and bowlers based on their career averages, and fielders and wicket-keepers based on the number of their catches and dismissals. The figures are complete to the end of the 1982 season and the full career records will be found in the main tables overleaf. The qualification for inclusion for batsmen and bowlers is 100 innings and 100 wickets respectively. Only those players likely to play first-class county cricket in 1983 have been included.

BATTING AND BOWLING

BATSMEN	Runs	Avge	100s	BOWLERS	Wkts	Avge
G. Boycott	42,269	56.28	132	J. Garner	490	17.32
Zaheer Abbas	30,069	53.84	95	M.D. Marshall	492	17.94
A.J. Lamb	11,458	50.92	27	G.S. Le Roux	413	19.24
C.H. Lloyd	27,334	48.98	70	D.L. Underwood	2,118	19.81
I.V.A. Richards	21,099	48.95	63	R.J. Hadlee	743	19.87
P.N. Kirsten	13,234	46.76	37	R. Illingworth	2,040	20.13
A.I. Kallicharran	22,781	44.49	57	W.W. Daniel	552	20.25
D.L. Amiss	35,158	43.24	82	A.M.E. Roberts	754	20.93
C.G. Greenidge	21,989	42.69	48	M. Hendrick	696	20.94
C.J. Tavaré	10,539	40.84	21	S.T. Clarke	409	21.13
C.E.B. Rice	15,386	40.17	27	C.E.B. Rice	679	21.50
J.G. Wright	12,220	40.76	30	C.M. Old	941	22.57

FIELDING AND WICKET-KEEPING

FIELDERS	Ct	WICKET-KEEPERS	Total	Ct	St
G.R.J. Roope	599	R.W. Taylor	1,526	1,359	167
K.W.R. Fletcher	549	A.P.E. Knott	1,213	1,090	123
D.S. Steele	488	R.W. Tolchard	984	868	116
C.T. Radley	442	E.W. Jones	908	816	92
R. Illingworth	435	D.L. Bairstow	795	684	101
J.H. Hampshire	420	D.J.S. Taylor	706	622	84
J.A. Ormrod	374	G. Sharp	572	492	80
C.G. Greenidge	340	G.W. Humpage	354	321	33
D.L. Amiss	336	D.J. Humphries	332	228	44
J.F. Steele	330	I.J. Gould	321	280	41
D. Lloyd	326	C.J. Richards	289	253	36
C.H. Lloyd	325	P.R. Downton	288	251	37

Wisden Cricketers' Almanack 1983

Edited by John Woodcock

The 120th edition of the cricket lover's 'bible' covers the 1982 season in its usual careful detail.

£9.95 hardcover
£8.95 paperback

Queen Anne Press
A division of Macdonald & Company

CAREER RECORDS
Compiled by Geoffrey Saulez

The following career records are for all players appearing in first-class cricket in the 1982 season. A few cricketers who did not appear for their counties in 1982, but who may do so in 1983, are also included.

Aggregates of 1,000 runs overseas are preceded by a + sign, e.g. D.L. Amiss 18+1.

The records of several Pakistan players are incomplete, owing to some scores in the seasons 1976-77 to 1979-80 not being available.

BATTING AND FIELDING

	M	I	NO	Runs	HS	Avge	100s	1000 runs in season	Ct	St
Abdul Qadir	97	122	26	1987	112	20.69	1	—	49	—
Abrahams, J.	144	216	27	4816	126	25.48	3	1	97	—
Acfield, D.L.	330	333	169	1430	42	8.71	—	—	109	—
Agnew, J.P.	47	49	7	389	56	9.26	—	—	16	—
Alleyne, H.L.	45	49	9	499	72	12.47	—	—	9	—
Allott, P.J.W.	74	67	21	577	52*	12.54	—	—	22	—
Amiss, D.L.	529	911	98	35158	262*	43.24	82	18+1	336	—
Anderson, I.J.	19	33	8	947	147	37.88	3	—	9	—
Anderson, I.S.	52	75	16	1192	103*	20.20	1	—	39	—
Armstrong, P.A.N.	1	2	0	34	34	17.00	—	—	—	—
Arnold, G.G.	365	379	90	3952	73	13.67	—	—	122	—
Asif Din	45	71	6	1733	102	26.66	1	—	25	—
Asif Iqbal	441	703	76	23375	196	37.28	45	7+2	304	—
Aslett, D.G.	18	32	5	982	146*	36.37	1	—	13	—
Athey, C.W.J.	143	236	20	6045	134	27.98	11	2	135	2
Bailey, M.J.	20	29	9	228	24	11.40	—	—	8	—
Bailey, R.J.	2	3	0	17	10	5.66	—	—	1	—
Bainbridge, P.	76	128	25	3103	105*	30.12	4	2	37	—
Bairstow, D.L.	311	447	86	8396	145	23.25	3	1	684	101
Balderstone, J.C.	306	479	49	14615	178*	33.98	23	8	167	—
Bamber, M.J.	1	2	0	58	31	29.00	—	—	—	—
Baptiste, E.A.E.	28	41	8	804	69*	24.36	—	—	18	—
Barclay, J.R.T.	203	342	32	7880	119	25.41	9	4	167	—
Barlow, G.D.	184	291	45	8402	177	34.15	15	5	96	—
Barnett, K.J.	76	107	15	2248	120	24.43	2	—	45	—
Barrington, W.E.J.	4	6	1	174	59	34.80	—	—	1	—
Barwick, S.R.	20	22	10	146	24	12.16	—	—	7	—
Benson, M.R.	46	79	10	2411	137	34.94	5	2	18	—
Birch, J.D.	122	181	31	3865	125	25.76	4	1	89	—
Boon, T.J.	34	56	6	1132	90	22.64	—	—	10	—
Booth, P.A.	1	1	1	0	0*	—	—	—	—	—
Bore, M.K.	135	133	46	693	37*	7.96	—	—	42	—
Botham, I.T.	203	312	25	9415	228	32.80	20	3	187	—
Boycott, G.	532	885	134	42269	261*	56.28	132	20+8	220	—
Boyd-Moss, R.J.	56	96	9	2550	139	20.31	5	1	26	—
Brassington, A.J.	122	150	43	856	35	8.00	—	—	207	47
Brearley, J.M.	454	767	102	25168	312*	37.84	45	11	418	12

196

	M	I	NO	Runs	HS	Avge	100s	1000 runs in season	Ct	St
Briers, N.E.	118	190	17	4767	119	27.55	8	2	44	—
Broad, B.C.	73	132	7	3743	129	29.94	5	2	29	—
Brown, A.	5	7	0	64	25	9.14	—	—	7	—
Brown, D.J.	390	446	111	4110	79	12.26	—	—	157	—
Brown, R.D.	28	53	3	1388	200*	27.76	3	—	36	9
Bryant, M.	2	2	0	6	6	3.00	—	—	1	—
Bullen, C.K.	1	—	—	—	—	—	—	—	—	—
Butchart, I.P.	5	7	0	106	54	15.14	—	—	4	—
Butcher, A.R.	198	333	33	9927	216*	33.09	19	4	87	—
Butcher, I.P.	8	11	3	238	71*	29.75	—	—	5	—
Butcher, M.S.	1	—	—	—	—	—	—	—	1	—
Butcher, R.O.	125	199	13	5396	197	29.01	8	1	140	1
Capel, D.J.	15	24	5	497	60*	26.15	—	—	9	—
Carrick, P.	211	262	50	4626	131*	21.82	3	—	107	—
Carter, R.M.	51	67	15	858	79	16.50	—	—	29	—
Cassidy, J.J.	1	1	0	0	0	0.00	—	—	—	—
Cheatle, R.G.L.	59	44	18	338	49	13.00	—	—	53	—
Chessher, J.R.	3	4	1	67	47	22.33	—	*	—	—
Childs, J.H.	138	127	68	441	34*	7.47	—	—	56	—
Clark, J.	13	16	3	104	29	8.00	—	—	13	—
Clarke, S.T.	106	117	18	1537	100*	15.52	1	—	51	—
Clift, P.B.	206	294	66	5230	88*	22.93	—	—	109	—
Clinton, G.S.	118	202	20	5415	172*	29.75	8	3	39	—
Close, D.B.	782	1218	170	34859	198	33.26	52	20	811	1
Cobb, R.A.	33	53	1	1083	64	20.82	—	—	19	—
Cockbain, I.	38	63	8	1165	98	21.18	—	—	18	—
Cook, C.R.	9	15	2	287	79	22.07	—	—	7	—
Cook, G.	289	508	35	14141	172	29.89	23	7	297	—
Cook, N.G.B.	96	94	32	792	75	12.77	—	—	60	—
Cooper, K.E.	113	111	23	742	38*	8.43	—	—	40	—
Corlett, S.C.	28	40	7	506	60	15.33	—	—	24	—
Cowan, R.S.	23	42	5	1252	143*	33.83	3	—	15	1
Cowans, N.G.	16	13	1	75	16	6.25	—	—	10	—
Cowdrey, C.S.	116	163	24	3760	101*	27.05	1	—	96	—
Cowley, N.G.	159	237	29	4374	109*	21.02	2	—	65	—
Croft, C.E.H.	118	131	50	853	46*	10.53	—	—	25	—
Crowe, M.D.	24	38	5	1127	150	34.15	2	—	29	—
Crowe, P.J.	1	2	0	11	11	5.50	—	—	—	—
Cumbes, J.	161	133	67	499	43	7.56	—	—	38	—
Cunningham, E.J.	4	6	2	26	11*	6.50	—	—	—	—
Curran, K.M.	9	12	4	172	55*	21.50	—	—	3	—
Curtis, I.J.	17	19	9	54	20*	5.40	—	—	4	—
Curtis, T.S.	19	31	6	524	59*	20.96	—	—	6	—
Daniel, W.W.	155	136	61	945	53*	12.60	—	—	37	—
Daniels, S.A.B.	16	23	10	227	73	17.46	—	—	7	—
Davies, A.G.	1	2	0	17	13	8.50	—	—	3	—
Davies, M.N.	2	1	0	0	0	0.00	—	—	1	—
Davies, T.	12	18	4	298	66*	21.28	—	—	28	2
Davis, M.R.	9	12	2	65	21*	6.50	—	—	4	—
Davis, W.W.	27	33	11	268	60	12.18	—	—	7	—

197

	M	I	NO	Runs	HS	Avge	100s	1000 runs in season	Ct	St
Davison, B.F.	389	639	58	23191	189	39.91	45	12	295	—
Denning, P.W.	243	403	38	10463	184	28.66	8	6	123	—
Dennis, S.J.	13	10	5	20	5*	4.00	—	—	4	—
Dilley, G.R.	98	106	39	1044	81	15.58	—	—	43	—
Doggart, S.J.G.	25	32	6	555	69*	21.34	—	—	10	—
D'Oliveira, D.B.	4	7	1	65	21	10.83	—	—	2	—
Donald, W.A.	4	6	1	75	34*	15.00	—	—	1	—
Doshi, D.R.	211	221	65	1264	44	8.10	—	—	54	—
Doughty, R.J.	6	7	1	75	29	12.50	—	—	2	—
Downton, P.R.	117	130	21	1929	90*	17.69	—	—	251	37
Dredge, C.H.	117	132	45	1239	56*	14.24	—	—	48	—
Dudhia, M.H.E.M.	2	1	0	0	0	0.00	—	—	—	—
Dudleston, B.	293	498	46	14689	202	32.49	32	8	234	7
Dutton, R.S.	6	6	4	7	7*	3.50	—	—	2	—
Dyer, R.I.H.B.	7	9	1	81	31*	10.12	—	—	3	—
Ealham, A.G.E.	305	466	68	10996	153	27.62	7	3	175	—
East, D.E.	37	49	11	669	78	17.60	—	—	86	14
East, R.E.	385	488	107	6728	113	17.65	1	—	245	—
Edbrooke, R.M.	1	2	1	100	84*	100.00	—	—	—	—
Edmonds, P.H.	263	348	60	5758	141*	19.99	2	—	251	—
Ehtesham-ud-Din	107	127	43	995	83	11.84	—	—	30	—
Ellcock, R.M.	1	2	1	13	13*	13.00	—	—	—	—
Ellis, R.G.P.	22	42	1	1285	105*	31.34	1	—	14	—
Ellison, C.C.	7	7	4	56	16	18.66	—	—	1	—
Ellison, R.M.	14	22	9	416	61*	32.00	—	—	6	—
Emburey, J.E.	180	211	55	3113	100*	19.95	1	—	166	—
Emery, K.S.D.	24	26	15	37	18*	3.36	—	—	3	—
Fairbrother, N.H.	1									
Fell, M.A.	10	18	0	315	108	17.50	1	—	9	—
Felton, N.A.	8	12	0	346	71	28.83	—	—	4	—
Ferreira, A.M.	94	140	22	3202	112*	27.13	2	—	45	—
Finney, R.J.	1	1	0	39	39	39.00	—	—	1	—
Fletcher, D.A.G.	99	176	21	3630	89	23.41	—	—	64	—
Fletcher, K.W.R.	601	989	143	32880	228*	38.86	57	18	549	—
Folley, I.	17	15	4	165	36	15.00	—	—	3	—
Forster, G.	5	4	2	45	22*	22.50	—	—	3	—
Foster, N.A.	7	6	3	74	36*	24.66	—	—	1	—
Fowler, G.	57	93	6	3233	150	37.16	9	2	37	5
Francis, D.A.	113	195	31	4008	142*	24.43	3	1	54	—
French, B.N.	120	151	34	1976	79	16.88	—	—	252	27
Gard, T.	18	16	6	161	51*	16.10	—	—	25	8
Garner, J.	111	117	25	1605	104	17.44	1	—	71	—
Garnham, M.A.	34	49	8	875	74	21.34	—	—	62	13
Gatting, M.W.	174	263	39	8725	192	38.95	16	4	156	—
Gavaskar, S.M.	269	440	45	20424	340	51.70	65	2+8	234	—
Gifford, N.	570	670	210	6302	89	13.70	—	—	282	—
Gilfillan, A.D.	3	4	1	40	31	13.33	—	—	—	—
Gladwin, C.	1	1	0	53	53	53.00	—	—	—	—
Goldie, C.F.E.	20	22	2	296	77	14.80	—	—	30	6

198

	M	I	NO	Runs	HS	Avge	100s	1000 runs in season	Ct	St
Gooch, G.A.	224	379	31	13711	205	39.39	31	6+1	195	—
Gould, I.J.	138	190	24	3615	128	21.77	1	—	280	41
Gower, D.I.	180	283	26	9812	200*	38.17	17	4	98	—
Graveney, D.A.	217	297	74	4230	119	18.96	2	—	101	—
Green, A.M.	18	32	1	883	99	28.48	—	—	8	—
Greenidge, C.G.	320	552	37	21989	273*	42.69	48	11	340	—
Greig, I.A.	88	121	13	2602	118*	24.09	2	—	56	—
Griffiths, B.J.	114	89	33	180	16	3.21	—	—	25	—
Griffiths, P.D.	1	2	0	1	1	0.50	—	—	—	—
Hacker, P.J.	71	77	30	449	35	9.55	—	—	16	—
Hadlee, R.J.	180	254	42	5461	142*	25.75	6	—	92	—
Halliday, M.	9	8	3	75	30	15.00	—	—	4	—
Halliday, S.J.	9	14	2	348	113*	29.00	—	—	3	—
Hampshire, J.H.	541	871	106	26676	183*	34.85	42	15	420	—
Hardie, B.R.	209	346	42	10460	162	34.40	13	7	184	—
Haroon Rashid	120	192	22	6080	153	35.76	14	0+2	105	—
Harris, M.J.	344	581	58	19196	201*	36.70	41	11	288	14
Hart, P.R.	3	5	0	23	11	4.60	—	—	1	—
Hartley, P.J.	3	4	1	31	16	10.33	—	—	1	—
Hartley, S.N.	59	93	16	1970	114	25.58	2	—	23	—
Hassan, S.B.	291	483	48	12896	182*	29.64	13	5	264	1
Hayes, F.C.	251	392	57	12141	187	36.24	20	6	163	—
Hayes, K.A.	21	35	3	894	152	27.93	1	—	7	—
Haynes, D.L.	75	124	10	4592	184	40.28	7	0+1	40	—
Hayward, R.E.	14	23	4	454	101*	23.89	1	—	7	—
Heath, J.R.P.	8	15	2	276	101*	25.09	1	—	2	—
Hemmings, E.E.	269	370	82	5995	127*	20.81	1	—	129	—
Hemsley, E.J.O.	243	389	57	9740	176*	29.33	8	1	180	—
Henderson, S.P.	33	52	7	998	209*	22.17	1	—	24	—
Hendrick, M.	243	241	96	1474	46	10.16	—	—	156	—
Heron, J.G.	56	106	5	2717	175	26.90	5	—	36	—
Higgs, K.	509	528	206	3637	98	11.29	—	—	311	—
Hignell, A.J.	150	252	30	6415	149*	28.89	9	2	144	—
Hill, A.	175	309	30	7922	160*	28.39	9	2	69	—
Hinks, S.G.	2	4	1	35	18	11.66	—	—	1	—
Hodgson, C.A.P.	4	7	0	182	87	26.00	—	—	2	—
Hodgson, K.I.	17	19	4	361	50	24.06	—	—	2	—
Hogg, V.R.	38	48	20	156	30	5.57	—	—	13	—
Hogg, W.	73	72	18	322	31	5.96	—	—	14	—
Holmes, G.C.	51	79	20	1280	100*	21.69	1	—	18	—
Hopkins, J.A.	188	333	20	8682	230	27.73	12	5	139	1
Hough, E.J.	3	2	1	4	4	4.00	—	—	—	—
Houghton, D.L.	26	47	3	976	87	22.18	—	—	48	6
Howarth, G.P.	259	454	36	13928	183	33.32	27	4	176	—
Hughes, D.P.	306	387	79	6973	126*	22.63	5	2	207	—
Hughes, S.P.	32	32	14	101	18	5.61	—	—	8	—
Humpage, G.W.	171	278	31	8871	254	35.91	16	5	321	33
Humphries, D.J.	132	189	32	3850	111*	24.52	2	—	228	44
Illingworth, N.J.B.	12	14	4	158	49	15.80	—	—	5	—
Illingworth, R.	766	1057	209	24063	162	28.37	22	8	435	—

199

	M	I	NO	Runs	HS	Avge	100s	1000 runs in season	Ct	St
Illingworth, R.K.	11	16	4	191	47*	15.91	—	—	5	—
Imran Khan	264	412	63	11534	170	33.04	19	3	82	—
Inchmore, J.D.	149	179	37	2310	113	16.26	1	—	50	—
Ingham, P.G.	8	14	0	290	64	20.71	—	—	—	—
Intikhab Alam	489	725	78	14331	182	22.14	9	—	228	—
Iqbal Qasim	121	123	31	1170	61	12.71	—	—	93	—
Jackman, R.D.	395	473	155	5593	92*	17.58	—	—	175	—
Jackson, P.B.	2	3	1	95	46	47.50	—	—	2	—
Jalaluddin	33	44	14	511	60*	17.03	—	—	8	—
James, K.D.	3	3	1	22	16	11.00	—	—	1	—
Jarvis, K.B.S.	160	111	46	177	12*	2.72	—	—	42	—
Jarvis, P.W.	7	5	2	12	7	4.00	—	—	5	—
Javed Miandad	244	402	67	17169	311	51.25	47	4+6	243	3
Jefferies, S.T.	27	32	8	519	63	21.62	—	—	12	—
Jesty, T.E.	320	509	66	13243	164*	29.89	21	5	183	1
Johnson, G.W.	324	513	55	11410	168	24.91	11	3	251	—
Johnson, P.	4	7	1	90	37*	15.00	—	—	—	—
Jones, A.	623	1131	70	34990	204*	32.97	55	22	281	—
Jones, A.L.	78	139	9	2636	88	20.27	—	—	41	—
Jones, A.N.	11	13	5	62	29	7.75	—	—	1	—
Jones, E.W.	390	573	114	8085	146*	17.61	3	—	816	92
Kallicharran, A.I.	352	573	61	22781	235	44.49	57	8+1	233	—
Kapil Dev	106	149	14	3803	193	28.17	6	—	64	—
Kemp, N.J.	18	19	4	210	46*	14.00	—	—	8	—
Kennedy, A.	150	243	20	6298	180	28.24	6	3	85	—
Ker, A.B.M.	2	3	0	123	65	41.00	—	—	2	—
King, C.L.	94	151	22	5030	163	38.99	11	1	82	—
Kirmani, S.M.H.	180	254	51	5561	116	27.39	3	—	239	85
Kirsten, P.N.	184	319	36	13234	228	46.76	37	5+1	117	—
Knight, R.D.V.	339	595	50	17029	165*	31.24	27	11	247	—
Knott, A.P.E.	455	669	118	16583	156	30.09	17	2	1090	123
Lamb, A.J.	164	278	53	11458	178	50.92	27	4	113	—
Lamb, T.M.	151	153	60	1204	77	12.94	—	—	40	—
Larkins, W.	199	341	24	10558	186	33.30	24	5	93	—
Lawrence, D.V.	2	—	—	—	—	—	—	—	—	—
Lawrence, M.P.	4	5	2	20	18	6.66	—	—	—	—
Lee, P.G.	202	164	68	779	26	8.11	—	—	29	—
Leiper, R.J.	2	4	0	53	49	13.25	—	—	2	—
le Roux, G.S.	104	132	43	2302	83	25.86	—	—	48	—
Lethbridge, C.	24	31	6	513	87*	20.60	—	—	10	—
Lever, J.K.	392	403	160	2607	91	10.72	—	—	151	—
Lewington, P.J.	72	73	21	383	34	7.36	—	—	31	—
Lilley, A.W.	28	44	2	1105	100*	26.30	1	—	13	—
Llewellyn, M.J.	136	215	30	4288	129*	23.17	3	—	87	—
Lloyd, B.J.	133	172	45	1496	48	11.77	—	—	83	—
Lloyd, C.H.	425	643	85	27334	242*	48.98	70	10+4	325	—
Lloyd, D.	397	637	71	18762	214*	33.14	37	11	326	—
Lloyd, T.A.	115	203	24	6102	138	34.08	8	3	71	—
Lloyds, J.W.	59	97	8	2323	132*	26.10	3	—	50	—

200

	M	I	NO	Runs	HS	Avge	100s	1000 runs in season	Ct	St
Louden, W.D.G.	1	1	0	21	21	21.00	—	—	1	—
Love, J.D.	120	198	29	5281	170*	31.24	10	1	70	—
Luddington, R.S.	10	14	1	290	65	22.30	—	—	5	1
Lumb, R.G.	225	374	27	10861	159	31.29	20	5	123	—
Lynch, M.A.	79	138	13	3256	141*	26.04	6	1	45	—
McCool, R.J.	1	2	0	19	12	9.50	—	—	1	—
McDermott, E.A.	1	2	0	18	18	9.00	—	—	1	—
McEvoy, M.S.A.	43	74	1	1371	67*	18.78	—	—	42	—
McEwan, K.S.	286	480	39	16886	218	38.29	41	9	256	7
McFarlane, L.	21	12	3	39	12	4.33	—	—	6	—
Mackintosh, K.S.	30	31	15	280	31	17.50	—	—	14	—
Madan Lal, S.	158	237	67	7536	223	44.32	18	—	101	—
Maguire, K.R.	3	3	0	3	2	1.00	—	—	—	—
Maher, B.J.M.	12	14	6	55	15*	6.87	—	—	19	2
Majid Khan	399	684	58	26699	241	42.65	70	8+3	404	—
Malhotra, A.	63	101	15	3639	224*	42.31	7	—	30	—
Mallender, N.A.	46	43	17	248	42	9.53	—	—	20	—
Malone, S.J.	23	22	8	127	23	9.07	—	—	5	—
Mansoor Akhtar	62	103	9	3765	224*	40.05	4	—	48	2
Marks, V.J.	158	242	35	5663	105	27.35	1	—	69	—
Marsden, R.	13	23	1	507	60	23.04	—	—	6	—
Marsh, S.	2	1	1	10	10*	—	—	—	6	—
Marshall, M.D.	118	155	19	2666	116*	19.60	2	—	43	—
Maru, R.J.	16	16	3	147	25	11.30	—	—	14	—
Maynard, C.	42	49	9	794	85	19.85	—	—	59	10
Mendis, G.D.	133	237	19	7080	204	32.47	10	3	66	1
Merry, W.G.	27	17	11	42	14*	7.00	—	—	6	—
Metson, C.P.	1	1	1	38	38*	—	—	—	1	—
Miller, A.J.T.	1	2	0	20	20	10.00	—	—	—	—
Miller, G.	219	323	50	7332	98*	26.85	—	—	154	—
Mills, J.P.C.	41	68	2	1585	111	24.01	1	—	14	—
Mohsin Khan	143	239	24	8670	246	40.32	24	1+2	106	—
Moir, D.G.	27	28	2	232	44	8.92	—	—	25	—
Monkhouse, G.	12	16	9	174	63*	24.85	—	—	5	—
Monteith, J.D.	26	37	5	435	78	13.59	—	—	20	—
Morris, H.	5	8	3	234	63	46.80	—	—	1	—
Morris, J.E.	1	2	0	18	12	9.00	—	—	—	—
Morton, W.A.	1	1	0	3	3	3.00	—	—	—	—
Moseley, E.A.	34	40	10	680	70*	22.66	—	—	11	—
Moseley, H.R.	213	217	94	1533	67	12.46	—	—	78	—
Moulding, R.P.	39	66	6	896	77*	14.93	—	—	16	—
Moxon, M.D.	13	23	0	715	116	31.08	2	—	8	—
Mudassar Nazar	133	221	21	9009	241	45.04	27	0+2	88	—
Mushtaq Mohammad	499	838	103	30974	303*	42.14	72	12+3	345	—
Nash, M.A.	331	467	66	7100	130	17.70	2	—	145	—
Nayak, S.V.	41	55	17	1131	100*	29.76	2	—	18	—
Neale, P.A.	149	258	31	7287	163*	32.10	12	4	62	—
Needham, A.	27	35	8	409	134*	15.14	1	—	12	—
Newman, P.G.	38	41	11	357	39*	11.90	—	—	10	—

201

	M	I	NO	Runs	HS	Avge	100s	1000 runs in season	Ct	St
Newport, P.J.	3	5	1	38	11	9.50	—	—	1	—
Nicholas, M.C.J.	68	117	18	3026	206*	30.56	6	1	35	—
Old, C.M.	329	406	81	6828	116	21.00	6	—	196	—
Oldham, S.	104	73	33	378	50	9.45	—	—	32	—
Oliver, P.R.	89	128	20	2679	171*	24.80	2	—	46	—
Ollis, R.L.	3	6	0	62	22	10.33	—	—	2	—
Ontong, R.C.	177	302	27	6986	152*	25.40	11	2	75	—
O'Reilly, P.M.	1	2	1	1	1*	1.00	—	—	—	—
Ormrod, J.A.	449	758	89	20985	204*	31.36	31	12	374	—
O'Shaughnessy, S.J.	29	42	11	874	62	28.19	—	—	6	—
Palmer, G.V.	1	2	0	33	27	16.50	—	—	—	—
Palmer, R.W.M.	10	8	5	20	12	6.66	—	—	3	—
Parkar, G.A.	35	60	6	2227	156	41.24	7	—	17	1
Parker, P.W.G.	161	276	42	8047	215	34.38	18	5	104	—
Parks, R.J.	55	72	16	913	64*	16.30	—	—	131	14
Parsons, G.J.	64	78	19	812	51	13.76	—	—	24	—
Patel, D.N.	137	210	16	4900	138	25.25	9	2	87	—
Patil, S.M.	53	81	5	2977	174	39.17	7	—	30	—
Pauline, D.B.	14	21	1	248	46	12.40	—	—	2	—
Payne, I.R.	17	23	1	141	29	6.40	—	—	15	—
Penn, C.	7	8	4	54	30	13.50	—	—	4	—
Perryman, S.P.	145	147	62	803	43	9.44	—	—	54	—
Phillip, N.	178	263	35	5672	134	24.87	1	—	56	—
Phillipson, C.P.	165	222	61	2977	87	18.49	—	—	134	—
Pigott, A.C.S.	52	60	12	635	55	13.22	—	—	18	—
Pocock, N.E.J.	88	133	12	2721	164	22.48	2	—	81	—
Pocock, P.I.	458	498	125	4321	75*	11.58	—	—	159	—
Pollock, A.J.	7	8	2	63	19	10.50	—	—	—	—
Pont, I.L.	4	7	1	32	16	5.33	—	—	1	—
Pont, K.R.	158	247	36	5259	113	24.92	5	—	83	—
Popplewell, N.F.M.	79	109	20	2004	135*	22.51	1	—	52	—
Potter, L.	15	27	3	874	118	36.41	2	—	8	—
Pridgeon, A.P.	136	130	58	631	34	8.76	—	—	40	—
Pringle, D.R.	67	96	19	2514	127*	32.64	5	—	26	—
Prior, J.A.	2	3	0	44	20	14.66	—	—	1	—
Pycroft, A.J.	29	53	7	1697	133	36.89	2	—	19	—
Radford, N.V.	44	55	14	907	76*	22.12	—	—	23	—
Radley, C.T.	449	720	100	21886	171	35.30	38	14	442	—
Ramage, A.	20	19	8	173	52	15.72	—	—	1	—
Randall, D.W.	264	451	40	14787	209	35.97	25	8	169	—
Randhir Singh	23	25	7	142	15	7.88	—	—	5	—
Rawlinson, H.T.	4	6	0	30	21	5.00	—	—	1	—
Rawson, P.W.E.	2	2	1	15	13	15.00	—	—	1	—
Reidy, B.W.	107	162	26	3641	131*	26.77	2	—	65	—
Rhind, P.A.	6	7	4	23	10	7.66	—	—	3	—
Rhodes, S.J.	1	—	—	—	—	—	—	—	—	—
Rice, C.E.B.	279	452	69	15386	246	40.17	27	8	217	—
Rice, J.M.	168	271	22	5091	161*	20.44	2	—	153	—
Richards, C.J.	135	161	38	2401	117*	19.52	1	—	253	36

202

	M	I	NO	Runs	HS	Avge	100s	1000 runs in season	Ct	St
Richards, I.V.A.	280	462	31	21099	291	48.95	63	9+3	266	1
Ridge, S.P.	11	15	6	71	22	7.88	—	—	3	—
Roberts, A.M.E.	193	247	57	2872	63	15.11	—	—	46	—
Robinson, R.T.	57	101	14	2540	138	29.19	2	—	33	—
Roebuck, P.M.	160	267	43	7053	158	31.48	5	2	87	—
Romaines, P.W.	20	33	3	665	186	22.16	1	—	6	—
Roope, G.R.J.	401	644	129	19037	171	36.96	26	8	599	2
Rose, B.C.	220	370	40	11156	205	33.80	22	8	111	—
Rowe, C.J.C.	147	233	39	5297	147*	27.30	6	2	53	—
Roy, P.	29	49	3	1599	160*	34.76	5	—	12	—
Russell, R.C.	5	7	2	82	41	16.40	—	—	11	3
Russom, N.	24	33	14	633	79*	33.31	—	—	6	—
Sadiq Mohammad	361	634	37	22096	203	37.01	44	7+2	297	—
Saleem Yousuf	34	54	2	1737	115	33.40	4	—	81	12
Salim Malik	28	48	6	1543	126*	36.73	4	—	14	—
Sarfraz Nawaz	277	342	67	5342	90	19.42	—	—	156	—
Saxelby, K.	22	24	8	201	59*	12.56	—	—	7	—
Scott, C.J.	46	51	13	262	27*	6.89	—	—	94	10
Scott, C.W.	3	4	1	45	17*	15.00	—	—	4	1
Scott, G.M.	1									
Scott, M.S.	25	48	1	1086	109	23.10	1	—	9	—
Selvey, M.W.W.	239	236	77	2044	67	12.85	—	—	65	—
Sharp, G.	261	347	72	5439	94	19.77	—	—	492	80
Sharp, K.	78	128	12	3189	116	27.49	4	—	26	—
Shastri, R.J.	35	49	9	988	134	24.70	1	—	25	—
Shepherd, J.N.	374	538	93	11444	170	25.71	8	1	261	—
Short, J.F.	9	15	2	478	114	36.76	1	—	9	—
Sidebottom, A.	106	117	25	1816	124	19.73	1	—	32	—
Sikander Bakht	105	107	38	925	60*	13.40	—	—	43	—
Simmons, J.	321	389	110	6526	112	23.39	3	—	253	—
Simpkins, D.P.	1	2	1	1	1*	1.00	—	—	—	—
Slack, W.N.	81	136	11	4253	248*	34.02	5	2	49	—
Slocombe, P.A.	128	216	27	5416	132	28.65	7	2	60	—
Small, G.C.	62	74	15	625	57*	10.59	—	—	17	—
Smith, C.L.	49	86	12	2573	130	34.77	6	1	29	—
Smith, D.J.	6	5	0	4	2	0.80	—	—	6	—
Smith, D.M. (Sy)	128	195	44	4472	160	29.61	6	1	83	—
Smith, D.M. (Wa)	3	4	1	48	27	16.00	—	—	1	—
Smith, K.D.	144	250	23	6650	140	29.29	7	3	59	—
Smith, P.A.	10	16	1	383	68	25.53	—	—	7	—
Smith, R.A.	11	19	1	400	91	22.22	—	—	5	—
Snodgrass, D.L.	1	1	0	6	6	6.00	—	—	1	—
Southern, J.W.	149	166	66	1507	61*	15.07	—	—	51	—
Speak, G.J.	5	6	4	27	15*	13.50	—	—	3	—
Spelman, G.D.	7	7	1	9	4	1.50	—	—	2	—
Steele, D.S.	450	742	105	21138	140*	33.18	30	10	488	—
Steele, J.F.	307	509	56	13342	195	29.45	20	6	330	—
Stephenson, F.D.	18	25	2	484	165	21.04	1	—	10	—
Stevenson, G.B.	147	179	29	3230	115*	21.53	2	—	63	—
Stevenson, K.	139	158	55	969	33	9.40	—	—	46	—
Stewart, A.J.	2	4	0	35	16	8.75	—	—	7	—

	M	I	NO	Runs	HS	Avge	100s	1000 runs in season	Ct	St
Stovold, A.W.	201	358	19	10097	212*	29.78	9	4	204	43
Stovold, M.W.	25	37	6	518	75*	16.70	—	—	5	—
Such, P.M.	8	9	3	3	2	0.50	—	—	7	—
Surridge, D.	34	28	16	103	14*	8.58	—	—	7	—
Sutcliffe, S.P.	36	47	11	141	20	3.91	—	—	5	—
Swan, R.G.	3	6	1	136	66	27.20	—	—	1	—
Tahir, Naqqash	30	33	3	595	60	19.83	—	—	14	—
Tavare, C.J.	176	296	38	10539	168*	40.84	21	6	183	—
Taylor, D.J.S.	302	420	95	7404	179	22.78	4	1	622	84
Taylor, L.B.	102	82	38	313	25	7.11	—	—	24	—
Taylor, N.R.	46	81	10	2242	143*	31.57	4	1	28	—
Taylor, N.S.	4	1	1	0	0*	—	—	—	1	—
Taylor, R.W.	581	799	147	10967	100	16.82	1	—	1359	167
Taylor, T.J.	14	17	7	115	28*	11.50	—	—	2	—
Tedstone, G.A.	3	5	2	45	18*	15.00	—	—	4	1
Terry, V.P.	19	29	4	369	94*	14.76	—	—	9	—
Thomas, D.J.	64	87	19	1010	64	14.85	—	—	22	—
Thomas, J.G.	15	22	3	259	84	13.63	—	—	7	—
Titmus, F.J.	792	1142	208	21588	137*	23.11	6	8	474	—
Todd, P.A.	156	276	16	7168	178	27.56	8	3	105	—
Tolchard, R.W.	457	645	182	14513	126*	31.34	12	—	868	116
Tomlins, K.P.	45	63	7	1496	146	26.71	2	—	27	—
Toogood, G.J.	9	18	4	392	83	28.00	—	—	4	—
Torrens, R.	6	8	1	42	17	6.00	—	—	1	—
Traicos, A.J.	67	99	43	722	43	12.89	—	—	56	—
Trembath, C.R.	2	1	1	8	8*	—	—	—	1	—
Tremlett, T.M.	63	101	13	1815	88	20.62	—	—	29	—
Tunnicliffe, C.J.	133	151	30	1631	82*	13.47	—	—	62	—
Turner, D.R.	316	527	46	13472	181*	28.00	20	6	162	—
Turner, G.M.	452	787	101	34213	311*	49.87	103	15+3	406	—
Turner, S.	327	470	93	8887	121	23.57	4	—	206	—
Underwood, D.L.	555	586	162	3990	80	9.41	—	—	233	—
Varey, D.W.	12	22	4	629	156*	34.94	1	—	8	—
Varey, J.G.	7	12	5	239	68	34.14	—	—	2	—
Vengsarkar, D.B.	128	196	19	8344	210	47.14	22	0+2	105	—
Viswanath, G.R.	265	420	36	16162	247	42.08	40	0+5	201	—
Wallace, G.C.	16	30	2	757	111	27.03	1	—	8	—
Waller, C.E.	207	213	83	1288	51*	9.90	—	—	112	—
Wallwork, M.A.	1	—	—	—	—	—	—	—	3	—
Warner, A.E.	11	17	2	287	67	19.13	—	—	2	—
Warner, C.J.	6	10	1	187	55	20.77	—	—	5	—
Wasim Bari	266	337	89	5462	177	22.02	2	—	620	139
Wasim Raja	208	322	45	9826	165	35.47	13	0+1	129	—
Waterton, S.N.V.	13	14	2	160	40*	13.33	—	—	22	4
Watkinson, M.	1	—	—	—	—	—	—	—	—	—
Watson, R.G.	1	2	0	15	11	7.50	—	—	—	—
Watts, A.	1	1	0	0	0	0.00	—	—	1	—
Webster, A.J.	9	11	5	81	25	13.50	—	—	3	—

	M	I	NO	Runs	HS	Avge	100s	1000 runs in season	Ct	St
Weightman, N.I.	4	6	0	175	105	29.16	1	—	3	—
Weir, R.	4	8	2	187	65	31.16	—	—	1	—
Wells, A.P.	7	12	3	311	70	34.55	—	—	3	—
Wells, C.M.	64	101	13	2869	135	32.60	5	2	20	—
Wenlock, D.A.	10	13	4	148	62	16.44	—	—	3	—
Weston, M.J.	24	41	2	841	93	21.56	—	—	9	—
Whiteley, J.P.	45	38	17	231	20	11.00	—	—	21	—
Wild, D.J.	14	19	5	241	30	17.21	—	—	2	—
Willey, P.	334	547	82	13274	227	28.54	20	3	131	—
Williams, N.F.	12	11	5	112	27*	18.66	—	—	2	—
Williams, R.G.	136	219	22	5613	175*	28.49	11	4	53	—
Willis, R.G.D.	269	284	123	2358	72	14.64	—	—	113	—
Willows, A.	4	3	1	5	4	2.50	—	—	—	—
Wills, R.T.	2	3	0	91	48	30.33	—	—	—	—
Wilson, P.H.L.	46	37	18	201	29	10.57	—	—	7	—
Windaybank, S.J.	15	19	4	385	53	25.66	—	—	3	—
Wood, B.	354	589	75	17431	198	33.91	30	8	283	—
Wood, L.J.	2	2	0	5	5	2.50	—	—	—	—
Woolmer, R.A.	328	509	71	14350	203	32.76	29	5	228	1
Wootton, S.H.	9	13	2	207	77	18.81	—	—	4	—
Wright, A.J.	10	19	2	399	65	23.47	—	—	3	—
Wright, J.G.	185	330	25	12220	190	40.06	30	5	109	—
Yadav, N.S.	45	46	14	602	49	18.81	—	—	15	—
Yardley, T.J.	260	390	69	8287	135	25.81	5	1	232	2
Yashpal Sharma	91	146	33	5376	201*	47.57	12	—	42	1
Younis Ahmed	390	656	98	21708	221*	38.90	36	11	219	—
Zaheer Abbas	383	648	79	30069	274	52.84	95	11+5	242	—

BOWLING

Players who have not bowled in first-class cricket are omitted from this list.

	Runs	Wkts	Avge	BB	5 wI	10 wM	100 wkts in season
Abdul Qadir	8934	470	19.08	8-29	37	7	—
Abrahams, J.	1567	30	52.23	3-27	—	—	—
Acfield, D.L.	21624	787	27.47	8-55	28	3	—
Agnew, J.P.	3103	102	30.42	6-70	2	—	—
Alleyne, H.L.	3701	139	26.62	8-43	5	2	—
Allott, P.J.W.	5274	186	28.35	8-48	8	—	—
Amiss, D.L.	718	18	39.88	3-21	—	—	—
Anderson, I.J.	249	17	14.64	5-21	1	—	—
Anderson, I.S.	690	14	49.28	4-35	—	—	—
Arnold, G.G.	24761	1130	21.91	8-41	46	3	1
Asif Din	1499	25	59.96	5-100	1	—	—
Asif Iqbal	8776	291	30.15	6-45	5	—	—

205

	Runs	Wkts	Avge	BB	5 wI	10 wM	100 wkts in season
Aslett, D.G.	343	7	49.00	4-119	—	—	—
Athey, C.W.J.	950	18	52.77	3-38	—	—	—
Bailey, M.J.	996	18	55.33	5-89	1	—	—
Bainbridge, P.	2727	74	36.85	6-59	2	—	—
Bairstow, D.L.	181	5	36.20	3-82	—	—	—
Balderstone, J.C.	7709	298	25.86	6-25	5	—	—
Baptiste, E.A.E.	1864	50	37.28	5-37	1	—	—
Barclay, J.R.T.	7161	240	29.83	6-61	7	1	—
Barlow, G.D.	52	3	17.33	1-6	—	—	—
Barnett, K.J.	1338	18	74.33	4-76	—	—	—
Barwick, S.R.	1114	39	28.56	5-44	1	—	—
Benson, M.R.	56	0	—	—	—	—	—
Birch, J.D.	1835	38	48.28	6-64	1	—	—
Boon, T.J.	57	0	—	—	—	—	—
Booth, P.A.	22	0	—	—	—	—	—
Bore, M.K.	9405	319	29.48	8-89	8	—	—
Botham, I.T.	17669	726	24.33	8-34	43	7	1
Boycott, G.	1360	44	30.90	4-14	—	—	—
Boyd-Moss, R.J.	999	23	43.43	4-42	—	—	—
Brassington, A.J.	10	0	—	—	—	—	—
Brearley, J.M.	192	3	64.00	1-6	—	—	—
Briers, N.E.	334	10	33.40	2-11	—	—	—
Broad, B.C.	656	11	59.63	2-14	—	—	—
Brown, D.J.	28961	1165	24.85	8-60	46	5	—
Bryant, M.	158	2	79.00	1-29	—	—	—
Bullen, C.K.	29	0	—	—	—	—	—
Butchart, I.P.	76	4	19.00	2-22	—	—	—
Butcher, A.R.	3710	94	39.46	6-48	1	—	—
Butcher, M.S.	2	0	—	—	—	—	—
Butcher, R.O.	56	0	—	—	—	—	—
Capel, D.J.	438	6	73.00	2-14	—	—	—
Carrick, P.	15548	537	28.95	8-33	24	2	—
Carter, R.M.	1492	38	39.26	4-27	—	—	—
Cassidy, J.J.	12	0	—	—	—	—	—
Cheatle, R.G.L.	3303	104	31.75	6-32	6	—	—
Childs, J.H.	10967	358	30.63	9-56	19	2	—
Clark, J.	800	43	18.60	4-10	—	—	—
Clarke, S.T.	8645	409	21.13	6-39	22	2	—
Clift, P.B.	13638	544	25.06	8-17	18	1	—
Clinton, G.S.	97	4	24.75	2-8	—	—	—
Close, D.B.	30836	1167	26.42	8-41	43	3	2
Cobb, R.A.	5	0	—	—	—	—	—
Cockbain, I.	14	0	—	—	—	—	—
Cook, G.	349	6	58.16	2-18	—	—	—
Cook, N.G.B.	7348	281	26.14	7-63	14	1	—
Cooper, K.E.	7327	263	27.85	6-32	6	—	—
Corlett, S.C.	1935	59	32.79	7-82	3	—	—
Cowan, R.S.	771	9	85.66	2-75	—	—	—
Cowans, N.G.	962	43	22.37	5-28	3	—	—

	Runs	Wkts	Avge	BB	5 wI	10 wM	100 wkts in season
Cowdrey, C.S.	1210	33	36.66	3-17	—	—	—
Cowley, N.G.	8260	230	35.91	6-48	4	—	—
Croft, C.E.H.	10277	419	24.52	8-29	17	1	—
Crowe, M.D.	187	4	46.75	2-8	—	—	—
Crowe, P.J.	121	1	121.00	1-105	—	—	—
Cumbes, J.	11447	379	30.20	6-24	13	—	—
Cunningham, E.J.	13	0	—	—	—	—	—
Curran, K.M.	441	18	24.50	4-33	—	—	—
Curtis, I.J.	1383	33	41.90	5-140	1	—	—
Curtis, T.S.	22	1	22.00	1-13	—	—	—
Daniel, W.W.	10573	522	20.25	9-61	23	5	—
Daniels, S.A.B.	1162	28	41.50	3-33	—	—	—
Davis, M.R.	481	12	40.08	3-36	—	—	—
Davis, W.W.	2595	86	30.17	7-101	2	—	—
Davison, B.F.	2617	82	31.91	5-52	1	—	—
Denning, P.W.	96	1	96.00	1-4	—	—	—
Dennis, S.J.	1092	38	28.73	5-35	2	—	—
Dilley, G.R.	6750	228	29.60	6-66	8	1	—
Doggart, S.J.G.	1379	22	62.68	3-54	—	—	—
Donald, W.A.	15	0	—	—	—	—	—
Doshi, D.R.	20714	803	25.79	7-29	36	5	1
Doughty, R.J.	588	17	34.58	6-43	1	—	—
Dredge, C.H.	8176	279	29.30	6-37	9	—	—
Dudhia, M.H.E.M.	71	5	14.20	2-13	—	—	—
Dudleston, B.	1201	43	27.93	4-6	—	—	—
Dutton, R.S.	261	1	261.00	1-45	—	—	—
Dyer, R.I.H.B.	2	0	—	—	—	—	—
Ealham, A.G.E.	189	3	63.00	1-1	—	—	—
East, R.E.	24997	983	25.42	8-30	48	10	—
Edmonds, P.H.	21178	852	24.85	8-80	34	6	—
Ehtesham-ud-Din	8235	400	20.58	8-45	32	6	—
Ellcock, R.M.	90	3	30.00	3-80	—	—	—
Ellis, R.G.P.	182	4	45.50	2-40	—	—	—
Ellison, C.C.	314	5	62.80	3-30	—	—	—
Ellison, R.M.	577	20	28.85	3-12	—	—	—
Emburey, J.E.	14359	606	23.69	7-36	35	8	—
Emery, K.S.D.	1969	83	23.72	6-51	3	1	—
Fell, M.A.	146	1	146.00	1-20	—	—	—
Ferreira, A.M.	7656	246	31.12	8-38	10	1	—
Finney, R.J.	40	1	40.00	1-37	—	—	—
Fletcher, D.A.G.	5691	207	27.49	6-31	5	1	—
Fletcher, K.W.R.	2167	50	43.34	5-41	1	—	—
Folley, I.	758	27	28.07	4-40	—	—	—
Forster, G.	275	4	68.75	2-30	—	—	—
Foster, N.A.	595	16	37.18	3-32	—	—	—
Fowler, G.	25	0	—	—	—	—	—
Francis, D.A.	6	0	—	—	—	—	—

	Runs	Wkts	Avge	BB	5 wI	10 wM	100 wkts in season
Garner, J.	8490	490	17.32	8-31	30	5	—
Gatting, M.W.	2125	87	24.42	5-34	2	—	—
Gavaskar, S.M.	1123	21	53.47	3-43	—	—	—
Gifford, N.	39244	1720	22.81	8-28	79	12	3
Gilfillan, A.D.	218	2	109.00	2-177	—	—	—
Gooch, G.A.	2952	83	35.56	7-14	2	—	—
Gould, I.J.	26	0	—	—	—	—	—
Gower, D.I.	78	4	19.50	3-47	—	—	—
Graveney, D.A.	14364	503	28.55	8-85	23	4	—
Green, A.M.	274	6	45.66	2-48	—	—	—
Greenidge, C.G.	438	16	27.37	5-49	1	—	—
Greig, I.A.	5218	197	26.48	7-43	7	2	—
Griffiths, B.J.	8484	298	28.46	8-50	9	—	—
Griffiths, P.D.	39	0	—	—	—	—	—
Hacker, P.J.	4792	153	31.32	6-35	4	—	—
Hadlee, R.J.	14767	743	19.87	7-23	43	5	1
Halliday, M.	485	22	22.04	5-39	1	—	—
Hampshire, J.H.	1633	30	54.43	7.52	2	—	—
Hardie, B.R.	80	2	40.00	2-39	—	—	—
Haroon Rashid	249	8	31.12	3-34	—	—	—
Harris, M.J.	3459	79	43.78	4-16	—	—	—
Hart, P.R.	140	2	70.00	1-22	—	—	—
Hartley, P.J.	215	2	107.50	2-45	—	—	—
Hartley, S.N.	1023	20	51.15	3-40	—	—	—
Hassan, S.B.	407	6	67.83	3-33	—	—	—
Hayes, F.C.	15	0	—	—	—	—	—
Hayes, K.A.	129	0	—	—	—	—	—
Haynes, D.L.	10	1	10.00	1-2	—	—	—
Hayward, R.E.	5	0	—	—	—	—	—
Hemmings, E.E.	21451	746	28.75	7-33	34	8	—
Hemsley, E.J.O.	2497	70	35.67	3-5	—	—	—
Henderson, S.P.	54	0	—	—	—	—	—
Hendrick, M.	14577	696	20.94	8-45	25	3	—
Heron, J.G.	17	0	—	—	—	—	—
Higgs, K.	36196	1531	23.64	7-19	49	5	5
Hignell, A.J.	184	3	61.33	2-13	—	—	—
Hill, A.	137	5	27.40	3-5	—	—	—
Hinks, S.G.	5	0	—	—	—	—	—
Hodgson, K.I.	1222	43	28.41	8-68	1	1	—
Hogg, V.R.	2938	109	26.95	6.78	2	—	—
Hogg, W.	5239	183	28.62	7-84	5	1	—
Holmes, G.C.	1017	26	39.11	5-86	1	—	—
Hopkins, J.A.	27	0	—	—	—	—	—
Hough, E.J.	233	12	19.41	4-48	—	—	—
Howarth, G.P.	3258	107	30.44	5-32	1	—	—
Hughes, D.P.	17737	603	29.41	7-24	20	2	—
Hughes, S.P.	2620	101	25.94	6-75	4	—	—
Humpage, G.W.	336	7	48.00	2-13	—	—	—

	Runs	Wkts	Avge	BB	5 wI	10 wM	100 wkts in season
Illingworth, N.J.B.	581	15	38.73	5-89	1	—	—
Illingworth, R.	41072	2040	20.13	9-42	104	11	10
Illingworth, R.K.	811	18	45.05	4-85	—	—	—
Imran Khan	21184	930	22.77	8-58	51	9	—
Inchmore, J.D.	10638	373	28.52	8-58	15	1	—
Intikhab Alam	43472	1571	27.67	8-54	85	13	1
Iqbal Qasim	10241	463	22.11	9-80	28	7	—
Jackman, R.D.	31706	1399	22.66	8-40	67	8	1
Jalaluddin	2540	113	22.47	4.43	6	1	—
James, K.D.	76	5	15.20	3-14	—	—	—
Jarvis, K.B.S.	12306	441	27.90	8-97	14	3	—
Jarvis, P.W.	508	8	63.50	2-24	—	—	—
Javed Miandad	5881	181	32.49	7-39	6	—	—
Jefferies, S.T.	2390	86	27.79	5-46	1	—	—
Jesty, T.E.	13574	515	26.35	7-75	18	—	—
Johnson, G.W.	14186	465	30.50	6-32	17	2	—
Jones, A.	333	3	111.00	1-24	—	—	—
Jones, A.L.	17	0	—	—	—	—	—
Jones, A.N.	491	23	21.34	4-33	—	—	—
Jones, E.W.	5	0	—	—	—	—	—
Kallicharran, A.I.	2470	52	47.50	4-48	—	—	—
Kapil Dev	9437	338	28.06	8-38	20	2	—
Kemp, N.J.	801	16	50.06	6-119	1	—	—
Kennedy, A.	398	10	39.80	3-58	—	—	—
King, C.L.	3532	113	31.25	5-91	4	—	—
Kirmani, S.M.H.	55	0	—	—	—	—	—
Kirsten, P.N.	2341	62	37.75	4-44	—	—	—
Knight, R.D.V.	11650	327	35.62	6-44	4	—	—
Knott, A.P.E.	87	2	43.50	1-5	—	—	—
Lamb, A.J.	92	4	23.00	1-1	—	—	—
Lamb, T.M.	10043	340	29.53	7-56	10	—	—
Larkins, W.	1071	27	39.66	3-34	—	—	—
Lawrence, D.V.	160	2	80.00	1-24	—	—	—
Lawrence, M.P.	366	2	183.00	1-32	—	—	—
Lee, P.G.	15339	599	25.60	8-34	29	7	2
le Roux, G.S.	7950	413	19.24	8-107	22	3	—
Lethbridge, C.	1478	36	41.05	5-68	1	—	—
Lever, J.K.	29183	1213	24.05	8-49	56	6	2
Lewington, P.J.	5705	191	29.86	7-52	6	—	—
Lilley, A.W.	10	0	—	—	—	—	—
Llewellyn, M.J.	615	23	26.73	4-35	—	—	—
Lloyd, B.J.	9257	226	40.96	8-70	3	—	—
Lloyd, C.H.	4104	114	36.00	4-48	—	—	—
Lloyd, D.	6772	220	30.78	7-38	4	1	—
Lloyd, T.A.	647	8	80.87	2-29	—	—	—
Lloyds, J.W.	2858	84	34.02	7-88	5	1	—

	Runs	Wkts	Avge	BB	5 wI	10 wM	100 wkts in season
Louden, W.D.G.	11	3	3.66	3-4	—	—	—
Love, J.D.	144	0	—	—	—	—	—
Lynch, M.A.	495	11	45.00	3-6	—	—	—
McCool, R.J.	63	0	—	—	—	—	—
McEvoy, M.S.A.	103	3	34.33	3-20	—	—	—
McEwan, K.S.	281	3	93.66	1-0	—	—	—
McFarlane, L.	1515	40	37.87	6-59	1	—	—
Mackintosh, K.S.	2045	59	34.66	6-61	1	—	—
Madan Lal, S.	10843	428	25.33	9-31	20	3	—
Maguire, K.R.	123	1	123.00	1-32	—	—	—
Majid Khan	7193	224	32.11	6-67	4	—	—
Malhotra, A.	73	1	73.00	1-37	—	—	—
Mallender, N.A.	3423	107	31.99	7-41	4	1	—
Malone, S.J.	1581	51	31.00	7-55	2	1	—
Mansoor Akhtar	182	3	60.66	1-16	—	—	—
Marks, V.J.	11332	339	33.42	7-51	14	—	—
Marshall, M.D.	8827	492	17.94	8-71	32	5	1
Maru, R.J.	766	23	33.30	4-30	—	—	—
Mendis, G.D.	11	0	—	—	—	—	—
Merry, W.G.	1554	49	31.71	4-24	—	—	—
Miller, G.	13497	542	24.90	8-70	25	6	—
Mills, J.P.C.	5	0	—	—	—	—	—
Mohsin Khan	460	11	41.81	2-16	—	—	—
Moir, D.G.	2357	82	28.74	6-63	4	—	—
Monkhouse, G.	619	19	32.57	3-40	—	—	—
Monteith, J.D.	1726	89	19.39	7-38	7	1	—
Morton, W.A.	82	2	41.00	1-38	—	—	—
Moseley, E.A.	2758	121	22.79	6-23	5	—	—
Moseley, H.R.	13668	557	24.53	6-34	16	1	—
Moxon, M.D.	23	0	—	—	—	—	—
Mudassar Nazar	2353	82	28.69	6-32	1	—	—
Mushtaq Mohammad	22662	935	24.23	7-18	39	2	—
Nash, M.A.	25448	989	25.73	9-56	45	5	—
Nayak, S.V.	2446	81	30.19	6-65	4	1	—
Neale, P.A.	190	1	190.00	1-15	—	—	—
Needham, A.	1668	32	52.12	5-91	1	—	—
Newman, P.G.	3008	94	32.00	5-51	1	—	—
Newport, P.J.	238	6	39.66	4-76	—	—	—
Nicholas, M.C.J.	85	2	42.50	1-4	—	—	—
Old, C.M.	21240	941	22.57	7-20	33	1	—
Oldham, S.	6994	220	31.79	7-78	4	—	—
Oliver, P.R.	2115	27	78.33	2-28	—	—	—
Ontong, R.C.	11165	366	30.50	7-60	11	2	—
O'Reilly, P.M.	14	1	14.00	1-14	—	—	—
Ormrod, J.A.	1094	25	43.76	5-27	1	—	—
O'Shaughnessy, S.J.	1125	39	28.84	4-66	—	—	—

	Runs	Wkts	Avge	BB	5 wI	10 wM	100 wkts in season
Palmer, G.V.	57	0	—	—	—	—	—
Palmer, R.W.M.	879	15	58.60	4-96	—	—	—
Parkar, G.A.	61	2	30.50	1-5	—	—	—
Parker, P.W.G.	471	8	58.87	2-23	—	—	—
Parks, R.J.	0	0	—	—	—	—	—
Parsons, G.J.	4517	135	33.45	5-25	1	—	—
Patel, D.N.	6905	190	36.34	7-46	8	—	—
Patil, S.M.	1207	34	35.50	4-58	—	—	—
Pauline, D.B.	22	0	—	—	—	—	—
Payne, I.R.	575	11	52.27	2-28	—	—	—
Penn, C.	327	7	46.71	2-11	—	—	—
Perryman, S.P.	10587	344	30.77	7-49	19	3	—
Phillip, N.	13171	530	24.85	7-33	21	2	—
Phillipson, C.P.	5213	153	34.07	6-56	4	—	—
Pigott, A.C.S.	3394	111	30.57	7-74	4	—	—
Pocock, N.E.J.	197	3	65.66	1-4	—	—	—
Pocock, P.I.	35594	1375	25.88	9-57	52	6	1
Pollock, A.J.	483	14	34.50	5-108	1	—	—
Pont, I.L.	302	3	100.66	2-107	—	—	—
Pont, K.R.	2478	78	31.76	5-17	2	—	—
Popplewell, N.F.M.	3128	72	43.44	5-33	1	—	—
Potter, L.	33	2	16.50	1-9	—	—	—
Pridgeon, A.P.	10299	279	36.91	7-35	4	1	—
Pringle, D.R.	3861	133	29.03	6-33	3	1	—
Prior, J.A.	56	0	—	—	—	—	—
Pycroft, A.J.	47	1	47.00	1-0	—	—	—
Radford, N.V.	3388	111	30.52	6-41	4	1	—
Radley, C.T.	111	6	18.50	1-0	—	—	—
Ramage, A.	1504	42	35.80	5-65	1	—	—
Randall, D.W.	142	3	47.33	3-15	—	—	—
Randhir Singh	2194	60	26.56	6-141	2	—	—
Rawlinson, H.T.	435	5	87.00	2-102	—	—	—
Rawson, P.W.E.	177	7	25.28	5-42	1	—	—
Reidy, B.W.	2508	60	41.80	5-61	1	—	—
Rhind, P.A.	332	6	55.33	3-62	—	—	—
Rice, C.E.B.	14601	679	21.50	7-62	20	1	—
Rice, J.M.	7707	230	33.50	7-48	3	—	—
Richards, C.J.	24	0	—	—	—	—	—
Richards, I.V.A.	5179	123	42.10	5-88	1	—	—
Ridge, S.P.	894	14	63.85	4-128	—	—	—
Roberts, A.M.E.	15784	754	20.93	8-47	38	5	1
Robinson, R.T.	93	2	46.50	1-22	—	—	—
Roebuck, P.M.	1979	42	47.11	6-50	1	—	—
Romaines, P.W.	9	0	—	—	—	—	—
Roope, G.R.J.	8395	225	37.31	5-14	4	—	—
Rose, B.C.	218	6	36.33	3-9	—	—	—
Rowe, C.J.C.	3199	78	41.01	6-46	3	1	—
Roy, P.	46	0	—	—	—	—	—
Russom, N.	1726	42	41.09	4-84	—	—	—

	Runs	Wkts	Avge	BB	5 wI	10 wM	100 wkts in season
Sadiq Mohammad	7070	221	31.99	7-34	7	—	—
Saleem Yousuf	16	1	16.00	1-16	—	—	—
Salim Malik	47	0	—	—	—	—	—
Sarfraz Nawaz	22627	941	24.04	9-86	46	4	1
Saxelby, K.	1294	51	25.37	4-18	—	—	—
Scott, M.S.	37	0	—	—	—	—	—
Selvey, M.W.W.	17582	685	25.66	7-20	34	4	—
Sharp, G.	68	1	68.00	1-47	—	—	—
Sharp, K.	41	0	—	—	—	—	—
Shastri, R.J.	2818	112	25.16	9-101	5	1	—
Shepherd, J.N.	27663	1016	27.22	8-40	49	2	—
Sidebottom, A.	5929	246	24.10	7-18	10	2	—
Sikander Bakht	8270	310	26.67	8-69	13	1	—
Simmons, J.	19031	691	27.54	7-59	21	2	—
Simpkins, D.P.	15	0	—	—	—	—	—
Slack, W.N.	281	12	23.41	3-17	—	—	—
Slocombe, P.A.	53	3	17.66	1-2	—	—	—
Small, G.C.	4590	133	34.51	7-68	2	—	—
Smith, C.L.	337	4	84.25	2-7	—	—	—
Smith, D.M. (Sy)	1443	27	53.44	3-40	—	—	—
Smith, D.M. (Wa)	157	1	157.00	1-55	—	—	—
Smith, K.D.	3	0	—	—	—	—	—
Smith, P.A.	536	10	53.60	2-12	—	—	—
Smith, R.A.	6	0	—	—	—	—	—
Snodgrass, D.L.	80	3	26.66	2-30	—	—	—
Southern, J.W.	11317	385	29.39	6-46	15	—	—
Speak, G.J.	230	1	230.00	1-78	—	—	—
Spelman, G.D.	357	10	35.70	2-27	—	—	—
Steele, D.S.	11951	494	24.19	8-29	22	3	—
Steele, J.F.	11482	456	25.17	7-29	12	—	—
Stephenson, F.D.	1435	77	18.63	6-19	5	1	—
Stevenson, G.B.	11389	403	28.26	8-57	16	2	—
Stevenson, K.	9880	334	29.58	7-22	15	—	—
Stovold, A.W.	86	2	43.00	1-0	—	—	—
Stovold, M.W.	19	0	—	—	—	—	—
Surridge, D.	2599	87	29.87	5-78	1	—	—
Sutcliffe, S.P.	3829	93	41.17	6-19	2	—	—
Tahir Naqqash	2066	69	29.94	9-45	3	—	—
Tavare, C.J.	272	2	136.00	1-20	—	—	—
Taylor, D.J.S.	16	0	—	—	—	—	—
Taylor, L.B.	7127	292	24.40	7-28	8	—	—
Taylor, N.R.	126	4	31.50	2-58	—	—	—
Taylor, N.S.	293	8	36.62	2-42	—	—	—
Taylor, R.W.	52	0	—	—	—	—	—
Taylor, T.J.	1272	37	34.37	5-81	2	—	—
Terry, V.P.	39	0	—	—	—	—	—
Thomas, D.J.	4605	128	35.97	6-84	2	—	—
Thomas, J.G.	1001	33	30.33	5-61	1	—	—
Titmus, F.J.	63313	2830	22.37	9-52	168	26	16
Todd, P.A.	3	0	—	—	—	—	—

212

	Runs	Wkts	Avge	BB	5 wI	10 wM	100 wkts in season
Tolchard, R.W.	34	1	34.00	1-4	—	—	—
Tomlins, K.P.	289	4	72.25	2-28	—	—	—
Toogood, G.J.	22	0	—	—	—	—	—
Torrens, R.	402	26	15.46	7-40	2	—	—
Traicos, A.J.	5469	165	33.14	6-66	5	—	—
Trembath, C.R.	219	6	36.50	5-91	1	—	—
Tremlett, T.M.	2241	80	28.01	5-30	2	—	—
Tunnicliffe, C.J.	8893	280	31.76	7-36	6	—	—
Turner, D.R.	323	9	35.88	2-7	—	—	—
Turner, G.M.	189	5	37.80	3-18	—	—	—
Turner, S.	19651	760	25.85	6-26	26	1	—
Underwood, D.L.	41970	2118	19.81	9-28	139	42	9
Varey, D.W.	4	0	—	—	—	—	—
Varey, J.G.	550	3	183.33	1-13	—	—	—
Vengsarkar, D.B.	41	0	—	—	—	—	—
Viswanath, G.R.	673	15	44.86	2-21	—	—	—
Wallace, G.C.	238	5	47.60	3-61	—	—	—
Waller, C.E.	14208	504	28.19	7-64	18	1	—
Warner, A.E.	707	19	37.21	4-73	—	—	—
Wasim Bari	30	1	30.00	1-11	—	—	—
Wasim Raja	13881	490	28.32	8-65	28	5	—
Watkinson, M.	45	1	45.00	1-24	—	—	—
Watts, A.	31	0	—	—	—	—	—
Webster, A.J.	734	15	48.93	5-87	1	—	—
Weightman, N.I.	4	0	—	—	—	—	—
Wells, A.P.	42	0	—	—	—	—	—
Wells, C.M.	1449	35	41.40	4-23	—	—	—
Wenlock, D.A.	268	7	38.28	3-50	—	—	—
Weston, M.J.	354	6	59.00	3-42	—	—	—
Whiteley, J.P.	2410	70	34.42	4-14	—	—	—
Wild, D.J.	488	7	69.71	2-15	—	—	—
Willey, P.	14225	491	28.97	7-37	20	3	—
Williams, N.F.	819	23	35.60	4-38	—	—	—
Williams, R.G.	5841	167	34.97	7-73	6	—	—
Willis, R.G.D.	19512	796	24.51	8-32	32	2	—
Willows, A.	242	8	30.25	4-33	—	—	—
Wilson, P.H.L.	2381	80	29.76	5-56	1	—	—
Wood, B.	9086	298	30.48	7-52	8	—	—
Wood, L.J.	182	4	45.50	4-124	—	—	—
Woolmer, R.A.	10647	405	26.28	7-47	12	1	—
Wootton, S.H.	7	0	—	—	—	—	—
Wright, J.G.	67	1	67.00	1-4	—	—	—
Yadav, N.S.	3864	110	35.12	6-64	1	—	—
Yardley, T.J.	38	0	—	—	—	—	—
Yashpal Sharma	633	20	31.65	3-98	—	—	—
Younis Ahmed	1605	39	41.15	4-10	—	—	—
Zaheer Abbas	828	25	33.12	5-15	1	—	—

THE 1982 FIRST-CLASS SEASON
STATISTICAL HIGHLIGHTS
Compiled by Brian Croudy

HIGHEST INNINGS TOTALS

616-6d	Kent v Oxford University at Oxford
594	England v India at The Oval (3rd Test)
536-7d	Surrey v Worcestershire at Worcester
523-4d	Warwickshire v Lancashire at Southport
502	Essex v Warwickshire at Colchester
501-1d	Worcestershire v Warwickshire at Worcester
498-7d	Lancashire v Warwickshire at Birmingham
478-5d	Middlesex v Oxford University at Oxford
473	Derbyshire v Yorkshire at Derby
467-4d	Pakistan v Worcestershire at Worcester
463	Somerset v Glamorgan at Taunton
461-5d	Middlesex v Yorkshire at Lords
458-8d	Hampshire v Lancashire at Southampton
450-2d	Pakistan v Sussex at Hove
450-9d	Surrey v Nottinghamshire at The Oval
449-6d	Essex v Northamptonshire at Northampton
447-7d	Warwickshire v India at Birmingham
447-8d	Warwickshire v Surrey at Birmingham
446	Warwickshire v Gloucestershire at Nuneaton
438-9d	Middlesex v Kent at Tunbridge Wells
438-5d	Somerset v Gloucestershire at Bristol
435-2d	Hampshire v Glamorgan at Portsmouth
434-5d	Gloucestershire v Warwickshire at Nuneaton
434-7d	Sussex v Kent at Hove
433	England v India at Lord's (1st Test)
428-8d	Pakistan v England at Lord's (2nd Test)
425	England v India at Manchester (2nd Test)
424-8d	Kent v Sussex at Tunbridge Wells
424	Yorkshire v Worcestershire at Sheffield
414-6d	Lancashire v Warwickshire at Southport
411-5d	Gloucestershire v Oxford University at Oxford
411-6d	Leicestershire v Glamorgan at Leicester
410	India v England at The Oval (3rd Test)
401-2d	Worcestershire v Oxford University at Oxford
401-9d	Surrey v Derbyshire at Derby
401	Northamptonshire v Gloucestershire at Bristol
400-5d	Northamptonshire v Derbyshire at Northampton
400-5d	Nottinghamshire v Derbyshire at Nottingham
400	Nottinghamshire v Leicestershire at Nottingham

LOWEST INNINGS TOTALS

43 (9)	Warwickshire v Sussex at Birmingham
56	Hampshire v Nottinghamshire at Nottingham
57	Somerset v Middlesex at Weston-super-Mare
57	Kent v Nottinghamshire at Nottingham
64	Worcestershire v Essex at Ilford

70	Gloucestershire v Sussex at Bristol
70 (9)	Nottinghamshire v Leicestershire at Leicester
70 (9)	Hampshire v Nottinghamshire at Nottingham
70 (9)	Gloucestershire v Leicestershire at Leicester
72	Somerset v Hampshire at Bournemouth
78	Somerset v Glamorgan at Taunton
84	Sussex v Northamptonshire at Eastbourne
84	Gloucestershire v Hampshire at Bournemouth
85 (9)	Worcestershire v Sussex at Hove
90	Kent v Middlesex at Tunbridge Wells
98	Gloucestershire v Sussex at Hastings
99	Hampshire v Gloucestershire at Bristol
99	Cambridge University v Essex at Cambridge

DOUBLE CENTURIES

311*	G.M. Turner for Worcestershire v Warwickshire at Worcester (County Record)
254	G.W. Humpage for Warwickshire v Lancashire at Southport
239*	G.M. Turner for Worcestershire v Oxford University at Oxford
235	A.I. Kallicharran for Warwickshire v Worcestershire at Worcester
230*	A.I. Kallicharran for Warwickshire v Lancashire at Southport
212*	A.W. Stovold for Gloucestershire v Northamptonshire at Northampton
211*	Mudassar Nazar for Pakistan v Sussex at Hove
210	A.I. Kallicharran for Warwickshire v Leicestershire at Leicester
209*	S.P. Henderson for Cambridge University v Middlesex at Cambridge
208	I.T. Botham for England v India at The Oval (3rd Test)
206*	M.C.J. Nicholas for Hampshire v Oxford University at Oxford
203*	Mohsin Khan for Pakistan v Leicestershire at Leicester
203*	W.N. Slack for Middlesex v Oxford University at Oxford
203	R.A. Woolmer for Kent v Sussex at Tunbridge Wells
200*	J.A. Ormrod for Worcestershire v Gloucestershire at Worcester
200	Mohsin Khan for Pakistan v England at Lord's (2nd Test)

OPENING BATSMAN CARRYING HIS BAT

157* (270)	C.G. Greenidge for Hampshire v Glamorgan at Cardiff
141* (259)	J.G. Wright for Derbyshire v Nottinghamshire at Chesterfield
118* (223)	W. Larkins for Northamptonshire v Yorkshire at Northampton
114* (246)	J.C. Balderstone for Leicestershire v Essex at Colchester

CENTURY IN EACH INNINGS

123 & 119	R.J. Boyd-Moss for Cambridge University v Warwickshire at Cambridge
126 & 128*	G. Fowler for Lancashire v Warwickshire at Southport
164* & 123*	P.N. Kirsten for Derbyshire v Surrey at Derby
132* & 102*	J.W. Lloyds for Somerset v Northamptonshire at Northampton
162* & 107	Zaheer Abbas for Gloucestershire v Lancashire at Gloucester

CENTURY BEFORE LUNCH

B.F. Davison for Leicestershire v Middlesex at Uxbridge
G.M. Turner for Worcestershire v Lancashire at Worcester
G.M. Turner for Worcestershire v Warwickshire at Worcester
Zaheer Abbas for Pakistan v Derbyshire at Chesterfield

FOUR CENTURIES IN AN INNINGS

126	R.A. Woolmer
127	N.R. Taylor
125	C.J. Tavaré
120	M.R. Benson

for Kent v Oxford University at Oxford

BATSMAN MONOPOLISING THE SCORE WHILST AT THE WICKET

93/102	M.J. Weston for Worcestershire v Pakistan at Worcester
104*/134	P.A. Todd for Nottinghamshire v Oxford University at Oxford
311*/501	G.M. Turner for Worcestershire v Warwickshire at Worcester

HIGHEST PARTNERSHIPS

470	4th	A.I. Kallicharran and G.W. Humpage for Warwickshire v Lancashire at Southport (English and County Record)
319	1st	Mudassar Nazar and Mohsin Khan for Pakistan v Sussex at Hove (Highest for Pakistan team in England)
316*	2nd	A.R. Butcher and D.M. Smith for Surrey v Warwickshire at Birmingham
291	1st	G.M. Turner and J.A. Ormrod for Worcestershire v Warwickshire at Worcester
278	1st	G. Cook and W. Larkins for Northamptonshire v Yorkshire at Middlesbrough
256*	6th	C.J. Tavaré and A.P.E. Knott for Kent v Essex at Chelmsford
251*	3rd	C.G. Greenidge and T.E. Jesty for Hampshire v Glamorgan at Portsmouth
246*	3rd	J.A. Ormrod and Younis Ahmed for Worcestershire v Gloucestershire at Worcester
242	1st	J.G. Wright and I.S. Anderson for Derbyshire v Yorkshire at Derby
241	3rd	W.N. Slack and K.P. Tomlins for Middlesex v Oxford University at Oxford
237	4th	M.W. Gatting and R.O. Butcher for Middlesex v Yorkshire at Leeds
232*	2nd	G.P. Howarth and D.M. Smith for Surrey v Yorkshire at The Oval
229	3rd	C.J. Tavaré and M.R. Benson for Kent v Oxford University at Oxford
228*	3rd	Mohsin Khan and Zaheer Abbas for Pakistan v Worcestershire at Worcester
227	1st	R.A. Woolmer and N.R. Taylor for Kent v Oxford University at Oxford
227	1st	A.R. Butcher and R.D.V. Knight for Surrey v Oxford University at Oxford
226*	1st	G. Fowler and D. Lloyd for Lancashire v Warwickshire at Southport
226	1st	Mohsin Khan and Mansoor Akhtar for Pakistan v Somerset at Taunton
225	2nd	A.R. Butcher and D.M. Smith for Surrey v Worcestershire at Worcester
222	5th	P.A. Slocombe and B.C. Rose for Somerset v Gloucestershire at Bristol
221*	3rd	Mudassar Nazar and Zaheer Abbas for Pakistan v Derbyshire at Chesterfield
220	4th	J.P.C. Mills and S.P. Henderson for Cambridge University v Middlesex at Cambridge
215	4th	A.T. Lamb and P. Willey for Northamptonshire v Oxford University at Oxford

210*	2nd	G.M. Turner and D.N. Patel for Worcestershire v Warwickshire at Worcester
207	3rd	J.C. Balderstone and B.F. Davison for Leicestershire v Glamorgan at Leicester
206	3rd	I.V.A. Richards and B.C. Rose for Somerset v Warwickshire at Birmingham
201	4th	R.C. Ontong and J.A. Hopkins for Glamorgan v Surrey at Guildford
172	10th	A. Needham and R.D. Jackman for Surrey v Lancashire at Manchester
149	10th	G. Boycott and G.B. Stevenson for Yorkshire v Warwickshire at Birmingham (County Record)
143	10th	T. Davies and S.A.B. Daniels for Glamorgan v Gloucestershire at Swansea (County Record)

No. 11 BATSMAN SCORING A CENTURY

115*	G.B. Stevenson for Yorkshire v Warwickshire at Birmingham

EIGHT WICKETS IN AN INNINGS

9-61	W.W. Daniel for Middlesex v Glamorgan at Swansea
8-56	A.M.E. Roberts for Leicestershire v Glamorgan at Leicester
8-68	K.I. Hodgson for Cambridge University v Glamorgan at Cambridge
8-70	G. Miller for Derbyshire v Leicestershire at Coalville
8-71	M.D. Marshall for Hampshire v Worcestershire at Southampton
8-80	P.H. Edmonds for Middlesex v Sussex at Lord's

THIRTEEN WICKETS IN A MATCH

14-94	(6-38 and 8-56) A.M.E. Roberts for Leicestershire v Glamorgan at Leicester
13 122	(7 44 and 6 78) Abdul Qadir for Pakistan v Sussex at Hove

FIVE CATCHES IN AN INNINGS BY A FIELDER

C.S. Cowdrey for Kent v Sussex at Hove
G.A. Gooch for Essex v Gloucestershire at Cheltenham

SIX CATCHES IN A MATCH BY A FIELDER

J. Abrahams for Lancashire v Nottinghamshire at Nottingham
C.S. Cowdrey for Kent v Sussex at Hove
G. Miller for Derbyshire v Somerset at Derby

SIX DISMISSALS AND OVER IN AN INNINGS BY A WICKET-KEEPER

7	D.L. Bairstow for Yorkshire v Derbyshire at Scarborough (Yorkshire Record)
6	B.N. French for Nottinghamshire v Essex at Nottingham
6	E.W. Jones for Glamorgan v Essex at Cardiff
6	A.P.E. Knott for Kent v Hampshire at Maidstone
6	D.J.S. Taylor for Somerset v Hampshire at Bath

EIGHT DISMISSALS AND OVER IN A MATCH BY A WICKET-KEEPER

11	(11 ct) D.L. Bairstow for Yorkshire v Derbyshire at Scarborough (equals World Record)
8	(8 ct) D.E. East for Essex v Derbyshire at Southend
8	(8 ct) E.W. Jones for Glamorgan v Essex at Cardiff
8	(7ct 1st) A.P.E. Knott for Kent v Leicestershire at Canterbury

FIRST TO TARGETS

1000 runs: M.W. Gatting on 26th June
2000 runs: A.I. Kallicharran on 14th September
100 wickets: M.D. Marshall on 25th August

MOST EXTRAS CONCEDED IN AN INNINGS

56 by Glamorgan v Hampshire at Portsmouth

FIRST-CLASS CRICKET RECORDS

COMPLETE TO END OF 1982 SEASON

Highest Innings Totals

1107	Victoria v New South Wales (Melbourne)	1926-27
1059	Victoria v Tasmania (Melbourne)	1922-23
951-7d	Sind v Baluchistan (Karachi)	1973-74
918	New South Wales v South Australia (Sydney)	1900-01
912-8d	Holkar v Mysore (Indore)	1945-46
910-6d	Railways v Dera Ismail Khan (Lahore)	1964-65
903-7d	England v Australia (Oval)	1938
887	Yorkshire v Warwickshire (Birmingham)	1896
849	England v West Indies (Kingston)	1929-30

NB. There are 22 instances of a side making 800 runs or more in an innings, the last occasion being 951-7 declared by Sind as above.

Lowest Innings Totals

12*	Oxford University v MCC and Ground (Oxford)	1877
12	Northamptonshire v Gloucestershire (Gloucester)	1907
13	Auckland v Canterbury (Auckland)	1877-78
13	Nottinghamshire v Yorkshire (Nottingham)	1901
15	MCC v Surrey (Lord's)	1839
15*	Victoria v MCC (Melbourne)	1903-04
15*	Northamptonshire v Yorkshire (Northampton)	1908
15	Hampshire v Warwickshire (Birmingham)	1922
16	Derbyshire v Nottinghamshire (Nottingham)	1879
16	MCC and Ground v Surrey (Lord's)	1872
16	Surrey v Nottinghamshire (Oval)	1880
16	Warwickshire v Kent (Tonbridge)	1913
16	Trinidad v Barbados (Bridgetown)	1941-42
16	Border v Natal (East London)	1959-60

*Batted one man short

NB. There are 25 instances of a side making less than 20 in an innings, the last occasion being 16 and 18 by Border v Natal at East London in 1959-60. The total of 34 is the lowest by one side in a match.

Highest Aggregates in a Match

2376	(38)	Bombay v Maharashtra (Poona)	1948-49
2078	(40)	Bombay v Holkar (Bombay)	1944-45
1981	(35)	South Africa v England (Durban)	1938-39
1929	(39)	New South Wales v South Australia (Sydney)	1925-26
1911	(34)	New South Wales v Victoria (Sydney)	1908-09
1905	(40)	Otago v Wellington (Dunedin)	1923-24

219

In England the highest are:

1723	(31)	England v Australia (Leeds) 5 day match	1948
1601	(29)	England v Australia (Lord's) 4 day match	1930
1507	(28)	England v West Indies (Oval) 5 day match	1976
1502	(28)	MCC v New Zealanders (Lord's)	1927
1499	(31)	T.N. Pearce's XI v Australians (Scarborough)	1961
1496	(24)	England v Australia (Nottingham) 4 day match	1938
1494	(37)	England v Australia (Oval) 4 day match	1934
1492	(33)	Worcestershire v Oxford U (Worcester)	1904
1477	(32)	Hampshire v Oxford U (Southampton)	1913
1477	(33)	England v South Africa (Oval) 4 day match	1947
1475	(27)	Northamptonshire v Surrey (Northampton)	1920

Lowest Aggregate in a Match

105	(31)	MCC v Australia (Lord's)	1878
134	(30)	England v The B's (Lord's)	1831
147	(40)	Kent v Sussex (Sevenoaks)	1828
149	(30)	England v Kent (Lord's)	1858
150	(30)	Cambridge Town v MCC (Chatteris)	1832
151	(30)	Canterbury v Otago (Christchurch)	1866-67
153	(37)	MCC v Sussex (Lord's)	1843
153	(31)	Otago v Canterbury (Dunedin)	1896-97
156	(30)	Nelson v Wellington (Nelson)	1885-86
158	(22)	Surrey v Worcestershire (Oval)	1954

Wickets that fell are given in parentheses.

Tie Matches

Due to the change of law made in 1948 for tie matches, a tie is now a rarity. The law states that only if the match is played out and the scores are equal is the result a tie.

The most recent tied matches are as follows:

Yorkshire (351-4d & 113) v Leicestershire (328 & 136) at Huddersfield	1954
Sussex (172 & 120) v Hampshire (153 & 139) at Eastbourne	1955
Victoria (244 & 197) v New South Wales (281 & 160) at Melbourne (St. Kilda)	1956-57
(The first tie in Sheffield Shield cricket)	
T.N. Pearce's XI (313-7d & 258) v New Zealanders (268 & 303-8d) at Scarborough	1958
Essex (364-6d & 176-8d) v Gloucestershire (329 & 211) at Leyton	1959
Australia (505 & 232) v West Indies (453 & 284) at Brisbane	1960-61
(The first tie in Test cricket)	
Bahawalpur (123 & 282) v Lahore B (127 & 278) at Bahawalpur	1961-62
Middlesex (327-5d & 123-9d v Hampshire (277 & 173) at Portsmouth	1967
England XI (312-8d & 190-3d) v England Under-25 XI (320-9d & 182) at Scarborough	1968
Yorkshire (106-9d & 207) v Middlesex (102 & 211) at Bradford	1973
Sussex (245 & 173-5d) v Essex (200-8d & 218) at Hove	1974
South Australia (431 & 171-7d) v Queensland (340-8d & 262) at Adelaide	1976-77
England XI (296-6d & 104) v Central Districts (198 & 202) at New Plymouth	1977-78
Peshawar (139 & 188) v Allied Bank (240 & 87) at Peshawar	1979-80

Highest Individual Scores

499	Hanif Mohammad, Karachi v Bahawalpur (Karachi)	1958-59
452*	D.G. Bradman, New South Wales v Queensland (Sydney)	1929-30
443*	B.B. Nimbalkar, Maharashtra v Kathiawar (Poona)	1948-49
437	W.H. Ponsford, Victoria v Queensland (Melbourne)	1927-28
429	W.H. Ponsford, Victoria v Tasmania (Melbourne)	1922-23
428	Aftab Baloch, Sind v Baluchistan (Karachi)	1973-74
424	A.C. MacLaren, Lancashire v Somerset (Taunton)	1895
385	B. Sutcliffe, Otago v Canterbury (Christchurch)	1952-53
383	C.W. Gregory, New South Wales v Queensland (Brisbane)	1906-07
369	D.G. Bradman, South Australia v Tasmania (Adelaide)	1935-36
365*	C. Hill, South Australia v New South Wales (Adelaide)	1900-01
365*	G.S. Sobers, West Indies v Pakistan (Kingston)	1957-58
364	L. Hutton, England v Australia (Oval)	1938
359*	V.M. Merchant, Bombay v Maharashtra (Bombay)	1943-44
359	R.B. Simpson, New South Wales v Queensland (Brisbane)	1963-64
357*	R. Abel, Surrey v Somerset (Oval)	1899
357	D.G. Bradman, South Australia v Victoria (Melbourne)	1935-36
356	B.A. Richards, South Australia v Western Australia (Perth)	1970-71
355	B. Sutcliffe, Otago v Auckland (Dunedin)	1949-50
352	W.H. Ponsford, Victoria v New South Wales (Melbourne)	1926-27
350	Rashid Israr, Habib Bank v National Bank (Lahore)	1976-77

NB. There are 93 instances of a batsman scoring 300 or more in an innings, the last occasion being 311* by G.M. Turner for Worcestershire v Warwickshire (Worcester) 1982.

Most Centuries in a Season

18	D.C.S. Compton	1947
16	J.B. Hobbs	1925
15	W.R. Hammond	1938
14	H. Sutcliffe	1932

Most Centuries in an Innings

6	for Holkar v Mysore (Indore)	1945-46
5	for New South Wales v South Australia (Sydney)	1900-01
5	for Australia v West Indies (Kingston)	1954-55

Most Centuries in Successive Innings

6	C.B. Fry	1901
6	D.G. Bradman	1938-39
6	M.J. Procter	1970-71
5	E.D. Weekes	1955-56

NB. The feat of scoring 4 centuries in successive innings has been achieved on 31 occasions.

Two Double Centuries in a Match

A.E. Fagg, 244 and 202* for Kent v Essex (Colchester)   1938

A Double Century and a Century in a Match

C.B. Fry, 125 and 229, Sussex v Surrey (Hove)   1900
W.W. Armstrong, 157* and 245, Victoria v South Australia (Melbourne) 1920-21
H.T.W. Hardinge, 207 and 102* for Kent v Surrey (Blackheath)   1921
C.P. Mead, 113 and 224, Hampshire v Sussex (Horsham)   1921
K.S. Duleepsinhji, 115 and 246, Sussex v Kent (Hastings)   1929
D.G. Bradman, 124 and 225, Woodfull's XI v Ryder's XI (Sydney)   1929-30
B. Sutcliffe, 243 and 100*, New Zealanders v Essex (Southend)   1949
M.R. Hallam, 210* and 157, Leicestershire v Glamorgan (Leicester)   1959
M.R. Hallam, 203* and 143* Leicestershire v Sussex (Worthing)   1961
Hanumant Singh, 109 and 213*, Rajasthan v Bombay (Bombay)   1966-67
Salahuddin, 256 and 102*, Karachi v East Pakistan (Karachi)   1968-69
K.D. Walters, 242 and 103, Australia v West Indies (Sydney)   1968-69
S.M. Gavaskar, 124 and 220, India v West Indies (Port of Spain)   1970-71
L.G. Rowe, 214 and 100*, West Indies v New Zealand (Kingston)   1971-72
G.S. Chappell, 247* and 133, Australia v New Zealand (Wellington)   1973-74
L. Baichan, 216* and 102, Berbice v Demerara (Georgetown)   1973-74
Zaheer Abbas, 216* and 156*, Gloucestershire v Surrey (Oval)   1976
Zaheer Abbas, 230* and 104*, Gloucestershire v Kent (Canterbury)   1976
Zaheer Abbas, 205* and 108*, Gloucestershire v Sussex (Cheltenham)   1977
Saadat Ali, 141 and 222, Income Tax v Multan (Multan)   1977-78
Talat Ali, 214* and 104, Pakistan International Airways v Punjab (Lahore) 1978-79
Shafiq Ahmed, 129 and 217*, National Bank v Muslim Commercial Bank
  (Karachi)   1978-79
D.W. Randall, 209 and 146, Nottinghamshire v Middlesex (Nottingham)   1979
Zaheer Abbas, 215* and 150*, Gloucestershire v Somerset (Bath)   1981

Two Centuries in a Match on Most Occasions

7 W.R. Hammond, Zaheer Abbas   6 J.B. Hobbs, G.M. Turner   5 C.B. Fry

Most Centuries

J.B. Hobbs, 197 (175 in England); E.H. Hendren, 170 (151); W.R. Hammond, 167 (134); C.P. Mead, 153 (145); H. Sutcliffe, 149 (135); F.E. Woolley, 145 (135); G. Boycott, 132 (105); L. Hutton, 129 (105); W.G. Grace, 124 (123); D.C.S. Compton, 123 (92); T.W. Graveney, 122 (91); D.G. Bradman, 117 (41); M.C. Cowdrey, 107 (80); A. Sandham, 107 (87); T.W. Hayward, 104 (100); J.H. Edrich, 103 (90); G.M. Turner, 103 (78); L.E.G. Ames, 102 (89); G.E. Tyldesley, 102 (94).

Highest Individual Batting Aggregate in a Season

Runs		Season	M	Innings	NO	HS	Avge	100s
3,816	D.C.S. Compton	1947	30	50	8	246	90.85	18
3,539	W.J. Edrich	1947	30	52	8	267*	80.43	12

NB. *The feat of scoring 3,000 runs in a season has been achieved on 28 occasions, the last instance being by W.E. Alley (3,019 runs, av. 59.96) in 1961.*
Since the reduction of the matches in the County Championship in 1969, the highest aggregate in a season is 2,554 runs (av. 75.11) by Zaheer Abbas in 1976.

Partnerships for First Wicket

561	Waheed Mirza and Mansoor Akhtar, Karachi Whites v Quetta (Karachi)	1976-77
555	H. Sutcliffe and P. Holmes, Yorkshire v Essex (Leyton)	1932
554	J.T. Brown and J. Tunnicliffe, Yorkshire v Derbyshire (Chesterfield)	1898
490	E.H. Bowley and J.G. Langridge, Sussex v Middlesex (Hove)	1933
456	W.H. Ponsford and E.R. Mayne, Victoria v Queensland (Melbourne)	1923-24
451*	S. Desai and R.M.H. Binny, Karnataka v Kerala (Chikmagalur)	1977-78
428	J.B. Hobbs and A. Sandham, Surrey v Oxford U (Oval)	1926
424	J.F.W. Nicholson and I.J. Siedle, Natal v Orange Free State (Bloemfontein)	1926-27
418	Kamal Najamuddin and Khalid Alvi, Karachi v Railways (Karachi)	1980-81
413	V. Mankad and P. Roy, India v New Zealand (Madras)	1955-56
405	C.P.S. Chauhan and M. Gupte, Maharashtra v Vidarbha (Poona)	1972-73

Partnerships for Second Wicket

465*	J.A. Jameson and R.B. Kanhai, Warwickshire v Gloucestershire (Birmingham)	1974
455	K.V. Bhandarkar and B.B. Nimbalkar, Maharashtra v Kathiawar (Poona)	1948-49
451	D.G. Bradman and W.H. Ponsford, Australia v England (Oval)	1934
446	C.C. Hunte and G.S. Sobers, West Indies v Pakistan (Kingston)	1957-58
429*	J.G. Dewes and G.H.G. Doggart, Cambridge U v Essex (Cambridge)	1949
426	Arshad Pervez and Mohsin Khan, Habib Bank v Income Tax Department (Lahore)	1977-78
398	W. Gunn and A. Shrewsbury, Nottinghamshire v Sussex (Nottingham)	1890

Partnerships for Third Wicket

456	Aslam Ali and Khalid Irtiza, United Bank v Multan (Karachi)	1975-76
445	P.E. Whitelaw and W.N. Carson, Auckland v Otago (Dunedin)	1936-37
434	J.B. Stollmeyer and G.E. Gomez, Trinidad v British Guiana (Port of Spain)	1946-47
424*	W.J. Edrich and D.C.S. Compton, Middlesex v Somerset (Lord's)	1948
410	R.S. Modi and L. Amarnath, India v Rest (Calcutta)	1946-47
399	R.T. Simpson and D.C.S. Compton, MCC v NE Transvaal (Benoni)	1948-49

Partnerships for Fourth Wicket

577	Gul Mahomed and V.S. Hazare, Baroda v Holkar (Baroda)	1946-47
574*	C.L. Walcott and F.M.M. Worrell, Barbados v Trinidad (Port of Spain)	1945-46
502*	F.M.M. Worrell and J.D.C. Goddard, Barbados v Trinidad (Bridgetown)	1943-44
470	A.I. Kallicharran and G.W. Humpage, Warwickshire v Lancashire (Southport)	1982
448	R. Abel and T.W. Hayward, Surrey v Yorkshire (Oval)	1899
424	I.S. Lee and S.O. Quin, Victoria v Tasmania (Melbourne)	1933-34
411	P.B.H. May and M.C. Cowdrey, England v West Indies (Birmingham)	1957
410	G. Abraham and B. Pandit, Kerala v Andhra (Palghat)	1959-60
402	W. Watson and T.W. Graveney, MCC v British Guiana (Georgetown)	1953-54
402	R.B. Kanhai and K. Ibadulla, Warwickshire v Nottinghamshire (Nottingham)	1968

223

Partnerships for Fifth Wicket

405	D.G. Bradman and S.G. Barnes, Australia v England (Sydney)	1946-47
397	W. Bardsley and C. Kellaway, New South Wales v South Australia (Sydney)	1920-21
393	E.G. Arnold and W.B. Burns, Worcestershire v Warwickshire (Birmingham)	1909
360	U.M. Merchant and M.N. Raiji, Bombay v Hyderabad (Bombay)	1947-48
355	Altaf Shah and Tanq Bashir, HBFC v Multan (Multan)	1976-77

Partnerships for Sixth Wicket

487*	G.A. Headley and C.C. Passailaigue, Jamaica v Lord Tennyson's XI (Kingston)	1931-32
428	W.W. Armstrong and M.A. Noble, Australians v Sussex (Hove)	1902
411	R.M. Poore and E.G. Wynyard, Hampshire v Somerset (Taunton)	1899
376	R. Subba Row and A. Lightfoot, Northamptonshire v Surrey (Oval)	1958
371	V.M. Merchant and R.S. Modi, Bombay v Maharashtra (Bombay)	1943-44

Partnerships for Seventh Wicket

347	D.S. Atkinson and C.C. Depeiza, West Indies v Australia (Bridgetown)	1954-55
344	K.S. Ranjitsinhji and W. Newham, Sussex v Essex (Leyton)	1902
340	K.J. Key and H. Philipson, Oxford U v Middlesex (Chiswick Park)	1887
336	F.C.W. Newman and C.R. Maxwell, Cahn's XI v Leicestershire (Nottingham)	1935
335	C.W. Andrews and E.C. Bensted, Queensland v New South Wales (Sydney)	1934-35

Partnerships for Eighth Wicket

433	V.T. Trumper and A. Sims, Australians v Canterbury (Christchurch)	1913-14
292	R. Peel and Lord Hawke, Yorkshire v Warwickshire (Birmingham)	1896
270	V.T. Trumper and E.P. Barbour, New South Wales v Victoria (Sydney)	1912-13
263	D.R. Wilcox and R.M. Taylor, Essex v Warwickshire (Southend)	1946
255	E.A.V. Williams and E.A. Martindale, Barbados v Trinidad (Bridgetown)	1935-36

Partnerships for Ninth Wicket

283	A.R. Warren and J. Chapman, Derbyshire v Warwickshire (Blackwell)	1910
251	J.W.H.T. Douglas and S.N. Hare, Essex v Derbyshire (Leyton)	1921
245	V.S. Hazare and N.D. Nagarwalla, Maharashtra v Baroda (Poona)	1939-40
239	H.B. Cave and I.B. Leggat, Central Districts v Otago (Dunedin)	1952-53
232	C. Hill and E. Walkley, South Australia v New South Wales (Adelaide)	1900-01

Partnerships for Tenth Wicket

307	A.F. Kippax and J.E.H. Hooker, New South Wales v Victoria (Melbourne)	1928-29
249	C.T. Sarwate and S.N. Bannerjee, Indians v Surrey (Oval)	1946
235	F.E. Woolley and A. Fielder, Kent v Worcestershire (Stourbridge)	1909
230	R.W. Nicholls and W. Roche, Middlesex v Kent (Lord's)	1899
228	R. Illingworth and K. Higgs, Leicestershire v Northamptonshire (Leicester)	1977
218	F.H. Vigar and T.P.B. Smith, Essex v Derbyshire (Chesterfield)	1947

BOWLING
Most Wickets in a Season

W		Season	M	O	M	R	Avge
304	A.P. Freeman	1928	37	1976.1	423	5489	18.05
298	A.P. Freeman	1933	33	2039	651	4549	15.26

NB. The feat of taking 250 wickets in a season has been achieved on 12 occasions, the last instance being by A.P. Freeman in 1933 as above. 200 or more wickets in a season have been taken on 59 occasions, the last instance being by G.A.R. Lock (212 wkts, avge 12.02) in 1957.

The most wickets taken in a season since the reduction of County Championship matches in 1969 are as follows.

W		Season	M	O	M	R	Avge
134	M.D. Marshall	1982	22	822	225	2108	15.73
131	L.R. Gibbs	1971	23	1024.1	295	2475	18.89
121	R.D. Jackman	1980	23	746.2	220	1864	15.40

NB. 100 wickets in a season have been taken on 32 occasions since 1969.

All Ten Wickets in an Innings

The feat has been achieved on 71 occasions.
On three occasions: A.P. Freeman, 1929, 1930 and 1931.
On two occasions: J.C. Laker, 1956, H. Verity, 1931 and 1932, V.E. Walker, 1859 and 1865.
Instances since the war:
W.E. Hollies, Warwickshire v Nottinghamshire (Birmingham) 1946; J.M. Sims of Middlesex playing for East v West (Kingston) 1948; J.K.R. Graveney, Gloucestershire v Derbyshire (Chesterfield) 1949; T.E. Bailey, Essex v Lancashire (Clacton) 1949; R. Berry, Lancashire v Worcestershire (Blackpool) 1953; S.P. Gupte, Bombay v Pakistan Services (Bombay), 1954-55; J.C. Laker, Surrey v Australians (Oval) 1956; J.C. Laker, England v Australia (Manchester) 1956; G.A.R. Lock, Surrey v Kent (Blackheath) 1956; K. Smales, Nottinghamshire v Gloucestershire (Stroud) 1956; P. Chatterjee, Bengal v Assam (Jorhat) 1956-57; J.D. Bannister, Warwickshire v Combined Services (Birmingham) 1959; A.J.G. Pearson, Cambridge U v Leicestershire (Loughborough) 1961; N.I. Thomson, Sussex v Warwickshire (Worthing) 1964; P.J. Allan, Queensland v Victoria (Melbourne) 1965-66; I. Brayshaw, Western Australia v Victoria (Perth) 1967-68; Shahid Mahmood, Karachi Whites v Khairpur (Karachi) 1969-70.

Nineteen Wickets in a Match

J.C. Laker 19-90 (9-37 and 10-53), England v Australia (Manchester) 1956.

Seventeen Wickets in a Match

The feat has been achieved on 18 occasions.

Instances between the two wars were: A.P. Freeman (for 67 runs), Kent v Sussex (Hove) 1922; F.C.L. Matthews (89 runs), Nottinghamshire v Northamptonshire (Nottingham) 1923; C.W.L. Parker (56 runs), Gloucestershire v Essex (Gloucester 1925; G.R. Cox (106 runs), Sussex v Warwickshire (Horsham) 1926; A.P. Freeman (92 runs), Kent v Warwickshire (Folkestone) 1932; H. Verity (91 runs), Yorkshire v Essex (Leyton) 1933; J.C. Clay (212 runs), Glamorgan v Worcestershire (Swansea) 1937; T.W.J. Goddard (106 runs), Gloucestershire v Kent (Bristol) 1939. There has been no instance since the last war.

Most Hat-tricks in a Career

7 D.V.P. Wright.

6 T.W.J. Goddard, C.W.L. Parker.

5 S. Haigh, V.W.C. Jupp, A.E.G. Rhodes, F.A. Tarrant.

NB.   Ten bowlers have achieved the feat on four occasions and 24 bowlers on three occasions.

The 'Double' Event

3,000 runs and 100 wickets: J.H. Parks, 1937.

2,000 runs and 200 wickets: G.H. Hirst, 1906.

2,000 runs and 100 wickets: F.E. Woolley (4), J.W. Hearne (3), G.H. Hirst (2), W. Rhodes (2), T.E. Bailey, D.E. Davies, W.G. Grace, G.L. Jessop, V.W.C. Jupp, James Langridge, F.A. Tarrant, C.L. Townsend, L.F. Townsend.

1,000 runs and 200 wickets: M.W. Tate (3), A.E. Trott (2), A.S. Kennedy.

Most 'Doubles': W. Rhodes (16), G.H. Hirst (14), V.W.C. Jupp (10).

'Double' in first season: D.B. Close, 1949. At the age of 18, Close is the youngest player ever to perform this feat.

The feat of scoring 1,000 runs and taking 100 wickets has been achieved on 302 occasions, the last instance being F.J. Titmus in 1967.

FIELDING

Most catches in a season:	78 W.R. Hammond	1928
	77 M.J. Stewart	1957
Most catches in a match:	10 W.R. Hammond, Gloucestershire v Surrey (Cheltenham)	1928
Most catches in an innings:	7 M.J. Stewart, Surrey v Northamptonshire (Northampton)	1957
	7 A.S. Brown, Gloucestershire v Nottinghamshire (Nottingham)	1966

WICKET-KEEPING

Most dismissals in a season:	127 (79ct, 48st), L.E.G. Ames	1929

NB.   The feat of making 100 dismissals in a season has been achieved on 12 occasions, the last instance being by R. Booth (100 dismissals–91ct, 9st) in 1964.

Most dismissals in a match:	12 E. Pooley (8 ct, 4 st) Surrey v Sussex (Oval)	1868
	12 D. Tallon (9 ct, 3 st), Queensland v New South Wales (Sydney)	1938-39
	12 H.B. Taber (9 ct, 3 st), New South Wales v South Australia (Adelaide)	1968-69
Most catches in a match:	11 A. Long, Surrey v Sussex (Hove)	1964
	11 R.W. Marsh, Western Australia v Victoria (Perth)	1975-76
	11 D.L. Bairstow, Yorkshire v Derbyshire (Scarborough)	1982
Most dismissals in an innings:	8 A.T.W. Grout (8 ct), Queensland v W. Australia (Brisbane)	1959-60

TEST CRICKET RECORDS

**COMPLETE TO THE END OF THE
AUSTRALIA v ENGLAND SERIES**

(but not including Pakistan v India)

HIGHEST INNINGS TOTALS

903-7d	England v Australia (Oval)	1938
849	England v West Indies (Kingston)	1929-30
790-3d	West Indies v Pakistan (Kingston)	1957-58
758-8d	Australia v West Indies (Kingston)	1954-55
729-6d	Australia v England (Lord's)	1930
701	Australia v England (Oval)	1934
695	Australia v England (Oval)	1930
687-8d	West Indies v England (Oval)	1976
681-8d	West Indies v England (Port of Spain)	1953-54
674	Australia v India (Adelaide)	1947-48
668	Australia v West Indies (Bridgetown)	1954-55
659-8d	Australia v England (Sydney)	1946-47
658-8d	England v Australia (Nottingham)	1938
657-8d	Pakistan v West Indies (Bridgetown)	1957-58
656-8d	Australia v England (Manchester)	1964
654-5	England v South Africa (Durban)	1938-39
652-8d	West Indies v England (Lord's)	1973
650-6d	Australia v West Indies (Bridgetown)	1964-65

The highest innings for the countries not mentioned above are:

644-7d	India v West Indies (Kanpur)	1978-79
622-9d	South Africa v Australia (Durban)	1969-70
551-9d	New Zealand v England (Lord's)	1973

NB. There are 44 instances of a side making 600 or more in an innings in a Test Match.

LOWEST INNINGS TOTALS

26	New Zealand v England (Auckland)	1954-55
30	South Africa v England (Port Elizabeth)	1895-96
30	South Africa v England (Birmingham)	1924
35	South Africa v England (Cape Town)	1898-99
36	Australia v England (Birmingham)	1902
36	South Africa v Australia (Melbourne)	1931-32
42	Australia v England (Sydney)	1887-88
42	New Zealand v Australia (Wellington)	1945-46
42†	India v England (Lord's)	1974
43	South Africa v England (Cape Town)	1888-89
44	Australia v England (Oval)	1896
45	England v Australia (Sydney)	1886-87
45	South Africa v Australia (Melbourne)	1931-32
47	South Africa v England (Cape Town)	1888-89
47	New Zealand v England (Lord's)	1958

†*Batted one man short*

The lowest innings for the countries not mentioned above are:

76	West Indies v Pakistan (Dacca)	1958-59
62	Pakistan v Australia (Perth)	1981-82

HIGHEST INDIVIDUAL INNINGS

365*	G.S. Sobers, West Indies v Pakistan (Kingston)	1957-58
364	L. Hutton, England v Australia (Oval)	1938
337	Hanif Mohammad, Pakistan v West Indies (Bridgetown)	1957-58
336*	W.R. Hammond, England v New Zealand (Auckland)	1932-33
334	D.G. Bradman, Australia v England (Leeds)	1930
325	A. Sandham, England v West Indies (Kingston)	1929-30
311	R.B. Simpson, Australia v England (Manchester)	1964
310*	J.H. Edrich, England v New Zealand (Leeds)	1965
307	R.M. Cowper, Australia v England (Melbourne)	1965-66
304	D.G. Bradman, Australia v England (Leeds)	1934
302	L.G. Rowe, West Indies v England (Bridgetown)	1973-74
299*	D.G. Bradman, Australia v South Africa (Adelaide)	1931-32
291	I.V.A. Richards, West Indies v England (Oval)	1976
287	R.E. Foster, England v Australia (Sydney)	1903-04
285*	P.B.H. May, England v West Indies (Birmingham)	1957
278	D.C.S. Compton, England v Pakistan (Nottingham)	1954
274	R.G. Pollock, South Africa v Australia (Durban)	1969-70
274	Zaheer Abbas, Pakistan v England (Birmingham)	1971
270*	G.A. Headley, West Indies v England (Kingston)	1934-35
270	D.G. Bradman, Australia v England (Melbourne)	1936-37
266	W.H. Ponsford, Australia v England (Oval)	1934
262*	D.L. Amiss, England v West Indies (Kingston)	1973-74
261	F.M.M. Worrell, West Indies v England (Nottingham)	1950
260	C.C. Hunte, West Indies v Pakistan (Kingston)	1957-58
259	G.M. Turner, New Zealand v West Indies (Georgetown)	1971-72
258	T.W. Graveney, England v West Indies (Nottingham)	1957
258	S.M. Nurse, West Indies v New Zealand (Christchurch)	1968-69
256	R.B. Kanhai, West Indies v India (Calcutta)	1958-59
256	K.F. Barrington, England v Australia (Manchester)	1964
255*	D.J. McGlew, South Africa v New Zealand (Wellington)	1952-53
254	D.G. Bradman, Australia v England (Leeds)	1930
251	W.R. Hammond, Australia v England (Sydney)	1928-29
250	K.D. Walters, Australia v New Zealand (Christchurch)	1976-77
250	S.F.A.F. Bacchus, West Indies v India (Kanpur)	1978-79

The highest individual innings for India is:

231	V. Mankad, India v New Zealand (Madras)	1955-56

NB. There are 124 instances of a double-century being scored in a Test Match.

HIGHEST RUN AGGREGATES IN A TEST RUBBER

R		Season	T	I	NO	HS	Avge	100s	50s
974	D.G. Bradman (A v E)	1930	5	7	0	334	139.14	4	—
905	W.R. Hammond (E v A)	1928-29	5	9	1	251	113.12	4	—
834	R.N. Harvey (A v SA)	1952-53	5	9	0	205	92.66	4	3
829	I.V.A. Richards (WI v E)	1976	4	7	0	291	118.42	3	2
827	C.L. Walcott (WI v A)	1954-55	5	10	0	155	82.70	5	2
824	G.S. Sobers (WI v P)	1957-58	5	8	2	365*	137.33	3	3
810	D.G. Bradman (A v E)	1936-37	5	9	0	270	90.00	3	1
806	D.G. Bradman (A v SA)	1931-32	5	5	1	299*	201.50	4	—
779	E.D. Weekes (WI v I)	1948-49	5	7	0	194	111.28	4	2
774	S.M. Gavaskar (I v WI)	1970-71	4	8	3	220	154.80	4	3
758	D.G. Bradman (A v E)	1934	5	8	0	304	94.75	2	1
753	D.C.S. Compton (E v SA)	1947	5	8	0	208	94.12	4	2

RECORD WICKET PARTNERSHIPS – ALL TEST CRICKET

1st	413	V. Mankad & P. Roy, I v NZ (Madras)	1955-56
2nd	451	W.H. Ponsford & D.G. Bradman, A v E (Oval)	1934
3rd	370	W.J. Edrich & D.C.S. Compton, E v SA (Lord's)	1947
4th	411	P.B.H. May & M.C. Cowdrey, E v WI (Birmingham)	1957
5th	405	S.G. Barnes & D.G. Bradman, A v E (Sydney)	1946-47
6th	346	J.H.W. Fingleton & D.G. Bradman, A v E (Melbourne)	1936-37
7th	347	D.S. Atkinson & C.C. Depeiza, WI v A (Bridgetown)	1954-55
8th	246	L.E.G. Ames & G.O.B. Allen, E v NZ (Lord's)	1931
9th	190	Asif Iqbal & Intikhab Alam, P v E (Oval)	1967
10th	151	B.F. Hastings & R.O. Collinge, NZ v P (Auckland)	1972-73

WICKET PARTNERSHIPS OF OVER 300

451	2nd W.H. Ponsford & D.G. Bradman, A v E (Oval)		1934
446	2nd C.C. Hunte & G.S. Sobers, WI v P (Kingston)		1957-58
413	1st V. Mankad & P. Roy, I v NZ (Madras)		1955-56
411	4th P.B.H. May & M.C. Cowdrey, E v WI (Birmingham)		1957
405	5th S.G. Barnes & D.B. Bradman, A v E (Sydney)		1946-47
399	4th G.S. Sobers & F.M.M. Worrell, WI v E (Bridgetown)		1959-60
388	4th W.H. Ponsford & D.G. Bradman, A v E (Leeds)		1934
387	1st G.M. Turner & T.W. Jarvis, NZ v WI (Georgetown)		1971-72
382	2nd L. Hutton & M. Leyland, E v A (Oval)		1938
382	1st W.M. Lawry & R.B. Simpson, A v WI (Bridgetown)		1964-65
370	3rd W.J. Edrich & D.C.S. Compton, E v SA (Lord's)		1947
369	2nd J.H. Edrich & K.F. Barrington, E v NZ (Leeds)		1965
359	1st L. Hutton & C. Washbrook, E v SA (Johannesburg)		1948-49
350	4th Mushtaq Mohammad & Asif Iqbal, P v NZ (Dunedin)		1972-73
347	7th D.S. Atkinson & C.C. Depeiza, WI v A (Bridgetown)		1954-55
346	6th J.H.W. Fingleton & D.G. Bradman, A v E (Melbourne)		1936-37
344*	2nd S.M. Gavaskar & D.B. Vengsarkar, I v WI (Calcutta)		1978-79
341	3rd E.J. Barlow & R.G. Pollock, SA v A (Adelaide)		1963-64
338	3rd E.D. Weekes & F.M.M. Worrell, WI v E (Port of Spain)		1953-54
336	4th W.M. Lawry & K.D. Walters, A v WI (Sydney)		1968-69
323	1st J.B. Hobbs & W. Rhodes, E v A (Melbourne)		1911-12
319	3rd A. Melville & A.D. Nourse, SA v E (Nottingham)		1947
316†	3rd G.R. Viswanath & Yashpal Sharma, I v E (Madras)		1981-82
308	7th Waqar Hasan & Imtiaz Ahmed, P v NZ (Lahore)		1955-56
303	I.V.A. Richards & A.I. Kallicharran, WI v E (Nottingham)		1976
301	2nd A.R. Morris & D.G. Bradman, A v E (Leeds)		1948

† 415 runs were added for this wicket in two separate partnerships. D.B. Vengsarkar retired hurt and was replaced by Yashpal Sharma after 99 runs had been added.

HAT-TRICKS

F.R. Spofforth	Australia v England (Melbourne)	1878-79
W. Bates	England v Australia (Melbourne)	1882-83
J. Briggs	England v Australia (Sydney)	1891-92
G.A. Lohmann	England v South Africa (Port Elizabeth)	1895-96
J.T. Hearne	England v Australia (Leeds)	1899
H. Trumble	Australia v England (Melbourne)	1901-02
H. Trumble	Australia v England (Melbourne)	1903-04
T.J. Matthews (2)*	Australia v South Africa (Manchester)	1912
M.J.C. Allom†	England v New Zealand (Christchurch)	1929-30
T.W.J. Goddard	England v South Africa (Johannesburg)	1938-39
P.J. Loader	England v West Indies (Leeds)	1957
L.F. Kline	Australia v South Africa (Cape Town)	1957-58
W.W. Hall	West Indies v Pakistan (Lahore)	1958-59
G.M. Griffin	South Africa v England (Lord's)	1960
L.R. Gibbs	West Indies v Australia (Adelaide)	1960-61
P.J. Petherick	New Zealand v Pakistan (Lahore)	1976-77

*In each innings. †Four wickets in five balls.

NINE OR TEN WICKETS IN AN INNINGS

10-53	J.C. Laker, England v Australia (Manchester)	1956
9-28	G.A. Lohmann, England v South Africa (Johannesburg)	1895-96
9-37	J.C. Laker, England v Australia (Manchester)	1956
9-69	J.M. Patel, India v Australia (Kanpur)	1959-60
9-86	Sarfraz Nawaz, Pakistan v Australia (Melbourne)	1978-79
9-95	J.M. Noreiga, West Indies v India (Port of Spain)	1970-71
9-102	S.P. Gupte, India v West Indies (Kanpur)	1958-59
9-103	S.F. Barnes, England v South Africa (Johannesburg)	1913-14
9-113	H.J. Tayfield, South Africa v England (Johannesburg)	1956-57
9-121	A.A. Mailey, Australia v England (Melbourne)	1920-21

NB.   There are 39 instances of a bowler taking 8 wickets in an innings in Tests.

FIFTEEN OR MORE WICKETS IN A MATCH

19-90	J.C. Laker, England v Australia (Manchester)	1956
17-159	S.F. Barnes, England v South Africa (Johannesburg)	1913-14
16-137	R.A.L. Massie, Australia v England (Lord's)	1972
15-28	J. Briggs, England v South Africa (Cape Town)	1888-89
15-45	G.A. Lohmann, England v South Africa (Port Elizabeth)	1895-96
15-99	C. Blythe, England v South Africa (Leeds)	1907
15-104	H. Verity, England v Australia (Lord's)	1934
15-124	W. Rhodes, England v Australia (Melbourne)	1903-04

NB.   There are 7 instances of a bowler taking 14 wickets in a Test Match.

HIGHEST WICKET AGGREGATES IN A TEST RUBBER

Wkts		Season	Tests	Balls	Mdns	Runs	Avge	5 wI	10 M
49	S.F. Barnes (E v SA)	1913–14	4	1356	56	536	10.93	7	3
46	J.C. Laker (E v A)	1956	5	1703	127	442	9.60	4	2
44	C.V. Grimmett (A v SA)	1935-36	5	2077	140	642	14.59	5	3
42	T.M. Alderman (A v E)	1981	6	1950	76	893	21.26	4	—
41	R.M. Hogg (A v E)	1978-79	6	1740	60	527	12.85	5	2
39	D.K. Lillee (A v E)	1981	6	1870	81	870	22.30	2	1
39	A.V. Bedser (E v A)	1953	5	1591	58	682	17.48	5	1
38	M.W. Tate (E v A)	1924-25	5	2528	62	881	23.18	5	1
37	W.J. Whitty (A v SA)	1910-11	5	1395	55	632	17.08	2	—
37	H.J. Tayfield (SA v E)	1956-57	5	2280	105	636	17.18	4	1
36	A.E.E. Vogler (SA v E)	1909-10	5	1349	33	783	21.75	4	1
36	A.A. Mailey (A v E)	1920-21	5	1465	27	946	26.27	4	2
35	G.A. Lohmann (E v SA)	1895-96	3	520	38	203	5.80	4	2
35	B.S. Chandrasekhar (I v E)	1972-73	5	1747	83	662	18.91	4	—

MOST WICKET-KEEPING DISMISSALS IN AN INNINGS

7 (7 ct)	Wasim Bari, Pakistan v New Zealand (Auckland)	1978-79
7 (7 ct)	R.W. Taylor, England v India (Bombay)	1979-80
6 (6 ct)	A.T.W. Grout, Australia v South Africa (Johannesburg)	1957-58
6 (6 ct)	D.T. Lindsay, South Africa v Australia (Johannesburg)	1966-67
6 (6 ct)	J.T. Murray, England v India (Lord's)	1967
6 (5 ct, 1 st)	S.M.H. Kirmani, India v New Zealand (Christchurch)	1975-76

MOST WICKET-KEEPING DISMISSALS IN A MATCH

10 (10 ct)	R.W. Taylor, England v India (Bombay)	1979-80

MOST WICKET-KEEPING DISMISSALS IN A SERIES

28 (28 ct)	R.W. Marsh, Australia v England	1982-83
26 (23 ct, 3 st)	J.H.B. Waite, South Africa v New Zealand	1961-62
26 (26 ct)	R.W. Marsh, Australia v West Indies	1975-76

HIGHEST WICKET-KEEPING DISMISSAL AGGREGATES

Total		Tests	Ct	St
334	R.W. Marsh (A)	91	322	12
269	A.P.E. Knott (E)	95	250	19
219	T.G. Evans (E)	91	173	46
189	D.L. Murray (WI)	62	181	8
187	A.T.W. Grout (A)	51	163	24
184	Wasim Bari (P)	67	160	24
151	R.W. Taylor (E)	47	144	7
141	J.H.B. Waite (SA)	50	124	17
137	S.M.H. Kirmani (I)	58	107	30
130	W.A.S. Oldfield (A)	54	78	52
114	J.M. Parks (E)	46	103	11

NB. Parks's figures include 2 catches as a fielder.

HIGHEST RUN AGGREGATES

Runs			Tests	Inns	NO	HS	Avge	100s	50s
8114	G. Boycott	(E)	108	193	23	246*	47.72	22	42
8032	G.S. Sobers	(WI)	93	160	21	365*	57.78	26	30
7624	M.C. Cowdrey	(E)	114	188	15	182	44.06	22	38
7249	W.R. Hammond	(E)	85	140	16	336*	58.45	22	24
6996	D.G. Bradman	(A)	52	80	10	334	99.94	29	13
6971	L. Hutton	(E)	79	138	15	364	56.67	19	33
6951	S.M. Gavaskar	(I)	79	139	10	221	53.88	25	30
6806	K.F. Barrington	(E)	82	131	15	256	58.67	20	35
6680	G.S. Chappell	(A)	81	144	18	247*	53.01	22	30
6227	R.B. Kanhai	(WI)	79	137	6	256	47.53	15	28
6149	R.N. Harvey	(A)	79	137	10	205	48.41	21	24
5946	G.R. Viswanath	(I)	85	147	10	222	43.40	14	34
5831	C.H. Lloyd	(WI)	85	143	10	242*	43.84	14	30
5807	D.C.S. Compton	(E)	78	131	15	278	50.06	17	28
5410	J.B. Hobbs	(E)	61	102	7	211	56.94	15	28
5357	K.D. Walters	(A)	74	125	14	250	48.26	15	33
5345	I.M. Chappell	(A)	75	136	10	196	42.42	14	26
5234	W.M. Lawry	(A)	67	123	12	210	47.15	13	27
5138	J.H. Edrich	(E)	77	127	9	310*	43.54	12	24
4882	T.W. Graveney	(E)	79	123	13	258	44.38	11	20
4869	R.B. Simpson	(A)	62	111	7	311	46.81	10	27
4737	I.R. Redpath	(A)	66	120	11	171	43.45	8	31
4555	H. Sutcliffe	(E)	54	84	9	194	60.73	16	23
4537	P.B.H. May	(E)	66	106	9	285*	46.77	13	22
4502	E.R. Dexter	(E)	62	102	8	205	47.89	9	27
4455	E.D. Weekes	(WI)	48	81	5	207	58.61	15	19
4399	A.I. Kallicharran	(WI)	66	109	10	187	44.43	12	21
4389	A.P.E. Knott	(E)	95	149	15	135	32.75	5	30
4334	R.C. Fredericks	(WI)	59	109	7	169	42.49	8	26
4129	I.V.A. Richards	(WI)	47	74	4	291	58.98	13	17
3931	Majid Khan	(P)	62	105	5	167	39.31	8	19
3915	Hanif Mohammad	(P)	55	97	8	337	43.98	12	15
3860	F.M.M. Worrell	(WI)	51	87	9	261	49.48	9	22
3798	C.L. Walcott	(WI)	44	74	7	220	56.68	15	14
3744	K.J. Hughes	(A)	56	100	6	213	39.82	8	19
3643	Mushtaq Mohammad	(P)	57	100	7	201	39.17	10	19
3631	P.R. Umrigar	(I)	59	94	8	223	42.22	12	14
3612	D.L. Amiss	(E)	50	88	10	262*	46.30	11	11

Runs			Tests	Inns	NO	HS	Avge	100s	50s
3599	A.W. Greig	(E)	58	93	4	148	40.43	8	20
3575	Asif Iqbal	(P)	58	99	7	175	38.85	11	12
3558	R.W. Marsh	(A)	91	144	11	132	26.75	3	16
3533	A.R. Morris	(A)	46	79	3	206	46.48	12	12
3525	E.H. Hendren	(E)	51	83	9	205*	47.63	7	21

HIGHEST WICKET AGGREGATES

Wkts			Tests	Balls	Runs	Avge	5 wI	10 wM
332	D.K. Lillee	(A)	64	16964	7753	23.25	22	7
309	L.R. Gibbs	(WI)	79	27115	8989	29.09	18	2
307	F.S. Trueman	(E)	67	15178	6625	21.57	17	3
297	D.L. Underwood	(E)	86	21860	7674	25.83	17	6
285	R.G.D. Willis	(E)	79	15301	7198	25.25	15	—
267	I.T. Botham	(E)	59	14050	6536	24.47	20	4
266	B.S. Bedi	(I)	67	21364	7637	28.71	14	1
252	J.B. Statham	(E)	70	16056	6261	24.84	9	1
248	R. Benaud	(A)	63	19108	6704	27.03	16	1
246	G.D. McKenzie	(A)	60	17681	7328	29.78	16	3
242	B.S. Chandrasekhar	(I)	58	15963	7199	29.74	16	2
236	A.V. Bedser	(E)	51	15918	5876	24.89	15	5
235	G.S. Sobers	(WI)	93	21599	7999	34.03	6	—
228	R.R. Lindwall	(A)	61	13650	5251	23.03	12	—
216	C.V. Grimmett	(A)	37	14513	5231	24.21	21	7
202	J.A. Snow	(E)	49	12021	5387	26.66	8	1
197	J.R. Thomson	(A)	49	10205	5326	27.03	8	—
193	J.C. Laker	(E)	46	12027	4101	21.24	9	3
192	W.W. Hall	(WI)	48	10421	5066	26.38	9	1
192	Imran Khan	(P)	43	11212	4758	24.78	12	2
189	S.F. Barnes	(E)	27	7873	3106	16.43	24	7
189	E.A.S. Prasanna	(I)	49	14353	5742	30.38	10	2
186	A.K. Davidson	(A)	44	11587	3819	20.53	14	2
174	G.A.R. Lock	(E)	49	13147	4451	25.58	9	3
173	A.M.E. Roberts	(WI)	40	9674	4481	25.90	10	2*
170	K.R. Miller	(A)	55	10461	3906	22.97	7	1
170	H.J. Tayfield	(SA)	37	13568	4405	25.91	14	2
169	R.J. Hadlee	(NZ)	38	9498	4464	26.41	13	3
165	Kapil Dev	(I)	42	9417	4827	29.25	12	1
162	V. Mankad	(I)	44	14686	5236	32.32	8	2
160	W.A. Johnston	(A)	40	11048	3826	23.91	7	—
158	S. Ramadhin	(WI)	43	13939	4579	28.98	10	1
155	M.W. Tate	(E)	39	12523	4055	26.16	7	1
153	F.J. Titmus	(E)	53	15118	4931	32.22	7	—

MOST TEST APPEARANCES FOR EACH COUNTRY

NB. The abandoned match at Melbourne in 1970-71 is excluded from these figures.

England

M.C. Cowdrey	114	W.R. Hammond	85
G. Boycott	108	K.F. Barrington	82
A.P.E. Knott	95	T.W. Graveney	79
T.G. Evans	91	L. Hutton	79
D.L. Underwood	86	R.G.D. Willis	79

232

Australia		South Africa	
R.W. Marsh	91	J.H.B. Waite	50
G.S. Chappell	81	A.W. Nourse	45
R.N. Harvey	79	B. Mitchell	42
I.M. Chappell	75	H.W. Taylor	42
K.D. Walters	74	T.L. Goddard	41
W.M. Lawry	67	R.A. McLean	40
I.R. Redpath	66	H.J. Tayfield	37
D.K. Lillee	64	D.J. McGlew	34
R. Benaud	63	A.D. Nourse	34
R.B. Simpson	62	E.J. Barlow	30

West Indies		New Zealand	
G.S. Sobers	93	B.E. Congdon	61
C.H. Lloyd	85	J.R. Reid	58
L.R. Gibbs	79	M.G. Burgess	50
R.B. Kanhai	79	B. Sutcliffe	42
A.I. Kallicharran	66	G.T. Dowling	39
D.L. Murray	62	G.M. Turner	39
R.C. Fredericks	59	R.J. Hadlee	38
F.M.M. Worrell	51	J.M. Parker	36
W.W. Hall	48	R.O. Collinge	35
E.D. Weekes	48	K.J. Wadsworth	33

India		Pakistan	
G.R. Viswanath	85	Wasim Bari	67
S.M. Gavaskar	79	Majid Khan	62
B.S. Bedi	67	Asif Iqbal	58
P.R. Umrigar	59	Mushtaq Mohammad	57
B.S. Chandrasekhar	58	Hanif Mohammad	55
S.M.H. Kirmani	58	Zaheer Abbas	52
C.G. Borde	55	Intikhab Alam	47
V.L. Manjrekar	55	Javed Miandad	46
D.B. Vengsarkar	52	Wasim Raja	44
S. Venkataraghavan	50	Sarfraz Nawaz	43
		Imran Khan	43

Most Centuries in Succession in Test Matches

5	E.D. Weekes, West Indies	1947-48 and 1948-49
4	J.H.W. Fingleton, Australia	1935-36 and 1936-37
4	A. Melville, South Africa	1938-39 and 1947

TEST CAREER RECORDS

(to the conclusion of the Australia v England series but not including Pakistan v India)

compiled by Brian Heald

ENGLAND

BATTING AND FIELDING

	M	I	NO	Runs	HS	Avge	100	50	Ct	St
P.J.W. Allott	5	6	2	119	52*	29.75	—	1	2	—
C.W.J. Athey	3	6	0	17	9	2.83	—	—	2	—
D.L. Amiss	50	88	10	3612	262*	46.30	11	11	24	—
D.L. Bairstow	4	7	1	125	59	20.83	—	1	12	1
I.T. Botham	59	92	3	3266	208	36.69	11	13	69	—
G. Boycott	108	193	23	8114	246*	47.72	22	42	33	—
A.R. Butcher	1	2	0	34	20	17.00	—	—	—	—
R.O. Butcher	3	5	0	71	32	14.20	—	—	3	—
G. Cook	7	13	0	203	66	15.61	—	2	9	—
N.G. Cowans	4	7	1	68	36	11.33	—	—	3	—
G.R. Dilley	16	25	7	313	56	17.38	—	2	4	—
P.R. Downton	4	7	1	59	26*	9.83	—	—	8	—
P.H. Edmonds	21	24	5	367	64	19.31	—	2	22	—
J.E. Emburey	22	33	6	326	57	12.07	—	1	15	—
K.W.R. Fletcher	59	96	14	3272	216	39.90	7	19	54	—
G. Fowler	4	8	0	302	86	37.75	—	3	2	—
M.W. Gatting	22	38	3	797	59	22.77	—	6	17	—
G.A. Gooch	42	75	4	2540	153	35.77	4	15	36	—
D.I. Gower	49	85	7	3338	200*	42.79	5	18	28	—
I.A. Greig	2	4	0	26	14	6.50	—	—	—	—
E.E. Hemmings	5	10	1	198	95	22.00	—	1	4	—
M. Hendrick	30	35	15	128	15	6.40	—	—	25	—
R.D. Jackman	4	6	0	42	17	7.00	—	—	—	—
A.P.E. Knott	95	149	15	4389	135	32.75	5	30	250	19
A.J. Lamb	11	21	1	669	107	33.45	1	4	6	—
W. Larkins	6	11	0	176	34	16.00	—	—	3	—
J.K. Lever	20	29	4	306	53	12.24	—	1	11	—
V.J. Marks	1	2	1	19	12*	19.00	—	—	—	—
G. Miller	32	47	4	1171	98*	27.23	—	7	15	—
C.M. Old	46	66	9	845	65	14.82	—	2	22	—
P.W.G. Parker	1	2	0	13	13	6.50	—	—	—	—
D.R. Pringle	7	11	2	166	47*	18.44	—	—	1	—
D.W. Randall	37	62	4	1879	174	32.39	5	9	25	—
B.C. Rose	9	16	2	358	70	25.57	—	2	4	—
G.B. Stevenson	2	2	1	28	27*	28.00	—	—	1	—
C.J. Tavaré	22	40	1	1290	149	33.07	1	10	15	—
R.W. Taylor	47	67	11	1010	97	18.03	—	3	144	7
D.L. Underwood	86	116	35	937	45*	11.56	—	—	44	—
P. Willey	20	38	5	923	102*	27.96	2	4	3	—
R.G.D. Willis	79	110	49	708	28*	11.60	—	—	33	—
R.A. Woolmer	19	34	2	1059	149	33.09	3	2	10	—

BOWLING

	Balls	Runs	Wkts	Avge	Best	5 wI	10 wM
P.J.W. Allott	696	414	6	69.00	2-17	—	—
I.T. Botham	14050	6536	267	24.47	8-34	20	4
G. Boycott	944	382	7	54.57	3-47	—	—
A.R. Butcher	12	9	0	—	—	—	—
G. Cook	42	27	0	—	—	—	—
N.G. Cowans	642	396	11	36.00	6-77	1	—
G.R. Dilley	2758	1401	45	31.13	4-24	—	—
P.H. Edmonds	4697	1512	55	27.49	7-66	2	—
J.E. Emburey	4981	1696	56	30.28	6-33	2	—
K.W.R. Fletcher	285	193	2	96.50	1-6	—	—
M.W. Gatting	92	39	0	—	—	—	—
G.A. Gooch	937	348	8	43.50	2-12	—	—
D.I. Gower	12	2	1	2.00	1-1	—	—
I.A. Greig	188	114	4	28.50	4-53	—	—
E.E. Hemmings	1468	558	12	46.50	3-68	—	—
M. Hendrick	6208	2248	87	25.83	4-28	—	—
R.D. Jackman	1070	445	14	31.78	4-110	—	—
A.J. Lamb	6	0	0	—	—	—	—
J.K. Lever	4115	1785	67	26.64	7-46	3	1
V.J. Marks	42	31	1	31.00	1-8	—	—
G. Miller	4981	1717	59	29.10	5-44	1	—
C.M. Old	8858	4020	143	28.17	7-50	4	—
D.R. Pringle	1091	495	11	45.00	2-16	—	—
D.W. Randall	16	3	0	—	—	—	—
G.B. Stevenson	312	183	5	36.60	3-111	—	—
C.J. Tavaré	12	11	0	—	—	—	—
R.W. Taylor	12	6	0	—	—	—	—
D.L. Underwood	21862	7674	297	25.83	8-51	17	6
P. Willey	1067	441	6	73.50	2-73	—	—
R.G.D. Willis	15301	7198	285	25.25	8-43	15	—
R.A. Woolmer	546	299	4	74.75	1-8	—	—

AUSTRALIA

BATTING AND FIELDING

	M	I	NO	Runs	HS	Avge	100	50	Ct	St
T.M. Alderman	16	21	11	51	12*	5-10	—	—	16	—
A.R. Border	50	90	15	3492	162	46.56	9	21	55	—
R.J. Bright	16	27	5	303	33	13.77	—	—	8	—
G.S. Chappell	81	144	18	6680	247*	53.01	22	30	114	—
T.M. Chappell	3	6	1	79	27	15.80	—	—	2	—
W.M. Darling	14	27	1	697	91	26.80	—	6	5	—
J. Dyson	27	52	7	1282	127*	28.48	2	5	10	—
J.D. Higgs	22	36	16	111	16	5.55	—	—	3	—
A.M.J. Hilditch	9	18	0	452	85	25.11	—	4	9	—
R.M. Hogg	25	41	7	272	36	8.00	—	—	5	—
D.W. Hookes	13	23	1	780	85	35.45	—	7	4	—
K.J. Hughes	56	100	6	3744	213	39.82	8	19	40	—
B.M. Laird	21	40	2	1341	92	35.28	—	11	16	—
G.F. Lawson	13	22	4	244	57*	13.55	—	2	4	—

235

	M	I	NO	Runs	HS	Avge	100	50	Ct	St
D.K. Lillee	64	86	22	874	73*	13.65	—	1	20	—
R.B. McCosker	25	46	5	1622	127	39.56	4	9	21	—
R.W. Marsh	91	144	11	3558	132	26.75	3	16	322	12
L.S. Pascoe	14	19	9	106	30*	10.60	—	—	2	—
C.G. Rackemann	1	1	0	4	4	4.00	—	—	1	—
G.M. Ritchie	3	6	1	206	106*	41.20	1	—	1	—
S.J. Rixon	10	19	3	341	54	21.31	—	2	31	4
P.R. Sleep	4	8	0	114	64	14.25	—	1	—	—
J.R. Thomson	49	69	16	641	49	12.09	—	—	19	—
P.M. Toohey	15	29	1	893	122	31.89	1	7	9	—
D.M. Wellham	4	7	0	221	103	31.57	1	—	1	—
K.C. Wessels	4	8	0	386	162	48.25	1	1	8	—
D.F. Whatmore	7	13	0	293	77	22.53	—	2	3	—
M.R. Whitney	2	4	0	4	4	1.00	—	—	—	—
J.M. Wiener	6	11	0	281	93	25.54	—	2	4	—
G.M. Wood	41	80	5	2550	126	34.00	7	11	32	—
K.J. Wright	10	18	5	219	55*	16.84	—	1	31	4
G.N. Yallop	32	61	3	2101	172	36.22	6	7	16	—
B. Yardley	32	54	4	978	74	19.56	—	4	30	—

BOWLING

	Balls	Runs	Wkts	Avge	Best	5 wI	10 wM
T.M. Alderman	4111	1890	66	28.63	6-135	4	—
A.R. Border	1379	502	14	35.85	3-20	—	—
R.J. Bright	3598	1343	37	36.29	7-87	3	1
G.S. Chappell	4937	1756	47	37.36	5-61	1	—
J.D. Higgs	4752	2057	66	31.16	7-143	2	—
R.M. Hogg	5297	2239	93	24.07	6.74	5	2
D.W. Hookes	78	35	0	—	—	—	—
K.J. Hughes	85	28	0	—	—	—	—
B.M. Laird	18	12	0	—	—	—	—
G.F. Lawson	2981	1402	59	23.76	7-81	5	1
D.K. Lillee	16904	7753	332	22.35	7-83	22	7
R.W. Marsh	60	51	0	—	—	—	—
L.S. Pascoe	3403	1668	64	26.06	5-59	1	—
C.G. Rackemann	200	96	2	48.00	2-61	—	—
P.R. Sleep	589	382	3	127.33	1-16	—	—
J.R. Thomson	10205	5326	197	27.03	6-46	8	—
P.M. Tooley	2	4	0	—	—	—	—
D.F. Whatmore	30	11	0	—	—	—	—
M.R. Whitney	468	246	5	49.20	2-50	—	—
J.M. Wiener	78	41	0	—	—	—	—
G.N. Yallop	192	116	1	116.00	1-21	—	—
B. Yardley	8603	3820	119	32.10	7-98	5	1

WEST INDIES

BATTING AND FIELDING

	M	I	NO	Runs	HS	Avge	100	50	Ct	St
S.F.A.F. Bacchus	19	30	0	782	250	26.06	1	3	17	—
P.J. Dujon	3	6	1	227	51	45.90	—	1	9	—
J. Garner	28	36	2	400	60	11.76	—	1	22	—
H.A. Gomes	22	35	2	1418	126	42.96	4	8	4	—
C.G. Greenidge	36	63	3	2569	134	42.81	5	19	39	—
D.L. Hayes	24	38	1	1431	184	38.67	3	8	13	—
M.A. Holding	31	44	8	434	58*	12.05	—	2	9	—
C.H. Lloyd	85	143	10	5831	242*	43.84	14	30	63	—
M.D. Marshall	12	16	1	126	45	8.40	—	—	5	—
R. Nanan	1	2	0	16	8	8.00	—	—	2	—
I.V.A. Richards	47	74	4	4129	291	58.98	13	17	48	—
A.M.E. Roberts	40	54	9	610	54	13.55	—	2	8	—

BOWLING

	Balls	Runs	Wkts	Avge	Best	5 wI	10 wM
S.F.A.F. Bacchus	6	3	0	—	—	—	—
J. Garner	6648	2560	124	20.64	6-56	2	—
H.A. Gomes	744	266	5	53.20	2-20	—	—
C.G. Greenidge	26	4	0	—	—	—	—
D.L. Haynes	18	8	1	8.00	1-2	—	—
M.A. Holding	7162	3194	139	22.97	8-92	10	2
C.H. Lloyd	1716	622	10	62.20	2-13	—	—
M.D. Marshall	2220	1084	34	31.88	4-25	—	—
R. Nanan	216	91	4	22.75	2-37	—	—
I.V.A. Richards	1924	703	13	54.07	2-20	—	—
A.M.E. Roberts	9674	4481	173	25.90	7-54	10	2

NEW ZEALAND

BATTING AND FIELDING

	M	I	NO	Runs	HS	Avge	100	50	Ct	St
R.W. Anderson	9	18	0	423	92	23.50	—	3	1	—
S.L. Boock	12	19	6	37	8	2.84	—	—	8	—
B.P. Bracewell	5	10	2	17	8	2.12	—	—	1	—
J.G. Bracewell	4	6	1	29	16	5.80	—	—	2	—
B.L. Cairns	26	42	6	575	52*	15.97	—	1	19	—
E.J. Chatfield	5	7	3	31	13*	7.75	—	—	—	—
J.V. Coney	18	31	5	805	82	30.96	—	7	18	—
M.D. Crowe	3	4	0	20	9	5.00	—	—	3	—
B.A. Edgar	18	32	1	1049	161	33.83	3	4	11	—
G.N. Edwards	8	15	0	377	55	25.13	—	3	7	—
R.J. Hadlee	38	66	8	1241	103	21.39	1	5	20	—
G.P. Howarth	28	51	5	1788	147	38.86	6	7	14	—
W.K. Lees	17	31	3	642	152	22.92	1	—	35	7
P.E. McEwan	3	6	0	56	21	9.33	—	—	3	—
J.F.M. Morrison	17	29	0	656	117	22.62	1	3	9	—
J.M. Parker	36	63	2	1498	121	24.55	3	5	30	—
J.F. Reid	4	7	1	269	123*	44.83	1	1	2	—
I.D.S. Smith	7	10	2	86	20	10.75	—	—	19	—
M.C. Snedden	6	6	2	72	32	18.00	—	—	2	—
G.B. Troup	12	15	6	43	13*	4.77	—	—	2	—
P.N. Webb	2	3	0	11	5	3.66	—	—	2	—
J.C. Wright	20	36	1	976	141	27.88	2	3	8	—

BOWLING

	Balls	Runs	Wkts	Avge	Best	5 wI	10 wM
S.L. Boock	2107	706	19	37.15	5-67	1	—
B.P. Bracewell	838	456	10	45.60	3-110	—	—
J.G. Bracewell	837	290	11	26.36	5-75	1	—
B.L. Cairns	6529	2478	72	34.41	6-85	4	—
E.J. Chatfield	1102	492	8	61.50	4-100	—	—
J.V. Coney	1107	360	10	36.00	3-28	—	—
M.D. Crowe	27	14	0	—	—	—	—
R.J. Hadlee	9498	4464	169	26.41	7-23	13	3
G.P. Howarth	500	235	3	78.33	1-13	—	—
W.K. Lees	5	4	0	—	—	—	—
J.F.M. Morrison	264	71	2	35.50	2-52	—	—
J.M. Parker	40	24	1	24.00	1-24	—	—
M.C. Snedden	870	426	11	38.72	2-40	—	—
G.B. Troup	2601	1114	34	32.76	6-95	1	1
J.G. Wright	6	2	0	—	—	—	—

INDIA

BATTING AND FIELDING

	M	I	NO	Runs	HS	Avge	100	50	Ct	St
M. Amarnath	26	45	3	1466	101*	34.90	2	9	23	—
Arun Lal	1	2	0	64	63	32.00	—	1	2	—
R.H.M. Binny	9	15	2	198	46	15.23	—	—	7	—
C.P.S. Chauhan	40	68	2	2084	97	31.57	—	16	38	—
D.R. Doshi	28	30	9	108	20	5.14	—	—	10	—
S.M. Gavaskar	79	139	10	6951	221	53.88	25	30	71	—
K.D. Ghavri	39	57	14	913	86	21.23	—	2	16	—
Kapil Dev	42	61	6	1821	126*	33.10	2	10	15	—
S.M.H. Kirmani	58	84	14	1889	101*	26.98	1	9	107	30
Kirti Azad	4	6	0	107	24	17.83	—	—	2	—
S. Madan Lal	26	41	9	595	55*	18.59	—	1	12	—
A. Malhotra	3	4	0	36	31	9.00	—	—	2	—
S.V. Nayak	2	3	1	19	11	9.50	—	—	1	—
G.A. Parkar	1	2	0	7	6	3.50	—	—	1	—
S.M. Patil	16	26	4	1081	174	49.13	3	5	8	—
P. Roy	2	3	1	71	60*	35.50	—	1	1	—
R.J. Shastri	12	16	3	281	93	21.61	—	2	7	—
R. Shukla	1	—	—	—	—	—	—	—	—	—
K. Srikkanth	4	6	0	119	65	19.83	—	1	1	—
T.E. Srinivasan	1	2	0	48	29	24.00	—	—	—	—
D.B. Vengsarkar	52	85	8	2964	157*	38.49	6	15	42	—
G.R. Viswanath	85	147	10	5946	222	43.40	14	34	62	—
N.S. Yadav	15	19	6	207	43	15.92	—	—	4	—
Yashpal Sharma	26	41	7	1217	140	35.79	2	6	8	—

BOWLING

	Balls	Runs	Wkts	Avge	Best	5 wI	10 wM
M. Amarnath	2506	1161	23	50.47	4-63	—	—
R.M.H. Binny	1133	632	15	42.13	3-53	—	—
C.P.S. Chauhan	174	106	2	53.00	1-4	—	—
D.R. Doshi	8387	2962	105	28.20	6-102	5	—
S.M. Gavaskar	304	163	1	163.00	1-34	—	—
K.D. Ghavri	7042	3656	109	33.54	5-33	4	—
Kapil Dev	9417	4827	165	29.25	7-56	12	1
Kirti Azad	294	158	1	158.00	1-35	—	—
S. Madan Lal	4162	1815	51	35.58	5-23	4	—
S.V. Nayak	231	132	1	132.00	1-16	—	—
S.M. Patil	633	238	9	26.44	2-28	—	—
R.J. Shastri	2979	1014	31	32.70	5-125	1	—
R. Shukla	294	152	2	76.00	2-82	—	—
K. Srikkanth	36	10	0	—	—	—	—
D.B. Vengsarkar	23	13	0	—	—	—	—
G.R. Viswanath	70	46	1	46.00	1-11	—	—
N.S. Yadav	3139	1449	41	35.34	4-35	—	—
Yashpal Sharma	18	1	0	—	—	—	—

PAKISTAN

BATTING AND FIELDING

	M	I	NO	Runs	HS	Avge	100	50	Ct	St
Abdul Qadir	14	19	3	217	29*	13.56	—	—	6	—
Ashraf Ali	2	3	2	132	58	132.00	—	1	4	2
Azhar Khan	1	1	0	14	14	14.00	—	—	—	—
Azmat Rana	1	1	0	49	49	49.00	—	—	—	—
Ehteshamuddin	5	3	1	2	2	1.00	—	—	2	—
Ejaz Fakih	2	4	0	63	34	15.75	—	—	—	—
Haroon Rashid	22	35	1	1217	153	35.79	3	5	16	—
Imran Khan	43	68	10	1606	123	27.86	1	5	12	—
Iqbal Qasim	34	40	12	269	56	9.60	—	1	26	—
Jalaluddin	1	—	—	—	—	—	—	—	1	—
Javed Miandad	46	77	13	3398	206	53.09	8	20	46	1
Majid Khan	62	105	5	3931	167	39.31	8	19	70	—
Mansoor Akhtar	10	18	2	444	111	27.75	1	2	7	—
Mohsin Khan	16	27	2	1175	200	47.00	3	3	15	—
Mudassar Nazar	29	46	3	1377	126	32.02	2	8	21	—
Rashid Khan	2	3	2	105	59	105.00	—	1	—	—
Rizwan-uz-Zaman	3	6	0	112	42	18.66	—	—	1	—
Sadiq Mohammad	41	74	2	2579	166	35.81	5	10	28	—
Saleem Yousuf	1	1	0	4	4	4.00	—	—	5	2
Salim Malik	2	4	1	139	100*	46.33	1	—	4	—
Sarfraz Nawaz	43	57	8	760	55	15.51	—	3	24	—
Shafiq Ahmed	6	10	1	99	27*	11.00	—	—	—	—
Sikander Bakht	25	34	12	137	22*	6.22	—	—	6	—
Tahir Naqqash	8	10	3	162	57	23.14	—	1	—	—
Taslim Arif	6	10	2	501	210*	62.62	1	2	6	3
Tauseef Ahmed	6	3	1	23	18	11.50	—	—	3	—
Wasim Bari	67	97	24	1191	85	16.31	—	5	160	24
Wasim Raja	44	73	12	2311	117*	37.88	2	16	12	—
Zaheer Abbas	52	88	6	3423	274	41.74	8	14	29	—

BOWLING

	Balls	Runs	Wkts	Avge	Best	5 wI	10 wM
Abdul Qadir	4094	1671	54	30.94	7-142	2	1
Azhar Khan	18	2	1	2.00	1-1	—	—
Ehteshamuddin	940	375	16	23.94	5-47	1	—
Ejaz Fakih	156	85	1	85.00	1-76	—	—
Haroon Rashid	8	3	0				
Imran Khan	11212	4758	192	24.78	8-58	12	2
Iqbal Qasim	8982	3301	112	29.47	7-47	4	2
Jalaluddin	210	92	5	18.40	3-77	—	—
Javed Miandad	1356	623	17	36.64	3-74	—	—
Majid Khan	3578	1452	27	53.77	4-45	—	—
Mohsin Khan	8	3	0				
Mudassar Nazar	1703	692	22	31.45	6-32	1	—
Rashid Khan	288	134	3	44.66	2-53	—	—
Rizwan-uz-Zaman	102	39	3	13.00	3-26	—	—
Sadiq Mohammad	199	98	0				
Sarfraz Nawaz	10581	4387	136	32.25	9-86	4	1

	Balls	Runs	Wkts	Avge	Best	5 wI	10 wM
Shafiq Ahmed	8	1	0	—	—	—	—
Sikander Bakht	4738	2305	66	34.92	8-69	3	1
Tahir Naqqash	1374	699	21	33.28	5-40	1	—
Taslim Arif	30	28	1	28.00	1-28	—	—
Tauseef Ahmed	1446	620	23	26.95	4-58	—	—
Wasim Bari	8	2	0	—	—	—	—
Wasim Raja	3055	1412	39	36.20	4-68	—	—
Zaheer Abbas	56	10	0	—	—	—	—

SRI LANKA

BATTING AND FIELDING

	M	I	NO	Runs	HS	Avge	100	50	Ct	St
A.L.F. de Mel	5	10	2	125	34	15.62	—	—	5	—
D.S. de Silva	5	10	2	213	49	26.62	—	—	1	—
G.R.A. de Silva	4	7	3	41	14	8.20	—	—	—	—
R.L. Dias	5	10	0	529	109	52.90	1	5	2	—
H.M. Goonatillahe	5	10	2	177	56	22.12	—	1	10	3
R.S.A. Jayasekera	1	2	0	2	2	1.00	—	—	—	—
L.W. Kaluperuma	2	4	1	12	11*	4.00	—	—	2	—
R.S. Madugalle	5	10	1	273	91*	30.33	—	2	5	—
L.R.D. Mendis	5	10	0	376	105	37.60	2	1	4	—
A.N. Ranasinghe	2	4	0	88	77	22.00	—	1	—	—
A. Ranatunga	4	8	0	144	54	18.00	—	1	1	—
J.R. Ratnayeke	3	6	1	54	24	10.80	—	—	—	—
B. Warnapura	4	8	0	96	38	12.00	—	—	2	—
S. Wettimuny	4	8	0	331	157	41.37	1	1	2	—
R.G.C.E. Wijesuriya	1	2	0	3	3	1.50	—	—	—	—

BOWLING

	Balls	Runs	Wkts	Avge	Best	5 wI	10 wM
A.L.F. de Mel	1149	792	23	34.43	5-68	1	—
D.S. de Silva	1517	775	23	33.69	5-59	1	—
G.R.A. de Silva	956	385	7	55.00	2-38	—	—
L.W. Kaluperuma	162	93	0	—	—	—	—
A.N. Ranasinghe	114	69	1	69.00	1-23	—	—
A. Ranatunga	6	12	0	—	—	—	—
J.R. Ratnayeke	442	301	5	60.20	3-121	—	—
B. Warnapura	90	46	0	—	—	—	—
S. Wettimuny	12	21	0	—	—	—	—
R.G.C.E. Wijesuriya	144	105	0	—	—	—	—

YOUNG CRICKETER OF THE YEAR

At the end of each season the members of the Cricket Writers' Club select by ballot the player they consider the best young cricketer of the season.

The selections to date are:

1950 R. Tattersall (Lancashire)	1966 D.L. Underwood (Kent)
1951 P.B.H. May (Surrey)	1967 A.W. Greig (Sussex)
1952 F.S. Trueman (Yorkshire)	1968 R.H.M. Cottam (Hampshire)
1953 M.C. Cowdrey (Kent)	1969 A. Ward (Derbyshire)
1954 P.J. Loader (Surrey)	1970 C.M. Old (Yorkshire)
1955 K.F. Barrington (Surrey)	1971 J. Whitehouse (Warwickshire)
1956 B. Taylor (Essex)	1972 D.R. Owen-Thomas (Surrey)
1957 M.J. Stewart (Surrey)	1973 M. Hendrick (Derbyshire)
1958 A.C.D. Ingleby-Mackenzie (Hampshire)	1974 P.H. Edmonds (Middlesex)
	1975 A. Kennedy (Lancashire)
1959 G. Pullar (Lancashire)	1976 G. Miller (Derbyshire)
1960 D.A. Allen (Gloucestershire)	1977 I.T. Botham (Somerset)
1961 P.H. Parfitt (Middlesex)	1978 D.I. Gower (Leicestershire)
1962 P.J. Sharpe (Yorkshire)	1979 P.W.G. Parker (Sussex)
1963 G. Boycott (Yorkshire)	1980 G.R. Dilley (Kent)
1964 J.M. Brearley (Middlesex)	1981 M.W. Gatting (Middlesex)
1965 A.P.E. Knott (Kent)	1982 W.G. Cowans (Middlesex)

NB. An additional award was made in 1980 to C.W.J. Athey (Yorkshire) as the best young batsman of the year.

SCORING OF POINTS IN THE SCHWEPPES CHAMPIONSHIP

The scheme is as follows:

(a) For a win, 16 points, plus any points scored in the first innings.

(b) In a tie, each side to score 8 points, plus any points scored in the first innings.

(c) If the scores are equal in a drawn match, the side batting in the fourth innings to score 8 points, plus any points scored in the first innings.

(d) First innings points (awarded only for performances in the first 100 overs of each innings and retained whatever the result of the match).

    (i) A maximum of 4 batting points to be available as follows: 150 to 199 runs – 1 point; 200 to 249 runs – 2 points; 250 to 299 runs – 3 points; 300 runs or over – 4 points.

    (ii) A maximum of 4 bowling points to be available as follows: 3-4 wickets taken – 1 point; 5-6 wickets taken – 2 points; 7-8 wickets taken – 3 points; 9-10 wickets taken – 4 points.

(e) If play starts when less than eight hours playing time remains and a one innings match is played, no first innings points shall be scored. The side winning on the one innings to score 12 points.

(f) The side which has the highest aggregate of points gained at the end of the season shall be the Champion County. Should any sides in the Schweppes Championship Table be equal on points, the side with most wins will have priority.

This isn't a bouncer!

Congratulations to Surrey on winning the NatWest Bank Trophy.

MINOR COUNTIES

BATTING AVERAGES
(Qualification: 8 Innings, Average 25.00)

Name	County	I	NO	Runs	HS	Avge
D.G. Ottley	Hertfordshire	11	3	605	108	75.63
Mudassar Nazar	Cheshire	8	1	422	110*	60.28
M.S. McEvoy	Cambridgeshire	19	2	961	140*	56.52
W.M. Osman	Hertfordshire	13	1	663	103	55.25
N.V. Radford	Lancashire II	9	4	275	74	55.00
S.G. Plumb	Norfolk	14	2	640	112*	53.33
S.R. Atkinson	Durham	12	2	505	155*	50.50
J.F. Harvey	Berkshire	20	7	636	96	48.92
M.L. Simmons	Berkshire	16	6	487	113*	48.70
R.V. Lewis	Dorset	17	2	726	114*	48.40
P.J. Garner	Oxfordshire	18	3	720	102*	48.00
J. Claughton	Berkshire	12	2	451	79	45.10
D.S. de Silva	Shropshire	14	3	489	109	44.45
R.L. Ollis	Somerset II	14	1	565	103*	43.46
S.C. Wundke	Cheshire	12	4	344	107*	43.00
G. Wallen	Devon	15	3	510	92*	42.50
D. Parry	Cambridgeshire	12	4	338	66	42.25
Mushtaq Mohammad	Staffordshire	18	1	703	98*	41.35
R.F. Howlett	Suffolk	18	4	567	61*	40.50
L. Baichan	Cumberland	13	1	472	95*	39.33
S.J. Halliday	Dorset	11	2	349	67	38.77
M.S.T. Dunstan	Cornwall	18	1	653	111	38.41
D.W. Varey	Cheshire	13	1	461	99*	38.41
J.G. Tolchard	Devon	11	0	407	94	37.00
S.M. Clements	Suffolk	20	4	586	95	36.62
P.J. Mir	Norfolk	15	5	366	89	36.60
D. Cartledge	Staffordshire	9	0	326	94	36.22
M.D. Nurton	Oxfordshire	14	2	431	69*	35.91
S. Greensword	Durham	16	2	501	65	35.78
J.S. Johnson	Shropshire	16	2	501	103*	35.78
G.D. Halliday	Northumberland	16	4	427	156*	35.58
G.I. Burgess	Wiltshire	19	0	676	115	35.57
P.D. Barker	Suffolk	20	3	603	108*	35.47
P.J. Sharpe	Norfolk	10	4	212	117*	35.33
P.A. Fowler	Oxfordshire	15	1	493	88	35.21
D.M. Daniels	Bedfordshire	19	3	563	63	35.18
B.L. Matthews	Devon	13	1	419	120*	34.91
R.D. Huggins	Norfolk	12	3	312	79*	34.67
C. Stone	Dorset	19	7	410	142*	34.16
G.V. Miller	Cambridgeshire	19	1	607	104*	33.72
F.L.Q. Handley	Norfolk	14	1	436	122	33.53
P. Dolphin	Bucks	24	4	666	100	33.30
P.A. Marshall	Staffordshire	11	1	366	65	33.27
P. Thorn	Wiltshire	18	3	495	109*	33.00
S.P. Henderson	Shropshire	10	2	256	67*	32.00
G.V. Palmer	Somerset II	9	1	253	75	31.62

Name	County	I	NO	Runs	HS	Avge
E.G. Willcock	Cornwall	16	1	471	130*	31.40
J. Wyatt	Somerset II	8	0	247	78	30.87
G. Robinson	Lincolnshire	16	0	489	119	30.56

BOWLING

(Qualification: 20 wickets. Average 24.00)

Name	County	Overs	Mdns	Runs	Wkts	Avge
T.H. Barnes	Norfolk	294.5	109	630	42	15.00
G.V. Palmer	Somerset II	148.5	37	418	27	15.48
D.S. de Silva	Shropshire	238	62	626	38	16.47
D.G. Gallop	Oxfordshire	126	35	367	21	17.48
R.O. Estwick	Lincolnshire	172.1	40	490	28	17.50
R.J. Gulliver	Wiltshire	185	67	457	26	17.57
R.M.O. Cooke	Cheshire	140.5	44	426	24	17.75
J. Johnston	Durham	205.3	60	459	25	18.36
R.N. Busby	Oxfordshire	188	53	460	25	18.40
R.L. Johns	Hertfordshire	124.1	34	372	20	18.60
C. Stone	Dorset	275.2	55	807	43	18.75
G.A. Cope	Lincolnshire	285.1	95	639	34	18.79
R.W. Flower	Staffordshire	285.2	112	624	33	18.90
R.A. Evans	Oxfordshire	271	81	627	32	19.59
P.J. Hayes	Suffolk	136.3	26	431	22	19.59
J.A. Smith	Shropshire	231	58	589	29	20.31
A.H. Watts	Cornwall	174.3	33	585	28	20.89
S.P. Davis	Durham	183.5	42	527	25	21.08
S.R. Porter	Oxfordshire	274	73	719	34	21.15
J.N. Graham	Northumberland	372.1	110	980	45	21.78
T.S. Smith	Hertfordshire	184.3	53	466	21	22.19
D. Crisp	Wiltshire	262	61	815	36	22.63
S. Greensword	Durham	217.4	90	453	20	22.65
D.A. Toseland	Cornwall	296.5	87	717	31	23.12
M. Brown	Cambridgeshire	225	44	717	31	23.12

PRINCIPAL FIXTURES 1983

Including play on Sunday

Wednesday 20 April

Cambridge: Cambridge U v Glam

Saturday 23 April

Cambridge: Cambridge U v Leics
Oxford: Oxford U v Lancs

Wednesday 27 April

Lord's: MCC v Middx
Cambridge: Cambridge U v Essex
Oxford: Oxford U v Somerset

Saturday 30 April

Schweppes Championship
Derby: *Derbys v Glos
Old Trafford: Lancs v Glam
Leicester: *Leics v Hants
Lord's: Middx v Essex
Trent Bridge: *Notts v Somerset
The Oval: *Surrey v Kent
Edgbaston: Warwicks v Northants
Worcester: *Worcs v Yorks
Other Match
Oxford: Oxford U v Sussex

Sunday 1 May

Old Trafford: Lancs v Glam (one day)

Wednesday 4 May

Schweppes Championship
Cardiff: Glam v Essex
Bristol: Glos v Surrey
Leicester: Leics v Derbys
Lord's: Middx v Lancs
Northampton: Northants v Hants
Taunton: Somerset v Worcs
Hove: Sussex v Notts
Headingley: Yorks v Warwicks
Other Match
Cambridge: Cambridge U v Kent

Saturday 7 May

Benson & Hedges Cup
Chesterfield: Derbys v Yorks
Southampton: Hants v Essex
Old Trafford: Lancs v Warwicks

Northampton: Northants v Glos
Taunton: Somerset v Sussex
The Oval: Surrey v Middx
Worcester: Worcs v Leics
Cambridge: Combined U v Kent

Sunday 8 May

John Player League
Southampton: Hants v Essex
Canterbury: Kent v Surrey
Old Trafford: Lancs v Derbys
Leicester: Leics v Worcs
Lord's: Middx v Glam
Northampton: Northants v Notts
Taunton: Somerset v Sussex
Edgbaston: Warwicks v Yorks

Wednesday 11 May

Schweppes Championship
Chesterfield: Derbys v Lancs
Chelmsford: Essex v Kent
Gloucester: Glos v Sussex
Southampton: Hants v Warwicks
Lord's: Middx v Yorks
Northampton: Northants v Notts
The Oval: Surrey v Leics
Worcester: Worcs v Somerset
Other Matches
Cambridge: Cambridge U v MCC
  (three days)
Oxford: Oxford U v Glam

Saturday 14 May

Benson & Hedges Cup
Chelmsford: Essex v Somerset
Gloucester: Glos v Leics
Canterbury: Kent v Middx
Hove: Sussex v Minor Counties
Edgbaston: Warwicks v Derbys
Bradford: Yorks v Notts
Aberdeen: Scotland v Worcs
Oxford: Combined U v Glam

Sunday 15 May

John Player League
Derby: Derbys v Northants
Chelmsford: Essex v Lancs
Swansea: Glam v Warwicks

246

Gloucester: Glos v Leics
Lord's: Middx v Hants
Trent Bridge: Notts v Somerset
Hove: Sussex v Kent
Headingley: Yorks v Surrey

Tuesday 17 May

Benson & Hedges Cup
Canterbury: Kent v Surrey
Leicester: Leics v Northants
Lord's: Middx v Glam
Trent Bridge: Notts v Derbys
Taunton: Somerset v Hants
Headingley: Yorks v Lancs
Glasgow (Titwood): Scotland v Glos
Slough: Minor Counties v Essex

Thursday 19 May

Benson & Hedges Cup
Derby: Derbys v Lancs
Chelmsford: Essex v Sussex
Cardiff: Glam v Surrey
Bournemouth: Hants v Minor
 Counties
Leicester: Leics v Scotland
Lord's: Middx v Combined U
Trent Bridge: Notts v Warwicks
Worcester: Worcs v Northants

Saturday 21 May

Benson & Hedges Cup
Swansea: Glam v Kent
Bristol: Glos v Worcs
Old Trafford: Lancs v Notts
Northampton: Northants v Scotland
The Oval: Surrey v Combined U
Hove: Sussex v Hants
Edgbaston: Warwicks v Yorks
Slough: Minor Counties v Somerset

Sunday 22 May

John Player League
Chelmsford: Essex v Derbys
Bournemouth: Hants v Northants
Leicester: Leics v Kent
The Oval: Surrey v Somerset
Edgbaston: Warwicks v Lancs
Worcester: Worcs v Glos
Hull: Yorks v Middx

Wednesday 25 May

Schweppes Championship
Southampton: Hants v Worcs

Leicester: Leics v Essex
Lord's: Middx v Glam
Taunton: Somerset v Sussex
The Oval: Surrey v Lancs
Edgbaston: Warwicks v Glos
Bradford: Yorks v Northants
Other Match
Oxford: Oxford U v MCC (three days)

Saturday 28 May

Schweppes Championship
Chelmsford: Essex v Surrey
Swansea: Glam v Glos
Canterbury: Kent v Hants
Old Trafford: Lancs v Yorks
Lord's: Middx v Sussex
Northampton: Northants v Leics
Trent Bridge: Notts v Derbys
Worcester: Worcs v Warwicks

Sunday 29 May

John Player League
Swansea: Glam v Lancs
Canterbury: Kent v Hants
Lord's: Middx v Sussex
Northampton: Northants v Leics
Trent Bridge: Notts v Surrey
Bradford: Yorks v Somerset
Other Match
Oxford: Oxford U v Free Foresters
 (three days)

Wednesday 1 June

Benson & Hedges Cup Quarter-Finals

Saturday 4 June

Schweppes Championship
Derby: Derbys v Hants
Dartford: Kent v Middx
Trent Bridge: Notts v Leics
Taunton: Somerset v Essex
Hove: Sussex v Worcs
Edgbaston: Warwicks v Lancs
Middlesbrough: Yorks v Glam
Other Match
Oxford: Oxford U v Combined
 Services (three days)

Sunday 5 June

John Player League
Bristol: Glos v Surrey
Old Trafford: Lancs v Northants

247

Lord's: Middx v Worcs
Trent Bridge: Notts v Glam
Taunton: Somerset v Essex
Coventry (Courtaulds): Warwicks v
  Derbys
Middlesbrough: Yorks v Hants

Wednesday 8 June

Schweppes Championship
Chelmsford: Essex v Notts
Bristol: Glos v Somerset
Bournemouth: Hants v Lancs
Leicester: Leics v Notts
Uxbridge: Middx v Derbys
Hove: Sussex v Kent
Worcester: Worcs v Surrey
Other Matches
Cambridge: Cambridge U v Warwicks
Oxford: Oxford U v Northants

Thursday 9 June

PRUDENTIAL CUP
Trent Bridge: Australia v Zimbabwe
The Oval: England v New Zealand
Swansea: Pakistan v Sri Lanka
Old Trafford: West Indies v India

Saturday 11 June

PRUDENTIAL CUP
Taunton: England v Sri Lanka
Leicester: India v Zimbabwe
Edgbaston: Pakistan v New Zealand
Headingley: West Indies v Australia
Schweppes Championship
Derby: Derbys v Leics
Cardiff: Glam v Warwicks
Tunbridge Wells: Kent v Essex
Old Trafford: Lancs v Notts
Northampton: Northants v Glos
The Oval: Surrey v Middx
Hove: Sussex v Somerset
Other Match
Oxford: Oxford U v Hants

Sunday 12 June

John Player League
Derby: Derbys v Leics
Chelmsford: Essex v Kent
Cardiff: Glam v Yorks
Old Trafford: Lancs v Notts
Northampton: Northants v Glos
The Oval: Surrey v Middx
Hove: Sussex v Warwicks

Monday 13 June

PRUDENTIAL CUP
Lord's: England v Pakistan
Trent Bridge: India v Australia
Bristol: New Zealand v Sri Lanka
Worcester: West Indies v Zimbabwe

Wednesday 15 June

PRUDENTIAL CUP
Edgbaston: England v New Zealand
The Oval: West Indies v India
Schweppes Championship
Derby: Derbys v Essex
Swansea: Glam v Somerset
Tunbridge Wells: Kent v Sussex
Old Trafford: Lancs v Warwicks
Leicester: Leics v Glos
Uxbridge: Middx v Hants
Trent Bridge: Notts v Surrey
Other Matches
Cambridge: Cambridge U v Northants
Oxford: Oxford U v Worcs

Thursday 16 June

PRUDENTIAL CUP
Southampton: Australia v Zimbabwe
Headingley: Pakistan v Sri Lanka

Saturday 18 June

PRUDENTIAL CUP
Old Trafford: England v Pakistan
Tunbridge Wells: India v Zimbabwe
Derby: New Zealand v Sri Lanka
Lord's: West Indies v Australia
Schweppes Championship
Bristol: Glos v Kent
Southampton: Hants v Yorks
Northampton: Northants v Warwicks
Bath: Somerset v Derbys
Horsham: Sussex v Lancs
Worcester: Worcs v Middx
Other Matches
Cambridge: Cambridge U v Notts
The Oval: *Surrey v Oxford U

Sunday 19 June

John Player League
Bristol: Glos v Kent
Basingstoke: Hants v Leics
Luton: Northants v Warwicks
Bath: Somerset v Glam
Horsham: Sussex v Lancs
Worcester: Worcs v Essex

Monday 20 June

PRUDENTIAL CUP
Chelmsford: Australia v India
Headingley: England v Sri Lanka
Trent Bridge: New Zealand v Pakistan
Edgbaston: West Indies v Zimbabwe

Wednesday 22 June

Old Trafford and The Oval:
PRUDENTIAL CUP SEMI-FINALS
Schweppes Championship
Ilford: Essex v Northants
Abergavenny: Glam v Worcs
Basingstoke: Hants v Sussex
Leicester: Leics v Surrey
Trent Bridge: Notts v Kent
Bath: Somerset v Glos
Sheffield: Yorks v Derbys
Other Matches
Cambridge: Cambridge U v Middx
Edgbaston: Warwicks v Oxford U

Saturday 25 June

Lord's:
PRUDENTIAL CUP FINAL
Schweppes Championship
Chesterfield: Derbys v Middx
Ilford: Essex v Sussex
Bristol: Glos v Hants
Hinckley: Leics v Glam
Trent Bridge: Notts v Lancs
The Oval: Surrey v Northants
Edgbaston: Warwicks v Yorks
Other Match
Worcester: Worcs v Cambridge U

Sunday 26 June

John Player League
Chesterfield: Derbys v Middx
Ilford: Essex v Sussex
Canterbury: Kent v Notts
Leicester: Leics v Glam
Bath: Somerset v Glos
East Molesey (Imber Crt): Surrey v
   Northants
Edgbaston: Warwicks v Hants
Worcester: Worcs v Yorks

Wednesday 29 June

Natwest Bank Trophy First Round
Reading: Berks v Yorks
Wisbech: Cambs v Middx

Bournemouth (Dean Park): Dorset v
   Essex
Chester-le-Street: Durham v Lancs
Bristol: Glos v Scotland
Hitchin: Herts v Hants
Dublin: Ireland v Sussex
Canterbury: Kent v Cheshire
Leicester: Leics v Devon
Sleaford: Lincs v Surrey
Norwich: Norfolk v Glam
Wellington: Shropshire v Somerset
Bury St. Edmunds: Suffolk v Derbys
Edgbaston: Warwicks v Oxfordshire
Swindon: Wilts v Northants
Worcester: Worcs v Notts
Other Match
Lord's: Oxford v Cambridge

Thursday 30 June

Portsmouth: Combined Services v
   New Zealand (two days)

Saturday 2 July

Schweppes Championship
Derby: Derbys v Worcs
Canterbury: Kent v Glam
Liverpool: Lancs v Hants
Trent Bridge: Notts v Essex
The Oval: Surrey v Glos
Hove: Sussex v Northants
Edgbaston: Warwicks v Middx
Harrogate: Yorks v Leics
Tourist Match
Taunton: *Somerset v New Zealand

Sunday 3 July

John Player League
Derby: Derbys v Worcs
Old Trafford: Lancs v Hants
Lord's: Middx v Glos
Trent Bridge: Notts v Essex
Hastings: Sussex v Northants
Scarborough: Yorks v Leics

Wednesday 6 July

Benson & Hedges Cup Semi-Finals
Tourist Match
Bristol: Glos v New Zealand (or
   another County if Glos in B & H
   Semi-final)
Other Matches
Harrogate: Tilcon Trophy (three days)

Saturday 9 July

Schweppes Championship
Cardiff: Glam v Sussex
Bristol: Glos v Derbys
Southampton: Hants v Surrey
Maidstone: Kent v Lancs
Leicester: Leics v Somerset
Northampton: Northants v Yorks
Nuneaton (Griff & Coton): Warwicks
  v Essex
Worcester: Worcs v Notts
Tourist Match
Lord's: *Middx v New Zealand

Sunday 10 July

John Player League
Cardiff: Glam v Sussex
Bristol: Glos v Derbys
Portsmouth: Hants v Surrey
Maidstone: Kent v Lancs
Leicester: Leics v Somerset
Tring: Northants v Yorks
Edgbaston: Warwicks v Essex
Hereford: Worcs v Notts

Wednesday 13 July

Schweppes Championship
Southend: Essex v Hants
Swansea: Glam v Lancs
Bristol: Glos v Middx
Maidstone: Kent v Somerset
Trent Bridge: Notts v Northants
Edgbaston: Warwicks v Derbys
Hereford: Worcs v Leics
Headingley: Yorks v Sussex

Thursday 14 July

THE OVAL: *ENGLAND V NEW
  ZEALAND
(First Cornhill Insurance Test Match)

Saturday 16 July

Schweppes Championship
Derby: *Derbys v Northants
Southend: Essex v Glam
Bournemouth: Hants v Notts
Old Trafford: Lancs v Worcs
Lord's: Middx v Leics
Taunton: Somerset v Surrey
Sheffield: Yorks v Kent

Sunday 17 July

John Player League
Southend: Essex v Glam
Bristol or Moreton-in-Marsh: Glos v
  Warwicks
Portsmouth: Hants v Notts
Old Trafford: Lancs v Worcs
Lord's: Middx v Leics
Scarborough: Yorks v Kent

Wednesday 20 July

NatWest Bank Trophy Second Round
Reading or Headingley: Berks or
  Yorks v Wilts or Yorks
Bournemouth Sports Club or
  Chelmsford: Dorset or Essex v Kent
  or Cheshire
Chester-le-Street or Old Trafford:
  Durham or Lancs v Shropshire or
  Somerset
Belfast or Hove: Ireland or Sussex v
  Worcs or Notts
Leicester or Torquay: Leics or Devon
  v Glos or Scotland
Lincoln or The Oval: Lincs or Surrey v
  Warwicks or Oxfordshire
Norwich or Swansea: Norfolk or Glam
  v Herts or Hants
Bury St. Edmunds or Derby: Suffolk
  or Derbys v Cambs or Middx
Tourist Match
Trent Bridge or Worcester: Notts or
  Worcs v New Zealand (loser of
  NatWest Trophy First Round Match)

Saturday 23 July

LORD'S: BENSON & HEDGES CUP
  FINAL
Tourist Match
Edgbaston: Warwicks v New Zealand
  (or another County if Warwicks in B
  & H Final)

Sunday 24 July

John Player League
Derby: Derbys v Notts
Canterbury: Kent v Middx
Leicester: Leics v Essex
Northampton: Northants v Glam
Taunton: Somerset v Hants
The Oval: Surrey v Lancs
Hove: Sussex v Yorks
Edgbaston: Warwicks v Worcs

Wednesday 27 July

Schweppes Championship
Portsmouth: Hants v Derbys
Southport: Lancs v Glos
Northampton: Northants v Somerset
The Oval: Surrey v Notts
Hove: Sussex v Essex
Edgbaston: Warwicks v Kent
Worcester: Worcs v Glam

Thursday 28 July

**HEADINGLEY: ENGLAND v NEW
ZEALAND
(Second Cornhill Insurance Test
Match)**

Saturday 30 July

Schweppes Championship
Chesterfield: Derbys v Kent
Swansea: Glam v Surrey
Portsmouth: Hants v Glos
Old Trafford: Lancs v Somerset
Leicester: Leics v Sussex
Lord's: Middx v Warwicks
Northampton: Northants v Worcs
Worksop: Notts v Yorks

Sunday 31 July

John Player League
Chesterfield: Derbys v Kent
Swansea: Glam v Surrey
Bournemouth: Hants v Glos
Old Trafford: Lancs v Somerset
Leicester: Leics v Sussex
Lord's: Middx v Warwicks
Trent Bridge: Notts v Yorks
Worcester: Worcs v Northants

Wednesday 3 August

NatWest Bank Trophy Quarter-Finals
Tourist Match
Northampton: Northants v New
Zealand (or another county if
Northants in NatWest Trophy
Quarter-final)

Friday 5 August

Lord's: England YC's v Australian
YC's
(First 'One-day International')
(Will only be played provided that, if
Middlesex drawn at 'Home' in
NatWest Trophy, their match is
completed within two days)

Saturday 6 August

Schweppes Championship
Chelmsford: Essex v Middx
Cheltenham: Glos v Glam
Canterbury: Kent v Worcs
Leicester: Leics v Notts
Weston-super-Mare: Somerset v
Northants
The Oval: Surrey v Warwicks
Eastbourne: Sussex v Derbys
Headingley: Yorks v Lancs
Tourist Match
Bournemouth: *Hants v New Zealand
Other Match
Trent Bridge: England YC's v
Australian YC's
(First 'Test Match') (four days)

Sunday 7 August

John Player League
Chelmsford: Essex v Middx
Cheltenham: Glos v Glam
Canterbury: Kent v Worcs
Leicester: Leics v Notts
Weston-super-Mare: Somerset v
Northants
The Oval: Surrey v Warwicks
Eastbourne: Sussex v Derbys
Headingley: Yorks v Lancs
Other Matches
Warwick Under-25 Semi-Finals (one
day),
(or Sunday 14 August)

Wednesday 10 August

Schweppes Championship
Chelmsford: Essex v Leics
Ebbw Vale: Glam v Notts
Cheltenham: Glos v Warwicks
Canterbury: Kent v Surrey
Northampton: Northants v Middx
Weston-super-Mare: Somerset v Yorks
Eastbourne: Sussex v Hants
Worcester: Worcs v Lancs

Thursday 11 August

LORD'S: ENGLAND v NEW ZEALAND
(Third Cornhill Insurance Test Match)

Saturday 13 August

Schweppes Championship
Derby: Derbys v Somerset
Cardiff: Glam v Kent
Cheltenham: Glos v Yorks
Old Trafford: Lancs v Middx
Wellingborough: Northants v Essex
Trent Bridge: Notts v Hants
Guildford: Surrey v Worcs
Edgbaston: Warwicks v Leics

Sunday 14 August

John Player League
Heanor: Derbys v Somerset
Cardiff: Glam v Kent
Cheltenham: Glos v Yorks
Old Trafford: Lancs v Middx
Wellingborough: Northants v Essex
Trent Bridge: Notts v Sussex
Guildford: Surrey v Worcs
Edgbaston: Warwicks v Leics
Other Matches
Warwick Under-25 Semi-Finals (one day)
(if not played on Sunday 7 August)

Wednesday 17 August

NatWest Bank Trophy Semi-Finals
Tourist Match
Chelmsford: Essex v New Zealand (or another County if Essex in NatWest Trophy Semi-Final)
Other Matches
Scarborough: England YC's v Australian YC's
(Second 'Test Match') (four days)
Glasgow (Titwood): Scotland v MCC (three days)

Saturday 20 August

Schweppes Championship
Colchester: Essex v Glos
Swansea: Glam v Derbys
Folkestone: Kent v Warwicks
Lord's: Middx v Somerset
Northampton: Northants v Lancs
Hove: Sussex v Surrey

Worcester: Worcs v Hants
Bradford: Yorks v Notts
Tourist Match
Leicester: *Leics v New Zealand

Sunday 21 August

John Player League
Colchester: Essex v Glos
Swansea: Glam v Derbys
Folkestone: Kent v Warwicks
Lord's: Middx v Somerset
Hove: Sussex v Surrey
Worcester: Worcs v Hants
Other Match
Edgbaston: Warwick Under-25 Competition Final (one day)

Monday 22 August

Derby: England YC's v Australian YC's
(Second 'One-day International')

Wednesday 24 August

Schweppes Championship
Colchester: Essex v Worcs
Bournemouth: Hants v Somerset
Folkestone: Kent v Leics
Blackpool: Lancs v Derbys
Lord's: Middx v Surrey
Northampton: Northants v Glam
Edgbaston: Warwicks v Sussex
Scarborough: Yorks v Glos

Thursday 25 August

TRENT BRIDGE: *ENGLAND v NEW ZEALAND
(Fourth Cornhill Insurance Test Match)

Saturday 27 August

Schweppes Championship
Chesterfield: Derbys v Yorks
Bristol: Glos v Notts
Bournemouth: Hants v Kent
Leicester: Leics v Northants
Taunton: Somerset v Glam
The Oval: Surrey v Essex
Hove: Sussex v Middx
Edgbaston: Warwicks v Worcs

252

Sunday 28 August

John Player League
Cardiff: Glam v Worcs
Bristol: Glos v Lancs
Southampton: Hants v Sussex
Milton Keynes: Northants v Middx
Taunton: Somerset v Kent
The Oval: Surrey v Essex
Edgbaston: Warwicks v Notts
Bradford: Yorks v Derbys

Wednesday 31 August

Schweppes Championship
Cardiff: Glam v Northants
Bristol: Glos v Worcs
Old Trafford: Lancs v Essex
Leicester: Leics v Kent
Trent Bridge: Notts v Warwicks
Taunton: Somerset v Hants
The Oval: Surrey v Sussex
Headingley: Yorks v Middx
Tourist Match
Scarborough: Brian Close's XI v New
   Zealand
Other Match
Canterbury: England YC's v
   Australian YC's
(Third 'Test Match') (four days)

Saturday 3 September

**LORD'S: NATWEST BANK
   TROPHY FINAL**

Sunday 4 September

John Player League
Derby: Derbys v Hants
Leicester: Leics v Surrey
Cleethorpes: Notts v Middx
Hove: Sussex v Glos
Worcester: Worcs v Somerset
Other Match
Scarborough: Yorks v Lancs
(Asda Cricket Challenge (one day)

Monday 5 September

Scarborough: Essex v Hants
Asda Cricket Challenge (one day)

Tuesday 6 September

Scarborough: Asda Cricket Challenge
   Final (one day)

Wednesday 7 September

Schweppes Championship
Derby: Derbys v Notts
Lord's: Middx v Northants
Taunton: Somerset v Kent
Hove: Sussex v Leics
Edgbaston: Warwicks v Glam
Worcester: Worcs v Glos
Scarborough: Yorks v Surrey

Saturday 10 September

Schweppes Championship
Chelmsford: Essex v Yorks
Southampton: Hants v Glam
Canterbury: Kent v Northants
Old Trafford: Lancs v Leics
Trent Bridge: Notts v Middx
Taunton: Somerset v Warwicks
The Oval: Surrey v Derbys
Worcester: Worcs v Sussex

Sunday 11 September

John Player League
Chelmsford: Essex v Yorks
Bournemouth: Hants v Glam
Canterbury: Kent v Northants
Old Trafford: Lancs v Leics
Trent Bridge: Notts v Glos
Taunton: Somerset v Warwicks
The Oval: Surrey v Derbys
Worcester: Worcs v Sussex

© Test and County Cricket Board 1983.

MINOR COUNTIES FIXTURES 1983
United Friendly Insurance County Championship
(Two Day Matches)

MAY *Western Division*
Sun   29   Berkshire v Shropshire: Reading University

JUNE
Sun   5   Shropshire v Cheshire: Wellington
Tues   14   Shropshire v Somerset II: St. Georges
Thurs 16   Cheshire v Somerset II: Chester (Boughton Hall)

JULY
Sun   3   Oxfordshire v Cheshire: Oxford (Morris Motors)
Sun   3   Bucks v Shropshire: Slough
Tues   5   Wiltshire v Cheshire: Swindon
Sun   10   Somerset II v Bucks: Taunton
Sun   17   Cornwall v Devon: Helston
Sun   17   Dorset v Bucks: Bournemouth (Sports Club)
Sun   17   Oxfordshire v Berkshire: Oxford (Christ Church)
Thurs 21   Devon v Dorset: Sidmouth
Sun   24   Oxfordshire v Bucks: Oxford (St. Edward's)
Sun   24   Cornwall v Berkshire: Truro
Sun   24   Cheshire v Dorset: Bowdon
Mon   25   Wiltshire v Somerset II: Chippenham
Tues   26   Devon v Berkshire: Exmouth
Tues   26   Shropshire v Dorset: Newport
Sun   31   Berkshire v Wiltshire: Reading (Courage)
Sun   31   Oxfordshire v Shropshire: Shipton-under-Wychwood

AUG
Mon   1   Cornwall v Bucks: Falmouth
Tues   2   Wiltshire v Shropshire: Trowbridge
Wed   3   Devon v Bucks: Torquay
Thurs   4   Berkshire v Dorset: Finchampstead
Mon   8   Somerset II v Devon: Taunton
Tues   9   Cheshire v Cornwall: Toft
Wed   10   Dorset v Somerset II: Bournemouth (Dean Park)
Wed   10   Wiltshire v Oxfordshire: Devizes
Thurs 11   Shropshire v Cornwall: Bridgnorth
Sun   14   Bucks v Cheshire: Stowe School
Mon   15   Wiltshire v Dorset: Salisbury (Bemeston)
Mon   15   Cornwall v Oxfordshire: St. Austell
Tues   16   Berkshire v Cheshire: Reading C.C.
Wed   17   Devon v Oxfordshire: Newton Abbot
Thurs 18   Somerset II v Berkshire: Weston-super-Mare (Westlands)
Sun   21   Bucks v Wiltshire: High Wycombe
Sun   21   Dorset v Oxfordshire: Canford School
Tues   23   Dorset v Cornwall: Weymouth
Tues   23   Cheshire v Devon: Nantwich
Tues   23   Somerset II v Oxfordshire: Keynsham
Thurs 25   Shropshire v Devon: Shrewsbury (London Road)
Thurs 25   Somerset II v Cornwall: Wells
Sun   28   Cornwall v Wiltshire: Wadebridge
Sun   28   Bucks v Berkshire: Amersham
Tues   30   Devon v Wiltshire: Bovey Tracey

254

Sun	29	Lincolnshire v Hertfordshire: Sleaford
Tues	31	Durham v Hertfordshire: Hartlepool

JUNE

Sun	5	Northumberland v Cambridgeshire: Bebwell Hill
Tues	7	Cumberland v Cambridgeshire: Carlisle
Sun	12	Lincolnshire v Cumberland: Bourne
Tues	14	Hertfordshire v Cumberland: Hitchin
Wed	15	Cambridgeshire v Norfolk: Wisbech
Sun	19	Northumberland v Lincolnshire: Jesmond
Sun	19	Durham v Norfolk: Chester-le-Street
Tues	21	Northumberland v Norfolk: Jesmond
Wed	22	Hertfordshire v Cambridgeshire: Watford
Sun	26	Staffordshire v Hertfordshire: Walsall

JULY

Sat	2	Hertfordshire v Bedfordshire: St. Albans (Clarence Park)
Wed	6	Staffordshire v Cambridgeshire: Knypersley
Sun	10	Cumberland v Staffordshire: Millom
Sun	10	Lincolnshire v Norfolk: Stamford
Tues	12	Northumberland v Cumberland: Jesmond
Sun	17	Bedfordshire v Lincolnshire: Bedford School
Wed	20	Suffolk v Cambridgeshire: Ipswich (G.R.E.)
Sun	24	Suffolk v Cumberland: Ipswich (G.R.E.)
Sun	24	Lincolnshire v Durham: Lincoln
Mon	25	Staffordshire v Northumberland: Brewood
Tues	26	Suffolk v Hertfordshire: Felixstowe
Tues	26	Cambridgeshire v Bedfordshire: Royston
Tues	26	Norfolk v Cumberland: Norwich (Lakenham)
Thurs	28	Norfolk v Bedfordshire: Norwich (Lakenham)
Sun	31	Durham v Northumberland: Durham City

AUG

Mon	1	Norfolk v Staffordshire: Norwich (Lakenham)
Wed	3	Suffolk v Staffordshire: Bury St. Edmunds
Wed	3	Norfolk v Hertfordshire: Norwich (Lakenham)
Wed	3	Cambridgeshire v Lincolnshire: March
Fri	5	Norfolk v Suffolk: Norwich (Lakenham)
Mon	8	Hertfordshire v Northumberland: Hertford (Balls Park)
Mon	8	Bedfordshire v Durham: Luton (Wardown Park)
Wed	10	Bedfordshire v Staffordshire: Dunstable
Wed	10	Cambridgeshire v Durham: Peterborough
Wed	10	Suffolk v Northumberland: Mildenhall
Sun	14	Northumberland v Bedfordshire: Jesmond
Sun	14	Lincolnshire v Suffolk: Grimsby
Mon	15	Staffordshire v Durham: Stone
Tues	16	Cumberland v Bedfordshire: Kendal
Sun	21	Staffordshire v Lincolnshire: Longton
Sun	21	Cumberland v Durham: Netherfield
Wed	24	Durham v Suffolk: Stockton-on-Tees
Sun	28	Bedfordshire v Suffolk: Southill Park

The top County in the Western Division will play the top County in the Eastern Division at Worcester in a one day match to decide the Championship.

ISBN 0 356 08592 9

© 1983 Queen Anne Press

Published in 1983 by
Queen Anne Press
Macdonald & Co (Publishers) Ltd
Maxwell House
Worship Street
London EC2

Filmset, printed and bound in
Great Britain by
Hazell Watson & Viney Ltd
Aylesbury, Bucks